Dealing with Drugs in Europe

Dealing with Drugs in Europe

An Investigation of European Drug Control Experiences:
France, the Netherlands and Sweden

Tim Boekhout van Solinge

Willem Pompe Institute for Criminal Law and Criminology
in co-operation with

BJu Legal Publishers
The Hague
2004

This volume first appeared as a Ph.D. dissertation from Utrecht University

Cover: Botanical drawings (papaver somniferum, coca and cannabis sativa),
by Chandra Brooks

Typography: Wieneke Matthijsse

ISBN 90-5454-518-6
NUR 824
www.bju.nl

Acknowledgements

First for the inspiration to work in the field of international drug control, I would like to thank Alain Labrousse, Founder and Director of the *Observatoire Géopolitique des Drogues* (OGD) in Paris. During a period of the 1990s, as a political geography student at the *Université de Paris–Sorbonne (Paris IV)* to obtain a *Diplôme d'Etudes Approfondies* (D.E.A.) I studied the international illicit drug economy, its massive scale and its intertwining with the economic and political worlds through Alain's publications. I would also like to give thanks to Herman van der Wusten, Political Geography Professor, and my M.A. supervisor at the University of Amsterdam for introducing me to Dr. Peter Cohen of the Centre for Drug Research (CEDRO). A great thanks goes to Dr. Peter Cohen for offering me the chance to do research in this field while spending several years at CEDRO in Amsterdam. I want to thank Peter for his original and critical thinking, which taught me to never take things for granted, even if most people accept it as 'truth'. Peter will remain my primary teacher on drug issues. A word of thanks also goes to Bob Keizer, former Director of the drug policy department of the Dutch Ministry of Public Health in The Hague. During his time as Director his department funded my first drug policy projects on France, Sweden, and the European Union. I would like to thank the Lindesmith Centre of the Open Society Institute in New York City for a grant enabling me to write a Ph.D. on international drug policy. Special thanks to Frank Bovenkerk for my position as lecturer and researcher in criminology at the Willem Pompe Institute for Criminal Law and Criminology in Utrecht. The Pompe Institute's intellectually open, critically thinking and stimulating academic environment offers me the freedom to explore new areas. With regard to my research I would like to thank all the people who participated through their work in France, the Netherlands, and Sweden. I would like to give special thanks to Chandra Brooks for proofreading, revisions and corrections of the text. I would also like to thank Cassandra York and Ted Goldberg for their critiques. I would like to extend my sincere gratitude to the professors of my Ph.D. Commission (Frank Bovenkerk, Chrisje Brants, Peter Cohen, Pierre Kopp, and Henrik Tham). Finally, I would like to thank my family and friends for supporting me.

Foreword

I was born in 1968, a year marked by great international upheaval: an escalation of both the war in Vietnam and demonstrations against it, the Soviet invasion of Czechoslovakia, the war in Biafra, and the assassinations of both Dr. Martin Luther King and Robert Kennedy in the United States. It was also the year in which young people around the world, especially university students, were asking for social change. In May 1968, the counter culture reached a climax in Paris, students and workers formed a coalition. From Paris, the revolutionary spirit sprang to other countries and cities in the world, making May 1968 an international event. 1968 is one of those years that stand out, a pivotal year that changed an era.[1]

One of the manifestations of the counter culture protest was the use of mostly illegal mind-altering drugs: cannabis, LSD, and to a lesser extent amphetamines, opium and heroin. Drugs became a symbol of the counter culture; their use was a sign of allegiance. The most common reaction from governments was one of disapproval. Especially since the counter culture was considered a threat to 'the establishment', so was the illegal drug use that symbolised it. A common reaction from governments therefore was to ban and suppress drug use.

In the beginning of the twenty-first century, more than a generation later, illegal drug use is well established in most Western and European societies. Drug use has spread from the counter culture to youth culture and society in general. In this study, the term 'modern drug use' is used to typify the spread of illegal drug use inside modern industrialised societies since the 1960s. Different drugs such as cannabis (marijuana and hashish), opium, LSD, amphetamines, heroin, cocaine, ecstasy and others appear, reappear, or disappear. A difference between modern drug use and that of the 1960s is that consumption is no longer confined to specific subcultures. Drugs are now being used by all segments of the population, irrespective to one's education, profession, class or political viewpoint.

---

1   See the book published by Magnum Photo: *1968, the year that moved the world*. Historian Eric Hobsbaum wrote the text of the book.

Countries have developed different approaches for dealing with the question of illegal drug use. The illegality of drugs is laid down in a series of international drug treaties, from 1912 to 1988, that have been signed by most countries. These UN Drug Conventions oblige countries to fight drugs through criminal law, the police and sometimes military. On the other hand, across Europe, the idea is increasingly being held that people who violate drug laws should not be punished severely. Care, treatment, and harm reduction policies have been set up. Some countries are moving towards the observation of drug use tolerance, such as in the case of recreational cannabis use.

Why countries have developed different approaches to the drug problem remains largely unclear. Despite public opinion, the reasons for these national variations cannot be explained by drug problems that differ in nature or scale. In this study it will be argued that national cultural traditions have greatly influenced how the question of illicit drug use is being dealt with. The study will explore justifications and rationalisations for the divergent, and even contradictory attitudes that distinguish the approaches to the drug questions of France, the Netherlands and Sweden, including underlying, sometimes less visible motives and influences.

Amsterdam and Utrecht,
Tim Boekhout van Solinge

Contents

Chapter 1 Drug Use and Drug Control

1.1	The United Nations World Drug Summit	1
1.2	Dealing with Psychoactive Substances	6
1.3	Global Drug Prohibition	14
1.4	National Varieties of Drug Prohibition	20

Chapter 2 From Global Prohibition to National Control

2.1	The Rise of Global Prohibition Regimes	33
2.2	The American Role in International Drug Control	39
2.3	The United Nations Drug Control Regime	45
2.4	European Drug Control	53
2.5	National Drug Control Trends in Europe	56

Chapter 3 Handling Drugs à la Française

3.1	Drugs in France	65
3.2	Geography, History, and the People	71
3.3	May 1968 and the 1970 drug legislation	79
3.4	Science and the Professionals	84
3.5	State Traditions of Law Enforcement and Central Rule	92

Chapter 4 Doing Drugs the Dutch Way

4.1	Introduction	105
4.2	Geography, History, and the People	109
4.3	Commissions and Professionals	116
4.4	Political and Legal Culture	124
4.5	Drug Trade and Drug Tolerance	132

Chapter 5 The Restrictive Swedish Model

5.1	Drugs in Sweden	143
5.2	Geography, History, and the People	148
5.3	A Restrictive Alcohol Policy	157

5.4   The Swedish Drug problem   165
5.5   The Symbolic Importance of the Drug Threat   174

Chapter 6 The Study of Drug Control Systems

6.1   Three Countries, Three Approaches   187
6.2   Diverging Perceptions and Constructions   189
6.3   Different Policies and Practices   192
6.4   Colliding Principles and Practices   200
6.5   National Drug Control Systems   209

References   223

Index   237

Chapter 1

Drug Use and Drug Control

1.1 The United Nations World Drug Summit

A World Drug Summit took place in New York in June 1998. A United Nations
General Assembly Special Session (UNGASS) was devoted specifically to the
drug problem, with the slogan "A Drug-Free World. We Can Do It".[1] Great
importance was attached to the summit: witness the presence of eight heads of
government and twenty-three heads of state, all of whom addressed the assembly, including the Presidents of the United States and France. Queen Silvia from
Sweden was also present, giving the introduction to a panel discussion on
"children, young people and drug abuse". UN Secretary-General Kofi Annan
spoke the opening words: "The proliferation of drugs over the past 30 years is
an example of the previously unimaginable becoming reality very quickly – a
tragic reality. It is my hope that when historians study the work of humankind
in the field of drug control they will write about the next few days as the point
where this trend was reversed. It is my hope they will record this as the time
when the international community found common ground in the mission to
create a drug-free world in the twenty-first century".[2]

The first government leader to speak after Annan was Bill Clinton, President
of the United States. Clinton stated his administration had provided the largest
anti-drug budget in history. The 1999 budget exceeded seventeen billion dollars,
of which six million would go towards demand reduction, the rest to interdiction
and law enforcement efforts. "We are determined to build a drug-free America
and to join with others to combat drugs around the world". Clinton announced
a media campaign against drugs: "Now, when our children turn on the television, surf the Internet, or listen to the radio, they will get the powerful message
that drugs are wrong and can kill them".

One of the first European representatives to speak was French President
Jacques Chirac, who made a quite dramatic appeal to the General Assembly: "I
expect our special session to give fresh world-wide impetus to the war on drugs.

---

1 See the web site of the UNGASS devoted to the World Drug Problem: «www.un.org/ga/20special».
2 UN Secretary-General Kofi Annan addressing UNGASS, June 8, 1998. Quotes from speeches are
   taken from United Nations General Assembly (1998), *20th Special Session, Official Records*.

The spread of this scourge is alarming. A real awakening to this fact is essential and an all-out offensive must be waged. Drugs corrupt. Drugs kill". In order to "counter attack on every front" this "world-girdling menace", Chirac proposed three principles for future action: co-responsibility between countries to simultaneously reduce demand and supply, solidarity among nations and with the addicts, and firmness, both at home and abroad. The French President expressed his belief in the "value and effectiveness of prohibitions" over which the state "must exercise its authority to ensure that they are respected". He closed with: "It is a crusade that must not cease until we have done away with this cancer that is eating away our societies. Our people must know that we will go all the way in this battle for life and that nothing will stop us."

Hans van Mierlo, Deputy Prime Minister and Minister for Foreign Affairs was speaking on behalf of the Netherlands. "Our primary aim is to protect health and social-well-being and to reduce the harm and risks associated with drug abuse. Within this context, we believe that drug users should not be criminalised for their habits, but, on the contrary, should be provided the help they need. (…) Our policy prevents drug users from going underground, where we cannot reach them. We have identified the various user groups and we know their habits. This has enabled us to develop targeted policy measures, which are more effective. By bringing it out into the open, drug use has become less glamorous. The clearest example of this is the use of opiates. For young people in the Netherlands now, heroin is for losers. Very few of them would think of trying it". Mr. Van Mierlo ended his speech with the words: "Whether the world will ever be completely free of drugs remains an open question. Control of drugs and drug-related problems seems a more attainable goal".

Margot Wallström, Minister of Health and Social Affairs, represented Sweden. She started by saying that she had met "boys and girls of no more than twenty years old who had already been treated several times for their drug addiction". "By international standards the drug problems in Sweden are relatively limited. But there is a increase in first-time recruitment for drug abuse and a growing interest among young people in testing different kinds of drugs." She continued: "The objective of Swedish drug policy is to create a drug-free society. It is supported by a broad consensus among the political parties in our Parliament. It is also a vision based on a positive, humanistic approach. Swedish drug policy has evolved over a long period of time. It is integrated into our social policy, which provides everybody with basic security through a system of general benefits". She ended with the words: "Let us not loose sight of our goal; a drug-free society. That is a responsibility we have to the younger generation as we lead our communities to the next millennium."

In total 150 speeches were given during the three-day UN summit. These speeches were meant to represent each country's approach towards the issue of illicit drugs. This is certainly true for the three European countries under focus in this study: France, the Netherlands, and Sweden. Quotes from representatives from these countries were chosen, as they show in a nutshell some characteristics of and differences between the approaches toward illicit drugs in these countries.

But of course, these types of speeches do not tell everything. They were political declarations, wrapped up in appropriately diplomatic phrases, partly aimed at the domestic market. They were also written toward a consensus reached beforehand over a so-called balanced approach of demand and supply reduction, in which Southern – producing – and Northern – consuming – countries had a shared responsibility.[3] Furthermore, a speech does not necessarily entirely cover a country's drug policy; its content is influenced by the speaker and by the government department that prepared it. In the French political system, for example, the President disposes of substantial powers that enable him to push forward some of his own ideas. This was indeed the case at UNGASS, as the French president did not mention the major changes French drug policy had just been going through, toward a more pragmatic, harm reduction approach. However, this also reflects French drug policy, as Chirac's personal experiences and ideas dominated official French views on drugs – though not practices – in the second half of the 1990s.

By taking a closer look at the language used in the three speeches, it becomes apparent that the drug question is perceived and constructed in different ways. Discourse analysis, a research technique from linguistics that has become a standard in cultural studies, shows that the language or discourse used to describe a phenomenon is never neutral, but that there is something behind the immediate surface. In other words, language reflects a world view. The debate over the relationship between discourse and the world has been a recurring theme in the history of philosophy. While for language theorists, how language and thought, language and culture, or discourse and society are interrelated, has been one of the main themes of research during the twentieth century.[4] The dominant idea among discourse analysts is that discourse not only reflects a world-view, but also helps in shaping the world as it is experienced. In other words, discourse both reflects and creates human beings' world views. Discourse analysis can be applied to the three speeches of UNGASS. Appropriate methodologies for analysing them would be content analysis – to look at the wording – and critical discourse analysis – to unravel some of the

3 Generally speaking, most of the production of illicit drugs (cannabis, cocaine and heroine) is found in the poorer, Southern part of the world, whilst the big consumption markets, at least in value, are found in the richer North. Although still true in general terms, since some years substantial consumption can be observed in the South (e.g. heroin use in Pakistan), while production has increased in the North (Europe and North America), in particular of cannabis and synthetic drugs.
4 Discourse analysis developed different methods for the study of language-in-use and enables to look at the speeches' differences in a more systematic and fundamental way, such as by looking at which language is used (naming and wording), what is said and what is not, the text structure, how the subject is represented, and more generally, why the text is the way it is. See Johnstone (2002) *Discourse Analysis*, 30, and Titscher et al. (2000), *Methods of Text and Discourse Analysis*, 59-60. With thanks to Dr. Ted Sanders of the Utrecht Institute of Linguistics for explaining some key concepts.

ideology and culture behind the discourse, since as Foucault showed, discourse is one of the principal activities through which ideology is circulated and reproduced.[5]

A striking element in the (French spoken) speech of President Chirac is the abundant use of dramatic and military language. Dramatic words carrying a negative and frightening connotation such as danger, scourge, evil, menace, and cancer, are employed to describe drugs. They are presented as a major threat to society and are being connected with phenomena such as infectious diseases, death, violence, delinquency, corruption, crime, and Mafia. Every aspect of the drug question is phrased in problematic and negative terms, while the use of drugs is only perceived in terms of addiction. Drugs "choose their first victims among the most susceptible teenagers as they emerge from childhood", they "are reaching an ever-larger and ever-younger population", then "have them in their power" and "lead them down the road of death". Not only are drugs portrayed as being inherently dangerous and problematic, they also foster "powerful, internationally organised crime interests which not only master the latest technology but laugh at international borders" and "maintain globe-spanning networks, gangs, and even armies", while the money is used for other "criminal and terrorist activities". Chirac's answer to this "world-girdling menace" is framed in military terms: "In every corner of the world is must be realised the United Nations is battle-ready for the fight against drugs. (...) We must counter attack on every front (...) the hostile forces that we must battle".

The speech of the Dutch Foreign Minister is of a totally different tone and outlook. It is not so principle, but merely pragmatic in nature. Instead of using negative, emotional words and rhetoric to describe the world drug problem, the Dutch speech is generally positive and practical. It states it is possible "to tackle the drug problem effectively (...) by an integrated and balanced approach that includes both demand reduction and supply reduction". The speech focuses on international actions such as crop eradication, alternative development, and international co-operation against drug trafficking and money laundering in the Caribbean. In the speech, most emphasis is put on health and harm reduction measures and indicators, such as by addressing "some of the experiences of the Netherlands' demand reduction policy", which primary aim is "to protect the health and social well-being and to reduce the risks associated with drug abuse". Drug prevention, the treatment system, and harm reduction measures such as methadone and needle exchange programmes "have not lead to more intrave-nous use", but to "fewer people sharing needles" and to low "morbidity and mortality rates among drug users". In the Dutch view, drug users should not be criminalised: instead of seeing them go underground, it would be better to have it occur in the open where they could be more easily reached.

The Swedish speech is idealistic and worrisome in tone. It begins somewhat

---

5   Foucault (1972), *The Archaeology of Knowledge*, 7.

emotionally, by describing young people in drug treatment who fell into the trap of drugs. Her description includes girls "falling in love with an older boy with drug problems, then dropping out of school, and then turning to crime, et cetera", and boys "from well-to-do families" who were "just curious and wanted to experiment". Idealism appears as the Swedish objective of a drug-free society, and that is clearly put forward in the speech. Swedish drug use may still be low from an international perspective, but among young people it is on the increase. Of more concern though is the international cultural context around drugs. A large part of the speech is devoted to the "intense international promotion of illicit drug use and of pro-drug messages", (…) transmitted world-wide in a matter of seconds and tend to be embedded in a cultural context, accompanied by music and fashion. The marketing is often aimed directly at young persons and promotes the view that drugs are fun and exciting." The best insurance toward "those very dangerous trends that threaten the structure of our societies and our basic cultural values" is "to maintain a negative attitude toward drug abuse among the general public. Solidarity with disadvantaged, vulnerable groups and concern for our children and young people require that. It is also an issue of democracy and preservation of democratic right."

The three speeches show that three different discourses are used to describe the world drug problem. In the French speech drugs were presented as a major threat to society and the world at large. Considering the importance attached to laws and their enforcement, and the emphasis put on "firmness" in order to curb the evil that drugs represent, the speech can be labelled authoritarian. It can also be considered a French security discourse (*discours de sécurité*), not unusual in French politics. Since metaphors are never culturally independent, the abundant metaphorical use of military terms only magnifies this security dimension.[6] In the Dutch speech on the other hand, the drug problem was presented almost entirely in public health terms. Using health indicators, it was argued the drug problem is controllable: "We in the Netherlands believe that we are on the right track, encouraged as we are by results and figures". In discussing new strategies the speech continued: "let us not get trapped in ideological disputes of the past. Let us instead base our discussions on facts and the practical experiences we have gained over the years". The goal of a drug-free world is hereby questioned: "control of drugs and drug-related problems seems a more attainable goal". In the Swedish speech the ongoing belief in the goal of a drug-free society appeared strong, despite the observed increase in drug use in Sweden itself. The main drug threat was presented as cultural in nature. More specifically, the 'pro-drug' messages that are increasingly transmitted via international popular culture were seen to undermine the Swedish goal of a drug-free society. This is why the speech highlights what is called "massive propaganda" for drugs, as internationalised culture is felt to exude an atmosphere that threatens Swedish

---

6   Lakoff & Johnson (1980), *Metaphors we live by.*

society. The Swedes do not seek a military solution to this perceived threat, but instead, work through social democratic welfare measures. Solidarity with disadvantaged groups and the integration of drug policy into the social policy "which provides everybody with basic security through a system of general benefits" is the focus of their approach.

The three discourses reflect different ways of regarding drugs and the world drug problem. Not only are different words employed, the ideological and theoretical assumptions behind them appear to vary, too. This means, in fact, that the representatives of the three countries are speaking different 'languages', which in turn may lead to confusion. These fundamental differences in perception and approaches will be explored by this study. Before embarking down that road, it is first useful to look at drug use and drug control policies in a large, historical perspective.

1.2 Dealing with Psychoactive Substances

As far as is known, mankind has always used drugs – or to give a more generic name: psychoactive or mind-altering substances. In an historical sense these substances were usually ingested in the form of psychoactive plants.[7] The use of psychoactive substances is not unique to humans; animals, such as elephants, apes, goats, dogs, mongooses and even birds, occasionally intoxicate themselves with alcohol, cannabis, or hallucinogens.[8] Some researchers adhere to the theory that psychoactive plants, especially hallucinogenic mushrooms, played a crucial role in the origin of religion.[9] Even human evolution, in particular, the development from apes to the more intelligent humans has been linked to the use of psychoactive substances.[10] Anthropologists think early man learned about

---

7   For a comprehensive overview of the plants being used all over the world by different (traditional) people, see the book by Schultes & Hofmann (1979), *Plants of the Gods*. Schultes, who died in 2001, was botany professor at Harvard Medical school and director of the Harvard Botanical Museum. Hofmann was the discoverer of LSD.
8   By eating fruits, preferable rotten, that will ferment in the stomach, the animals will become alcohol intoxicated, in other words, drunk. Elephants especially like a special type of palm fruit, which they can smell from a distance and will sometimes run for it. Contrary to man, however, the animal intoxication is always temporary, probably because continued intoxication might make surviving more difficult, such as by becoming more vulnerable to predators. For a study on animal drug use, see Siegel (1989), *Intoxication*. A BBC documentary of December 2002 showed monkeys who had developed the habit of finishing cocktails left by tourists on beach tables. The monkey's alcohol use had been studied and the documentary stated the distribution of use patterns was comparable to man: most monkeys were occasional drinkers, 5% was considered abuser/alcoholic, whilst another minority abstained.
9   See for instance Wasson et al. (1978), *Persephone's Quest: Entheogens and the Origins of Religion*. Lévi-Strauss (1973: 273) commented in *Les champignons dans la culture* on Wasson's earlier work and described it as 'pan mycism', the tendency to explain everything through (magic) mushrooms. For a good overview (in Dutch) see Lemaire (1995), *Godenspijs of duivelsbrood*, 132.
10 For the latter theory see McKenna (1993), *Foods of the Gods: the Search for the Original Tree of Knowledge*.

medicines and drugs by observing animals using plants. The legendary story in this regard is the discovery of coffee in the Ethiopian highlands around 900 AD, when a herd of goats became abnormally frisky after eating the bright red fruit of a tree.[11] With the exception of people that live in the Arctic where no plants grow (Inuit and Aleut), every human culture in every age of history has used one or more psychoactive drugs. Since it is so common and widespread, some call it a universal or basic human activity.[12] Ample references to drug use in ancient times exist, some in the texts of great historiographers.

The use of cannabis can be traced back approximately 10,000 years, from the moment man planted crops. That it has many uses goes a long way in explaining why cannabis has been cultivated almost everywhere in the world.[13] In ancient China, cannabis had multitudinous uses: as a plant fibre, a food plant (one of the major grains), a medicinal plant, and as a psychoactive plant.[14] In the pharmacopoeia of the Chinese king Chen-Nong of 2,700 BC cannabis is mentioned as a sedative and treatment for mental alienation.[15] The Chinese emperors ate their cannabis, or brewed it in their tea.[16]

Archaeological excavations in Israel revealed cannabis and opium had been produced there since 1400 BC.[17] Cannabis was used to ease menstrual cramps and was offered to women during childbirth.[18] In the ancient Middle East, cannabis – in Hebrew *kaneh bosm* – was often utilised in the form of cannabis-based oil, the recipe of which can be found in the Hebrew and Aramaic versions of the Old Testament. In Exodus 30: 22-23, God directed Moses to make a holy oil composed of "myrrh, sweet cinnamon, kaneh bosm, and kassia".[19] In 2003,

---

11 Siegel & Jarvick (1975), 'Drug-Induced Hallucinations in Animals and Man', 83-87.
12 Weil & Rosen (1993), *From Chocolate to Morphine*, 10.
13 The book *Cannabis Culture*, edited by Vera Rubin (1975), collects some of the papers presented at the IX International Congress of Anthropological and Ethnological Sciences. It gives an overview of cannabis use in a broad range of societies. *Plants of the Gods* by Schultes & Hofmann (1979) is another authoritative book on this subject.
14 Li (1975), 'The Origin and Use of Cannabis in Eastern Asia: Their Linguistic-Cultural Implications', 51-75.
15 Van de Wijngaart (1991), *Competing Perspectives on Drug Use*, 12.
16 Lyman & Potter (1996), *Drugs in Society*, 4.
17 In August 2002, the *Jerusalem Post* reported that researchers from Hebrew University had found ancient ceramic pots containing residues of cannabis and opium, some of which dated back as far as 1400 BC. See Keyser (2002), 'Israel centre of ancient drug trade'.
18 In central Israel, the skeleton of a 14-year-old girl was found who had died in childbirth around 390 AD. On her stomach was found a substance that turned out to be a mixture of hashish, dried seeds, fruits, and common reeds. The use of cannabis for childbirth continued until the nineteenth century, when new drugs were developed.
19 Anthropology professor Sula Benet explained that the original Hebrew text of the Old Testament contains several references to hemp, both as incense, which was an integral part of religious celebration, and as an intoxicant. She further noted that in many translation of the Bible's original Hebrew, kaneh bosm is variously and erroneously translated as 'calamus' (a fragrant marsh plant) or by the vague term 'aromatic reed'. Benet retraced the translation error of calamus to the oldest Greek translation of the Hebrew Bible in the third century BC, an error that was repeated in many other translations, including Martin Luther's. See Benet (1975), 'Early Diffusion and Folk Uses of Hemp', 40-41. See also Kaplan (1981), *The Living Torah: The Five Books of Moses and the Haftarot*.

a debate was sparked when the question arose as to whether Christ (which means the anointed one) had been using this cannabis-based anointing oil in his healings.[20] Significantly, the relationship between religion and psychoactive substances is not as far fetched as it may first appear. In a recent published book, Huston Smith, one of the world's leading religious scholars, delves into the relationship between religion and psychoactive plants as spiritual catalysts, for which the word entheogens is used.[21]

The first reference to cannabis use in Europe is found in the work of the great historiographer Herodotus, who was writing around 450 BC. In his *Histories*, about the Scythians living North of the Black Sea, Herodotus recorded that cannabis grew wild in Thrace and was also cultivated for its fibre, which was used for weaving.[22] He also described how the Scythians used cannabis as a euphoriant by taking a cannabis 'vapour bath', which led the users, "delighted, to shout for joy".[23] In Western Europe, during the pre-Roman as well as the Roman period, it is well documented that there was widespread use of cannabis, at least for commercial purposes. Stefanis makes mention of cannabis that had been grown in the Rhône valley region and had been used to make rope for the navy of Hieron II of Syracuse (third century BC). Documented as well, is that the sails and canvas of the Roman galleys were also made from cannabis fibre.[24]

For more than 8,000 years, the opium poppy, whose milky sap is used as the basis for heroin and other opiates, has been cultivated for this pain-relieving property.[25] In Mesopotamia, Sumerian tablets, dating from 5,000 BC, speak of a herb called 'the joy plant' which historians presume to be opium. Homer (900 BC) wrote about the use of opium in *The Iliad*, while Hippocrates (450 BC), the father of modern medicine, recommended drinking the seed of the opium poppy combined with nettle. Until the present day, the opium plant has remained an

20 Bennett (2002) claims in 'The Plant of Kindness: Cannabis and Christianity' published in the cannabis magazine *High Times* that Jesus Christ and his apostles may have used a cannabis-based anointing oil to cure people with crippling diseases and other physical and mental problems. Church representatives reacted with denial, but Boston University Classics professor Ruck (2003) reacted in a *Sunday Times* article ('Was there a whiff of cannabis about Jesus?') it might well have been the case. Besides archaeological indications, he writes, the scriptures make mention of cannabis oil used for medical and visionary use. Apostle Mark describes Jesus as casting out demons and healing by the use of this holy chrism, and early Christian documents found in Egypt, thought to be a more accurate record than the New Testament, portray Jesus as an ecstatic rebel sage who preached enlightenment through rituals involving magical plants.
21 Smith (2000*), Cleansing the Doors of Perception.* Smith is also the author of the *World's Religions*, which is since some thirty years considered a standard work.
22 Stefanis et al. (1975), 'Sociocultural and Epidemiological Aspects of Hashish Use in Greece', 304.
23 Herodotus wrote in *The Histories* (IV: 74-75) the following about the cannabis 'vapour bath': "The Scythians, as I said, take some of this hemp-seed, and, creeping under the felt coverings, throw it upon the red-hot stones; immediately it smokes, and gives out such a vapour as no Grecian vapour-bath can exceed; the Scythians, delighted, shout for joy, and this vapour serves them instead of a water-bath; for they never by any chance wash their bodies with water.
24 Stefanis et al. (1975), 'Sociocultural and Epidemiological Aspects of Hashish Use in Greece', 303.
25 Van de Wijngaart (1991), *Competing Perspectives on Drug Use*, 12.

important source for pain relief along with morphine, whose opiate effect is close to that of heroin. Even with a virtual pharmacopoeia of new synthetic pain-relieving drugs on the market today, morphine is still considered by many to be the 'queen' of the painkillers.

The use of the coca leaf, from which cocaine is derived, dates back to approximately 1,000 BC in South America. No written records exist, but stone and ceramic artefacts portray persons with a bulge in the cheek, referring to coca chewing. Much earlier, around 3,000 BC, the Chinese were already familiar with the stimulant ephedrine, which is close to amphetamines. The use of another group of mind-altering substances, hallucinogens such as magic mushrooms and the peyote cactus, can be traced back more than 2000 years in the Americas. In Europe, the use of cocaine and hallucinogens does not have such a long history, but their use goes back further than commonly thought. Research published in 2001 revealed several seventeenth century smoking pipes, including some found in the garden of William Shakespeare, containing residue of cannabis, cocaine and myristic acid, a hallucinogen found in nutmeg. It is not proven that any of the pipes were actually used by Shakespeare, but the results support the view that at least one hallucinogen was accessible to him and other seventeenth century writers.[26]

Alcohol use, finally, has been known among civilisations on all continents. It distinguishes itself from the earlier mentioned substances in the sense that knowledge and use of a particular plant is not required for the effect to be produced, but instead, knowledge of a process.[27] "Alcohol has always been the most commonly used drug because the consumption of fermented juices easily produces interesting and pleasant variations from ordinary consciousness".[28] In Ancient Egypt, beer was the most important popular drink, whereas wine was a more exclusive commodity, as it had to be imported. In a later era, the Egyptians produced wine themselves. Documentation for this production has been gleaned from a hieroglyphic depiction of a winepress dating from 3,200 BC.[29] The Greek produced wine on a commercial basis and bottled it in amphorae, a practice followed by the Romans, who introduced the taxation.

---

26 Thackeray et al. (2001), 'Chemical analysis of residues from seventeenth-century clay pipes from Stratford-upon-Avon and environs'. Of the pipes that were found in Shakespeare's garden, several tested positive for cannabis. One of the cocaine pipes came from 'Harvard house,' the home of the mother from John Harvard, after whom Harvard University was named. Thackeray started the pipe study after coming across a reference to the "noted weed" in Sonnet 76 of Shakespeare's poems, which he thought might be Shakespeare alluding to his use of cannabis. See Smillie (2001), 'Did Shakespeare Puff on "Noted Weed"'.
27 Essential for the process of fermenting farinaceous cereals or sugary fruits, respectively yielding beer and wine, is the fungus yeast. In *From Chocolate to Morphine* Weil & Rosen (1993: 53) explain that yeast are simple, one-celled forms of life everywhere, such as in the air and on skins of many fruits. To grow and multiply, yeast cells need water, sugar, and warmth. They keep on growing till they have used up all the sugar, or until the alcohol concentration kills them
28 Weil (1986), *The Natural Mind*, 17.
29 Gerritsen (1993), *De politieke economie van de roes*, 25.

Human organisations and the construction of boundaries, social rules prescribing what is allowed and what not, whether through a community, society, church or modern State, have always existed. This also applies to the use of psychoactive substances; regulations for their use were developed in either formal or informal ways. "Usually the use of certain drugs is approved and integrated into the life of a tribe, community, or nation, sometimes in formal rituals and ceremonies".[30] Confinement of use to a particular context, sometimes under the guidance of a shaman, is one method of controlling and regulating the use within a community. In more complex societies, formal and sometimes institutionalised regulations have developed. As early as ancient Babylon, for example, there were legal controls in place for the control of alcohol use: the Code of Hammurabi (1,700 BC.) included censure of public intoxication.[31] During the seventh dynasty of ancient Egypt two centuries later, opium addiction was thought to be morally corrupting, and rules were established to limit opium use.

While the use of psychoactive substances may be found almost universally among humans in different times and places, the approval of certain types of drugs, and the disapproval of others, differs greatly from one culture to the other. Andrew Weil and Winifred Rosen give several examples in their book *From Chocolate to Morphine*, such as some early Muslim sects encouraging the use of coffee in religious rites, while invoking strict prohibitions against alcohol. Conversely, when coffee came to Europe in the seventeenth century, the Roman Catholic Church opposed it as an evil drug, but continued to regard wine as a traditional sacrament.[32]

Different attitudes have also existed toward tobacco. When Columbus brought the plant from America to Europe, it provoked such strong reactions that some countries installed the death penalty for users.[33] In the twentieth century tobacco was initially seen as a source of State revenue, and some States took the production and sales in their own hands through monopolies on growing and rules about distribution. In the first half of the twentieth century, authorities even advocated tobacco smoking in the belief it promoted concentration and relaxation.[34] The positive qualities attributed to smoking were depicted in movies of the 1930 and 1940s, with characters who were constantly smoking. During World War II, American soldiers had cigarettes as standard issue in their rations, and when they liberated parts of Europe cigarettes became a symbol of

---

30 Weil & Rosen (1993), *From Chocolate to Morphine*, 10.
31 Lyman and Potter (1996), *Drugs in Society*, 4.
32 Weil and Rosen (1993), *From Chocolate to Morphine*, 11.
33 As Weil & Rosen (1993: 53) point out in their book, *From Chocolate to Morphine,* tobacco in the 1500s was different and differently used than today's tobacco. It was occasionally smoked in order to alter consciousness. The harsh tobacco was smoked by inhaling it very deeply, but because it was so harsh, it could not be smoked often enough to develop tolerance and addiction. Still, authorities were upset about it, and considered it as a new source of evil and tried to prohibit it.
34 Weil & Rosen (1993), *From Chocolate to Morphine*, 53.

freedom. Up until the 1950s, doctors still appeared in cigarette advertisements promoting particular brands as 'soothing the throat'. In the second half of the twentieth century, however, tobacco increasingly came to be seen as posing a health hazard, resulting in stricter regulations for its use and sale. Hence, in only a few decades, a major shift in attitude toward tobacco smoking took place. Despite its general negative reputation, tobacco is still legal everywhere in the world. It also appears a valued commodity economically, as production continues to be subsidised in Europe and North America.

The current social reactions toward another plant, cannabis, although usually smoked in the same way as tobacco, are very different. Although cannabis use historically goes back further than tobacco, and was geographically much more widespread,[35] it is prohibited by governments throughout the world, as well as often being deemed 'deviant'. This social disapproval has been laid down in national laws and a person found smoking it can be penalised either by the enforcement of drug laws or by social sanctions, such as being fired or expelled from school. Although punitive actions such as these have become commonplace in most societies, other approaches do still exist. In India for example, cannabis is not only smoked but also eaten and drunk in the form of bhang, a mixture of cannabis and milk, yoghurt or fruit juices. Bhang can be bought from street vendors or at bus and train stations and its use is socially accepted. Its use is prescribed by social custom and religious usage, such as by priests, and at weddings it is often expected that bhang be served.[36]

Alcohol is socially accepted and used in most countries of the world. In some cultures, such as in the Islamic world, however, it is not tolerated. In India, traditionally a religious (Hindu) aversion exists toward alcohol, but use is increasing among urban and westernised Indians. In Europe, after being generally accepted for centuries, it increasingly came to be seen as problematic during the second half of the nineteenth century. All kinds of social ills were attributed to it, and national and international efforts were made for its prohibition.[37] In the first half of the twentieth century, a partial alcohol ban was realised. A handful of Western countries (Iceland, Finland, and of course, the United States which is the most known example) initiated some sort of alcohol prohibition for a number of years. Most African countries maintained alcohol prohibition for the first four decades of the twentieth century.[38] Islamic countries

---

35 As far as known, tobacco only occurred in South America until Columbus brought it to Europe.

36 Clinard & Meier (1979), *Sociology of Deviant Behavior*, 281. Considering this tradition of cannabis use, the strict control regime of the 1961 convention did not immediately apply to India and Pakistan. Bruun et al. write in *The Gentlemen's Club* (1975: 200) that the 1961 convention included transitional provisions, allowing countries like India and Pakistan that cannabis be used non-medically for twenty-five years.

37 Levine (1978), *Demon of the Middle Class: Self-control, Liquor, and the Ideology of Temperance in 19th Century America.*

38 Alcohol prohibition in Africa, decided about by the European colonial powers and only directed towards the natives, is not much known. Its background will be briefly discussed in the next chapter. See also Bruun et al. (1976), *The Gentlemen's Club.*

continue banning alcohol, but in Catholic, Southern European countries, alcohol is socially and culturally highly valued, and, for example, considered indispensable for a dinner. These different attitudes sometimes lead to diplomatic problems, such as when an Islamic leader visits a Southern European country and demands that no wine be served during dinner. In October 2002, this led to the cancelling of the protocol dinner King Juan Carlos had intended to offer to Iranian President Khatami who was on an official visit to Spain.

These examples show that attitudes toward psychoactive substances differ greatly in time and place. This is also true for today's illicit drugs, with disapproval being the prevailing idea and norm since the twentieth century. Prior to that, however, this was very different. In the nineteenth century for example, the legal substances opium, coca, their derivatives, and to a lesser extent cannabis, were popular and widely used both for medicinal and recreational purposes. Opium, which had been used as a general medicine for centuries, was one of the most widely used substances in medical practice until far into the nineteenth century.[39] In the words of Yale medical historian David Musto: "It was used in its crude form as an ingredient of multi-drug prescriptions, or in such abstracts as laudanum, that contained alcohol, or as 'black drop', containing no alcohol. Valued for its calming effect and soporific effects, opium was also used as a specific against gastrointestinal illnesses such as cholera, food poisoning, and parasites". Its relatively mild psychological effect when taken by mouth or as part of a more complex prescription was enhanced by frequent use, and the drug was supplied freely by physicians.[40] Coca became popular in Europe and America in the form of tonics and wines. The best known of these cocaine drinks was Coca-Cola,[41] while another was the Bordeaux wine Vin Mariani, a wine that also contained cocaine and which could lay claim to kings, presidents and popes among its avid consumers.[42]

Nineteenth century technological inventions in the drug production process, however, changed the kind of products: the isolation of morphine and heroin from opium, the isolation of cocaine from the coca plant, and the perfection of methods of hypodermic injection in the mid-nineteenth century. In a first stage these innovations revolutionised medical applications. Cocaine became the first local anaesthetic to be used in medical surgery.[43] In the 1880s, cocaine came to be seen as a panacea and doctors began to prescribe it for a variety of medical problems, including dependence on opiates and alcohol. In the United States, Musto writes, cocaine achieved popularity as a general tonic, for sinusitis and

39 De Kort (1995), *Tussen patiënt en delinquent,* 33.
40 Musto (1999), *The American Disease. Origins of Narcotics Control*, 1.
41 As Weil & Rosen (1993: 45) note in *From Chocolate to Morphine*, the Coca-Cola Company took cocaine out of its drinks in the early twentieth century. It continues to use the coca leaves for the drink though, from which a drug-free extract is used as a flavour.
42 Nadelmann (1990), 'Global prohibition regimes', 510.
43 Weil & Rosen (1993), *From Chocolate to Morphine*, 45.

hay fever, and as a cure for the opium, morphine and alcohol habits.[44] Learned journals published accounts which fell just short of advising unlimited intake of cocaine, while neurologist William Hammond, former Surgeon General of the army, "swore by it and took a wineglass of it with each meal". Sigmund Freud is a well-known proponent of cocaine as a general tonic and addiction cure. Freud publishing several cocaine papers during the 1880s.[45]

However, at the end of the century the phenomena of 'cocainism' was discovered and medical applications of cocaine were being restricted. Doctors started looking for other local anaesthetics, leaving cocaine only to be used for certain operations. Morphine was first hailed too, as it proved to be useful – and still is – in the medical treatment of pain. Later in the century physicians discovered morphine was addictive and as a cure to 'morphinism', German pharmaceutical company Bayer brought heroin on the market, which was also used as a cough suppressant. Until the early twentieth century, heroin was advertised in newspapers and magazines, until it became increasingly clear it also had some dependency creating properties.

Gradually, a distinction was being made between the uses of drugs for medical or recreational purposes. If prescribed by physicians, they were viewed as beneficial, but the same drugs in the hand of the lay public were considered harmful.[46] Public health policies emerged and it was decided drugs should no longer be left to the free market. Concern over easy prescriptions and wide-spread use of cocaine and opiate derivatives led to stricter rules, such as government controls over their distribution, or to the monopolisation of physicians and pharmacists on their prescription. The easy access of the public came to be limited, and sometimes prohibited.

As will be further explained in the next chapter, the concern over harmful potential of drugs, however, was not the main reason for their ultimate international prohibition. Consumption of opiates was quite common in the United States, Britain, and elsewhere during the nineteenth century, and much of it was properly viewed as benign.[47] In the nineteenth century industrial age, opium and alcohol were both widely used, but alcohol and alcoholism was generally considered a much bigger problem or vice than opiates and cocaine.[48] This explains why, at the time, there were many more national and international movements against alcohol than against drugs. Still, as already mentioned, alcohol prohibition would only take shape in a limited form. Drugs on the other

---

44 Cocaine was used as a remedy for sinusitis, as when it is sniffed, the cocaine crystals shrink mucous membranes and drain sinuses. In the nineteenth century, cocaine became the official remedy of the American Hay Fever Association. See Musto (1999), *The American Disease,* 7-8.
45 Musto (1999), *The American Disease,* 7. Freud's three cocaine papers were published in the 1880s in Vienna and were later translated and published in English (see Musto's footnote 18 on pp. 305-306).
46 De Kort (1995), *Tussen patiënt en delinquent,* 6.
47 Nadelmann (1990), 'Global prohibition regimes', 505.
48 See Berridge & Edwards (1981), *Opium and the People.*

hand were to be subject of an international prohibition regime, starting off in the beginning of the twentieth century.

1.3 Global Drug Prohibition

The world-wide illegality of drugs is something most people today take for granted and do not really question. They seem to unconsciously accept it, without realising it once was a decision to make them illegal. Drug prohibition can therefore be labelled, in Emile Durkheim's terms, a 'social fact'. Durkheim defined social facts as "any way of acting, whether fixed or not, capable of exerting over the individual an external constraint".[49] As American sociologist Harry Levine explained, "social facts exist outside of our consciousness – they exist whether we recognise them or not, and they have real effects, real consequences".[50] This indeed applies to the phenomenon of global drug prohibition, a world-wide system structured by a series of three international treaties that are supervised by the UN. Most countries of the world have signed these treaties, resulting in legal constraints regarding the production, sale, possession, and in some cases consumption of drugs. "Every country criminalises production and sale of cannabis, cocaine and opiates (except for limited medical use). Most countries criminalise both the production and sale of some other psychoactive substances, as well as holding criminal simple possession of small amounts of the prohibited substances".[51] These laws are enforced by police and military. Individuals not respecting these constraints may have to face the consequences, which often results in legal sanctions.

Global drug prohibition may be a social fact today, in an historical sense the illegality of drugs is not obvious at all, but a relatively recent phenomenon. Efforts to internationally control the substances that today are called illicit drugs are less than a century old. It was during the twentieth century that, in gradual steps, drugs have become internationally prohibited. The first step was taken in China, and was related to a Chinese problem. The book *The Gentlemen's Club: International Control of Drugs and Alcohol,* a standard work on international drug control by the Scandinavian authors Kettil Bruun, Lynn Pan and Ingemar Rexed, puts it as follows: "International drug control was initiated in response to a specific problem in a specific area of the world – opium in China".[52] In 1909, the Shanghai Opium Commission met, attended by representatives from thirteen countries, with the aim of arriving at a stricter opium regime. As this

49 Durkheim (1982), *The Rules of the Sociological Method*, 59. Originally published in French in 1895.
50 Levine (1997), 'The Secret of World-Wide Drug Prohibition'. See also Levine (2003), 'Global drug prohibition: its uses and crises', a commentary in the special issue of the *International Journal of Drug Policy* of April 2003 dedicated to the UN drug conventions.
51 Levine (2003), 'Global drug prohibition: its uses and crises', 145.
52 Bruun et al. (1975), *The Gentlemen's Club: International Control of Drugs and Alcohol*, 28.

conference took the form of a Commission, its recommendations were not binding. Then, in December 1911, the first opium conference took place in The Hague, which one month later, resulted in the 1912 convention on opium.[53] In addition to opium, its derivatives morphine and heroin were declared illegal, as well as cocaine. The 1912 convention marks the beginning of the international drug control regime that is based on drug prohibition.

International drug control took full effect after World War II, when the United Nations had been founded and assumed international drug control functions. Some earlier drug treaties were put together, which eventually lead to the 1961 Single Convention on Narcotic Drugs. The Single Convention was set up to control the listed narcotic substances, which are mostly plant-based, such as opium, cannabis and coca. Ten years later a second treaty followed, which was called the 1971 Convention against Psychotropic Substances. Aimed at controlling the so-called psychotropic substances, this second treaty lists mostly synthetic substances such as amphetamines, hallucinogens, barbiturates, tranquillisers, as well as some plant-based substances not listed in 1961. Finally, in 1988 a third drug convention followed, which was called the 1988 Convention against Illicit Trafficking in Drugs and Psychotropic Substances. This third treaty does not focus on substances, but more on international drug trafficking, for which reasons it includes provisions on matters such as extradition, mutual legal assistance and money laundering.[54] An important provision of the 1988 treaty is that it obliges states to establish as criminal offences all actions with regard to the substances listed in the 1961 and 1971 treaties, such as production, transport, import, export, distribution, transport, including possession and purchasing. Hence, only the consumption of the listed substances is exempted here from being obligatory criminalised by signatory States.

The three UN drugs conventions are generally regarded as the basis for international drugs policy. They determine that the production, manufacture, possession and use of the listed substances must be limited to medical and scientific purposes. Over the years, the number of listed substances has grown substantially. Whereas at the first international drug control meeting in 1909 only opium was on the agenda, in 1912, four substances were declared illegal, a number that by the end of the twentieth century had increased to some 250. And, whereas the first drug convention of 1912 was signed by 34 states, almost a century later almost all countries in the world have signed the drug conventions.[55] It is therefore possible to speak of a drug prohibition system that has become truly global in scope. As a result, "the production, sale, and even

---

53 As the next chapter will explain further, it was actually a series of conferences that were held in the Hague, not only in 1912 but also in 1913 and 1914.

54 For all provisions and more details see De Ruyver et al. (2002), *Multidisciplinary Drug Policies and the UN Drug Treaties*.

55 177 States are party of the 1961 convention, 171 are party of the 1971 convention, and the 1988 convention has been ratified by 162 States. For a full overview, see Annex 3 of De Ruyver et al. (2002), *Multidisciplinary Drug Policies and the UN Drug Treaties*, 153-156.

possession of cannabis, cocaine, and most opiates, hallucinogens, barbiturates, amphetamines, and tranquillisers outside strictly regulated medical and scientific channels are now punished with criminal sanctions in virtually every nation".[56]

It is unusual for consumer commodities to be declared illegal internationally. An examination of the reasons that drugs have come under this international control regime has been subjected to study, to some extent, but is certainly not part of the public consciousness.[57] Until recently, Levine points out, the term 'drug prohibition' was rarely used by governments, the news media, or academics. Yet these factors, combined, have led to a passive acceptance of the global (UN) prohibition system, and thus, in a sense, have rendered it nearly imperceptible.[58] The rather complex history of drug prohibition will be more fully discussed in the next chapter – suffice to mention here that, surprisingly, international drug prohibition did not result from a careful analysis and well-considered scientific considerations over the health hazards drugs pose. Certain substances, for example, did not become illegal when they had been found to be even far more dangerous than others that remained legal. The most striking example of this is alcohol. In the history of drug prohibition, other forces have been at work, with certain drugs sometimes being used in a larger political power play. The complete history of all the participants involved is not yet fully known, such as the extent of the role of pharmaceutical companies, or other lobbies such as manufacturers of synthetic textiles and plastics that had an interest in prohibiting a useful substance like hemp.[59]

What is known though about the reasons for international drug prohibition is that moral judgements and political opportunism were behind it. From the very beginning the United States have been the driving force behind the process of international drug prohibition, which was related to external commercial and political considerations, but which had its domestic political reasons as well.[60] This does not mean it has been an American 'conspiracy' to declare drugs illegal. That the United States was able to promulgate their domestic norms to the international level, is no more than a reflection of their acquired hegemonic

56 Nadelmann (1990), 'Global prohibition regimes', 503.
57 Classic academic books in this regard are the earlier quoted work of Bruun et al. (1975), *The Gentlemen's Club* and Musto (1973), *The American Disease*. A recent study is done by Bewley-Taylor (1999), *The United States and International Drug Control, 1909-1997*.
58 Levine (2003), 'Global drug prohibition: its uses and crises', 145.
59 *The Gentlemen's Club* refers in its title to the small group of men, just over a dozen in number, who all have central positions in the machinery of the UN international drug control system. One of the things these gentlemen have in common is their many connections to pharmaceutical companies, an interesting point the book does not further explore. The precise history of the prohibition of cannabis – including the prohibition of the much useful and much used industrial hemp – and the role of certain interests groups such as chemical, paper, and cotton industry is not fully described yet. In *The Emperor Wears no Clothes*, Herer (2000) refers to the role of manufacturers of synthetic textiles and plastics, such as Dupont.
60 See Bewley-Taylor (1999), *The United States and International Drug Control, 1909-1997*.

position in the world. Hence, in a sense, the American norms became globalised and during the twentieth century it became the dominant international norm to consider drugs as morally bad and their use as deviant.[61] It should be noted though, that this strict view on drugs is not shared by all Americans.

Drug prohibition was given a new push with the 'drug epidemic' of the 1960s and 1970s, especially when young people in Western countries suddenly became interested in using illicit drugs. Owing to their membership in the counter culture or 'protest generation', the most common reaction of governments was to design new, more stringent, national drug legislations, which in many cases have been in force until today. This explains why, in many Western countries, current drug legislation dates from about 1970.

It is this increasing use of drugs, seen rising since the 1960s and continuing through 1970s, that is the starting point of this study. This type of drug use is labelled 'modern drug use' for the purposes of this study, because it is a new type of drug use, one that is no longer confined to specific – often artistic and deviant – circles as was the case before the 1960s. While it was the protest generation of the 1960s and 1970s that first introduced illicit drug use into modern western societies, a generation later use has expanded into mainstream populations to become, generally speaking, a part of international youth culture. Hence, what started off initially as an expression of a specific subculture, the counter culture, developed during the 1980s and 1990s into a more general social phenomenon, without any political, ideological or 'protest' associations attached to it. In other words, what once was a meaningful appendage to a political statement and the lifestyle associated with social change, has turned into an apolitical international socio-cultural phenomenon, mostly but not exclusively observed in Western societies. Modern drug use has expanded with an increasing number of users involving new illegal substances on the market today that were not available to users a generation ago. In some industrialised and urbanised societies, drug use has been more or less normalised; that is to say, it has found a general popular acceptance within society to the extent that use or experimentation is considered quite normal for young people. They are aware of the fact that the substances are illegal, but they themselves often consider illegal drugs to be available, without seeing a real difference – besides the legal status – between drugs and substances like tobacco and alcohol.

However, most politicians and policy makers still adhere to a strict interpretation of the law, that drugs are illegal, as well as conforming to the idea of drug prohibition as a social and legal fact. A common approach had developed in the last century, which led to an international political consensus among governments of almost all countries in the world, that the best way to deal with drugs was to prohibit them, and to fight them. This is why Kofi Annan's stressed the

---

61 See the excellent article by Nadelmann (1990), 'Global prohibition regimes', in which he rightly notes that, surprisingly, international norms have not been studied a lot.

common ground of global drug prohibition in his opening words to the World Drug Summit UNGASS quoted at the beginning of this chapter. When politicians discuss drugs today, the politically accepted and correct norm has been to use robust anti-drug language and rhetoric.[62] Former American President Bill Clinton for example announced a major new media campaign that would give American children the "powerful message that drugs are wrong and can kill them". In general terms, the drug summit largely reconfirmed the commitment to existing policy and a new push was given to intensify the fight against drugs. The United Nations Drug Control Programme (UNDCP) unfolded a 'Strategy for Coca and Opium Poppy Elimination' (SCOPE), with the aim of totally eradicating illicit drug production for the purpose of attaining a drug-free world.

The international political consensus over the illegality of drugs is so strong that it has become difficult to discuss alternatives, or to evaluate current international policy. The original impetus for UNGASS had, however, been a Mexican request to have a summit on the effectiveness and viability of international drug control strategies over the past decade.[63] The year 1998 was chosen as it marked ten years after the last drug convention of 1988. By doing so, the Mexican government represented the viewpoints of the governments of a number of Southern producing and transit countries that are of the opinion they get too much of the blame for the world drug problem and pay too high a price in the fight against it. Since the United States is a big and highly profitable drug market, Mexico, its southern neighbour, is an important transit country therefore suffering the negative 'spill over' of the American War on Drugs. As Mexican president Zedillo said during his UNGASS speech: "It is our men and women who die first combating drug trafficking. It is our communities that are first to suffer from violence, and our institutions that are undermined by corruption. It is our governments that are the first to have to shift valuable resources needed to fight poverty to serve as the first bulwark in this war".[64] However, during the official preliminary consultations Mexico's idea for an evaluation of international drug control strategies received too little support from several Western countries, in particular the United States, and the United Nations Drug Control Programme (UNDCP) itself. The prospect of an evaluation or review was therefore dropped from the agenda.[65]

The only serious criticism of global drug prohibition came from the outside. On the first day of UNGASS, an open letter signed by hundreds of academics, business people, intellectuals, and politicians, including former UN Secretary-General Perez de Cuellar was published in a two-page advertisement in the *New*

62 See Boekhout van Solinge (2002), *Drugs and Decision-Making in the European Union.*
63 See Jelsma (2003), 'Drugs in the UN system: the unwritten history of the 1998 United Nations General Assembly Special Session on drugs', 182-183.
64 United Nations General Assembly (1998), *20th Special Session Official Records.*
65 For a detailed account of this political trajectory leading to UNGASS, see Jelsma (2003), 'Drugs in the UN system: the unwritten history of the 1998 United Nations General Assembly Special Session on drugs', 181-195.

York Times, addressed to UN Secretary-General Kofi Annan.[66] The core of its message being: "We believe that the global war on drugs is causing more harm than drug abuse itself".[67] In short, the letter claimed the cure as being worse than the disease. In the international media, the criticism expressed by the letter overshadowed the UNDCP plans to reach a drug-free world within ten years, which would imply an intensification of the fight against drugs. At the summit itself, however, such arguments were not part of the official debates.

The convergence toward a common drug policy approach based on consensus over the prohibition of drugs is also observed in the European Union. Drugs are illegal in all its member States and all have signed the three UN drug conventions. The UN drug treaties have actually been incorporated into what is known as the EU's 'acquis' or legal foundations. This implies that the ratification of these drug conventions has become a condition for EU membership. With the completion of the European Union in 1993, drug policy has become part of EU competence.[68] As a result, EU member states are increasingly taking common measures in the area of drug policy, such as so-called joint actions, and the making of several EU drug action and strategy plans. As a result, it has become difficult for Member States to deviate too much from the others and they increasingly have to adjust their policies to one another. It is, however, in the sphere of external relations that the EU is most active where drugs are concerned. The EU has become an active promoter of the UN drug conventions, as it systematically brings drug-related issues into virtually all political dialogues with third countries (non-members) or regional organisations. Third countries, in particular those in the South, have to fulfil a number of conditions if they want some form of co-operation with the EU and the taking of drug-related measures has become one of them.[69]

Despite these common measures, the European Union has not decided (yet) whether it wishes to have a common drug policy. The question of harmonising drug policies of the EU member states was a recurring theme in the 1980s and 1990s. It was first discussed in the context of the Schengen agreement, but eventually a political solution was found by invoking the UN drugs conventions, the ratification of which should be regarded as a guarantee for the harmonised

---

66 The open letter was signed by some 600 people; besides many academics, writers, intellectuals, (former) politicians, it included former presidents, (prime) ministers, business people, and a number of Nobel laureates.

67 For the full text of the open letter and its signatories, see «www.drugpolicy.org/events/archive/conferences/ungass/letter».

68 After the Maastricht summit in 1991, the Treaty on European Union, or EU Treaty – and by the media often called Maastricht Treaty – was signed in 1992 and entered into effect in 1993. Ever since, policy areas have been added to the EU's areas of competence, which are organised in the second and third pillar, respectively external (foreign policy and defence) and internal affairs (justice and home affairs).

69 Boekhout van Solinge (2002), *Drugs and Decision-Making in the European Union*.

legislation.[70] Eventually, it was adopted as a general principal that if a country's drugs policy deviates from that of others, all parties must take measures to limit the impact of this discrepancy on those other countries. Then, in 1995 and 1996, a series of study conferences organised by the European Commission, Council, and Parliament on the EU Member States' drug laws found that the national drug laws approached each other sufficiently.[71] The discussions on the comparability of drug legislation focused on implementation as well as the legislation itself. The conferences reached the conclusion that there was no need to harmonise drugs legislations, which displayed enough similarities and scope for action against drugs. Harmonisation would have no added value.[72]

All this suggests the drug policies of the countries of the European Union are converging. Within the Union, member states now have to gear their drug policies to one another, while toward the outside, the third countries, the EU has the tendency to speak with one voice. The three UN drug conventions have come to serve as a formal basis for policy and a guarantee for sufficient harmonised drug legislations, and their ratification is actively promoted toward third countries.[73] In short, looking at the formal positions and the decisions that are being made within the EU, a common European drug policy approach seems to be developing.

1.4 National Varieties of Drug Prohibition

With a political and ideological consensus having been reached regarding drug prohibition in the twentieth century, the existence of other approaches has nearly been forgotten. The historical examples given earlier show that attitudes toward psychoactive substances varied in time and place and that different regulatory regimes existed, both for today's legal, as well as illegal substances.

---

70 The Schengen Agreement dates from 1985, and its object is to accomplish the free movement of persons, goods and services. To achieve this, the Schengen countries strive to abolish all controls along their inner frontiers. The Schengen countries therefore decided to endeavour to harmonise their legislation on drugs, arms and explosives, but the harmonisation of legislation on drugs was a stumbling block in the negotiations. The question arose of which national legislation or practice should be adopted as the standard. Eventually a political solution was found by invoking the UN drugs conventions.

71 The Task Force of the European Commission had decided to take stock of member states' drugs legislation. The overview was given by De Ruyver (1996), *Identification of differences in drug penal legislation in the member states of the European Union*, which study was subsequently discussed at conferences in 1995 and 1996.

72 "It is proposed to identify areas where greater co-operation would help to resolve the practical problems encountered by Member States when applying the legislation. This approach is regarded as more effective and realistic than a possible harmonisation of national legislations. More in-depth co-operation will lead to greater approximation in practice". See European Parliament, Spanish Presidency & European Commission (1996), *Conference on Drugs Policy. Summary of discussions and conclusions*. Brussels, December 7-8 1995 – March 25-26 1996, p. 36.

73 While it is true that most countries have signed the UN drug conventions, not all have signed all three of them.

This study focuses upon illicit drugs, but with the awareness that twentieth century global drug prohibition severely limited the range of possibilities for regulation. In a broader historical and theoretical perspective, many more drug regulatory models can be distinguished.

David Bewley-Taylor identified three ideal types of drug control policies: the libertarian approach, prohibition, and regulation.[74] In the first, *libertarian* approach, all drugs are freely available with no formal laws or controls whatsoever. In a historical sense, the libertarian approach is the one that existed for the longest period of time. The second category is *prohibition*. In this legalistic response, laws are designed to achieve the total prohibition of all production, trafficking, sale, possession, and use of drugs for other than medical and scientific purposes. This type of response is most commonly associated with the United States and it has spread to become the dominant and global regime. The third category, occupying the middle ground between the former two, is a policy of *regulation*. In such a system drug use is permitted under specified legal constraints that are reinforced by criminal sanctions. The United Kingdom pursued such a regulative drug policy until the 1960s with its 'medico-centric' approach, allowing General Practitioners to prescribe heroin.[75] Other historical examples of the regulation model are the governmental opium regulation systems that used to be in place in Asia, such as in Indonesia when it was under Dutch rule, and in French Indochina, and the Kingdom of Siam, now Thailand. The French system of regulating cannabis and tobacco in Morocco was in place from 1914-1952, and also fits under the heading of regulation. However, a distinction can be made here, in that it was not under the control of a government monopoly, but instead, was controlled by a group of French and European banks. This group was led by the *Banque de Paris and des Pays-Bas* (later renamed *Paribas*), and to which cannabis sales were granted as a concession. In fact, as Yann Bisiou showed, the French introduced several governmental monopoly systems. In addition to Morocco, the French also maintained a tobacco and cannabis monopoly system in Tunisia from 1881 to 1954. In the French possessions in India, government monopolies existed on opium, cannabis and cannabis derivatives such as hashish between 1846 and 1954, while in Oceania, an opium monopoly was in place from 1877 to 1922.[76]

In the second half of twentieth century, those regulatory systems ceased to exist. Since almost all countries have ratified the drug conventions of 1961, 1971, and 1988, the three ideal types of drug control policies just mentioned have become theoretical concepts that no longer exist in practice. In fact, of

---

74 Bewley-Taylor (1999), *The United States and International Drug Control, 1909-1997*, 4.
75 Bewley-Taylor (1999), *The United States and International Drug Control, 1909-1997*, 4.
76 Bisiou (1999), 'Histoire des politiques criminelles. Le cas des régies françaises des stupéfiants', 89-98. Bisiou's article is based on his Ph.D. thesis of 1994: *Les monopoles des stupéfiants* (University Paris X – Nanterre). Bisiou also mentions a government monopoly on cannabis seems to have existed Lebanon when it was a French protectorate, but he did not find the confirmation of it.

Bewley-Taylor's classifications of drug policy ideal types, only the second type, that of the prohibitionist approach, remains in practice. This has given rise to the situation as it exists today, in which all national drug policies are to be found on one side of the spectrum of policy approaches – that of prohibition.

American sociologists Craig Reinarman and Harry Levine also discuss different drug control possibilities under today's international prohibition. In their book *Crack in America*, they suggest that the varieties of drug prohibition could be seen as existing along a continuum.[77] At one end of the continuum are the most criminalised and punitive forms of drug prohibition that heavily rely on the arrest and incarceration of people for possessing, dealing or using illicit drugs. The other end of the continuum is formed by less harsh forms of drug prohibition, such as decriminalised and regulated forms of drug prohibition. These more tolerant forms of drug prohibition allow for public health policies reducing drug use harm, they arrest and imprison a much smaller part of the drug users, or they have decriminalised personal possession of some drugs. Punitive prohibition and regulatory prohibition can be considered ideal types forming the two ends of the drug policy continuum under global drug prohibition.

Reinarman and Levine consider the drug policy of the United States to be the best-known example of criminalised or punitive prohibition. American drug prohibition heavily relies upon arresting and imprisoning people for possession and use of illicit drugs, or for small-scale dealing.[78] This punitive type of prohibition gives long prison sentences for repeated possession, use, and small-scale distribution of illicit drugs, and many drug laws explicitly remove sentencing discretion from judges and do not allow for probation or parole.[79] The 1986 Anti-Drug Abuse Act established mandatory minimum sentences, which led to a substantial increase in the amount of drug law violators subjected to incarceration. In 1988, a similarly titled act was passed, which reinstalled the death penalty for major drug traffickers in some circumstances.[80] The United States now has nearly half a million people in prison for violating its drug laws. Most of them, poor and from racial minorities, are imprisoned for possession of an illicit drug or intent to sell small quantities. The mandatory federal penalty for possessing five grams of crack-cocaine for a first offence, for example, is five years in prison with no parole.[81]

Reinarman and Levine consider the drug policy of the Netherlands, and in particular, its cannabis policy, to be the best known example of the other end of

---

77 Reinarman and Levine (1997), *Crack in America*, 322. See also the article by Levine (2003), 'Global drug prohibition: its uses and crises', 146.
78 Reinarman and Levine (1997), *Crack in America*, 322
79 Levine (2003), 'Global drug prohibition: its uses and crises', 146.
80 Musto (1999), *The American Disease*, vii (foreword to the third edition).
81 See Levine (2003), 'Global drug prohibition: its uses and crises', 146, who adds that the mandatory federal penalty for possessing five grams of crack-cocaine, for a first offence, is five years in prison with no parole.

the drug prohibition continuum, representing a decriminalised and regulated form of drug prohibition. Technically speaking, cannabis possession and distribution remain illegal in the Netherlands, as required of any country which is a signatory to the UN drug conventions. Additionally, national legislation and policy in the Netherlands also limit the prosecution of the approximately 800 'coffee shops' that are licensed to sell small quantities of cannabis for on- and off-premises personal use. Under these policies, the coffee shops are permitted to operate as long as they are orderly and stay within well-defined limits that are monitored and enforced by the police. "Even as the cannabis sales are open, routine, and *appear* to be completely legal, importing and commercially producing this cannabis remains illegal. As a result, the coffee shops have always been supplied, as the Dutch say, through the 'back door'. This is still formally drug prohibition and the Netherlands prosecute importers (smugglers), dealers and commercial growers who handle large quantities of cannabis".[82] This type of regulatory prohibition as put into practice by the Dutch represents the farthest any country has been able to go within the current structures of global drug prohibition.

As Levine further explains, the prohibition policies of other Western countries exist along a continuum that ranges from the heavily criminalised crack-cocaine policies of the United States to the regulated cannabis prohibition of the Netherlands. No Western or democratic country has ever imposed forms of drug prohibition as criminalised and punitive as the United States, though some undemocratic countries have drug laws that are even harsher. Additionally, beginning in the early 1990s, clearly the drug policies in Europe, Canada and Australia and elsewhere have been shifting away from the criminalised end of the drug prohibition continuum.[83]

An additional and more practical way to formulate the drug policy continuum within the framework of global drug prohibition is by using the policy spectrum in which one side is formed by law enforcement and criminal justice, and the other by care and treatment. All national drug policies have, at least in theory, a dual character: they all have both a criminal justice and a health dimension. Since drug users are using illegal substances, the drug question is a criminal justice issue. At the same time, however, it is thought drug users might need help or treatment, for which reason, care and treatment policies have been also set up. In order words, the drug question is considered both a criminal justice and a public health problem. This punish-help spectrum is large, however, and the form it takes, in practice, differs greatly from country to country. In punitive models such as the United States, the emphasis is clearly placed upon punishment, with far less emphasis placed upon the availability of care and treatment programs. The current trend has seen countries decide to move away

---

82 See Levine (2003), 'Global drug prohibition: its uses and crises', 146.
83 Levine (2003), 'Global drug prohibition: its uses and crises', 146.

from the criminalised end of drug prohibition, and increasingly, to consider drug use as more of a health problem, rather than as a criminal problem. More precisely, as will be discussed further in the next chapter, beginning in approximately 1990 and continuing unabated as of this writing in 2004, a clear policy trend has emerged toward 'harm reduction'. This represents 'damage control', both for the user and society. This trend has been observed among the fifteen countries that formed the European Union until May 2004. This policy response means that the primary aim of the policy has shifted from an effort to reduce illegal drug use, per se, but instead, the new objective has become to reduce the (medical) harm that is associated with illegal drug use, such as infectious diseases. It was the arrival of AIDS in the second half of the 1980s, necessitating the recognition that intravenous drug users had been infected by sharing needles, that prompted countries to adopt this more pragmatic response.

If the drug policy continuum under global drug prohibition as described by Reinarman and Levine is applied to Europe, the Dutch type of prohibition, with harm reduction defined as its primary objective, can be identified as the clearest European example of a health oriented approach. On the other end of the spectrum, no Western country has had a form of drug prohibition as punitive as that of the United States, therefore no European equivalent can be found. In that respect, the European drug policy continuum is less broad in range – in particular, less punitive and more health-oriented. The European country whose drug policy comes closest to American drug prohibition is Sweden, which sets the drug-free society as its clear objective, and which has increasingly used criminalisation as a control strategy. Although Swedish drug policy as compared to American drug policy is not punitive to the degree found in the United States, but offers much more in the way of treatment possibilities, it is the European country where drug prohibition is found in the most extreme and uncompromising form. This is best shown by the fact that Swedish authorities have difficulty in accepting the pragmatic concept of harm reduction. The two poles of the European drug policy continuum are therefore formed by drug policies of the Netherlands and Sweden. The drug policies of other European countries are situated between these two poles.

But despite their commonalties, the European drug policies also differ considerably and offer many varieties. Whereas the origin and background of American drug policy has been studied and described extensively, the drug policies of European have been subjected to far less scrutiny. Clearly, academics, politicians, and professionals are amply informed as to the various European national drug policies and how they differ considerably in practice. But deeper analyses of underlying differences, which ultimately led to the development and pursuit of different public responses, are generally not known, and in fact, lacking scrutiny, remain relatively obscure. Descriptions of national drug policies do exist, of course, such as the overviews that the European Monitoring Centre for Drugs and Drugs Addiction (EMCDDA) in Lisbon distributes every year.[84] However, these generally are limited to offering statistics about prevalence and superficial descriptions of trends and policy measures, without giving in-depth explanations why certain measures were implemented. Similarly, academic studies have also been conducted, but even within the various disciplines related to drug policy, comprehensive in-depth studies, for the most part, have been absent.[85] In general, it can be said that it is rare that studies examine drug control in a broader social, political and cultural perspective; most studies of drug control are largely descriptive, and typically, have fallen short of probing for deeper explanations. This study wishes to fill that gap, and by doing so, make a contribution to the available knowledge with regard to national and international drug control policies in modern, industrialised societies. This study, therefore, sets out to analyse why countries have developed different drug policies. To achieve this goal, three rich European countries with long democratic and welfare state traditions, all of which are members of the European Union, will be taken into consideration. This study will look at modalities for handling drug related issues, as well as mechanisms within their respective societies, including a multiplicity of internal social, cultural and political attitudes that have led to the decisions taken by various countries in addressing the phenomenon. A concerted effort will be made to contextualise and explain the consequent variations in approach to state management and administration of drug policies.

France, the Netherlands and Sweden have been chosen for this undertaking. Although each country is reacting to the same – or at least greatly similar – phenomenon of modern drug use, each of these three countries has developed a distinct national drug policy. Examination of the drug discourses in France, the Netherlands, and Sweden, presented in the beginning of this introduction, indicate that major differences can be identified – despite the attainment of a consensus about the world-wide illegality of drugs and the measures taken within the context of the UN and EU. In their speeches for UNGASS, the representatives of the three European countries addressed the same subject of illicit drugs entirely differently. Each discourse stands for another way of evaluating and approaching the drug issue. As will be shown in the next chapters of this study, substantial differences can be identified between the three countries' drug policies.

The drug policies of France, the Netherlands and Sweden were selected because their drug policies cover the European drug policy continuum under drug prohibition. The two extremes of this continuum are formed by the drug policies of the Netherlands and Sweden. The fact that they constitute the

84 See also EMCCDA (2002), *Prosecution of drug users in Europe*, which analyses and describes the responses of the criminal-justice systems to drug offenders throughout Europe.
85 Studies in English on national drug policies that can be mentioned in this regard include, for example Korf (1995), *Dutch Treat*, Leuw & Haen Marshall (Eds.) (1994), *Between Prohibition and Legalization,* and Tops (2001), *A society with or without drugs?*

extremes of policy formation, makes these two public responses to illegal drug use interesting cases appropriate for this study. The two drug policies are even more interesting as in both countries a large number of politicians and policy makers believe in their rightness and effectiveness. This belief is so strong that in both countries it is feared that future increased EU co-operation might force them to give up some aspects of their policy. Paradoxically, while in the Netherlands the liberal, de facto decriminalised cannabis policy is considered as one of examples that have had positive results, in Sweden this is considered true for the restrictive and criminalised cannabis policy.

France is presented as the third country of this study because its drug policy is exemplary of the European trend toward changing drug practices that has been seen since the 1980s, and increasingly, in the 1990s. As noted earlier, the general trend in Europe and elsewhere in the industrialised Western world has been that drug policies are shifting away from the criminalised end of the drug prohibition continuum. Traditionally, the French public response to modern drug use was largely one of criminalised drug prohibition, but it has partly shifted away from that toward more drug-use tolerance and pragmatism. In the early 1990s, the concept of harm reduction was embraced and policies of that kind were set up in a short period of time. This makes the French case of specific interest, since the shift from criminalised toward less harsh forms of drug prohibition has been particularly obvious. The strict French drug legislation has not changed and drug users are still arrested, but the way of looking at drugs has changed, as is illustrated by the fact that a 1999 governmental report put heroin and alcohol in the same category of 'most dangerous drugs', to the dismay of the French wine and restaurant culture.[86] Although this does not mean alcohol will be treated in the same way as heroin (or vice versa), it does reflect a more harm reduction oriented and public health thinking.[87]

It is tempting to think the variations in national responses to modern drug use are due to different drug problems – in nature or in scale. For example, the extent of drug use or a certain type of drugs being used and leading to more damage could explain a different – more pragmatic – policy response. However, when looking at the most used illicit drug, cannabis, no logical relationship can be found between the extent of use and the policy response. Of the three countries under discussion, France has the highest recent cannabis use among young adults (17%), Sweden the lowest (1%), and the Netherlands (9.8%) occupies a middle position.[88] When considering problematic drug use, no such

---

86 Rocques (1999), *La dangerosité des drogues*.
87 In the sense that it points at the harm associated with the use of different substances, irrespective of their legal status. For the French policy towards alcohol and drugs, this legal difference remains, of course, crucial.
88 For young adults, the EMCDDA uses the range 15-34 years. Recent year is understood here as having used during the year prior to the interview. See EMCDDA (2002), *Annual Report*, 12 (figure 2).

correlation can be found either. In France and the Netherlands, the primary problem drug since the 1970s has been heroin. In Sweden on the other hand, this has long been the stimulant amphetamine. This very fact, however, does not explain the restrictive Swedish approach and its drug-free society aim, as amphetamine cannot be said to be more be significantly more dangerous than heroin. In reverse, that the Netherlands has a liberal and harm reduction policy cannot be explained either by the extent of the problem, since where problem users are concerned, it has the lowest figures of the EU.[89] Nor can it be said that greater drug-related harm, such as HIV infections or drug-related deaths, has led to the adoption of harm reduction in the Netherlands. More such harm can actually be found in France and in Sweden. In France, the high morbidity (HIV infections) and mortality (overdoses) led to the adoption of harm reduction in the early 1990s. In Sweden on the other hand, where the number of overdoses has been steadily rising, creating the highest per capita number of overdoses, it did *not* lead to the adoption of harm reduction as a policy strategy. Hence, when the general public responses of European countries toward illegal drugs are considered, no overall logical relationship can be established with their levels of drug use or drug problems.

At the level of the European Union, a clear link between countries' drug problems and their public responses cannot be established either. The European Monitoring Centre for Drugs and Drug Addiction (EMCDDA) looked into the correlation between the prevalence, or extent, of drug use and the relative harshness of a county's control regime. Former EMCDDA chair Mike Trace declared in this regard: "We have found no link across fifteen Member States between the robustness of their policy and the level of prevalence. There are some countries with high prevalence and harsh policies, some countries with low prevalence and harsh policies, and still other countries with low prevalence and liberal policies. There is no link, there is no rational link".[90]

In short, the form the drug policy of a county takes is not directly influenced by the extent of the drug problem, nor is there empirical evidence that a national drug policy has any substantial impact on the prevalence of drug use.[91] Gradual differences of course can be identified, but generally speaking Western countries have all basically been confronted with the same phenomenon of drug use, to which they react in different ways. If differences in the nature and extent of the drug problem cannot explain national variations in policy responses, what then?

89 EMCCDA (2002), *Annual Report*, 15 (figure 5).
90 Mike Trace thus declared in his testimony for a Special UK Home Affairs responsible for evaluating UK drug policy. See House of Commons, Home Affairs Committee (2002), *The government's Drugs Policy: Is it working?*, 6. Trace was also former deputy UK Anti-Drugs Coordinator.
91 What drug policy, however, certainly does have an impact on are the *conditions* under which drugs are being used.

The longer American experience in drug use and drug policy, which has been studied much more than European drug policies, gives some clues. It may be tempting to understand the strong repressive law enforcement oriented drug policy of the United States by looking at its large drug problem, such as inner city social problems and drug-related crime. A more profound analysis would be, however, to point to the conservative and punitive aspects of American society in general. But since American drug policy has been studied much more than European drug policies, it is now known it cannot be understood without looking at cultural factors. In his famous nineteenth century study on democracy in the United States, Alexis de Tocqueville already wrote that cultural principles, traditions and customs are just as important as laws.[92] Numerous American studies show that the repressive approach toward drugs should be understood in the context of the complicated race and power relations of the United States.[93] From its inception American drug policy has had a clear ethnic component. As will be explained in more detail in the next chapter, certain substances have become prohibited in the United States, exactly because they were associated with a particular ethnic minority group.

The smoking of opium came under prohibition in California in the late nineteenth century, because it was primarily used by Chinese, a group that was considered a threat to white society.[94] Cocaine was associated with Afro-Americans rebelling against segregation and oppression in the American South. During the 1920s and 1930s, marijuana was mostly used by Mexican immigrants. Horrible crimes were attributed to marijuana and its Mexican purveyors, which led to the labelling of marijuana as the 'killer weed' and, in 1937, to prohibition of its use.[95] To the list of substances being used by a minority or not-dominant group, and prohibited in a later stage by a dominant group, alcohol should also be added. Many White Anglo-Saxon Protestant Americans identified alcohol and its ills with the fearsome flow of millions of Catholic and Jewish immigrants, some of who had a tradition of alcohol drinking like the Irish, Italians and Poles. This ethnic dimension of power relations in American society is one of the background factors that led to American alcohol prohibition of 1920-1933.[96] Of course, the ethnic dimension is not the sole explanatory factor of American drug policy, but it certainly is one of the primary ones.

In this study it will be argued that national cultural traditions in handling social problems have greatly influenced the way the question of illicit drugs is being dealt with. The American drug experience and the three European drug discourses show there are vast cultural differences in interpretation of drug policy, as this study will reveal. The concept of culture is, of course, as cultural

92 Tocqueville (1981), *De la démocratie en Amérique I*, 392 (first published in 1835).
93 See Musto (1999), *The American Disease*, and Reinarman and Levine (1997), *Crack in America*.
94 Nadelmann (1990), 'Global prohibition regimes', 506.
95 Musto (1999), *The American Disease*, 224-229.
96 See Clark (1976), *Deliver Us From Evil. An Interpretation of American Prohibition*.

studies pioneer Raymond Williams noted, one of the most complicated words in English language.[97] The relatively new discipline, cultural studies, is devoted in part to discourse and the regulation of language, which can be attributed to the influence of French philosopher Michel Foucault. "From Foucault, cultural studies has derived the idea of discourse as a regulated way of speaking that defines and produces objects of knowledge, thereby governing what topics are talked about and practices conducted. For Foucault, discourse constructs, defines, and produces objects of knowledge in a intelligible way while at the same time excluding other ways of reasoning as unintelligible".[98] This probably explains why it is that although the same terminology is used to describe aspects of the drug question, policy makers, professionals, and politicians from the various countries often do not understand each other's approaches. National drug policies all show some internal logic but they appear to reason from different perspectives. As such, the different drug policy discourses referenced in the beginning of this chapter stand for different interpretations of the drug question, which in turn leads to misunderstanding and miscommunication between those who are involved in drug policy.

In order to really understand a national drug policy and its ideological and theoretical underpinnings, the wider context in which this policy evolved has to be taken into consideration. In this study it will be demonstrated that drug policies constitute complex constructions, which have developed in culturally and historically specific ways and that have been shaped within the boundaries of public concern, social policies and health and legal systems.[99] The different parts of every construction form some kind of overall system or drug policy paradigm through which its practitioners filter and interpret information. Given this complexity and the interplay of its components, the term 'national drug control system' is employed. In this study, the expression 'drug control system' has been adopted instead of the more commonly used term drug policy since the first indicates more precisely the intended direction taken within this thesis.[100]

This study thus unravels the constructions of national drug control systems and explains why countries deal with drugs the way they do. It will examine why France, the Netherlands and Sweden react to the same phenomenon of illicit drug use in different ways. It will explore justifications and rationalisations for the divergent, and even contradictory attitudes that distinguish French,

---

97 Williams (1983), *Keywords.*
98 Barker & Galasinski (2001), *Cultural Studies and Discourse Analysis*, 12.
99 See Peter Cohen's foreword to Boekhout van Solinge (1997), *The Swedish Drug Control System.*
100 The term drug control system is preferred over 'drug policy 'or 'drug control' as the drug control described in this study is, in fact, the form of a system, complex interplay or whole. The actual form a general public response takes towards the illicit drugs phenomenon, is influenced by other factors as well, some of which are outside the direct scope of illicit drugs. In this study it is argued that drug control systems are complex systems with a social, cultural, economic and political dimension.

Dutch, and Swedish approaches to drug use, including underlying, sometimes less visible political motives and influences.

The methodology used for this study is as follows. In order to understand a drug control system from within and subsequently describe it, a large variety of different sources were consulted. To begin with, this study is partly based on earlier work, such as the studies on Dutch, French and Swedish drug policy, as well as a study on drug control of the European Union.[101] For these earlier studies, as well as for the underlying one, it was essential to study general literature on the three countries and their drug policies. Moreover, a large number of people were interviewed, mostly policy makers and practitioners, in France, the Netherlands and Sweden, as well in as in EU 'capital' Brussels. In all three countries fieldwork was done, where many different drug users were met as well as some drug dealers, although this is not so much reflected in the underlying study. In this study, fieldwork data or insights merely have the role of supportive data, or as a way to clarify a point.[102]

Since the underlying study is about three different national constructions of the illegal drug question, a central question of this study was to distinguish, in a Foucauldian methodological sense, the different persons or parties that have had definition power in the process of constructing national drug control systems. In other words, the three drug control systems had to be 'de-constructed' to identify the influential and determining factors, individuals or organisations that make up these drug control systems. By studying academic studies and governmental reports, and by interviewing key persons, an effort has been made to identify these different factors.

The organisation of this study is as follows. Chapter two provides a historical overview of international drug control, which is essential in understanding the range of possibilities countries have at their disposal to deal with drug issues. In general a lot can be learned from history. The history of global drug prohibition has remained largely unknown to most academics and informed readers. The following chapter is an overview of this peculiar and interesting history and serves as a stage to view the variations of drug control in Europe. Chapters three, four and five describe and analyse the drug policies respectively of France, the Netherlands, and Sweden. These country chapters clarify why in each of these individual European countries culturally distinctive approaches were developed in order to deal with the phenomenon of modern drug use. Each of the three country chapters in this book starts with a short, general description of the geography, history and the people of the country in question. These

---

101 See the earlier books, reports and articles on drug issues by Boekhout van Solinge: *Standpunten drugsproblematiek (1995)*, 'Le cannabis en France' (1995), *L'héroïne, la cocaïne et le crack en France* (1996), *The Swedish Drug Control System* (1997), 'Dutch Drug Policy in a European Context' (1999), *Op de pof* (2001), and *Drugs and Decision-Making in the European Union* (2002).
102 In the studies mentioned in the previous footnote, more fieldwork data can be found.

country sections serve as a general background against which the drug policy should be placed. The writing of a country section is a delicate and difficult task, as it is almost impossible to not fall back in stereotypes. On the other hand, stereotypes are useful as they usually carry some truth and at times are painfully accurate. Finally, chapter six analyses the differences between the three approaches, the political problems evolving from these differences, and offers deeper explanations for the existence of the different ways in which these European countries deal with drug issues.

Chapter 2

From Global Prohibition to National Control

2.1 The Rise of Global Prohibition Regimes

International efforts to regulate and control elements and activities within societies are not unique to drugs. The development of international arrangements for drug control, in fact, parallels other forms of international co-operation that emerged during the nineteen and twentieth century.[1] International drug control can be considered within the larger context of internationalism, a nineteenth century concept based upon the idea that countries should have friendly relations and work together, jointly addressing activities or areas of concern.

In his article 'Global prohibition regimes', Ethan Nadelmann analyses the evolution of norms in international society, describing the dynamics by which these norms emerge, evolve, and expand. Nadelmann refers specifically to norms of a special classification, namely those "which prohibit, both in international law and in the domestic criminal law of states, the involvement of state and non-state actors in particular activities". Both the substance of these norms, and the processes by which they are enforced, are institutionalised in powerful global prohibition regimes. By way of example, Nadelmann examines: piracy and pirateering, the African slave trade, the white slave trade, and psychoactive substances, which have all come under a global prohibition regime.[2]

Piracy, practised officially or unofficially by European governments for more than a hundred years has gradually undergone a transformation from a national industry into an international threat.[3] During the eighteenth and nineteenth centuries measures were increasingly taken to suppress piracy by European governments – particularly the British. Privateering, or government-sanctioned piracy during wartime, was a practice that occurred regularly during the first half of the nineteenth century. By signing the 1856 Declaration of Paris, Great Britain, France, Russia, Prussia, Austria, Sardinia and the Ottoman High Porte formally abolished privateering. At the time, the United States refused to accede, insisting that its small navy required the option of privateering. As the

1   Bruun et al. (1975), *The Gentlemen's Club*, 7.
2   Nadelmann (1990), 'Global prohibition regimes'.
3   Nadelmann (1990), 'Global prohibition regimes', 488, based on C. M. Senior (1976), *A Nation of Pirates: English Piracy in Its Heyday*, 149.

United States navy grew during the second half of the nineteenth century so did the notion that privateering was no longer an acceptable mode of warfare. The United States government was eventually led to outlawing the practice of privateering. As a result, a once customary form of waging war had been eliminated by the end of the nineteenth century.[4] The agreement to end privateering represents one of the earliest examples of international co-operation leading to a global regime coming into effect.

Representing another example of the potential power of global regimes was the international concern over the African slave trade in the nineteenth century. The emancipation movement to abolish slavery began in the United Kingdom with the British Parliament's banning of the slave trade in 1807 and its abolishment from British colonies in 1833.[5] France abolished slavery in 1848, the Netherlands in 1863, Spain in 1886, and Brazil in 1888.

Throughout the nineteenth and into the twentieth century, the British government devoted naval, diplomatic, and economic resources towards the antislavery campaign. Britain also promoted its campaign through multilateral negotiations at international conferences, such as at the 1814-1815 Paris Peace conference, and at the Congresses of Vienna (1815), wherein it tried to achieve multilateral condemnation of the slave trade.[6] At these conferences, the first agreements were put forward to punish states not willing to abolish the slave trade. In a later stage, multilateral treaties strengthened and expanded the global criminalisation of the slave trade. The most important of these conferences was the Brussels Conference of 1889-1890, where eighteen states declared their intention to put an end to the African slave trade. In the twentieth century, the League of Nations undertook efforts toward the abolishment of slavery, work that was later continued by the United Nations.[7]

During the second half of the nineteenth century efforts were made to terminate the practices of white slavery and the white slave trade. The term white slavery referred to the system of licensed prostitution – for some it referred to all prostitution – as it existed in Europe and the United States. The white slave trade referred to the recruitment and trade in woman and children by force or by fraud. The campaign against the white slave led to conferences and agreements condemning the practice, notably the Agreement for the Suppres-

---

4   Nadelmann (1990), 'Global prohibition regimes', 489.
5   Some authors argue that the British, in abolishing slavery, were primarily motivated by economic and not humanitarian reasons. Economic considerations did play a role, as the country shifted from mercantilism to industrial capitalism and someone like Adam Smith argued that slavery was a highly inefficient economic system. However, as Nadelmann (1990: 493) summarises "fundamental impetus behind Britain's reversal on slavery and its subsequent efforts to suppress the slave trade, most historians on the subject have concluded, was a moral one derived in good part from religious and humanitarian impulses and the principles of Enlightenment and based not only on pity, (…) but also on the idea of the natural rights of man."
6   Nadelmann (1990), 'Global prohibition regimes', 492.
7   The UN Declaration of Human Rights, adopted by the General Assembly in 1948, contains a provision prohibiting slavery or trading in slaves.

sion of the White Slave Trade. Signed in Paris in 1904, it would later be ratified by approximately one hundred governments.[8]

Alcohol, as previously mentioned, was another of the nineteenth century concerns. The preoccupation with this issue had its roots in the widespread alcohol use, alcoholism, and the manifestation of alcohol related problems, especially among the poor working classes of the industrialised cities. Males in particular spent a relatively big part of their salary on alcohol, leaving less money to feed and clothe their family. Combined with the already difficult living conditions (poverty, housing, hygiene, illiteracy) of the pauperised working classes, alcohol was considered a vice that should be fought. There were also economic reasons for concern over alcohol. Industrial accidents caused by alcohol intoxication were not uncommon, making it clear that alcohol use did not mix well with the increasingly mechanised production methods of industrialisation.[9]

The Temperance Movement gained increased support in the nineteenth century, becoming the largest enduring mass movement of that century in the United States.[10] The first local American Temperance Society was founded in 1808; twenty-five years later, the movement had expanded to six thousand local societies, with a total of one million members. After the American state of Maine passed the first alcohol prohibition law in 1851, the movement pushed on internationally, spreading to Ireland, England, and the Scandinavian countries. The first international alcoholism congress was held in Paris in 1878. This was followed, in 1906, by the establishment of an international association. By 1910, membership in this association had grown to twenty-seven countries, with the strongest support coming from Islamic countries.[11]

For religious reasons, Islamic countries had instituted bans on alcohol. Of the Western countries, only a handful achieved full national bans on alcohol. Even when national bans were established, their duration was limited: Iceland (1909-1934), Finland (1919-1932), and the United States (1920-1933).[12] During

---

8 Nadelmann (1990), 'Global prohibition regimes', 515.
9 Gerritsen (1993), *De politieke economie van de roes*, 134.
10 Levine (1978), *Demon of the Middle Class: Self-control, Liquor, and the Ideology of Temperance in 19th Century America*, 44.
11 Bruun et al. (1975), *The Gentlemen's Club*, 8.
12 The Icelandic and Finnish alcohol prohibitions are much less known cases than the American one. With Icelandic alcohol prohibition ending, it was apparently 'forgotten' to legalise beer, as a result of which it remained illegal for long, until 1989 when the beer prohibition was repealed. See Olafsdottir (1998), 'The Dynamics of Shifts in Alcoholic Beverage Preference: Effects of the Legalization of Beer in Iceland' and Olafsdottir (1999), 'The Entrance of Beer into a Persistent Spirits Culture'. Finland's alcohol prohibition started in 1919, two years after independence. Finnish Parliament had passed prohibition a number of times, in 1907, 1909, 1911, and 1914, but each time the (Russian) tsar rejected it. Prohibition ended in 1932, after an advisory referendum showed extensive public dissatisfaction with its consequences. The International Edition of Finnish daily *Helsingin Sanomat* (9 April 2002) reported alcohol consumption had not only increased during prohibition (from 1.5 to 2 litres pure alcohol per capita), it also had made drinking more intoxication-oriented.

the first four decades of the twentieth century, an international agreement for alcohol control existed throughout most of Africa, banning distilled liquors. This had less to do with a general acceptance of the dangers associated with distilled liquors than with its connection with slavery. Exceptions were made for the non-native population of Africa, based not on the belief that the dangers were with liquor, but in the characteristics of the African people, accounting for the dangerous results of drinking.[13] Some Western countries instituted partial alcohol prohibition, such as Sweden (1917-1955), which put forth a ration system allowing the (male) head of the household to buy a certain quota of alcohol.[14] Most Islamic countries have remained 'dry' to this day.

An international or global ban on alcohol did not occur. Trials existed to get support for international control of alcohol, especially through the League of Nations, but they did not receive significant support. An important reason for this was that most Western countries were not enthusiastic about international alcohol control, in part because it would reduce tax revenues. Furthermore, an alcohol ban was largely blocked by resistance based in wine-growing countries, adding to the ideological conflict between prohibitionists and anti-prohibitionists, which also hampered it.[15] In short, the global consensus required to attain and sustain an alcohol prohibition regime could not be attained.[16]

However, opium prohibition followed quite a different course, and did not meet the same kind of powerful opposition. In the nineteenth century, opium was considered a lesser problem as compared to alcohol – for which reason there were fewer anti-opium movements. This meant these groups initially had less political leverage than gained by the anti-alcohol movements, which were widespread. The anti-opium movement originated in Britain and arose after the 1840-1842 opium war between Britain and China. The target was initially the British-Indian-Chinese opium trade.[17] In 1874, the Society for the Suppression of the Opium Trade was founded in London. However, the anti-opium movement received increasing political support in Britain until the end of the

---

13 See Bruun et al. (1975), *The Gentlemen's Club*, 16, where they write about the 1889-90 Brussels Act, under which colonial powers in Africa agreed to take measures against the slave trade. "This almost forgotten act also had a chapter (6) on 'Restrictive Measures Concerning the Traffic in Spirituous Liquor'; the regulations, which were valid for all Africa, except for north of latitude 200 N and south of 220 S latitude. The Act obliged signatory countries to take necessary steps to bar the introduction of liquor." In 1919, at St. Germain-en-Laye, a Convention on the Liquor Traffic in Africa was adopted, reiterated the stipulations of the Brussels Act. See chapter 12 of Bruun et al. (1975) for the history of international alcohol control endeavours.

14 See further chapter 5 on Swedish drug policy.

15 Bruun et al. (1975), *The Gentlemen's Club*, 180.

16 Nadelmann (1990), 'Global prohibition regimes', 510.

17 Bruun et al. (1975), *The Gentlemen's Club*, 9. The background of this war as follows. China was the big market for opium, which was mainly traded by Britons from India to China. Around the 1840s, Chinese resistance grew about the British opium trade and China wanted to stop it, but Britain insisted on free trade. Ultimately, the conflict led to a war, won by Britain, and resulting in a continuation of the British opium trade to China. The war did, however, lead to increased criticism on the trade in Britain itself.

nineteenth century. In China and the United States, anti-opium movements were also launched.

In the twentieth century, anti-opium efforts led to the Shanghai Opium Commission of 1909, the first international meeting to discuss international drug control. Of primary importance in the development of an international opium prohibition regime would be the support of the United States. As will be explained in section 2.2, the basis of the American anti-opium position was a combination of moral arguments set against a backdrop of rife with economic and political interests.

Several conclusions can be drawn from comparing different efforts to secure international or global prohibition regimes that have been discussed in this section. The regime against piracy can be considered the first global prohibition regime. The regimes against slavery and the slave trade added new dimensions that have been replicated in more recent global prohibition regimes. In the words of Nadelmann:

> "The regime to ban the slave trade was the first regime to be institutionalised in a series of international conventions signed by the vast majority of governments; it was the first in which blatantly moral impulses were a key factor and transnational moral entrepreneurs played leading roles; it was the first to criminalise international commerce in a particular 'commodity'; and it was the first to evolve into a far more ambitious regime aimed at the criminalisation of all activities involving the production, sale, and use of that 'commodity' in every country".[18]

Another conclusion that can be drawn from global prohibition regimes is that their rise seems to follow eighteenth century enlightenment thinking, resulting in concrete measures during the nineteenth century. These regimes should therefore be interpreted as representing progress in human history and milestones of international co-operation. The establishment of new norms would then mean a new step in the evolution of man, making clear which activities are no longer acceptable, but are henceforth to be considered deviant. "It is, in short, impossible to explain the abolition of slavery throughout the world during the past two centuries without emphasising the powerful role of shared moral notions derived primarily from the religious and secular principles of the Enlightenment".[19] This argumentation of the evolution of norms may be true to some extent – it certainly is for the question of slavery – but the explanation is more complex.

When studying more closely the norms on which prohibition regimes are based, it is observed that they do not always find general acceptance throughout the world. The spread of these norms onto the global level reflects the power relations between countries in the world at a particular moment. In attempting to understand the global spread of these norms in the evolution of global

18 Nadelmann (1990), 'Global prohibition regimes', 497.
19 Nadelmann (1990), 'Global prohibition regimes', 497.

society, the centrality of Western Europe initially, and later, the ascension to centrality of the United States during the twentieth century, cannot be over-emphasised.

> "To an extent virtually unprecedented in world history, a few European States and the United States proved successful in proselytising to diverse societies, shaping the moral views of substantial sectors of elite opinion outside their borders, and imposing their norms on foreign regimes around the world (...) Some Asian States, for instance, might have opted for a different global regime that legitimised the use of opium; some African and Asian States for a regime legitimising cannabis; many Muslim States for a regime prohibiting alcohol; and some Latin American States for a regime that sanctioned coca".[20]

A correlation can thus be observed between a hegemon, the world's dominant country during a particular period, and the measures that were then taken internationally. Economic and military domination often go hand in hand with political and cultural domination, allowing the hegemonic country to spread its agenda to other parts of the world.[21] In the nineteenth century Britain was the most dominant country in the world, it took the lead in forging regimes against both piracy and the slave trade, and managed to expand the British norms to a generalised, world scale. The United States took over Britain's position as world hegemon in the beginning of the twentieth century.[22] Consequently, the global norms evolving at the end of nineteenth, and especially the early twentieth century, were to reflect those of the new hegemonic power, the United States.

The role of subsequent hegemonies explains why it was not alcohol, but opium, which came under a global prohibition regime. Alcohol use was considered a greater problem than opium use, thereby giving the Temperance Movement wider support than the anti-opium movement. The Temperance Movement was largely an American invention: it had only limited influence in Britain which was then the world's hegemon. At that time the United States did not yet have enough power to transform its anti-alcohol stance into an internationally accepted program. The anti-opium movement arose in Britain, largely levelled against the British opium trade. However, Britain's hegemony was descending at the end of the nineteenth century as the movement began to gain in influence. In the same period, an increasingly critical stance towards opium was developing in the United States. It is fair to say that the British anti-opium movement would have had less success without American backing.[23] The United States position on an international ban on opium should therefore be seen in the context of the hegemony shifting from Britain to the Unites States around 1900. The country that would suffer most from an international ban on opium was Britain, the United States' main economic rival.

---

20 Nadelmann (1990), 'Global prohibition regimes', 484 and 511.
21 See the remarkable book by political geographer Peter Taylor (1996), *The Way the Modern World Works: World Hegemony to World Imperialism.*
22 See Taylor (1996), *The Way the Modern World Works: World Hegemony to World Imperialism.*
23 Bruun et al. (1975), *The Gentlemen's Club*, 8.

2.2 The American Role in International Drug Control

The preceding section attests to the decisive role played by the United States in the establishment of opium prohibition. In fact, during the entire history of international drug control, the United States has played such a prominent role that it is described as "the principal force".[24] The actions of the United States were key in the genesis of the international drug control regime at the beginning of the twentieth century. Beginning with the 1909 Shanghai Opium Commission, and the Hague Convention of 1912, the United States has continued to dominate its further development, including the latest UN drug convention of 1988, and beyond. This section attempts to explain the background of the United States' strict position on drugs. Various internal, domestic political causes will first be taken under consideration, followed by the more important and decisive external considerations related to policy and commercial interests.

Compared to European countries around 1900, the United States had a relatively large number of opiates users at the time, not only at home, but also in the Philippine archipelago acquired in 1898 after the American-Spanish War.[25] In the United States itself, the use of opiates were widespread, most of which was properly viewed as benign. Opiates were often consumed in the form of liquids such as laudanum, particularly among older white women in the South.[26] Going against this tide were 'moral crusaders' who considered the use of opium as being morally corrupt. Anti-opium campaigners, such as the Episcopal bishop Charles Brent in the Philippines, did not limit their arguments to opium, but considered as vices a wider range of activities including tobacco use, alcohol consumption, and prostitution. These campaigners played a central role in inspiring the passage of federal and state prohibition laws for opiates, cocaine, alcohol, cigarettes, and more.[27]

Decisive in the creation of American drug legislation were a series of 'drug scares', moral panics over drug use. In their book, *Crack in America*, Reinarman and Levine survey drug scares in the United States, describing them as "phenomena in their own right, quite apart from drug use and drug problems". They show how a particular drug is used as a scapegoat by attempting to link it to a group that is seen as problematic, such as immigrants, ethnic minorities, or rebellious youth.[28] The best known drug scare focused on alcohol. The nineteenth century anti-alcohol movement blamed alcohol for a large proportion of

---

24 The term 'principal force' is borrowed from the title of chapter 10: 'The United States – the Principal Force', of *The Gentlemen's Club* by Bruun et al. (1975).
25 When the United States gained possession of the Philippine archipelago it was confronted with the use of opium among both the Filipino and Chinese population. In 1905, Congress eventually decided to ban the use of opium by Filipinos with immediate effect, while the ban for the Chinese population would take effect three years later. See Musto (1999), *The American Disease*.
26 Laudanum was a well-known tincture containing opium.
27 Nadelmann (1990), 'Global prohibition regimes', 506.
28 Reinarman & Levine (1997), *Crack in America*, 1.

the poverty, crime, violence and moral degeneration in the United States. This anti-alcohol movement culminated in Prohibition (1920-1933), which its advocates praised as a panacea for society's ills. Part of the setting of this anti-alcohol movement was, in fact, a cultural conflict between the dominantly white Protestants and the more recently arrived Catholic immigrants such as the Irish, Italians and Poles, among whom alcohol consumption was much more prevalent.

At the end of the nineteenth century, an opium scare occurred in California, resulting in the ban of opium smoking, which was more of a Chinese practice. This ban had unmistakable racial undertones: it was prompted not so much by problems associated with opium use as by the general anti-Chinese agitation in California. America's west coast had a large Chinese population, most of whom had been hired as contract labourers on the railways and goldmines. With the depletion of the mines and the completion of the railway lines, the last quarter of the nineteenth century fell into an economic recession. In this increasingly tight labour market the Chinese, who tended to work for low pay, were increasingly perceived as a threat to Americans of European origin.[29] This led to the demonisation of Chinese people in the public mind, associations between Chinatown communities, opium, prostitution and gambling. The Chinese and their custom of opium smoking were closely watched.[30] The Chinese were alleged to be using opium to entice white women into sexual slavery. Although opiate use was far more common among white Americans than in the Chinese community at the end of the nineteenth century, it was, above all, the *smoking* of opium by the Chinese that was seen as a problem. It was suggested that opium smoking was one of the ways in which the Chinese were attempting to undermine American society so it became a focus for general anti-Chinese sentiments. Many forms of antagonism arose to drive the Chinese out or to at least isolate them.[31] This demonisation prompted the introduction of the first legislation against opium in the country, a law prohibiting the smoking of opium, enacted by the San Francisco municipal authority in 1875.

At the beginning of the twentieth century, cocaine and several cocaine-containing drinks, including Coca-Cola, came to be associated with Black Americans. Cocaine was especially feared in the American South where it was thought that black cocaine users might become "oblivious of their prescribed bounds and attack white society", they feared that blacks would rise above their place in society.[32] Black Americans purportedly became incredibly powerful and wild after using cocaine. To incapacitate "cocaine crazed Negroes", Musto writes, some Southern police stations switched from .32 to .38 calibre revolvers.

---

29 The low status of the Chinese at the time can even be seen in the comics of cowboy hero *Lucky Luke*.
30 Musto (1999), *The American Disease*, 5-6.
31 Musto (1999), *The American Disease*, 6.
32 Musto (1999), *The American Disease*, 6-7.

Another popular rumour was that Black Americans were raping white women under the influence of cocaine. David Musto concludes that this cocaine scare resulted not from problems in cocaine use, but from white fears of black rebellion against segregation and oppression. These cocaine myths gave one more excuse to continue the repression of blacks.[33]

Another drug scare arose in the 1930s, this time concerning marijuana. Harry Anslinger, who headed the alcohol prohibition task force during Prohibition, was later appointed head of the Federal Bureau of Narcotics. In his zeal to ban marijuana, he published propaganda describing murders committed by people under its influence. Since marijuana was mostly used by Mexicans at the time, they became the new focus of this anxiety: marijuana allegedly made them violent. Anslinger further alarmed the public by training attention to the growing popularity the 'killer weed' was gaining among young white Americans. In 1937, the result of this 'reefer madness' scare, engineered almost single-handedly by Anslinger, led the U.S. Congress to declare marijuana illegal.

Notwithstanding these moral panics in American society the United States' policy on drugs stemmed, first and foremost, from the country's new hegemonic status: its war against Spain in 1898 had yielded as newly annexed territories Cuba, Puerto Rico and the Philippines. With these new overseas possessions the United States had become a political and economic world power. As a nation with a strong economic agenda, the United States recognised that it would still have to compete with several European powers for expanding markets in the Far East.

One of the reasons that the United States had conquered the Philippines was to use it as a bridgehead for the huge Chinese market. However, the trading ties between the United States and China were marked by friction. "What united China and the United States was their common adversary – the European colonial powers, and Britain in particular. By emphasising its aversion to the colonial opium trade, the United States was able to distinguish itself from its European rivals."[34]

Fifty years after losing the opium wars to Britain in the mid-nineteenth century, a vigorously nationalistic anti-opium mood prevailed in China. The nationalists, in particular, wanted to reopen debate on the opium trade. The Americans presented themselves as the ideal partners to help the Chinese with their opium problem, starting with the implementation of an international ban. By currying favour with the Chinese, they hoped to gain access to their vast economic market. An international ban on opium would not be necessarily bad for the United States, since the country hardest hit by it would be Britain, its main commercial rival. Bruun et al. summarise it as follows: "The United States

---

33   Musto (1999), *The American Disease*, 7. See also Reinarman & Levine (1997), *Crack in America*, 7.
34   Gerritsen (1993), *De politieke economie van de roes*.

adopted an anti-opium standpoint partly because there were economic reasons for doing so: it was a way of eroding the European domination of the trade with China. Thus the objectives of the moral crusaders coincided with, and were reinforced by economic objectives".

To this end, in the Philippines, Bishop Brent was one of the anti-opium advocates. One of his counterparts in the United States was Hamilton Wright, a politically connected physician who had specialised in tropical diseases. As Musto writes, these anti-opium activists – or moral crusaders – persuaded President Theodore Roosevelt that "a humanitarian movement to ease the burden of opium in China would help his long-range goals: to mollify Chinese resentment against America, put the British in a less favourable light, and support Chinese antagonism against European entrenchment".[35]

It appears that foreign policy and commercial considerations were the prime motives in the United States' active role in international drug control. Tellingly, the United States did not introduce its own federal legislation in this area – the Smoking Opium Exclusion Act – until 1909, the year in which the Shanghai Opium Commission was convened. Since the United States was advocating a ban on drugs, it attempted to protect its credibility on the international political stage by showing that it was putting its theories into practice at home. Taylor summarised the American motivation for the anti-drug campaign as follows:

> "Though morally inspired and promoted by the United States with missionary vigour, the anti-drug campaign was carried out within a highly political context. (…) From the standpoint of the United States, the movement was conceived within the framework of a broad interpretation of the open door policy in regard to China. (…) The United States desired a strong, stable, and prosperous China able to resist the incursions of foreign powers and providing opportunities for mutually profitable trade relations".[36]

In retrospect, there had not only been moral, economic and political consider-ations that have moved the United States in taking their position on drugs. Nadelmann states "that moral and emotional factors related to neither political nor economic advantage but instead involving religious beliefs, humanitarian sentiments, faith in universalism, compassion, conscience, paternalism, fear, prejudice, and the compulsion to proselytise, can and do play important roles in

---

35 Musto (1999), *The American Disease*, Musto explains a major role was played in persuading Roosevelt by moral crusaders like the Episcopal bishop in the Philippines, Charles Brent, and Hamilton Wright. Arnold H. Taylor writes about Wright that "to him, more than to any other individual, must go the greatest share of the credit for the success of American efforts in the anti-opium drive in the first two decades of the twentieth century". Taylor also adds it was Bishop Brent who gave the movement the character or a moral crusade. See Taylor (1968), *American diplomacy and the narcotics traffic, 1900-1939*, 54-58.

36 Taylor (1969), *American diplomacy and the narcotics traffic*, preface on vii and 28-29. The interest in the Chinese market also appears clearly from *The American Disease* by Musto (1999). He starts chapter two by describing how, at the close of the nineteenth century, the Far East beckoned as a market for American investors: "According to enthusiastic calculations, a pair of shoes sold to each Chinese would keep American shoe factories busy for years."

the creation and the evolution of international regimes".[37] In the case of international drug control, he points out that the United States efforts have been driven by fears of deviant drug use, moralistic abhorrence of recreational use of psychoactive substances other than alcohol and tobacco, a sense of righteousness, as well as the aforementioned compulsion to proselytise.[38]

In the twentieth century, the American standard of drug prohibition was taken to the international level and became the accepted international standard. Bewley-Taylor notes it is widely acknowledged that the United States' exploited its hegemonic position to create multilateral regimes in the fields of trade and money, as demonstrated by Bretton Woods monetary system and the General Agreement on Tariffs and Trade (GATT). "While these regimes enjoy significant attention, the global prohibition system, a product of the same international political environment, remains largely ignored".[39] In many countries, early drug legislation was "powerfully shaped by the example set by the United States".[40] Throughout the twentieth century, the United States remained the main driving force behind the consolidation and extension of the global drug prohibition regime.[41] Wherever necessary the United States used its world dominance to put pressure on countries, or they manoeuvred in intelligent albeit discreetly diplomatic ways at international conferences.[42] *The Gentlemen's Club* gives a lucid account of the United States' dominant influence on international drugs policy until the 1970s. The authors write that it is common knowledge that the United States has pressured countries into signing the UN drugs conventions or into enacting drugs legislation.[43] More recent examples exist of the United States pressuring or criticising other governments over their drug policies: the British and Dutch for their emphasis on public health approaches to the drug problem, the Colombians to silence the debate on legalisation, and more recently, the Australian government to abandon plans for an experiment with medically prescribed heroin.[44]

The American formula by which prohibition should be effectuated, such as through repressive and even military means, has spread internationally as well as. Even the American rhetoric of the 'War on Drugs' has globalised.[45] Since

---

37 Nadelmann (1990), 'Global prohibition regimes', 480.
38 Nadelmann (1990), 'Global prohibition regimes', 508.
39 Bewley-Taylor (1999), *The United States and International Drug Control, 1909-1997*, 55.
40 Nadelmann (1990), 'Global prohibition regimes', 509. See also Bewley-Taylor (1999), *The United States and International Drug Control, 1909-1997*.
41 Nadelmann (1990), 'Global prohibition regimes', 507-510. See also Bruun et al. (1975), *The Gentlemen's Club*, in particular 132-148. For a more detailed accounts see Bewley-Taylor (1999), *The United States and International Drug Control, 1909-1997*. See also Friman (1996), *Narco-Diplomacy*.
42 See Friman (1996), *NarcoDiplomacy*.
43 Bruun et al. (1975), *The Gentlemen's Club*, 141.
44 See respectively Nadelmann (1990), 'Global prohibition regimes', 509; Bewley-Taylor (1999), *The United States and International Drug Control, 1909-1997*, 169. The Australian case happened in the late 1990s.
45 Nadelmann (1990), 'Global prohibition regimes', 503.

the early 1990s, The American Drug Enforcement Administration (DEA), with
some three hundred agents dispatched throughout more than forty countries, has
now played the role of global enforcer and advocate of U.S. drug policies and
as well as global conventions. It is a role comparable to that of the British navy
on behalf of Britain's campaigns against piracy and slavery in earlier
centuries.[46]

At the institutional level of international drug control, the influence of the
United States is also clear. Bewley-Taylor has described in detail the influence
of the United States' on UN drug control, in both formal and informal ways.[47]
Their influence has been enormous, not only in drafting UN drug conventions,
but also in creating control organs and influencing ideas and knowledge on
drugs.[48] Bewley-Taylor mentions the 1992-1994 Cocaine Project of the World
Health Organisation (WHO), the largest study of cocaine use ever conducted. It
produced some unexpected conclusions, such as that occasional use causes
generally few problems and that health problems from legal drugs such as
alcohol and tobacco are greater than those from cocaine. The report of the WHO
Cocaine Project was never published; rumours at the UN suggested the United
States had threatened to withdraw funding if it were to be published. Among
cocaine experts and other researchers it has become known that the United
States pressured WHO to suppress publication.[49] The United States is also said
to have stopped publication of data from a WHO background study on cannabis
which suggested it was less harmful than alcohol or tobacco. *The New Scientist*
released this story, which the WHO later denied in a press release.[50]

Finally, it was the United States that blocked Mexico's candidacy for
Presidency of the preparatory meetings for the UN General Assembly Special
Session on Drugs (UNGASS). As explained in the first chapter, Mexico had
played a key role in its preparations – and now wished to hold the presidency.
Its candidacy was supported by Latin American and Caribbean countries, but
was blocked because the United States was concerned about Mexico's more
recent 'critical' tone, which contributed to the fact that Mexico's original
proposal for an evaluation of international drug control policy was dropped, and
that UNGASS turned into a reconfirmation of the global drug prohibition
system.[51]

46 Nadelmann (1990), 'Global prohibition regimes', 509.
47 Bewley-Taylor (1999), *The United States and International Drug Control, 1909-1997*, 55.
48 Nadelmann (1993), *Cops Across Borders*.
49 Bewley-Taylor mentions of rumours circulating at UN drug control head quarters in Vienna. See:
    Bewley-Taylor (1999), *The United States and International Drug Control, 1909-1997*, 169-170.
    For a more precise description of the U.S. threat on WHO, see Jelsma (2003), 'Drugs in the UN
    system: the unwritten history of 1998 United Nations General Assembly Special Session on drugs',
    188-190.
50 *New Scientist* (1998a), 'High Anxities'. What the WHO does not want you to know about
    cannabis'.
51 Jelsma (2003), 'Drugs in the UN system: the unwritten history of 1998 United Nations General
    Assembly Special Session on drugs'.

2.3 The United Nations Drug Control Regime

As previously stated, the history of the international ban on drugs began with the meeting of the Shanghai Opium Commission in 1909, attended by representatives from thirteen countries, with the aim of arriving at a stricter international policy on opium. The United States, Britain, and China "naturally dominated" the commission. The groundwork for the meeting and the documentation prepared in advance largely followed the format that had been carefully lain by American diplomatic efforts. Other views were expressed, but did not carry enough weight to influence the decision-making. For example, Sir Cecil Clementi Smith, the senior British delegate "maintained that the declared policy in India, of regulation rather than prohibition was quite the wiser one".[52] The delegation of the Netherlands made the only non-American proposal, to consider the state monopoly, such as it existed in the Dutch East Indies, as the most effective way of regulation, which the British resisted, stating such could not be determined beforehand. The Dutch resolution was never voted upon, but it did find its way into a printed document of the proceedings, with the remark that every country should see for itself whether a state monopoly was the most appropriate form of self-regulation.[53]

The conference ended with the adoption of nine resolutions, some dealing with the Chinese opium question, others with international trade. One resolution called for a general suppression of opium smoking (opium eating was not mentioned). Another resolution, a compromise between Britain and the United States, stated that the use of opium for other than medical purposes was held by "almost every participating country" to be "a matter for prohibition or careful regulation".[54] A resolution Bruun et al. call "surprising and maybe more important" concerned the problem of morphine and the injunction to take drastic measures to control its use.[55] Because this conference took the form of a Commission, its recommendations were not binding. However, it was to have far-reaching consequences in subsequent years as it would lead to the Hague Opium Convention in 1912.[56]

In December 1911, the first opium conference took place in the Hague, resulting one month later, in the Hague Opium Convention of 1912. In 1913 and 1914, additional opium conferences were held, for which reason it is sometimes referred to as a series of opium conferences. The Hague Opium Convention, the first treaty to attempt to control drugs by world-wide agreement, marks the

---

52 Taylor (1969), *American diplomacy and the narcotics traffic*, 68.
53 De Kort (1995), *Tussen patiënt en delinquent*, 65.
54 Bruun et al. (1975), *The Gentlemen's Club*, 11.
55 Bruun et al. (1975), *The Gentlemen's Club*, 11.
56 Bruun et al. (1975), *The Gentlemen's Club*, 9. For a detailed description, see Musto (1999), *The American Disease*. See also Bachman & Coppel (1989), *La drogue dans le monde*, 267-274, and De Kort (1995), *Tussen patiënt en delinquent*, 62-80.

beginning of the international drug control regime as in effect today.[57] Just as in Shanghai, the United States made the preparations. Britain, afraid to lose their trade interest in the east, attempted to introduce tactics to slow the process down, such as their effort to bring about a postponement of the meeting and a reformulation of the agenda in order to include cocaine and morphine as well.[58] Italy tried to include cannabis, but this was rejected, while the Germans, the leading drug manufacturing country, tried unsuccessfully to have cocaine excluded from the agenda.[59] At the Hague Opium Convention of 1912, it was eventually decided to set up international control for four substances: opium, morphine, heroin and cocaine. Germany did succeed in introducing a postponement however, by demanding that the convention must have universal signature before going into effect. The outcome of this unusual ratification procedure was that the Hague Convention saw a delay in implementation; for the most part, this would happen shortly after World War I.

It was through their ratification of the Versailles Peace Treaty in 1919 that a large number of countries became party to the Hague Convention.[60] Prior to the end of World War I some saw the Peace Conference as a convenient vehicle by which nations could be brought into the anti-opium movement. The British brought up this idea, which the Americans quickly embraced as a way to secure wider adhesion to and enforcement of the 1912 Convention. Both the British and American delegations to the Peace Conference agreed that the time and occasion were opportune for taking steps to put the Hague Convention into operation. Eventually it was the American draft that was executed: by signing

---

57 Taylor adds it was generally agreed that the Hague was a distinct advance in the anti-opium movement, that it represented a new standard of international morality in that the participating powers agreed to help each other in the solution of a problem that was beyond the control of any individual state, and that it firmly established the principle of the necessity of such international co-operation. See Taylor (1969), *American diplomacy and the narcotics traffic*, 108. See also Musto (1997), 'International drug control: historical aspects and future challenges', 165.

58 Originally, the British had objected to an international opium conference but eventually they agreed on the condition morphine and cocaine were included. "The British, alarmed at the flooding of their Far Eastern Possessions with morphine and cocaine, had insisted upon an investigation of the manufacture and traffic in these drugs as a *sine qua non* of their participation in the conference. The British delegation therefore came armed with strong proposals to deal with this problem". See Taylor (1968), *American diplomacy and the narcotics traffic*, 101.

59 Italy only participated in the first day's session. For the German situation, see also chapter two of Friman (1996), *NarcoDiplomacy*, and see Taylor, who noted that the delegation most responsible for watering down the British proposal regarding manufactured drugs like morphine and cocaine was the German. "The German chemical industry had put much pressure on the German government not to attend the conference. Germany was a major manufacturer of opium derivatives and had almost a monopoly on cocaine production. The German delegation therefore was out to scuttle any strong measures that might jeopardise the favoured position of the German manufacturers". German delegates were adamantly opposed to having their government make any pledges in regard to the control and restriction in these drugs while others might remain free to do as they like. See Taylor (1969), *American diplomacy and the narcotics traffic*, 102-106.

60 Germany and Turkey, countries on the losing side in World War I, were forced to sign on in Versailles in 1919, and in doing so, both lost important commercial interests in the market of cocaine and opiates (morphine).

the peace treaty, the Hague Opium Convention was also signed and ratified.[61] American president Woodrow Wilson was an important player at the Versailles Peace Conference, where the decision was made to create the League of Nations. In the Covenant, it was stated that the League was to have "the general supervision over agreements with regard to the traffic in opium and other dangerous drugs". The League's first assembly saw to the creation of an Advisory Committee on Traffic in Opium and Other Dangerous Drugs. The United States, neither a member of the League, nor a member of the consultative committee, manoeuvred to actively participate in a 'consultative capacity'.[62]

A global drug approach gradually started to evolve, which would increasingly affect individual national approaches towards drugs. While 1909 and 1912 had seen important advancements leading up to this process, the 1919 Peace Conference unveiled its new stance, through which it would accomplish two important objectives. First, it gave the League of Nations an administrative role in international drug control. Second, in signing the Versailles Treaty, as previously mentioned, countries would automatically become signatory to the 1912 Hague convention. It is no coincidence that the first national drug legislations in Europe date from this period, when countries translated the international control regime into their national legislations.

Throughout the 1920s and 1930s more international drug conventions were signed. Not only had the tally of countries signing drug international conventions increased, the number of substances declared illegal increased as well. The British slowing down tactics had already led to the inclusion of cocaine and morphine in the Hague Convention.[63] In 1925, at the Geneva Opium Convention, cannabis was introduced to the growing list of controlled substances, despite the fact that it had not been an item on the agenda and no documents were made available on the issue. The first international meeting of 1909 was held to discuss opium. The first international drug treaty three years later included four substances, opium, its derivatives morphine and heroin, and cocaine. In 1925, the number of controlled substances grew to seven, in 1931 the number grew to seventeen, and by 1948, the list now numbered thirty-six.[64]

Following World War II international drug control went into full effect. Responsibility for international drug control was transferred from the League of Nations to the United Nations. The number of drug conventions and control

---

61 In the British draft, the powers would promise to ratify the Convention immediately and put in into effect after signing Versailles. The American draft would become Article 295 of the Treaty of Versailles. See Taylor (1969), *American diplomacy and the narcotics traffic*, 141-143.

62 Bruun et al. (1975), *The Gentlemen's Club*, 13.

63 Friman (1996), *NarcoDiplomacy*.

64 With the number of drug conventions and its list of illegal substances on the rise, new international control organisations had to be created, such as the Permanent Central Opium Board, later renamed the Permanent Central Narcotics Board (PCNB). At the 1931 convention, the Drug Supervisory Board (DSB) had been created with the task of setting up a system of estimates regarding national drug requirements, imports and manufacture.

organs further increased. In 1946, the Commission of Narcotic Drugs (CND) was formed, in which the representative Member States were authorised to map out the main contours of UN drug policy, later be confirmed by the UN's Economic and Social Council. In 1946, the International Health Conference in New York founded the World Health Organisation (WHO). Additional protocols were established respectively on synthetic drugs (Paris 1948) and on the production of raw materials (New York 1953). The Permanent Central Narcotics Board (CBD) and the Drug Supervisory Board (DSB) merged in 1968 to form the International Narcotics Control Board (INCB). Following these post-war treaties of 1948 and 1953, the total number of drug treaties had become nine, with some of them overlapping, which made the international control regime somewhat confusing.[65]

The aim of the 1961 Single Convention on Narcotic Drugs was to amalgamate all the drug conventions in existence up to that point, and organise them into a single, unified policy vehicle.[66] Article two was expressly devised to control the cultivation, production, manufacture, export, import, distribution of, trade in, use of, and possession of narcotic substances for other than medical and scientific purposes. More than one hundred mostly plant-based substances and their derivatives were mentioned in the convention, including opium, coca, and cannabis. For cannabis, the 1961 Single Convention meant a new policy, namely prohibition.[67] Also on the basis of the 1961 Single Convention the decision was taken to create the International Narcotics Control Board (INCB), a control organisation with members serving in their personal capacity, independent from governments and the United Nations, responsible for monitoring compliance with the drugs conventions. The International Narcotics Control Board was established in 1968.[68]

Ten years after the Single Convention, a second drug convention was signed, the Convention against Psychotropic Substances (1971), which would control 'psychotropic' substances and their derivatives, depressants and stimulants of

---

65 De Kort (1995), *Tussen patiënt en delinquent*, 78-79.

66 The official title of the convention is '1961 Single Convention on Narcotic Drugs, as amended by the 1972 Protocol. The latter protocol to the convention strengthens the 1961 convention as it calls for increased efforts to prevent illicit production of, traffic in, and use of narcotics. It also highlights the need to provide treatment and rehabilitation services to drug users, "which may be considered instead of, or in addition to imprisonment in cases involving individuals who have committed a drug offence." See United Nations International Drug Control Programme (1997), *World Drug Report*, 168.

67 At the 1925 Geneva Convention, cannabis had come under a limited form of international control, but the Single Convention meant prohibition. Whereas in 1925 it was an Egyptian suggestion to control cannabis, it was the United States that had been promoting international prohibition of cannabis since the 1930s, which culminated in its inclusion in the 1961 Single Convention. See Bruun et al. (1975), *The Gentlemen's Club*, 17 and 181-203.

68 For the INCB see Bruun et al. (1975), *The Gentlemen's Club*, in particular chapter 6. For more recent accounts see also Fazey (2002), *The INCB and the Wizard of Oz*, and Fazey (2003), 'The Commission on Narcotics Drugs and the United Nations International Drug Control Programme: politics, policies and prospects for change'.

the central nervous system (including tranquillisers, barbiturates, and amphetamines) as well as hallucinogens (such as LSD).[69] Simply put, while the 1961 convention concerned itself mostly with the control of plant-based drugs, the treaty of 1971 was mostly aimed at synthetic drugs.[70] The total number of controlled substances now exceeded one hundred. Following the legal precedent set in the 1961 treaty, all use of the aforementioned substances listed in the 1971 convention was henceforth limited exclusively to scientific and medical purposes. Substances have continually been added to the 1961 and 1971 Drug Conventions; in 1995, the number of controlled substances totalled 245.[71]

Finally, the Convention against Illicit Traffic in Narcotic Drugs and Psychotropic Substances (1988) was signed. As its title indicates, this convention does not focus on substances, but is specifically concerned with the international trafficking of the substances mentioned in the 1961 and 1971 conventions. The 1988 treaty also contains provisions on related aspects enabling international co-operation between countries, such as extradition, mutual legal assistance, money laundering, and forfeiture of proceeds derived from illicit drug trafficking. The 1988 treaty has important penal provisions on signatory countries. The main thrust of the convention was to obligate signatory states to criminalise: cultivation, production, sale, import, export, possession and purchase of the listed narcotic or psychotropic substances. Article three of the 1988 convention explicitly imposes the obligation to criminalise the demand side, while the 1961 and 1971 conventions focused on the supply side. These provisions in the 1988 convention reflect an attempt to reach a political balance between producer and consumer countries. In addition to the former policy of obligating producing countries to suppress supply, consuming countries now fell under the obligation to suppress the demand for drugs.[72]

In *The Gentlemen's Club,* Bruun et al. describe the first seventy years of international drug control documented with extensive interviews and case studies. The authors paint a detailed picture of the considerable influence exerted by international drug control agencies. In particular, its account of the 'Gentlemen's Club', describes how a handful of men managed to greatly influence the regime of international drug control.[73] Many of these key players were diplomats, law enforcement officers, or health administrators. More important to note are the personal friendships these individuals maintained, and their relationship to the pharmaceutical industry.[74] Through their participation in key organisations such as CND, WHO, and INCB, they are the players who,

---

69 Bruun et al. (1975), *The Gentlemen's Club,* 17.
70 The 1971 convention also prohibited some plant-based substances that were not prohibited (yet) by 1961, such as mescaline, the subject of Huxley's *The Doors of Perception.*
71 United Nations International Drug Control Programme (1997), *World Drug Report,* 163.
72 De Ruyver et al. (2002), *Multidisciplinary Drug Policies and the UN Drug Treaties,* 11-12.
73 For the descriptions of these influential men, see Bruun et al. (1975), *The Gentlemen's Club,* 118-131.
74 Bruun et al. (1975), *The Gentlemen's Club,* 128.

sometimes through informal means, have 'created' the international policy on drugs.

The Gentlemen's Club makes for a dismal read. It is a tale of ill-conceived priorities, disputes about the powers of organisations, conflicting national interests, the influence of the pharmaceutical lobby, and the lack of expert knowledge among the leaders of decision-making bodies. The book also provides an interesting view on the workings of these international organisations, including the influence they exerted upon the working procedures of the policy-making and administrative apparatus. The authors describe the ways, often arbitrary, in which the priorities of these individuals and the people they represent, have found their way to the agenda, subsequently taking on a life of their own. The book also makes evident the influence that could be exerted by a single individual. As case in point, Harry Anslinger not only played a decisive role in American policy, but was also a leading player in the drafting of international drug policy, particularly with regard to cannabis.[75]

With more international drug control institutions being created, more institutional interests have arisen that not only consolidated, but also served to fuel the global prohibition regime even more. In 1991, the United Nations Drug Control Programme (UNDCP) was founded, acting as the administrative and executive branch of UN drug policy. UNDCP also serves as secretary for the International Narcotics Control Board (INCB), the independent agency that monitors compliance with drug conventions. In 1997, the Italian Pino Arlacchi became the new head of the UNDCP. In his function as UN Under Secretary General, Arlacchi decided that UNDCP would became part of the United Nations Office for Drug Control and Crime Prevention (ODCCP). However, in 2002, Arlacchi was forced to resign under pressure arising from a corruption-related scandal. He was succeeded by another Italian, Antonio Mario Costa, an economist and former Secretary General of the European Bank for Reconstruction and Development. In practice the UN drug control office has been led by Italian nationals since its origin in 1992.[76] Italy was the major donor in the past, and continues to be one of the major donors to the UN drug control programme. Under Costa's leadership, the United Nations Office on Drug Control and Crime Prevention (ODCCP) was renamed the United Nations Office on Drugs and Crime (UNODC), which is now the umbrella organisation that makes up the United Nations Drug Control Programme (UNDCP) and the Centre for International Crime Prevention.

---

75 For a detailed account on the influence of Harry Anslinger in the international drug control system, see Bewley-Taylor (1999), *The United States and International Drug Control, 1909-1997.*
76 The first executive director of the UN drug control programme was Giorgio Giacomelli (1992-1995), who was succeeded by Pino Arlacchi (1997-2002). Antonio Costa is in office since May 2002.

The UNDCP functions officially on the administrative and executive side and does make UN drug policy as such (this is the task of the CND),[77] but it adds its own dynamic to global drug prohibition. The UNDCP tries to get as many countries as possible to sign the UN drug conventions, which includes using measures to influence the drug policies of countries. The UNDCP, in its attempt to influence EU drug policy, has also created an office in Brussels. The UNDCP considers the UN conventions as the basis for international action; the more countries to sign and implement them, the more effectively drugs can be fought.[78] The impression exists, however, that the UNDCP is trying to secure the signatures of additional countries to the drug treaties because of its own, institutionalised interests, namely in investing itself with more authority and power. The fact that the UNDCP has been found to misrepresent drug use statistics, or has even been known to manipulate them, such as in the *UN World Drug Report 2000*, reinforces this impression.[79] The UNDCP is increasingly presenting itself as a hard-line defender of drug prohibition. Tellingly, consumption of illicit substances is referred to exclusively as 'abuse' in all its publications; the more neutral term 'drug use' is non-existent. The UNDCP seems to be an organisation striving to validate its existence by illustrating the dangers of drugs and denouncing liberal drug policies which they claim to have devastating effects. In light of the increased criticism towards the UN drug conventions and the UN drug control organs, the organisation seems to have more reasons to do so.[80]

The International Narcotics Control Board (INCB) can also be said to be not as independent as it intended to be. Officially the INCB is an independent monitoring agency concerned with the compliance of countries signed on to the drugs conventions, in practice it has proven itself to be a strict interpreter of the treaties. The INCB's interpretation of the UN drug conventions is generally narrow and statements in its yearly report are sometimes more political than factual.[81] It has nearly become ritual for the INCB to rebuke a number of Western countries with harm reduction measures, such as heroin prescription programs and users rooms. Injection rooms in Australia were criticised because they were seen as 'giving up' in their fight against drugs.[82] It also has become

---

77 The main contours of UN drug policy are shaped by the Commission on Narcotic Drugs (CND), representing all nations. These contours are later to be confirmed in the UN's Economic and Social Council (ECOSOC).

78 Boekhout van Solinge (2002), *Drugs and Decision-Making in the European Union*.

79 United Nations Office for Drug Control and Crime Prevention (2000), *World Drug Report 2000*. See also chapter six about the report by Rossi (2001), *World Drug Report 2000: Contents, Omissions and Distortions*.

80 See Fazey (2003), 'The Commission on Narcotics Drugs and the United Nations International Drug Control Programme'. See also the other articles on UN drug control in this special issue of the *International Journal of Drug Policy* 14 (2003).

81 See also the editorial of the special issue of the *International Journal of Drug Policy* 14 (2003) 141-143, that mentions the "unique interpretation" of the Drug Conventions by the INCB.

82 When presenting the 2002 INCB report, the above criticism was made by President Ghodse (at a press conference in London on 25th February 2003). Ghodse is originally from Iran but works in London at St. George's Hospital Medical School.

routine to criticise countries for taking more lenient approaches toward drug use. Professor Hamid Ghodse, President of the INCB, has criticised Britain's policy to make cannabis possession a non-arrestable offence, suggesting that this measure could contribute to cannabis becoming as widespread as tobacco. He added this could lead to the psychiatric hospitals being filled with people with cannabis problems. "This is what the Board is trying to advocate: that the recreational use of these drugs is something that has caused problems and difficulties – that is why they are controlled".[83]

The INCB has received serious criticism and difficulty maintaining its credibility and goodwill because of its strict interpretation of the drug conventions. Its yearly rebuking of Australia, Canada, the Netherlands, Switzerland, and most recently the United Kingdom for more tolerance towards drugs have been rebuffed by many. Countries with harm reduction policies, such as Switzerland, have opposed to INCB's condemnation of medically prescribed heroin, whereas the UN drug conventions allow the use of controlled substances for medical or scientific purposes. Professor Cindy Fazey, former head of UNDCP Demand Reduction, states that the INCB actually exceeds its mandate:

> "The INCB has deliberately and systematically 'talked up' its role over many years, beyond any authority it has ever been given. The Board now comments on national policy and clinical practice when neither is within the Board's remit of competence. Its functions are closely defined and limited; yet it has arrogated to itself a position of pseudo power and has tried to usurp the policy functions of the Commission on Narcotics Drugs without authority".[84]

It is, however, the UN drug control organisation UNODC (the former UNDCP) that has been exposed to the most criticism. Over the last few years, UNODC has been plagued by scandals and mismanagement. In the 1990s, a money embezzlement scandal occurred in the head office for West Africa, which was then moved from the Ivory Coast to Senegal. Although the affair never became public, subsequent budgets were substantially cut by donor countries.[85] When Pino Arlacchi became head of the UNODC mismanagement and corruption scandals mounted and took on new dimensions. The scandals led to the resignation of several highly placed civil servants, pull-back of money by the Dutch government, and to an official UN investigation launched from UN headquarters in New York that eventually resulted in Arlacchi's resignation from his post in February 2002. Arlacchi was succeeded by Costa, under whose leadership a

---

83   Quote from article on BBC web site («news.bbc.co.uk»): Mark Doyle (2003), *New drugs laws 'send wrong signal'*.

84   Fazey (2002), *The INCB and the Wizard of Oz*, 20.

85   The author was informed of this affair while interviewing for a job application at the UNDCP office in Dakar, Senegal. At the time (1995), Boutros Boutros-Ghali was UN Secretary-General, and a relative or acquaintance of Boutros-Ghali headed the UNDCP office in Ivory Coast. There were 'rumours' of embezzlement at this UNDCP office and the consequent financially difficult position of this UNDCP office. In order to hide the affair, apparently the head office was moved from Ivory Coast to Senegal.

new scandal arose when the newly appointed head of Demand Reduction, Mike Trace, was forced to resign after Sweden objected to his continued participation. Sweden exerted pressure to withdraw their funds because Trace was involved in a programme that supported decriminalisation and challenged international drug prohibition.[86]

During the last few years there has been increased criticism about UN drug policy. The criticism is not only levelled against the drug conventions, but also against the drug control organisations involved.[87] During the UN Special Session on Drugs (UNGASS) in 1998, hundreds of notable public figures signed an open letter to Kofi Annan, published in the *New York Times*, with the request of opening a debate on international drug control. Five years later at the UNGASS midterm review in Vienna, several NGOs voiced protest against the UN drug control policy. Included in these protests were former high-ranking UNDCP employees who had shifted position and joined the ranks of the international drug reform movement. Also joining the protest were a number of noted scholars specialising in international drug control, showing that an international drug reform movement is clearly taking shape and is increasingly challenging the concept of global drug prohibition.[88]

Despite criticism expressed of UN drug control policy, the countries represented in the Commission on Narcotic Drugs (CND) still solidly support the UN drug conventions, and the ideas brought forth, such as freeing the world from the scourge of drugs, remained solidly intact.[89] This has led to the awkward situation where it is understood that privately officials now agree that it is unrealistic to expect to eradicate drugs from the planet, "as soon as they sit down in the conference halls in Vienna and New York, they shift into consensus-mode and the majority of the officials are swept along in a ritual of rhetoric while the minority prefers to keep as low a profile as possible".[90]

2.4 European Drug Control

Since the mid-1990s, the European Union has become an active player in the international drug field. The 1993 Treaty on European Union – often called

---

86 In September 2002, Trace had sent an e-mail to Aryah Neier, President of the Open Society Institute (OSI), an organisation funded by philanthropist and drug policy reformer, George Soros. Trace's e-mail was published by the British *Daily Mail*.

87 Cohen speaks in this respect of a conservative 'drug prohibition church'. See Cohen (2003),'The drug prohibition church and the adventure of reformation'.

88 Some of the scholars are part of the recently established *Senlis Council*, that wishes to open the debate on possible alternatives to the current international drug control regime.

89 The 1961 Convention states that "addiction to narcotic drugs constitutes a serious evil for the individual and is fraught with social and economic danger to mankind." See Bruun et al. (1975), *The Gentlemen's Club*, 39. The slogan for UNGASS 1988 was 'A Drug-Free World. We Can Do It'.

90 Jelsma (2003), 'Drugs in the UN system: the unwritten history of 1998 United Nations General Assembly Special Session on drugs', 188-190.

Maastricht Treaty – extended the co-operation between EU's Member States. Drugs, along with many other new areas, were brought within the EU's competence. Since then the drug issue has been on the agendas of numerous EU forums. An important reason for the prominence of drugs on the EU's political agenda is the close relationship between drugs and organised crime. Criminal organisations derive their income from a variety of sources, drugs appear to be among the most important. The demand that organised crime be tackled is therefore put forward as an important reason to fight drugs.[91]

Since 1993, the policy areas in which the EU has competence have been divided into three 'pillars', discussing drugs in each. The first pillar consists of the 'old' European Community (EC). The second pillar deals with the Common Foreign and Security Policy. The third deals with Justice and Home Affairs. In the first pillar discussions on drug issues arise relating to development co-operation, and to Community health measures adopted to complement Member States' actions at national levels. In accordance with the principle of 'subsidiarity', public health is largely a matter of domestic policy for the Member States.[92] The Commission may take complementary measures in the realms of prevention and the dissemination of public information. In addition, certain other aspects of drugs are discussed in the first pillar, such as precursors and money laundering.

The EU is especially active in the area of drug control externally, in its relations with 'third countries', non EU-members. Drugs and human rights are among the subjects that are routinely raised. The EU upholds actions to combat drugs and the respect for human rights as key conditions for co-operation. The Commission raises the subject in talks on development co-operation, and the Council does so in the second and third pillar. Since all Member States have signed the UN drug conventions, they have become part of the EU's 'acquis' or legal basis. This explains why signing them has become a condition for EU accession. The EU also adopted a policy of encouraging all countries to sign the UN drugs conventions. This applies not only to applicant countries, whose capacity to act effectively against drugs is an important condition for accession, but to all countries that want to do business with the EU.

Although many measures are taken on drug issues in the different EU bodies (Commission, Parliament, and especially Council), most aspects of drug policy still fall primarily under the competence of the Member States. The EU only takes complementary measures to these. The most obvious examples of 'internal' EU drug measures are the so-called joint actions, but their exact legal status

---

91 Boekhout van Solinge (2002), *Drugs and Decision-Making in the European Union*, 81-84.
92 Subsidiarity is an EU term and basically means that Community action is taken only if it has added value compared to policymaking at national level. Article 3B of the Treaty on European Union states the Commission takes action only "if and insofar as the objectives of the proposed action cannot be sufficiently achieved by the Member States and can therefore, by reason of the scale or effects of the proposed action, be better achieved by the Community".

and implications are not yet entirely clear. Up to now, two joint actions have been taken on drugs, one on legislation and the other on an early warning mechanism for synthetic drugs. The first involved mutual adjustments to legislation and practices, although this has remained something of a paper tiger. In 1997, a second joint action followed, setting up an early warning mechanism for new synthetic drugs. This system makes it possible to react quickly to the appearance of any new synthetic substance on the market, to make a rapid risk assessment as to whether or not the new substance should be banned.[93]

The question of harmonisation of anti-drugs legislation and implementation has been on the EU agenda for a while, but harmonisation has not been achieved as it has proved too politically sensitive. In order to maintain some common basis of an EU drug policy, the EU regularly invokes the UN conventions. When Member States fail to reach agreement on common drug policy measures, the UN drug conventions (as EU 'acquis') are exercised by default.

AS the EU emerges as a new player in international drug control, it has begun to exert its influence over the arena where international drugs policy is made: the UN Commission on Narcotic Drugs (CND) and its executive agency, the UNODC). Expansion of this influence can be expected as EU countries are contributing an increasingly large proportion of the UN drug control budget – their share has reached 70%.[94] The EU's growing influence was noticeable at the last (UNGASS), which convened in June 1998 to deliberate on the global drug problem. The largely European emphasis on demand reduction clearly gained ground in relation to the American law enforcement approach that had been more traditional in UN circles hitherto. Prior to UNGASS, countries had already reached agreement in the CND on the guiding principles of demand reduction, which included reducing the negative effects of drug use or 'harm reduction' – though not yet referred to as such it has become incorporated *de facto* into UN drugs policy. It is fairly impossible formally to use the phrase 'harm reduction' in UN texts, which remains consistent with the longstanding approach demanded by and practised in the United States. The UN still follows the American usage of defining all use of illicit drugs as 'abuse'. Nonetheless, it is fair to say that the United States no longer plays the all-important role in international drug control that it had for almost the entire twentieth century. The countries of the South and the Member States of the EU are making their voices heard more clearly than before. In this respect, the EU remains too divided to exert itself as an organisation; it may do so in the future, if Member States can agree on a uniform approach.

93 Boekhout van Solinge (2002), *Drugs and Decision-Making in the European Union*, 123-126.
94 The United Nations Office for Drugs Control and Crime Prevention – UN/ODCCP (1999), *European-United Nations partnerships against perils*, 11. This page displays a table showing the sums of money that countries donate to the UNDCP.

2.5 National Drug Control Trends in Europe

While the drug issue has been a much discussed subject in various EU bodies since the early 1990s, it became a real political issue for most European countries during the 1960s, when young people starting using illicit substances, called drugs, or dope. To most people, these drugs were relatively 'new' and unknown psychoactive substances. Cannabis became the most popular drug in use, followed to a lesser degree by LSD, amphetamines, opium and heroin. In the 1960s, the use of drugs was clearly taking place in the context of the counter and hippie culture by artists and progressive university students. The counter culture in its efforts to overthrow 'the establishment' in all areas of their lifestyles embraced the use of mind-altering substances as a means of opening consciousness and exploring new realms. A further means of distinguishing themselves from their parents' generation and of their use of alcohol, was by the use of these 'new' exotic and exciting – mostly illegal – substances.

Confronted with the new phenomenon of illicit drug use during the 1960s and 1970s, authorities' most common reaction was to reject this bohemian manifestation of drug use. Since the counter culture was considered a threat by the establishment, so was the drug use symbolising it. In the United States, cannabis was thought to make people unpatriotic, as the marijuana smokers protested against the war in Vietnam.[95] Even if drugs were not considered a threat they were at least classified as 'unwelcome'. The first and direct practical measure resulting from this attitude was the introduction of new national drug legislations. Most European countries had signed the earlier conventions, just prior too or directly after World War I, therefore national drug legislation was already in place, but relatively unused. The rise in drug use during the 1960s and 1970s led most Western countries – including the three countries under discussion in this thesis – to design new drug legislation.

Although LSD was an integral part of the hippie movement and cannabis became the most widely used substance within the counter culture at large.[96] Cannabis was already categorised as illegal in most national drug laws following the 1961 UN convention or earlier international drug treaties. In the 1960s, new, popular drugs among the counter culture such as LSD and amphetamines were often not yet illegal. Therefore, it became normal for governments to declare them illegal as well as they emerged. Under the second UN drug convention in 1971, amphetamines and LSD became internationally controlled. LSD led to a number of accidents such as people jumping out of windows

---

95 It should be added that the drug control dynamic in the United States, maintained or reinforced by the illegal status of cannabis, gave the government a way of suppressing behaviour of dissidents, such as Vietnam protestors, or as a way to intervene in and control problematic (ghetto) neighbourhoods.

96 On substance use in the early formation of the counter and hippie culture, including the 'Beat' subculture of the 1950s that experienced with peyote and LSD, see McGlothlin (1975), 'Socio-cultural Factors in Marihuana Use in The United States', 532-539.

believing that they could fly! LSD These accidents happened rarely but were seized upon and exploited by the media.[97] Because of fears of adverse reactions and 'bad-acid-trips' many stayed away from LSD.

Dr. Andrew Weil, author of *The Natural Mind* describes the experience of anxiety and panic reactions under the influence of mind-altering substances. In *The Natural Mind* he wrote that any drug may trigger a panic reaction, but the panic does not seem to have much basis in pharmacology rather. It is not the direct effect of the drug that causes anxiety and panic so much so as the person's perception of what he feels the drug is doing to him. Dr. Weil mentions a study by sociologist, Howard Becker who observes that the incidents of such intense panic and anxiety occurring diminished as these drugs became more widely used and their applications better understood:

> "Becker explained the change as an expression of change in expectations (set) toward the drug. When marijuana first appeared in the country it was an unknown quantity. There was no established ritual for its use, no body of folklore to suggest to people what they would experience when they smoked it. Consequently, first-time users in the 1920s probably were much more anxious than their counterparts ten years later, and some of those who expected to lose control did lose control. But as the drug spread across the nation through the non-white and Bohemian underground, as it became familiar, individual sets toward it included less anxiety, and panic reactions became correspondingly less frequent. In 1967, when every large city hospital was seeing many bad LSD trips (and most psychiatrists were calling them toxic psychoses), Becker predicted that these, too, would decline in frequency as LSD use increased. And, indeed, this is just what happened".[98]

Amphetamines and heroin were making their first notable appearance in the early or mid-1970s in most European countries along with other substances used among the counter culture. Since these drugs were relatively new to most, they experimented at times without sufficient knowledge about the exact differences between them.[99] Of course they had first hand experiences and anecdotal information, but since the effect of a drug is also dependent on the individual's psychological state as well as the circumstances,[100] the exact effects different drugs would have on people was something they had to find out for themselves. These first drug users were on the 'front line' and some paid high prices and found themselves with difficult to quit habits. This was especially the case with

---

97 As the American Weil rightly predicted in the early 1970s, the number of fatal accidents dropped quickly after some LSD incidents, hence after it became known there was a certain risk involved in LSD use. See Weil (1986), *The Natural Mind* (originally published in 1972).

98 See Weil (1986), *The Natural Mind*, 51-54. Weil did not refer to Becker's famous book *Outsiders* of 1963, but to his article 'History, Culture, and Subjective Experience: An Exploration of the Social Bases of Drug-Induced Experiences', published in *Journal of Health and Social Behaviour* 8:3 (1967).

99 A situation comparable to, for example Central and Eastern Europe, where different illicit drugs have arrived on the market without much general knowledge about the substances and their different effects.

100 These insights were introduced by Zinberg (1984), *Drug, Set, & Setting.*

heroin and to a lesser extent amphetamine users. Most early heroin users were unaware of the fact that if an opiate such as heroin is used for a period of weeks or months, and one day it is not available, it is quite unpleasant and problematic for most users. In that sense, opiates can be compared to cigarettes or coffee: if used on a daily basis over a long period, the (sudden) non-availability may be experienced as problematic.[101] Heroin users sometimes describe withdrawal symptoms as being 'sick'. This is actually the main problem with heroin; in itself it has low toxicity and does not do much harm to the body, but when the body and mind are used to it, they react when it is not available. William Burroughs, who used heroin for decades, offered a graphic description of the withdrawal symptoms he encountered on the day he first found himself deprived of heroin, in his book *Junky*. He creates clear depictions of the many different ways in which a heroin user can experience withdrawal symptoms. For some it is a real sickness, for others it is not much more than episodes of intense sweating.[102]

Even after this first 'generation' of heroin users, heroin would continue to find new users in later decades. Whereas the first heroin use took place against the background of the counter culture, the increase in heroin use of later decades often – but certainly not only – reflects a more problematic, psychological, or psychiatric in nature background of use rather than innocence of the drug's qualities. However, this does not deny the fact that some heroin use is also associated with a decision of the user to be deviant and transgressive. Part of the allure of heroin use, therefore, is not merely that it affects one's mind and emotions, but that use can also reflect a desire or need to engage in scandalous, dangerous, and outsider behaviour.

In certain countries, areas or cities heroin has occasionally taken on near 'epidemic' proportions. Scotland in the mid-1990s as portrayed in the film *Trainspotting* is an example of this. It may be difficult for the reader who is well integrated into society to imagine how young people feel when they are socially excluded and possess few opportunities for self-improvement making heroin an attractive functional alternative. Some countries or cities in Eastern Europe, including Russia, also suffer from similar heroin 'epidemics'. On the social level particularly in urban areas, these cases can be explained by facts such as high unemployment, social exclusion and social deprivation giving the individual a 'good' reason for intoxication. Although this correlation has been made clear by researchers and social workers for some time, it has only been officially recognised in recent years.[103] This correlation also explains why (recent)

---

101 Imagine, for example, what happens if suddenly, one day, no coffee would be available at the office.
102 Burroughs (1953), *Junky*.
103 National governments and politicians often find it hard to acknowledge this relationship. It was in its 1999 annual report that the EMCDDA for the first time stated a correlation exists between problematic drug use and areas of social deprivation, but the EMCDDA added it should not be oversimplified. See EMCDDA (1999), *Annual Report*, 10.

immigrant groups who are found more often among the lower strata of society are often highly represented among problem users. In most countries, intravenous use (injecting with a needle) is the most common form of use, but other techniques exists as well, for example smoking – also known as 'chasing the dragon'.[104] Heroin continues to be the main problem drug of the different illegal substances that are used in Europe.

Another substance associated with problematic use is amphetamine. This substance can be consumed in different ways (snorting, swallowing, injecting and smoking), but intravenous use is the mode of ingestion most commonly found among compulsive and problematic users in Europe.[105] In parts of Scandinavia, such as Sweden, amphetamine is the main problem drug, although heroin has been on the rise since the 1990s. The most recent problem drug on the European market is a crack, a smoke-able form of cocaine. Crack was introduced on the American market in the 1980s, and in the 1990s use increased in Europe.

The EMCDDA defines problem drug use as "injecting drug use or long-duration/regular use of opiates, cocaine and/or amphetamines".[106] Generally, countries base their number of problem drug users on those drug users seeking care and treatment from institutions, or on law enforcement statistics.[107] In the European Union, the rate per 1,000 inhabitants aged 15-64 ranged from two to three problem users (Belgium, Germany, the Netherlands) to between five and eight problem users (Italy, Portugal, United Kingdom) to 9.3 (Luxembourg).[108] Thus the number of heroin users suggested by these European Union statistics[109] represent their numbers as being anywhere between 500,000 and one million.[110] Per country this would mean that the number of people estimated to be dependent on heroin is under 0.5% of the general population.

The way in which different countries dealt with these problematic drug users was mostly repressive. Most national drug legislation posses a dual character of punitive repression as well as the possibility of care and treatment. In practice, based on the concept of drug use being undesirable, the emphasis was placed on its being banned and repressed. This changed during the second half of the

---

104 In the Netherlands, smoking is the most common technique of using heroine. The organisation Mainline set up a 'Switch Campaign' to stimulate users to switch from injecting to smoking as it involves less health risks. A recent techniques in safer drug use is rectal injection (without a needle), which is being promoted in Belgium as well in London, where the 'Up Your Bum' campaign was started. See Schmidt & Van der Spek (2003), *Ins & Outs*.

105 Amphetamines, especially methamphetamines, can also be smoked but this not a common technique in Europe. In the United States it is called 'ice', in Thailand 'ya ba'.

106 EMCCDA (2001), *Annual Report*, 11.

107 Of course, countries and institutions register in different ways and definitions differ between cou tries as well, which makes comparisons difficult. Still, despite these methodological comparison flaws, the available statistics give an idea about the extent of problematic drug use.

108 See EMCDDA (2003), *Annual Report*, figure 5.

109 These figures are representing the fifteen countries that then formed the European Union up until 2004 when ten other countries joined.

110 EMCDDA (1996), *Annual Report*, 8.

1980s and 1990s when the drug problem became a public health issue. The emergence of AIDS as an epidemic in 1985 forced many authorities into a more pragmatic attitude towards intravenous drug use. HIV was discovered to have infected substantial numbers of intravenous drug users in European countries. Countries with weak public health policies recognised HIV infection problems too late to take preventative measures. In some Southern European countries with poor public health policies half of the intravenous drug users were esti-mated to be zero-positive. These numbers were so substantial that the authorities realised that the prevalence and spread of HIV among intravenous drug users posed a more serious threat to public health because these users were spreading the virus outside of the drug injecting population through sexual activity.

In the late 1980s and early 1990s, harm reduction movements in different countries were a response to the growing threat of HIV. Harm reduction is a policy approach that focuses on limiting the harm associated with drug use, implying nominal acceptance of drug use. Fierce drug policy debates began in many European countries regarding whether or not the authorities should take pragmatic preventative measures which would accept and somehow facilitate intravenous drug use in order to curb the rise of AIDS. Most European Union countries took the eventual outcome of the debate as the official recognition that intravenous drug use should be primarily considered a public health issue. Over the course of the 1990s, this general change of perception led to the rise of harm reduction as a new international drug policy model. In the 1990s the approach of harm reduction spread throughout the entire European Union, particularly to cities where local authorities were confronted with drug problems and sought workable solutions. Methadone and needle exchange programmes were the first and most visible indicators of the move towards harm reduction.

In the 1990s an international trend took place indicating a rise in recreational drug use in most Western countries, from North America to Europe to Australia. This period can be compared to the late 1960s when drug use was increasing. The contrast between today and the1960s is that the variety of drugs has grown. In the 1990s, many 'new' drugs appeared on the market that quickly grew in popularity such as ecstasy (MDMA) and amphetamines, as well as their derivatives.

A significant difference between drug use in the 1960s and drug use today is that the use of illicit drugs is no longer confined to specific subcultures. Illicit drug use has become well established in the Western world, yet it remains a behaviour that is mostly limited to younger groups, as comparative research indicates that few people continue using illicit drugs after the age of thirty-five.[111] Many consider a period of drug experimentation a normal phase of

111 See Cohen & Kaal (2001), *The irrelevance of drug policy. Patterns and careers of experienced cannabis use in the populations of Amsterdam, San Francisco and Bremen.* Especially the data on Amsterdam are significant, as buying cannabis in this city is very easy, which means there are no legal constraints for users to quit.

adolescence, a rite of passage through which most emerge unscathed.[112] One possible explanation for this change in perception is the greater availability of information about the different substances enabling users to make more conscious decisions, which are less likely to result in problematic dosages and use patterns. Drugs are now used by all segments of the population, irrespective of education, profession, politics or social standing.

In several Western countries between 10% and 35% of the general population has experience with illicit drugs. In the European Union, cannabis, in the form of marijuana or hashish, is the illicit drug of choice, both in terms of lifetime experience and in terms of recent use.[113] EMCDDA data indicate that cannabis lifetime use in the adult population (15-64 years old) ranges from 10% to 25%, current use (in epidemiological terms referred to as 'last month use') varies from 0.5% to 5%. Logically, in younger segments of the population drug use figures are much higher than in the general population. The proportion of 18-year old school students who admit to having tried cannabis, ranges from approximately 10 to 50% or more in some Western countries.[114] Due to the generation effect, this means that the experience with illicit drug use in the general population will gradually grow. As far as recent use is concerned, roughly 10 to 20% of 15-16 year old students are said to have used drugs during the last month.[115]

In regard to recreational drug use the attitudes and policies in Europe are shifting towards pragmatism. It seems that the more pragmatic and less punitive approach to problematic drug use of the 1980s and 1990s was being extended to recreational drug use as well. Since the latter types of drug use increased during the 1990s amongst young people who were otherwise not committing any other crimes outside of the buying and possessing of prohibited drugs, policy makers in a growing number of European and non-European countries have adopted more pragmatic and liberal policies.

The 1998 EMCDDA's annual report contained a special item on cannabis, "one of the most controversial policy issues in the EU countries". The following trends were observed: "some countries or regions tolerate some forms of cannabis possession and consumption; some countries apply less severe penalties when cannabis is involved in the offence; even in countries where the formal legislation is severe concerning penalising cannabis offences, there are increasingly pragmatic approaches to the implementation of drug legislation".[116]

---

112 Weil & Rosen (1993), *From Chocolate to Morphine*, 5.
113 EMCCDA (2001), *Annual Report*, 7. Here is referred to the fifteen members of the EU, as was the situation until May 2004.
114 The 50% figure is reached with respect to the cannabis lifetime prevalence among older teenagers in Australia, France, United Kingdom (England and Wales), and United States.
115 According to EMCCDA data over 1999, cannabis use in the last month for 15-16 year olds was 14% in the Netherlands, 15% in Ireland, 16% in the UK, 22% in France 22% (in the United States 19%).
116 EMCDDA (1998), *Annual Report*, 77-78.

In the 1999 annual report, a similar observation was made: "Developments in European drug policies and new legal approaches towards illicit drugs show a shift towards decriminalising some behaviours linked to consuming and possessing drugs for personal use, notably when this is related to drug dependence. Most Member States reject extreme solutions –such as full legalisation or harsh repression – but continue to prohibit drug consumption while modifying the penalties and measures applied to it."[117]

This more pragmatic attitude towards recreational drug use may be interpreted as harm reduction. The underlying reason for the decriminalisation of recreational drug use is often that the criminalisation is considered disproportionate or more harmful than the act of using drugs. In the past, most policy makers had only one message – abstinence, but abstinence did not work in accordance with the reality that people continued to use drugs. Harm reduction fills the void between 'abstinence' and the reality of drug usage. In the twenty-first century, harm reduction has become the dominant strategy for dealing with drugs in Europe. However owing to their being signatories to the UN conventions that limit their autonomy on the matter, all countries still formally prohibit the possession of drugs.

The 1990s witnessed the rise in the use of synthetic drugs. In fact, these drugs represent the most recent and rapidly expanding drug use. A lot of this rise in synthetic drug use was taking place in new social environments such as raves.[118] Rave culture became an international wave spreading across the face of the planet,[119] particularly in Western countries where it began in post-industrial Detroit and Chicago in the late 1980s.[120] Via the international tourist and travellers communities of Goa (India) and Ibiza (Spain),[121] raves reached the United Kingdom in the summer of 1988 – known as the Second Summer of Love.[122] From London raves spread to Manchester where they gained further momentum and spilled out over the English countryside where massive raves were held in fields and warehouses. From the United Kingdom and Spain, raves

---

117 EMCDDA (1999), *Extended annual report*, 19.
118 Since this music and dance culture is a recent and changing phenomenon with new trends and currents constantly arising and disappearing, different names are being used. The precise meaning also differs between countries; what in one country is the umbrella term (e.g. techno in France) is a side current in another. Trance is generally considered a specific, more psychedelic form, with both a mainstream and a subcultural (Goa trance) variety.
119 It remains dominant in the western world though, but spread out to Asia (especially Japan) and South and Central America as well, with party people travelling as far as the heart of the Amazon, such as to Brazil's city Manaus in the summer of 2003. In this same period the rave culture is also peaking in parts of Central and Eastern Europe. Spanish party island Ibiza got a Thai equivalent in the island Ko Pha-Ngan, famous for its full moon parties visited every month by thousands of visitors from all corners. Before, the full moon party phenomenon had grown big in the Indian coastal party place Goa, famous for its 'neo hippie' Goa trance music.
120 Acid house was the first term used for this new music coming out of Chicago, while techno came more from Detroit.
121 Adelaars (1991), *Ecstasy*.
122 1967 was the first Summer of Love.

quickly spread across Europe, to places such as Belgium, the Netherlands, Germany, France and so on.[123] Despite its American origins, rave music only gained popularity in the United States following its success in Europe.

Rave music and dancing are faster and of longer duration than disco. Stimulants such as ecstasy (MDMA) are taken to enhance and intensify dancing all night to rave beats.[124] Similar to how young people engage in social alcohol drinking, this type of drug usage was often confined to certain party settings in the weekends. Following the popularity of ecstasy, many other substances would appear on the market such as the re-emergence of LSD and an entire range of chemical varieties, facilitated by the work of the 'chemical couple' Alexander and Anne Shulgin.[125]

In the 1990s policy makers in all European countries found themselves confronted with the phenomenon of hundreds of thousands of young people raving every weekend, a substantial number of whom were taking ecstasy or other (stimulant) drugs. Some countries reacted by repressive means, while others implemented harm reduction measures such as pill testing.[126] In 1997, the European Union installed an early warning system that identifies the risks of new drugs that appear on the market, and then recommends if the substances should be controlled or not.

In closing, since the 1960s and 1970s, important changes have occurred in Europe both in the official perception of drug use and in how drugs should be dealt with. While the primary goal towards drugs in the 1960s and 1970s was to criminalise and ban them from society, since the 1990s more pragmatic approaches are developing which are leading, in practice, to less punitive responses towards drug use. This increased pragmatism is also apparent by the fact that harm reduction policies have sprung up in most European countries, especially at the local level where drug problems are most manifest. This

---

123 Whereas Amsterdam was more following London, in Rotterdam a specific hard core variety developed that was much faster than normal house music, 'gabber'. From the Netherlands it spread to the UK and became known as 'gabba'. In this more working class dance culture it was not MDMA but amphetamine that was mostly used. Berlin became famous for its Love Parade that was first held in 1989, a year after the British Summer of Love and the same year as the fall of the Berlin Wall. It gradually grew to a yearly parade with more than one million street ravers, and is sometimes referred to as the biggest 'ecstasy market'.

124 For books on the rave culture and drug use see for example Reynolds (1998), *Energy Flash: A Journey through Rave Music and Dance Culture*, or (in Dutch) Adelaars (1991), *Ecstasy*. The last letter A in the chemical name MDMA stands for amphetamine. Speed is more the (old) street name for amphetamine, see e.g. Grinspoon & Hedblom (1975), *The Speed Culture: Amphetamine Use and Abuse in America*.

125 Shulgin (1991), *PiHKAL*. This thick book is referred to as 'the bible' for synthetic drugs lovers and manufacturers, as it gives an overview of many possible chemical combinations, with their effects of different dosages, since the Shulgins like trying them out and report about their experiences into their advanced age.

126 By informing people about the potential risks fatalities could be reduced. Pill testing prevents the use of pills with a dangerous composition. Snother measure is modifying the circumstances under which the substances were being used (for example by making sure adequate water is available for ravers).

European fits into a larger international trend moving towards more pragmatic approaches to the drug question. A sign of this international trend is the rise of the international harm reduction movement.

While this chapter described the background of drug prohibition, outlining the contours of international and European drug control, the following three chapters will delve more closely into how France, the Netherlands and Sweden are giving shape to their respective drug policies. More importantly, the three country chapters will explain why these three European countries deal in different ways with psychoactive substances that are increasingly used in their societies while remaining illegal.

Chapter 3

Handling Drugs à la Française

3.1 Drugs in France

Wine is closely associated with French culture. As Sanche de Gramont notes in his *the French*, the grape has become one of those common denominators that unite Frenchmen, along with language, and the epic past of France.[1] Although it is more of a cliché to think of the French as being all *bon vivants*, conventional wisdom suggests that the French do know how to appreciate their *petits plaisirs*. Eating and drinking are part of life's little pleasures; they are highlights of the day, preferably enjoyed in company.[2] France has highly refined its wine and food culture with rules governing all aspect of eating, from rituals for the different courses to which wine belongs with which dish to how the setting of the table. Many books are written about food and wine as well as these being a popular subject of regular discussion.

The French do not have the reputation of being big consumers when it comes to illegal drugs. The *French Connection* immortalised and romanticised the Marseille based heroin laboratories and trafficking network that catered to the American heroin market until it was dismantled in the early 1970s. The *French Connection* is notably the most famous or infamous 'drug link' to France. Still, compared to other European countries, the French seem to have a longer history of drug use, and in the finest French tradition, they not only used drugs but also published studies and discussions.

It was during Napoleon's 1798 expedition to Egypt that troops discovered hashish.[3] Although consumption and possession were soon banned, this did not prevent cannabis from being brought back to France. This led to the gradual popularisation of hashish in Europe, particularly in France. Regular imports of hashish followed the expedition which soon made it possible to purchase at any pharmacy. In the 1840s, Physician Jacques-Joseph Moreau described hashish' effects as being an intellectual intoxication that was preferable to that of

---

1   De Gramont (1970), *the French*, 358.
2   Chavannes (2000a), *Frankrijk achter de schermen*, 31.
3   This particular nineteenth century French cannabis history is based on the book *Cannabis The Hip History of Hemp* by Green (2002), of which an edited extract ('Spoonfuls of Paradise'), was published in *The Guardian* of 12 October 2002.

alcohol. Moreau then met philosopher and writer Théophile Gautier who was part of the romanticism movement. Via Gautier, a number of leading Parisian writers and artists would get to know cannabis such as Alexandre Dumas, Gérard de Nerval, Victor Hugo, Honoré de Balzac, Charles Baudelaire, Eugène Delacroix and many others. They called themselves the *Club des Hachichins*. Dressed in Arab clothing they met in the gothic Pimodan House – also known as the Hôtel Lauzun – where they drank strong coffee laced with hashish, or they smoke the hashish in a pipe. Some of these writers used cannabis to get inspiration or they felt inspired to write about its effects, of which Baudelaire's *Les paradis artificiels* (1860) a comparison of hashish and wine "as means of expanding individuality" is the most known.[4]

A visit to a quality Parisian book shop shows that quite an amazing selection of French books on drugs exists even today, not only from professionals such as psychiatrists, but also from lawyers, academics, and activists. The underground press has translated several classic academic books on drugs into French. The CIRC, the slightly provocative cannabis organisation, has also published serious scientific works. France was notably one of the first European countries to have a famous personality advocating drug use, poet and actor Antonin Artaud. In the 1930s Artaud wrote about the usage of American indigenous hallucinogens (peyote), long before Aldous Huxley introduced the English speaking world to his experiences with mescaline in *The Doors of Perception* (1954).[5] During the 1990s, France housed the only independent research centre on international drug trafficking in the world, the *Observatoire Géopolitique des Drogues* (OGD), also known as the Geopolitical Drug Dispatch, which published newsletters, books, an atlas and a dictionary.[6] The subject of drugs occurs regularly in the French media: television, newspapers, and the much read weekly's.[7] In general terms, drugs – particularly cannabis, are an issue that often finds its way into the public forum, and is then hotly debated.

A diffuse picture emerges when it comes to the extent of drug use in France today in comparison to other countries. With regard to the extent of problem drug use, the current available data on the use of illicit drugs in Europe suggest

4   Green (2002) also gives other titles, such as *Hashish Wine Opium* by Gautier and Baudelaire, the book *De Hachish et de l'Alienation Mentale - Études Psychologiques* by Moreau, and the essay by Gautier whom Green considers the best informant: 'Le Club des Hachichins', published in the *Revue des Deux Mondes* in 1846. Green quotes Gautier, who wrote in an essay on Baudelaire: "It is possible and even probable that Baudelaire did try hashish once or twice by way of physiological experiment, but he never made continuous use of it".
5   In the 1960s it became a cult book and inspired Jim Morrisson for the name of his group *The Doors*.
6   See «www.ogd.org for publications and on-line reports». The OGD ceased to exist after 2000.
7   At the governmental drug policy institution MILDT a special collection was made at the occasion of an open day of media covers on drugs in 2000 called *Drogues à la une*. This cover collection is interesting as shows the ways drugs are discussed in the press and visually reflects the changes of thinking France has been going through over the last ten years.

that France' ranking is in the middle.[8] France finds itself ranking higher in European numbers when it comes to the most generally used illicit drug, cannabis.[9] French press regularly reminds its readers that several million French people use or have used cannabis. A recent French Senate report put their number at 9.5 million.[10] A 2000 survey involving a large number of seventeen years olds showed that almost half of them had already used illicit drugs.[11] A year later, when they were eighteen, more than half of them had used drugs.[12] To the dismay of some politicians this gave France the European lead in the spread of drug use among young people. Many parents realised with a shock that one in two of their older teenagers – hence, their child or his or her best friend – had already tried drugs.

There seems to exist something like a 'drug culture' among French youth. For many of them, there is something exciting and attractive about drugs.[13] The expression '*La fumette*' is used commonly by French youth for a cannabis joint – usually a mixture of tobacco and hashish. Many young people feel they have to try it, as if it is a part of growing up, like a rite of passage. In the streets of Paris as well as in southern cities, cannabis can be smelled quite regularly.[14] An expression often heard in the public debate is the *banalisation* of cannabis use among the youth; this term suggests that its use has become common or normal. Despite its illegal status, many French youth find cannabis less harmful than alcohol and tobacco.[15] Surveys show French youth generally know little about wine and are not so interested in knowing more about what they consider part of their parents' world, a universe from which they want to distance themselves.[16] The older French generations can have extensive nearly professionally

---

8   See the data on problem drug use in countries of the EU: «www.emcdda.org» In the 2002 annual report, France had an estimated 4.4 problem drug users per 1000 inhabitants aged 15-64, which puts it in the middle range.

9   A problem here though, is that major differences can be identified between different surveys, which can be due to poor or different methodologies. See Boekhout van Solinge (1997b), 'Drugs in France: Prevalence of Use and Drug Seizures'.

10   AFP (2003), *Cannabis, héroine, ecstasy: la hausse de la consommation en chiffres*, press release of 4 June 2003, based on Sénat (2003), *Drogue: l'autre cancer*.

11   This survey, Escapad 2000, was held when in May 2000 14,000 French youth, most of them 17, and some of them 18 or 19, were called upon in connection with the replacement of the French military service for males into a civil service for all youth. It offered a unique possibility to question an age cohort about their drug use. The survey showed that at the age of 17, 41% of the girls and 50% of the boys had used cannabis. See: Beck et al. (2000), *Regards sur la fin de l'adolescence (ESCAPAD 2000)*.

12   In 2001, the ESCAPAD study found 45% of the girls and 56% of the boys had used cannabis. On average, first experimentation occurs in the beginning of the sixteenth year. See «www.ofdt.org», or see Beck et al. (2001), *Santé, mode de vie et usage de drogue à 18 ans – ESCAPAD 2001*.

13   Boekhout van Solinge (1995), 'Le cannabis en France', 144.

14   Impression of the author, based on fieldwork and numerous visits to different quarters and areas.

15   Lemoine (2001), 'Un jeune sur deux a déjà fumé du hasch', based on ESCAPAD survey.

16   Chavannes (2000a), *Frankrijk achter de schermen*, 33, based on the findings of French sociologist Gérard Mermet who explains that the youth distance themselves from their parents' generation, which they consider responsible for the high unemployment. Consequently, they refuse to take over attributes of that older generation, such as wine. Mermet publishes every two year *Francoscopie*,

discussions about wines – their differences, characteristics and when to use each type – in the same manner as do young cannabis *connoisseurs*.

Despite the extent and *banalisation* of drug use (and of cannabis in particular) French authorities generally react in a repressive way towards the illicit drugs phenomenon. By French legal standards, the French drug legislation of 1970 is an exceptional law, a *loi d'exception*. France is one of the few countries that prohibits the *use* of drugs, even when occurring in the privacy of ones own home.[17] Putting drugs in a positive light is explicitly prohibited by an article in the drug legislation which considers this to be an act which incites the use of drugs.[18] Prevention workers complain that the article is so strict that it does not allow them to legally perform aspects of their work such as openly discussing drugs with users and addressing their positive and pleasurable effects. The strictness of this article also does not allow prevention workers to discuss safer methods of use, seeing how this could be interpreted as inciting people to use drugs.

French drug legislation is not only strict to the letter, but also in its application. The 1970 law offered the possibility of an alternative for penal action in the form of treatment, but in practice this was not often applied. Although guidelines of the Ministry of Justice recommended non-penal responses, the most common answer was still a punitive one.[19] The number of drug arrests has been growing constantly since 1970, and rose above 100,000 by the year 2000. The large majority of drug arrests concern cannabis users being arrested for 'use' or 'use-reselling'.[20] Several hundred people are incarcerated for the use of drugs, despite politicians' claims this is not, or should not be the case.[21] The incitation article against placing drugs in a positive light is regularly applied. French citizens and 'naïve' tourists are arrested for wearing T-shirts or earrings with cannabis leaves. It is on these same grounds that a hemp clothing fashion show was closed down some years ago in Paris, or more recently, in September 2003, that the ex president of a techno-music organisation, *Techno +*, was put on trial for putting harm reduction leaflets on their website, such as on safe snorting techniques.[22]

In line with the French culture of debate, the discussion on the depenalisation of cannabis use finds itself on the public discussion agenda. Thus it has been for many years that the question arises as to whether the consumption of

---

comment vivent les Français? ('Francoscope: how do the French live?').

17 Some drug legislations make the distinction between private and public use. The Belgian law does so, for example, whereas the French drug law did until 1970.

18 Article L3421-4 (formerly L-630) of the Public Health Act (*Code de la santé publique*).

19 As noticed already by the governmental commission chaired by Pelletier (1978) *Problèmes de la drogue*, quoted by Ehrenberg (1995), *L'individu incertain*, 98. See also further where an evaluation report is quoted.

20 ODFT (2000), 'Drogues et dependences: Indicateurs et tendances'.

21 OFDT (2002), *Drogues et dependences. Indicateurs et tendances 2002*, 49 and 56 (see table).

22 The safe snorting leaflet pointed at the health risks of nasal drug use, while the 'drug mix' leaflet informed about the risks using different drugs together. See «www.technoplus.org».

drugs should be depenalised. This public debate recurs typically in the media, most of which has long concluded it would be best to change what it believes is outdated as well as Europe's most repressive legislation. However, politicians are reluctant to change the drug legislation and often put forward the forbidden fruit argument: cannabis is attractive for young people to use just because it is illegal making it young people's temptation to transgress those laws. It is further argued that if the use of cannabis were de-penalised, young people would seek the transgression in other, more dangerous, substances. Another reason for the political unwillingness to change their drug law is that the issue of drugs is so much intertwined with the security theme that has been drummed into French politics, especially by right wing parties. Drug use and trade are prevalent in some of the suburban, lower class housing projects where large immigrant communities form. These suburbs underground economies are fed by drug wholesale areas.[23] Some notorious suburbs have turned into 'no-go' areas where security has become a big political issue. Being more lenient on drugs would be perceived as being soft on security, which does not sell well politically.

The differences in attitudes towards legal and illegal drugs are striking in France. For a long time, it proved difficult to discuss licit and illicit drugs together. When in the late 1990s a report of a government-appointed scientific commission – The Roques Commission – put alcohol in the same category as heroin, hell broke out in the wine and restaurant community.[24] How could such a culturally valued product such as wine, which has proven itself to be medically beneficial (known to decrease the risk of cardiovascular diseases), be put in the same category as the 'lethal' and illegal substance heroin? Psychoactive pharmaceuticals are easily prescribed and used. Until 1993, most of the tobacco in France was controlled and taxed by one large government-owned tobacco company, Seita which is an old and respected company.[25] Alcohol is considered an indistinguishable part of French culture that should be preserved and cherished.

Only recently, in the twenty-first century, official attitudes towards licit drugs have changed. The damage of alcohol is increasingly recognised, not only the physical harm, but also the 'social' damage, such as violence and automobile accidents due to driving under the influence. Drinking and driving have

---

23 See the study that compiles fieldwork on different areas in France: Conseil National des Villes (1994), *L'Économie souterraine de la drogue*. See also Duprez and Kokoreff (2000), *Les mondes de la drogue*.

24 Roques (1999), *La dangerosité des drogues*. The study on the dangers of both legal and illegal psychoactive substances was ordered by Under Minister for Health, Bernard Kouchner.

25 Seita stands for 'Societe Nationale d'Exploitation Industrielle de Tabacs et Allumettes' and was privatised in 1993. More than half of the stock is held by a vast number of small investors, including many of France's 35,000 tobacconists. There is no single large controlling interest, and government participation has fallen to 5%. See Bell (1999), *SEITA: Consolidated Cigar's French Connection*.

now been severely banned. In order to limit the dangers of tobacco smoking, the French government have considerably raised cigarette prices.

The use of illicit drugs is generally met by repression based on the 1970 drug legislation. Harm reduction officially became an integral aspect of French drug policy in 1993, thereafter measures were taken, such as expanding substitution treatment and needle exchange programmes. France, being one of the last European Union countries to opt for a harm reduction policy was still lagging behind.[26] In the mid-1990s, stimulated by the findings of a high level governmental commission headed by Medical Professor Roger Henrion, it was fully acknowledged that France lagged behind in taking harm reduction measures which had contributed to one in three French intravenous heroin users being infected by HIV.[27] The Henrion Report stated that French drug policy, "based on the idea of certainly not doing anything that may facilitate the life of drug addicts had led to a health and social catastrophe".[28]

It was during the second half of the 1990s that the change in approach began to bear fruit as French drug policy underwent substantial changes. Under the dynamic leadership of the new national drug policy co-ordinator Nicole Maestracci an impressive move was made to improve French harm reduction and prevention policies.[29] Over a relatively short period of time, a major paradigm shift was made from an ideological abstinence-based approach, to a more pragmatic harm reduction approach. Since 1999, this policy no longer focused solely on the dangers of illicit drugs, but now looked at all unhealthy or risky substance-taking behaviours, including tobacco, alcohol, psychoactive medicines and doping. Hence, a genuine public health policy began to develop breaking the taboo that legal and illegal drugs could not be discussed together. In 1999, the Ministry of Justice issued a guideline that enlarged possibilities for alternatives to sanctioning drug use, such as a warning or being directed to health services.[30]

Despite the paradigm shift in French drug policy, the changes go slowly and resistance still exists. Traditionally, the powerful Ministry of the Interior opposes a softer, health oriented approach, insisting on a strict law and order approach. While it is true that the police no longer arrest heroin users when leaving pharmacies with newly purchased syringes, the Interior Ministry is not really on board when it comes to the health and harm reduction emphasis of the drug question. Drug users, particularly cannabis smokers, are being arrested in

---

26 After the advent of Aids in the mid 1980s, most countries started taking measures in the late 1980s or early 1990s.

27 For figures see Boekhout van Solinge (1996), *L'héroïne, la cocaïne et le crack en France*, 189-193.

28 Henrion (1995), *Rapport de la commission de réflexion sur la drogue et la toxicomanie*, 58.

29 In France, the governmental drug control institution is called MILDT: Interdepartmental Mission for the Fight Against Drugs and Drug Addiction. Maestracci became the new MILDT director.

30 Ministère de l'Intérieur (1999), *Circulaire du 17 juin 1999. Les réponses judiciaires aux toxicomanies*.

growing number. Another factor at play is that drugs remain a politically sensitive issue and several French presidents have been active in promoting anti-drugs measures. The current right-wing President Jacques Chirac, is taking the promoting of anti-drugs measures further in his regular pattern of speaking out against the "drug peril".[31]

This chapter explores the origin and development of French drug policy as well as its strict and exceptional drug legislation. Following the American argumentation that drug and immigrant problems coexist their strict response can be explained by the complicated relationship between France and its North African population, among whom the use of hashish is traditionally more common and widespread.[32] In this light, France's strict drug prohibitionist approach could be based on the protection of what is considered typically French culture, against new and unknown cultures and habits. But as this chapter will shown, the root of the strict French reaction towards illicit drugs has not much to do with the immigration question, but more with internal French affairs. This chapter will also discuss the French debate on the de-penalisation of cannabis use as well as politicians' reluctance to do so. The shift in orientation from abstinence to harm reduction as a focus of policy will be described and the resistance from both professionals and politicians will be explained. Before going into these drug policy questions, the next section will focus on France itself and what appears to point towards a 'culture of ingestion'. It describes Frances rich and stormy history, the political tradition of a strong state and central rule, and will tentatively explain the French tastes for food, wine and other pleasures.

3.2 Geography, History, and the People

France is one the biggest and most centrally located countries in Western Europe touching both the Atlantic and Mediterranean. Because of its position, France has a wide variety of nature and landscapes and generally has a pleasant climate all of which the French are aware and proud of. The French sometimes say France has been naturally formed, not only by the seas, but also by the mountain chains, from the Pyrenees in the South (the border with Spain) to the Alps and Jura in the East (bordering Switzerland), while the country is separated from Germany by the Rhine. The French sometimes refer to their country as *l'Hexagone*, since the country indeed has a six-sided form, with three sides on

---

31 See for example his words spoken at UNGASS quoted in the Introduction.

32 American sociologist Harry Levine, hypothesising in a personal communication and discussion, 1996. It was explained earlier that the restrictive American drug policy had a clear racial undertone. The introduction of drug laws had little directly with drug problems, but more so with the fact that certain immigrant groups were using certain drugs. Controlling drugs was a way of controlling these groups. It could be hypothesised that this also explains the French response towards drugs, a resistance towards the 'Arab' hashish and a way of controlling the Arab population.

the sea and three on the land. "Which other people have made the shape of their country an aesthetic value and a source of moral satisfaction?" wonders Gramont.[33] The diverse French landscape offers possibilities for many forms of leisure activities, from nautical sports, skiing and mountain climbing to more modern sports such as rock climbing and speleology (cave climbing). The landscape combined with the pleasant Mediterranean climate in the southern half of the country, France is a popular tourist destination. With some seventy million visitors a year France is the world's first tourist destination.[34]

The country of France occupies a large territory with a great deal of country-side and thousands of small villages with almost sixty million inhabitants of whom a substantial number are living in urban areas, especially around Paris. One of the most important agricultural countries in Europe is France whose agriculture is also important to the rest of the world.[35] Land, its yield and the farmers who tend it are generally well respected in France.[36] Traditions such as fishing and hunting remain intact in the French countryside, which explains why the lobby organisation '*la peche et la chasse*' is, after agriculture, the second strongest political lobby in Paris.

Discussing Europe without illuminating the role of France on its history is difficult owing to how central the history of France is to that of Europe. French Kings have ruled other parts of Europe fighting many conflicts with its rulers. The Hundred Years War (against England) is one of the oldest French conflicts to be kept alive in the collective memory. The Hundred Years War ended in 1453 giving the French their first national hero, Jeanne d'Arc.[37] During the seventeenth century the French state was more firmly constructed under the reign of Henry IV later to be continued under the administrations of Cardinals Richelieu and Mazarin, and throughout the long reign of The Sun King, Louis XIV (1643-1715). The Sun King gave new impetus to French civilisation through his power and central rule, as well as through the literature, music and arts which flourished at his dazzling palace at Versailles.[38] The eighteenth century was a period of great colonial expansion, but it also led to conflicts with England over possessions in the New World. A series of wars from 1741-83

---

33 De Gramont (1970), *the French*, 3.
34 This figure includes tourists passing through France on their way to Spain and Portugal.
35 The importance of French agriculture is also clear in the politics of the European Union. Since half of the EU budget is spent of agriculture subsidies, France receives a big share of it and it is therefore the main opponent to agricultural reforms.
36 When farmers protest against high quotas of decreasing subsides by blocking roads, or dumping truck loads of agricultural produce in front of the city council, French citizens generally react with understanding.
37 It was however, only after her death in 1431 (burnt at the stake by the English) that her merits for the country were acknowledged and she was declared sainted. See Smith, 'Introduction. France in the Making' in Perry (Ed.) (1997), *Aspects of Contemporary France*, 4 and 420.
38 The political system established, or at least strongly consolidated, by Louis XIV was firmly centralist with a clear social hierarchy and convoluted etiquette, ensuring the will of the central government was enacted in the province. See Smith (1997), 'Introduction. France in the Making', 6-7.

bankrupted the state and led to the loss of a number of colonies in America and Asia.[39] At the same time, the country was internally attacked and undermined by the *philosophes* – Voltaire, Diderot, Rousseau, and Montesquieu – who attacked intolerance, obscurantism, and unenlightened absolutism.

The Revolution of 1789 was a landmark event because it first limited and later, in 1792, led to the overthrowing of the Bourbon monarchy. "The Revolution occurred, not quite by accident but certainly not in a premeditated way, because of a combination of governmental ineptitude and powerlessness, social injustice, economic crisis and reforming ambitions born out of the Enlightenment and the example of the American Revolution which had only recently taken place".[40] It was during the Revolution that the political terms Left and Right were invented.[41] It was also when the Declaration of the Rights of Man was voted as the preamble to the first written French Constitution.[42]

In 1799 Napoleon Bonaparte first seized power as the First Consul of the new regime, later in 1804 he became the first Emperor of France.[43] Napoleon's lasting legacy is in his creating the legislative, administrative, financial, judicial and religious foundations of France. For example, after 1806 he introduced the civil code, known as Code Napoleon, which acknowledged civil liberties for men. Under the principal of unifying centralism, Napoleon centralised the court system and reorganised French administration.[44] 1848 was a revolutionary year for Europe of which France was not excluded. In 1848 a new constitution was established and Louis-Napoleon Bonaparte was elected President of the Republic. In 1852 after devising a new Constitution, Louis-Napoleon Bonaparte was proclaimed Emperor carrying the title Napoleon III marking the beginning of the Second Empire.[45]

The Second Empire lasted until the French-German War of 1870, after which France entered its Third Republic. Not much later, during World War I (1914-18), France would be again at war with Germany, a rivalry to be repeated by World War II. These two big European countries fought three wars in seventy years, which explains why after 1945, the French-German friendship became the backbone of European co-operation and integration. The bloodshed of World War II led to the creation of the European Community and later

---

39 France fought the war of Austrian Succession (1741-48), the Seven Years War (1756-63) and the American War of Independence (1773-83).
40 Smith (1997), 'Introduction. France in the Making', 8.
41 Knapp and Write (2001: 2) explain in *The Government and Politics of France*: "Those noble members of the first National Assembly who wished to limit the powers of the monarch moved to sit with the commoners on the Left of the Assembly; those who still supported the abolutionism of what was shortly to become known as the *ancien régime* sat on the right."41
42 Even though, as De Gramont (1970: 104) notes in *the French*, many of the articles were subsequently violated by the practice of revolution.
43 Smith (1997), 'Introduction. France in the Making', 9.
44 The principle of centralism remained strong until being modified in the early 1980s under President Mitterrand's decentralisation policy.
45 Smith (1997), 'Introduction. France in the Making', 13.

European Union.[46] Co-operation would reduce the risk of war in Europe. As a first step the French and German coal and steel industries were put under a supra-national authority.

During World War II Charles De Gaulle became the symbol of French resistance, naturally he came to head the first French government following the war. De Gaulle desired a new constitution with a more powerful president, but the French people voted for a more traditional form of government. This explains why the Fourth Republic, founded in 1946, was only new in name. Disappointed, De Gaulle retreated from politics to write his memoirs from the French countryside. He would get his new constitution, but only twelve years later when a special appeal was made to him to solve the Algerian crisis of 1958 which brought France to the brink of a civil war.[47] De Gaulle accepted the role of Prime Minister, but on the condition that he could govern for six months without parliament. In the meantime he was to design a new constitution over which the people could decide through a referendum. In June 1958 De Gaulle headed the new government, in September the referendum was held and De Gaulle's plan was accepted. New parliamentarian elections were held, which were overwhelmingly won by the newly formed Gaullist party. A new Constitution was drawn, which gave substantial powers to the President, and limited those of Parliament. December 1958 Charles De Gaulle became the first President of the Fifth Republic.[48] De Gaulle's legacy in French politics goes beyond 'creating' the Fifth Republic, and establishing presidential power over parliament. According to De Gaulle, France should hold its rightful place in the world and play a role in world affairs.[49] After De Gaulle other French Presidents

---

46 Important Europeans in this regard were Robert Schumann from Germany and Jean Monnet from France.

47 In 1958, the nomination of Pflmlin as French Prime Minister led to a revolt of French *pieds noirs* and French soldiers in French Algeria, who think Pflmlin supports negotiations with the Algerian rebels, who fight for independence. In Algeria, French parachute general Massu headed a emergency committee and rumours were that parachutes would land in Paris. The threat of a civil war over an independent French Algeria now exists. The only man who considered to be able to end the crisis is 'strong man' and war hero general De Gaulle. Eventually he manages to control the French revolt in Algeria by giving a speech, broadcast on television in which he asks the rebels to put down the arms, which they do on 1st February 1960. De Gaulle's achievement is that Algeria becomes independent without leading to a French civil war. See Wesseling (1987), *Vele ideeën over Frankrijk*, 160-165.

48 The most significant feature of the Fifth Republic is that it allows for much executive (presidential and governmental) power and relatively little parliamentary power. Furthermore, the President is elected by universal suffrage and is responsible for the choice (and dismissal) of the Prime Minister with whom he consults to nominate the rest of the cabinet. The most controversial presidential power is that it allows him exceptional powers (generally defined as those 'required by the circumstances') for a certain period during a time of crisis. De Gaulle only used this once, in 1961 after a putsch by four general in Algeria. See Forbes et al. (2001), *Contemporary France*, 21.

49 De Gaulle gave France (back) pride, self-respect and *grandeur*. He had a 'certain idea of France', which he expressed in his books and speeches. Part of his vision on France is that it stood on itself, independent from the world powers. The clearest sign of this independence was the stepping out of NATO's integrated military structure in 1966 and the *force de frappe*, France's own atomic weapon. To the annoyance of the Americans, the French atomic defence is directed *tous azimuts*, in

continued the idea of France playing a major role in world politics. Reminiscent of when France was a world power and French was spoken internationally by nobility and the well educated, presidents and politicians have tried to follow in his footsteps, or have claimed to represent his legacy but none have managed to uphold the grandeur that De Gaulle gave to France. De Gaulle's rule came to an end a year after the student revolt of May 1968, which was also a protest against his generation.[50]

The history of France is characterised by a series of wars, revolutions and revolts, leaving France with the legacy of conflict: "Modern French history is driven by deep and often murderous political conflict in which Frenchmen kill Frenchmen and regimes were toppled by protest from the streets, defeat in war, or both. These events are remembered, and referred to regularly by contemporary politicians".[51] Every village square in France carries the national history, with a monument for the fallen placed across the village church.[52] Knapp and Wright add another trait to the political tradition: "But French history has also, paradoxically, been marked by the near-continuous presence, under successive regimes, of a strong, activist, often intrusive, state".[53] Jacobinism, the political philosophy which sprang out of the Revolution placed the interest of the state above all else. France has had strong and centralised rule during its different constitutions and types of government – often combined with grandeur.[54] The most lasting legacy of De Gaulle and Gaullism was the use of a strong, centralised state to establish political stability and the modernisation of the economy.[55]

all directions. For an excellent description and analysis of De Gaulle in Dutch, see Wesseling (1987), *Vele ideeën over Frankrijk*, 158-178.

50 After the student revolt De Gaulle wanted to reform and decentralise France, for which he held a referendum, which was seen as a political choice for or against him, as De Gaulle said he would retreat in case of a defeat. Prime Minister Georges Pompidou who had negotiated with the unions and had managed to reach an agreement, also became candidate and he eventually beat De Gaulle. As promised De Gaulle retreated from politics the next day. A year later, in 1970, De Gaulle died.

51 Knapp & Wright (2001), *The Government and Politics of France*, 2. Chavannes (2000a: 50) adds in *Frankrijk achter de schermen* that every village square carries French history, a cross from the church is the monument for the fallen. Counting from 1870, France has been involved in five wars in less then a century: the French-German War, World Wars I and II, the Indo-Chinese War and the Algerian War.

52 Chavannes (2000a) *Frankrijk achter de schermen*, 50. From 1870 onwards, France has been involved in five wars in less then a century: the French-German war, World War I and II, the Indo-Chinese war and the Algerian War.

53 Knapp & Wright (2001), *The Government and Politics of France*, 2.

54 Sun King Louis XIV gave it a very personal interpretation by saying he himself was the state ("*l'Etat, c'est moi*"), but also several other heads of states have given their rule some grandeur. While the last socialist president François Mitterrand, gave the French Presidency something 'royal' with the many prestigious projects he initiated, current president Jacques Chirac tries to give France back prestige and a place in international politics. This became clear from French policy towards Iraq as it challenged, also as a permanent member of the UN Security Council, US foreign and military dominance and unilateralism.

55 Forbes et al. make the remark that according to many, Gaullism is a type of Bonapartism, a reference to the populist-authoritarian rule of Napoleon Bonaparte and Louis Napoleon. See Forbes et al. (2001), *Contemporary France*, 20-21.

The idea of France and a strong state being inseparable is so strongly rooted that De Gaulle's successor, George Pompidou, said "France would not exist without a state".[56] In the French view, the role of the state is not only seen as a vehicle for functions such as defence, public order, justice, education and so on, but also as the architect of the nation. These views on the primal role of the state in French history are also reflected in the state's contemporary role and its autonomy and primacy in relation both to sub-national levels of government and to civil society in general.[57]

Under the central rule of France an active education policy aided the rapid spread of the French language throughout French held territory.[58] Pride in Frances diversity, history, achievements, traditions, food and culture is taught in French schools explaining why there is such pride and awareness of their culture and themselves – sometimes viewed as arrogance.

Art, culture and the artists themselves are respected and sometimes worshipped in France in ways not seen in other countries. France has had a tradition of intellectuals, usually writers or philosophers since 1898 when the novelist Emile Zola wrote an open accusation letter to the French president over the Dreyfus affaire in his *J'accuse*. Intellectuals play an active role in public debate by writing articles in newspapers and pamphlets, or through radio and television programmes.[59] The debate is considered important In France. A famous quotation illustrating this is General De Gaulle's reaction when it was suggested that Jean-Paul Sartre be arrested for his criticism of France's policy in Algeria: "One does not arrest Voltaire".[60] The French seem to have a predilection for great men and great ideas partly owing to their political, intellectual and philosophical traditions: people who stand out and are idealised for greatness – whether they be kings, emperors, heroes, politicians, writers or philosophers. The drug field is no exception to this rule as it will be shown to have its own *pater intellectualis*.

The French Revolution and the Declaration of Rights of Man in 1789 have given the French the belief that the universal messages learned from these make France the 'cradle of human rights' and establish them at the forefront of the

---

56 Knapp & Wright (2001), *The Government and Politics of France*, 2.
57 Knapp & Wright (2001), *The Government and Politics of France*, 16.
58 It should be noted that in the mid-1990s, only a minority of the French really spoke French. See Weber (1979), *Peasants into Frenchmen. The modernization of rural France*.
59 Dreyfus was a Jewish artillery officer in the French army convicted of a crime he never committed. Although it was found out later that he had been falsely convicted, the army covered it up. The affair got world wide attention and the process that followed against the famous writer was covered by hundreds of journalists from all over the world.
60 Jean-Paul Sartre supported the Algerians in their independence, for which he was branded traitor. In 1960 Sartre signed an illegal petition denouncing the behaviour of the French military in Algeria, *Manifeste des 140*, which was published in Sartre's revue *Les Temps modernes*. When it was suggested to the General to jail Sartre for it upon his return from a trip to Algiers, the General spoke the famous words "On n'arrête pas Voltaire".

issue.[61] In the international political arena, the French intellectual tradition offers grand and visionary ideas explaining why they believe themselves to deserve a leadership role in Europe.[62] The French also believe that they posses a special cultural position internationally. The French introduced the notion of 'cultural exception' as protection against the overwhelming American Holly-wood culture when the OECD (an organisation of rich countries) was trying to stimulate free trade. The French were given an exception from free trade in the area of culture which included music, film and the arts. Their argument in defence of 'cultural exception' was that their culture and art were not solely marketable as economic products (like the American mass marketing of popular culture) but are aspects of French culture, which gives them the right to protect and subsidise these 'products'.

Visitors to France are struck by the general appreciation given to their food and drink by the French. It is common in Southern European Latin culture to respect food and drink by talking about their pleasures and virtues and in taking time to enjoy them. The French describe their homeland as one that ordains the good life: *le pays de bien vivre*. Peter Mayle's best-seller *A Year in Provence* romanticises *le pays de bien vivre* and describes life in the South of France as moving at a slower pace, being less business oriented and where people take the time to enjoy life. The locals drink their coffee or wine in the village-square under the shade of the plane trees and the cafes seem to always be full of people as if they do not have to work.

It was mentioned in the introduction of this chapter that the French like the 'petits plaisirs' which refers not only to ingesting pleasurable substances such as food, drink and drugs, dining and cinema (more film is seen in France than anywhere else) but extending further to the art of seduction and sexuality. Meals such as lunch and diner serve important social functions where the participants, whether they be family, friends or business contacts take the time to discuss all manner of topics. French meals are often concluded with cheese, of which the French have hundreds of different types – enough, the French say, to have another cheese every day. Gastronomy is of such social importance that it is common for an office employee to dine in restaurants daily where the bill is paid with a special ticket (partially paid for by their employer) making lunch in a restaurant part of the conditions of employment.

In Latin culture meals are accompanied by wine. The Greek introduced the vine to France, but the French turned wine cultivation into an art. The birth of France began with wine, notes Gramont with irony: "The history of the French

---

61 As declared by former Minister of Foreign Affairs, Hubert Védrine to the correspondent of Dutch daily *NRC Handelsblad*, Chavannes (2000a), *Frankrijk achter de schermen*, 98.
62 Which France has played to some extent. Since the origin of European cooperation and with reputed politicians such as Monnet and Shuman, and with its strong administrative tradition and qualified civil servants, France has been a leading participant of European cooperation and has tried to develop a vision about Europe.

nation begins not with a banquet, but with a glass of wine. The Frankish King Clovis won the support of the Church when he converted to Catholicism and took communion from the bishop of Rhimes with a glass of non-sparkling champagne".[63] The vine is the favoured symbol in French decorative art. Wine was believed by kings to be a cure for their indigestion and generals believed it won wars. Even saints drank wine and had wines named after them, like Saint-Emilion and Saint-Estephe, and Joan of Arc liked it in her soup.[64] Normally, wines are named after the place of their geographical origin. Some wines, such as the fine sparkling wine Champagne, have acquired such a world-wide reputation that outside of France few know it is named after its region.

France, with a yearly production of fifty to sixty million hectolitres ranks just above Italy as the world's main wine producer. France is responsible for 20% of world wine production.[65] Besides producing large quantities of wine, the French are also big wine consumers, drinking 15% of the world's wine. The French and Italians combined drink 29% of all wine, while Europe as a whole consumes 70% of it. France remains one of the world's main consumers with some 56 litres a year per capital.[66] Still, over the last few decades, French alcohol consumption has decreased considerably. In the late 1990s the average per capita wine consumption was 60 litres compared to 73 litres in 1990, and 120 litres in the 1970s, when the French and Italians still drank 50% of the wine in the world.[67] Strikingly, the decrease in wine consumption is especially attributable to younger people.[68] The French are also big tobacco smokers. More than a third of the population, almost twenty million people, smoke. Half of the French in the age range of 15-24 smoke making this the highest figure in the European Union for this age range.

The French are also consuming large amounts of licit, pharmaceutical drugs such as anti-depressants, hypnotics, sedatives, and anxiolytics which are easily prescribed by their physicians.[69] In fact, the French are (among) the world's biggest per capita consumers of these drugs.[70] In French medical practice and

---

63   De Gramont (1970), *the French*, 357-358.
64   De Gramont (1970), *the French*, 357-359.
65   In 2001 France produced 56.2 million hectolitres of wine (20%), while Italy produced 51.5 million (19%). The two stand out as the world's leading wine producers, largely surpassing the third and fourth producers, Spain and the United States.
66   According to the *Wine Specatator* («www.winespecatator.com») of 28 April 2003, France's per capita wine consumption was 56 liters.
67   Based on 'la baisse actuelle de la consommation d'alcool', in Mignon (1993), *Les 'toxicomanies légales' (alcool, tabac, médicaments)*, 16-19, and on Chavannes (2000a), *Frankrijk achter de schermen*, 32-33. Italians drank nearly 50% of all wine.
68   Mignon (1993), *les 'toxicomanies légales' (alcool, tabac, médicaments)*, 18.
69   See the series of articles on this subject in *Le Monde* of 6 September 2004, such as 'Pourquoi les Français consomment toujours plus de psychotropes'.
70   See the remark by Ehrenberg that the French are (after Belgium) the biggest consumer of tranquillisers in the Western world and the biggest consumers of prescription drugs in general. See Mignon (1993), *Les 'toxicomanies légales' (alcool, tabac, médicaments)*, 18. According to the *Le Monde* article in the previous footnote, the French would be the biggest consumers of 'psychotropic pharmaceuticals'.

culture, patients usually expect to leave the doctor's surgery with a prescription. The extensive use of over-the-counter and prescription drugs explains why the lit green pharmacy cross is so visible and present in street scenes, from large cities to small villages. This also explains why many French medicine cabinets at home are filled with drugs.

When looking at drug use from the much wider perspective of the ingestion of pleasurable substances, the French seem to have developed a particular taste. Alcohol use has been going down steadily which has been largely attributed to the fact that young people are drinking less. Considering the existence of a cannabis culture and the popularity of cannabis consumption among the youth some of whom are consuming heavily,[71] it could be argued that the decrease in alcohol consumption parallels the increase in cannabis consumption. This could mean that cannabis use is partly replacing alcohol use. It does seem that younger French people have added illicit drugs to the list of pleasurable substances that can be ingested. The moderate shift from alcohol to cannabis use may give a better understanding of the increase in illicit drug use but it does not explain why the authorities react so fiercely against it. As will be shown in the next section, part of the explanation lies in the turbulent events of May 1968.

3.3 May 1968 and the 1970 drug legislation

The 1960s are generally considered to be a decade of student protest and of social and political change. Young people not only protested against the war in Vietnam, but against the old fashioned values of the ruling generation, its materialism and political faults, which had not only led to Vietnam, but also to World War II and the Cold War.[72] Since the beginnings of the counter culture in the 1960s, student protest movements sprang up in many places, mostly in the western world but also beyond its borders. In France protesting took on a different more dramatic and violent form compared to student revolts across the globe. May 1968 became a world event, giving impetus to student protests not only in Europe, but also as far away as Mexico and South Korea.

The historical overview made clear that changes in French society usually are not gradual, but come with shocks. More than once a revolution was necessary in order to change things – which leads some French to say: we are a people of revolutions – and May 1968 was almost a revolution. An opinion poll held for the French monthly *L'Histoire* in November 1998, showed that the

---

71 See the study conducted on heavy cannabis consumption patterns in a Paris suburb that found young people smoking hashish-tobacco joints in numbers comparable to the number of cigarettes of regular tobacco smokers. See S. Aquatias et al. (1997), *l'usage dur des drogues douces. Recherche sur la consommation de cannabis dans la banlieue parisienne.*
72 See Wesseling (1987), *Vele ideeën over Frankrijk*, 175, quoting B.E. Brown (1974), *Protest in Paris. Anatomy of a Revolt.*

French that after World War II the French consider May 1968 to be the second most dramatic event of the twentieth century.[73] What distinguished the Paris revolt in 1968 from many other student revolts was their alliance with another dissatisfied group – the working class. The students wanted to change society, whereas the workers and their unions only wanted to spread wealth more equally. Playing in the background was France still being somewhat old-fashioned and authoritarian. "French society was stiflingly bureaucratic and over-centralised and the social structure and social culture were frustratingly inflexible", Hewlett writes.[74] Sociologist Michel Crozier described French society as "*la société bloquée*", while political activist and analyst Régis Debray described France in the 1960s as "*la France à deux vitesses*" with the economy cruising in a high gear and social aspects of France stuck in a low gear. Hewlett explains it well:

> "One the one hand, economically France had undergone tremendous modernising changes since the Second World War, which included an impressive growth in Gross National product (GDP), the concentration of capital, the 'feminisation' of the labour force and the vast increase in the number of graduates, whose historical task it was to oversee further economic development. On the other hand there still was a backward, paternalistic system of industrial relations where the *patronat* virtually refused to talk to the trade unions, an education system where relations between teachers and students were archaic, despite the massive expansion of student numbers, the traditional model of the family where patriarchy reigned, cultural and legal constraints on relations between the sexes which were out of date and, last but not least, the paternalistic and authoritarian nature of Gaullism itself".[75]

Historian Wesseling describes how the university students protests began. The French Ministry of Education has large say on education and on all matters regarding universities which meant that for the students, resistance against the university authorities was equal to resisting the government. From just outside of Paris at the University of Nanterre in early May of 1968, the protests spread to the Sorbonne in the heart of Paris where students occupied the Sorbonne's courtyard until they were evicted by the police. The student protests then went to the streets, which led to demonstrations, barricades, occupations, and riots with the police. On the eleventh of May, the police decided to conduct a big and violent offensive against the students, which led to hundreds being arrested and wounded. The students then sought the support of the workers with whom they had declared solidarity. 14 May 1968 strikes and occupations began and within a few weeks ten million French people, representing a substantial part of the labour force, were on strike throughout the country, almost causing public life to come to a standstill. All in all, May 1968 meant a three-week general strike,

---

73 Chavannes (2000a), *Frankrijk achter de schermen*, 60. World War II is by far considered the most drastic event of the twentieth century. It is followed by May 1968, the fall of the Soviet Union, World War I, European unification and decolonisation.
74 Hewlett (2001), 'Politics in France', 7.
75 Hewlett (2001), 'Politics in France', 7.

a virtual governmental power vacuum, economic power paralysis – and almost a revolution. President De Gaulle left Paris 'without declaration' to visit the French army in Germany led by General Massud in order to reassure himself of his support.[76] In 1971, André Hoyles described the atmosphere as follows:

> "In May-June 1968, with the breakdown of normal communication – press, radio, television – everybody was talking to everybody, in university lecture theatres and cafés and on the streets (this was, of course, more true in large towns than villages, of Paris than the provinces, of young people than of old). For a short while, there was an impression of liberation from the constraints of normal life, an awakening, for people normally held down by routine. Theatre companies, journalists, writers, television personalities who visited the occupied factories and universities, were struck by the overwhelming response of their audiences. People became aware of the censorship of the government-controlled radio and television, of the cultural desert in which they were kept".[77]

Eventually, the strike and revolt came to an end because of the different goals sought by the students and workers. Since the workers did not want to radically change society, the government started negotiating with their unions and offered a substantial increase in income. The unions accepted the proposals, isolating the students and the revolt practically came to a halt. It is debatable whether or not there were substantial changes in France following May 1968. As Hoyles put it: "But romanticizing is of no avail: the wave of excitement was followed by what may appear to be a return to the old state of affairs. (...) Censorship remained. But if there were no *measurable* change, a new consciousness does exist, however diffuse".[78] The barrier of communication had been shaken, in secondary schools discipline and syllabuses were transformed, and schools became more open to the outside world. Also, the introduction of participation in factories and schools reflected a change of attitude. In short, May 1968 did mean a change, but not to the extent it is sometimes suggested by the people who were actively involved.

May 1968 meant a change in the perception of how illicit drugs were viewed. The authorities perceived the rise in drug use during the late 1960s as being a part of the 1968 protest movement although from the protesters' point of view the desire for political change was the most important aspect. The political ramifications to the main events of May 1968 became the authorities' reaction to the illicit drug use phenomenon. Surprisingly, France's historical experiences with drug use and drugs control were forgotten in their formation of drug legislation in 1970. In French Indochina, France had a state monopoly on opium. In Morocco the sales of hashish were granted as a concession to a group of banks. In the 1920s the number of cocaine users in Greater Paris was

---

76 Wesseling (1987), *Vele ideeën over Frankrijk*, 175-176.
77 Hoyles (1971), 'Social Structures', 20.
78 Hoyles (1971), 'Social Structures', 20.

estimated at 80,000.[79] Without mention of the above history, the authorities explanation for their attitude towards illicit drugs came from the 1960s counter culture. In 1969 a young woman had a lethal overdose at the popular seaside resort Bandol – known as the Bandol drama – which dramatised the drug situation.[80]

The 1995 Henrion Commission report recognised that French drug legislation was adopted in a period characterised by student movements, and that some drugs had come to symbolise those movements. Henrion report continues that the 1970 drug legislation was meant as a barrier against the protest movement which some interpreted as the dissolution of morals.[81] Bergeron explained there also were political motivations, by "fusioning drugs and the left wing protestors, it is possible to discredit and demonise the fight of a political adversary".[82] The French authorities therefore reacted vehemently in order to halt the drug 'catastrophe' and just before the closing of the year, the *Assemblée Nationale* unanimously adopted *loi d'exception*, the exceptional law of 31 December 1970.

Jacqueline Bernat de Célis gave an overview of the origin of French drug legislation and of the Parliamentary debates in the *Assemblée* which led to this law. The fact that illicit substances were being used was not the determining factor for making a new drug legislation. Of course, the fact that the authorities wished to stop the increase in drug use played a part, but the different specialists consulted in the period prior to the adoption of the new law pointed out that the increase in drug use was not so dramatic as presented by some. Much more important with regard to illicit drug use at the end of the 1960s were three other developments that Bernat de Célis identified. First, there were new products on the market, such as cannabis and LSD which users and physicians were not informed of the effects of. Secondly, the drug use phenomenon was on the rise. The third most important and worrisome development was that drug use was a phenomenon that mostly involved the young.[83] The fact that the authorities vehemently wanted to suppress this new and growing phenomenon by enacting strong drug legislation cannot be dissociated from their recent memories of 1968 in 1970 when the law was voted in.

Drug use was considered deviant, non-conformist behaviour. In itself, private drug use was not forbidden in France until the drug legislation of 1970; it had only been illegal when occurring in the company of others. Because groups of youths were using drugs, it was considered a threat to the 'social order', a regularly recurring term in the parliamentary debates.[84] In other words, drugs were perceived as a social danger, as a sign of the protest cultures

79   Bernat de Célis (1992), *Fallait-il créer un délit d'usage illicite de stupéfiants?*, 110.
80   See Bergeron (1999), *L'État et la toxicomanie*, 24.
81   Henrion (1995), *Rapport de la commission de réflexion sur la drogue et la toxicomanie*, 24.
82   Bergeron (1999), *L'État et la toxicomanie*, 25.
83   Bernat de Célis (1992), *Fallait-il créer un délit d'usage illicite de stupéfiants?*, 110.
84   Ehrenberg (1995), *L'individu incertain*, 73.

resisting and rejecting accepted norms and values. The French psychiatrist Olievenstein, an influential consultant on the *Assemblée* said: "It is the exalting sensation to do something forbidden and to oppose the world of adults".[85]

The 1970 drug legislation substantially increased penalties for drug law violations. In addition it criminalised the private use of drugs which became punishable by up to six months imprisonment and prohibited the 'incitation of use'. This law did not differentiate substances, or types of use be they occasional or problematic. The unusual and tough character of this law appeared in the rules for taking a person into custody. Whereas custody would normally be for a maximum of 24 hours or with the consent of the prosecutor custody could be extended to 48 hours, in the case of illicit drugs, custody can be extended to 96 hours. The new drug legislation was not entirely repressive because it offered the alternative of anonymous care and treatment (*injonction thérapeutique*) for first time offenders – an option that was seldom put into practice.[86] Bergeron describes the nature of the law as being largely repressive in that it lay the foundation for a political philosophy that made those importing, selling and using drugs outlaws, effectively creating a War on Drugs.[87]

Parliamentarians were aware of the exceptional character of the 1970 drug law in regard to civil liberties. The believed that because of the social security and support offered by the state, society in return can impose certain limits regarding that to which a person can subject his or her own body".[88] More important than civil liberties, was the consensus reached among the legislators over the 'slackening of morals' and the 'malaise of the youth' symbolized by drug use. To justify the loss of civil liberties it was argued that the user by virtue of his decision to be 'abdicated to artificial paradises' he therefore can be said to have lost title to a big part of his right of liberty.[89] Moreover, drug use was considered an epidemic that was being spread through propaganda. In a statement by The Rapporteur from the Senate Commission on Social Affairs, 'surprise parties' are described as places of communal experimentation which sometimes created additional clients which deliberately contributed to the degradation of our society.[90]

---

85 Bernat de Célis (1992), *Fallait-il créer un délit dúsage illicite de stupéfiants*, 120. In French Olievenstein's words were "c'est l'exaltante sensation de faire quelque chose de défendu et de s'opposer ainsi au monde des adultes".

86 See the evaluation of the *injonction thérapeutique*: by Setbon & De Calan (2000), *L'Injonction thérapeutique*, which shows that only 5.5% of the cases of drug users being directed to *injonction thérapeutique* are put into practice.

87 Bergeron (1999), *L'État et la toxicomanie*, 29.

88 Ehrenberg (1995), *L'individu incertain*, 72-74.

89 The latter expression is a reference to Baudelaire's *Les paradis artificiels*. The politician's quotes come from Ehrenberg (1995), *L'individu incertain*, 72-74, who also looked at the debates in the Senate.

90 The politician's quotes come from Ehrenberg (1995), *L'individu incertain*, 72-74, who examined the debates in the Senat and who studied some additional parliamentary reports than the ones Bernat de Célis, (1992) based her work on.

Sociologist Alain Ehrenberg sees the influence of May 1968 on the creation of the strict drug legislation, but he also notes underlying causes. According to Ehrenberg, drug use was a marginal social and health problem at the time but the reason for it being considered problematic was that it created tension between private and public life. Ehrenberg considers the status of the citizen to be at the core of the anti-drug policy. The republican state tradition prescribes that citizens have to conform to the civic norm as part of their civic duties, to which personal *'passions'* are subordinate. The drug use of the 1960s collided with this political tradition, as private *'passions'* were now being seen publicly by young people who were collectively using drugs. In this new development, Ehrenberg sees *'passions'* appearing instead of being suppressed. This new phenomenon, of private lives becoming concrete experiences for the entire French population, with youths becoming more autonomous, and a new style of political participation – all these tendencies clash with the general concept of politics and the role of the state in France. It has structured a drug policy that reposes on the golden triangle of abstinence as a foundation, detoxification as an objective for the consumer, and the eradication of drugs from society.[91] It thus explains the civic rather than health dimension of French drug policy and it is where Ehrenberg sees the explanation for the difficulty of integrating health emergencies like AIDS. The reasons that have structured the drug policy were not to protect individuals against themselves, but protecting the civic norm itself.[92]

3.4 Science and the Professionals

The French illicit drug use phenomenon of the 1960s was thus perceived in the context of the counter culture, which manifested itself more violently than in other countries. Psychiatrist Claude Olievenstein was quoted earlier as one of the specialists consulted by the parliamentarians to explain why young people were using drugs, for which he put forward the forbidden fruit argument: young people wish to transgress laws as a way to oppose to the parents and their world. As Ehrenberg notes, clinicians at the time often spoke about the retreat of initiation rituals at the adolescent age and the desire to transgress interdicts at the moment, as Olievenstein writes, "when sexual interdicts vacillate (at least verbally) and when the parents admit this transgression". It is this transgression, Olievenstein states, that he considers to be at the origin of the youth's choice for (illegal) drugs and of the rejection of (allowed) alcohol.[93] Olievenstein was to lead the first specialised centre for drug addicts in the early 1970s and would

---

91   Ehrenberg (1995), *L'individu incertain*, 70.
92   Ehrenberg (1995), *L'individu incertain*, 71.
93   Olievenstein (1973), *Écrits sur la toxicomanie*, 25 and Olievenstein (1970), *La drogue*, 112,
       quoted by Ehrenberg (1995), *L'individu incertain*, 102.

later become the grand old man of French thinking on drugs until the early 1990s.

Claude Olievenstein began in the 1960s as an assistant psychiatrist at the Villejuif Hospital just outside Paris. In 1970 he wrote a book, *La drogue*, and became one of the first medical professionals writing on the subject at the time. In the late 1960s he began to appear on radio and television and in the press. By using his media talents, Olievenstein built legitimacy for his interventions. In his excellent study on the peculiar French care and treatment system, Henri Bergeron describes Olievenstein as being convinced of the necessity of creating specific structures for drug users, for which he regularly made pleas in the media. According to Olievenstein, the drug users had a mental disposition, behaviours and lifestyles that were particular enough that they required a special therapy that was so specific that they could not be dealt with in normal hospitals. Therefore, he considered it inevitable that special structures be created for them. Olievenstein also pleaded for the creation of a constitution for this specialised profession, since "drug addiction is something particular, different from alcoholism." Although Olievenstein's ideas met with opposition, they were accepted by the government. Health Minister Boulin opened the first specialised institution for drug addicts, Marmottan, with Olievenstein in charge. By doing so, the government went against the advice of the traditional experts of the psychiatric sector, and notably against the advice of an *ad hoc* commission created with the purpose of seeing whether a specialised institution was necessary. Bergeron concluded that all things considered, the creation of Marmottan resulted from the combination of political will to demonstrate specific action regarding drug users in conjunction with the wishes of a clinician.[94]

The existence of Marmottan as a specialised centre would have tremendous influence on the new generation of specialists in drug addiction. Marmottan immediately became the reference in all of France. Olievenstein established himself as 'the' expert in the field and became the spokesperson when opinions were needed. Health Minister Boulin made Olievenstein one of his privileged interlocutors. By the early 1970s, Olievenstein was progressively becoming the mediator incumbent who would construct the public care and treatment policy for drug addicts. In short, Olievenstein became the spokesperson for this entire sector of professionals as well as for the drug users themselves.[95]

In the 1970s the French medical tradition was devoted to curative means for the treatment of medical problems. This medical tradition was also applied to the new psychiatric field of drug addiction. There needed to be a cure for drug addiction which would leave the user drug-free. Also influential in the approach being applied to drug addiction was the anti-psychiatric ideology which became influential after May of 1968. In France, the anti-psychiatry movement criticised

94 Bergeron (1999), *L'État et la toxicomanie*, 35-38.
95 Bergeron (1999), *L'État et la toxicomanie*, 93.

(normal) psychiatric ideology because of the notion of normality, which it considered to be a myth. Rather than denouncing those outside of the law such as revolutionaries, gangsters, and drug users, the anti-psychiatry movement gave them privileged standing. Liberty became the new ethical keyword of a number of specialists working in the field. Those who had formally been marginalised and outlawed had to be liberated from the stigma society had placed upon them. Moreover, their suffering had to be heard and dealt with – the idea was no longer to be against them, but with them, and for them. What distinguished the French anti-psychiatry movement from those in other countries was its alliance with psychoanalysis. This trend developed further in the 1980s and the 'psychoanalisation' of care and treatment interventions for drug users became a French specialisation.[96]

In the French care and treatment model there was little room for substitution programmes (such as methadone) and therapeutic communities – although these exist as common treatment practices in many other western countries. In the late 1970s there were two experimental methadone programmes with space for fifty participants. Some argued for an extension of methadone programmes but most specialists opposed it. Because of their view that drug use was a symptom of the suffering born out of traumas of early youth, using methadone as an intervention was seen as nothing more than treating the symptoms without addressing the psychopathological troubles at the core of the 'addiction'. The psychiatrists argued that methadone distribution would only replace one opiate product (heroin) by the other (methadone). Several psychiatrists, such as Olievenstein's deputy Francis Curtet, spoke out against methadone by stating hat doctors should not become "dealers".[97] This view won the discussion over methadone and by the mid-1970s, the methadone discussion was neutralised; methadone use remained marginal and no-one pleaded for an extension. The 1978 government report by Pelletier, ordered by President Valéry Giscard d'Estaing, affirmed the consensus on the rejection of more methadone programmes officially.

In France, Henri Bergeron explained, a specific care and treatment paradigm developed which was a combination of anti-psychiatry and psychoanalysis. This paradigm dominated the field. It is in the existence of this French paradigm where Bergeron found the answer to one of his main research questions, namely why is it that harm reduction programmes, such as extensive methadone programmes, were introduced so late in France – in the 1990s – and why did both the state and the large majority of specialists refuse this tool for so long which in many other countries was presented as an indispensable complement to the care and treatment of drug users. The goal of the state was the eradication of drugs from society while the treatment sector believed in abstinence as the final goal of treatment. Owing to the collective goal of the state and the treat-

96   Bergeron (1999), *L'État et la toxicomanie*, 66.
97   Coppel (2002), *Peut-on civiliser les drogues?*, 253.

ment sector being abstinence, the possibilities for care and treatment were severely limited. In the French paradigm, drug use could only be seen in terms of deviance and individual suffering. The cure for drug addiction should be sought in dealing with the underlying causes of the individuals suffering rather than allopathic treatment of the sufferers' symptoms. This view eventually led to the institutionalisation of a therapeutic care and treatment model that focused on the curative aspects of the intervention paying little attention to a preventative and palliative policy to which methadone treatment is related.[98]

There are several reasons why the French could develop and practice such a dominant care and treatment paradigm compared to their European counterparts. The first reason for this is that the French have a national health care system. In these centralised traditions, health care falls under the responsibility of the state. Although health services exist at the level of departments,[99] they merely execute what is decided at the national level and do not have many possibilities for innovations and new approaches. On the national level decisions are made about measures and treatment. Second, following the passing of the 1970s drug law, the French state more or less granted the monopoly for care and treatment of drug users to psychiatrists, many of whom, as mentioned, belonged to the anti-psychiatry movement, which had psychoanalysis as its theoretical basis. Generally speaking, psychoanalysis is very popular in France, as is shown by the popularity of psychoanalysts Lacan and Freud, who are read and quoted more in France than in other western countries. A third, related reason is that the psychiatrists assigned as specialists, had the freedom to define and construct the drug problem to a great extent. From their monopolistic position, their views were never seriously challenged by other professional groups (such as criminologists, lawyers, psychologists or other physiciens) with alternative views and theories on drug use. Drug users themselves having already 'lost their freedom' to drugs were also not taken seriously enough to make contributions to the debate. Consequently the "progressive formation of a community of public policy" developed consisting of different actors, having frequent contact and feeding opinions more or less comparable. Some professional actors became legitimate experts, representing the whole specialised field at the civil service responsible for the dossier, the Health Ministry.[100]

Within the French drug paradigm, drug use was interpreted as a sign of an individual problem, which manifests itself through transgression. Drug use was seen as an individuals problem rather than viewing it in perspective to its larger social context. This was essentially a clinical perspective, and the only treatment

---

98 Bergeron (1999), *L'État et la toxicomanie*, 14.
99 France is administratively divided into almost one hundred *départements*, some of which are overseas. This division into departments is, in fact, based on the old Roman administrative and military division. The size of a department was determined by how far soldiers could reach within one day's march from their centrally located garrison, which today has become the prefecture of the department.
100 Bergeron (1999), *L'État et la toxicomanie*, 15.

possibility was individual therapy. This French approach to drug use left little room for harm reduction measures. Speaking more generally, the clinical and cure oriented approach in which French specialists viewed drug addiction left very little opportunity for public health initiatives, or alternative approaches which can be well illustrated by the Schwartzenberg affair in 1998. Schwartzenberg was a cancer expert appointed by the Under Minister of Health for the Rocard government. Schwartzenberg was forced to resign from office after declaring on television that perhaps state heroin prescription was preferable to purchase on the illegal market. Schwartzenberg's statement was the opposite of the official French drug policy based on abstinence, detoxification and eradication.[101]

According to Bergeron, the existence of a consensus regarding the nature of the problem and the policy to be pursued which was that abstinence was the normative horizon-explains why harm reduction never got a chance. Olievenstein reacted in *Le Monde* to Schwartzenberg's heroin prescription plan by saying in that the Dutch and Spanish experiences of semi-legalisation should be a warning to proceed cautiously.[102] A few years later, in 1992, psychiatrist Francis Curtet vehemently opposed needle exchange programmes. During a debate at a conference, Curtet asked the rhetorical question whether therapeutic goals should be abandoned: "Should we give up now, should we leave users to their addiction?"[103] Curtet not only opposed harm reduction for ideological reasons, but also for practical ones, as he believed France was the country that "through an extensive care and treatment network had best managed to contain addiction. What now matters is to convince our European partners".[104] It is probably to these kind of remarks which the Henrion commission referred in its report, when stating that the intellectual prestige of some specialists masked the poor means available in the care and treatment sector, which gave many citizens the impression that there was a balanced policy.[105]

Whether it be stubbornness, conceit or ignorance, the consequences of sticking to the French drug paradigm and persistently opposing it to harm reduction measures without studying their beneficial effects in other countries, became fully clear in the early 1990s. The refusal to start needle exchange programmes had contributed to France having the largest number of AIDS cases in the European Union, of whom a substantial number were related to intravenous drug use. In the early 1990s several studies found that nationally approximately 30% of intravenous (mostly heroin) drug users were infected. The number of yearly overdoses, estimated at between 500 and 1,000, also appeared

---

101 To quote again Alain Ehrenberg (1995: 70) who described French drug policy as "the golden triangle of abstinence as a foundation, detoxification as an objective for the consumer, and the eradication of drugs from society".
102 Stengers & Ralet (1991), *Drogues. Le défi hollandais*, 11-12.
103 Coppel (1996), 'Les intervenants en toxicomaine, le sida et la réduction des risques en France', 77.
104 Coppel (1996), 'Les intervenants en toxicomaine, le sida et la réduction des risques en France', 77.
105 Henrion (1995), *Rapport de la commission de réflexion sur la drogue et la toxicomanie*, 12.

high in an international perspective, and it seemed, at least partially attributable to substitution programmes being virtually absent.[106] In any case, the figures pointed at the poor health situation of (intravenous) drug users in France. It is this hard data that led the Henrion Commission to make the statement that French drug policy, "based on the idea of certainly not doing anything that may facilitate the life of drug addicts had led to a health and social catastrophe".[107] The discovery of this disaster painfully revealed three aspects of the French drug use phenomenon and the way in which it was dealt.

The first problem is that it showed the absence of a real public health policy. Since French medical practice was heavily curative, it could happen that possible health threats either passed without recognition or were underestimated. A famous example of this, was the 'haemophilia affair', where a number of hemophiliacs were infected with HIV through blood transfusions tainted by the virus. Another example of this appeared after the 1986 Chernobyl disaster. According to French authorities as the time, it seemed as if the radioactive plume stopped at their border: "French territory, because of the remoteness, has remained totally free of the deposition of radio-nuclides in consequence of the accident of the nuclear power plant of Chernobyl," declared the French Ministry of Agriculture on 6 May 1986.[108] While Germany and other Western European countries took measures to protect the population by forbidding consumption of certain foods and drinks, the French authorities announced the wind had pushed away the radioactive cloud and that it would not cross the French border.[109] Since this nuclear threat was so greatly underestimated, measures that should have been taken, were not.[110] Later on when it appeared that there had been radioactive contamination, it was too late implement measures to reduce the amount of radio-nuclides entering the food chain. Finally, a more recent example of the weak public health tradition is the large number of deaths (15,000) during the August 2003 heat wave, when Health Minister Jean-

---

106 See Boekhout van Solinge (1996), *L'héroïne, la cocaïne et le crack en France,* 189-193, which gives a detailed discussion of both morbidity (infections) and mortality (overdoses) figures of drug users in France. It also discusses regional differences. For example, in the South of France and in suburban areas around Paris about half of the population had been HIV infected, while the prevalence was much lower in the north and north east.

107 Henrion (1995), *Rapport de la commission de réflexion sur la drogue et la toxicomanie,* 58. Interestingly, before chairing the commission Henrion was opposed to any drug liberalisation, but after working for nine months on the subject he changed his position and now favours cannabis legalisation.

108 WISE (1991), 'Worldwide Contamination. Environmental monitoring since Chernobyl'.

109 See the press release of AFP (2002) of 24 February 2002: *La CRIIRAD publie un atlas des retombées de Tchernobyl.* With thanks to Frans Trautmann of the Trimbos Insitute for pointing at the French reaction towards Chernobyl.

110 What may have influenced the French short-sightedness and lack of public health view on the Chernobyl disaster is the general importance of nuclear energy in France. France is the only country in Western Europe where nuclear plants supply the majority of energy. Nuclear power is also of prime political importance as it symbolises the independence of the army and state from other nuclear powers.

François Mattei and the Raffarin Government were criticised for doing too little too late. An official report described what happened as a "health catastrophe" and found that health authorities were not fully aware of the unfolding crisis on the ground: "An adequate alert, watch, and information system would have allowed those involved to act more quickly in implementing measures to adapt the health care system," said the report.[111]

Ehrenberg sees the cause for the French medical field not being adequately prepared for the AIDS epidemic in the 1980s as being the absence of an adequate public health policy.[112] The Henrion Report adds that these drug users, ignorant of being zero-positive, infected a large number of non-drug users, making this a real public health threat. Anne Coppel has shown that the first time the journal for medical drug specialists makes mention of AIDS was in 1987, and yet it would take until 1990 that methadone and needle exchange were discussed for the first time.[113]

Secondly, by the sole governing of care and treatment by specialists, general practitioners were given the impression that drug users were not their affair. As consequence of this, drug users had less access to basic care than did other citizens. It should be added to this that general practitioners were mostly ill-informed in the areas of drug use and addiction to which medical training paid little attention. Paradoxically, the Henrion Report concludes that the monopoli-sation of drug care and treatment by specialists led to an under-medicalisation of drug users.

A third aspect of the French view on drugs was that the socio-economic dimension of problematic drug use was entirely overlooked. The French paradigm limited drug problems to individual problems. Part of the paradigm and a regularly recurring phrase was that drug addiction occurred in all social strata.[114] Although this is true in a literal sense, it denies the fact that problem-atic drug use is much more prevalent in the lower than in the higher strata. And, in those lower strata, ethnic minorities seem to be over-represented among the population of problem users. This is not particularly new to researchers, and can be observed in many other western countries, but in France it is difficult to say so openly. One reason for this is that post World War II the French prefer to not mention ethnicity, but rather to speak in terms of nationality and citizenship. When one is born on French soil one is French in both nationality and French perception, irrespective of the parental or ethnic background. Although the

---

111 See BBC news of 8 September 2003: «news.bbc.co.uk/2/hi/europe/3091244.stm». Different European countries had a large death toll because of the heath wave, such as the Netherlands (1,400), Portugal (1,300), United Kingdom (900) and Spain (100), but France stood out with an estimate of 11,000 which later amounted to 15,000. Health Minister Mattei resisted calls to step down, but Surgeon-General Lucien Abenheim resigned on 18 August over the crisis.
112 Ehrenberg (1996), 'Comment vivre avec les drogues? Questions de recherche et enjeux politique', 13.
113 Coppel (1996), 'Les intervenants en toxicomaine, le sida et la réduction des risques en France', 84.
114 The often used phrase in French is: 'La toxicomanie touche toutes les couches sociales'.

relationship between problematic drug use and minority groups can be derived from some French reports, it is rarely openly recognised as such. Another factor is the difficult racial and religious relationships in a traditionally Catholic country that now has five million Muslims and where the extreme right gets approximately twenty percent of the votes. Mentioning ethnicity might further feed the alleged relationship between social problems and minority groups that the extreme right is pushing. Visits to drug treatment clinics and disadvantaged areas as well as field work such as in Greater Paris and Lille clarify the relationship between social deprivation and problematic drug use undeniable.[115]

Eventually, in the 1990s, it was fully recognised that French care and treatment were lagging behind. A sharp about-face was made in 1994 when the focus of drug policy officially changed into harm reduction. It was AIDS that had changed the face of the French drug problem and which gave the push for taking more pragmatic measures. The medical drug specialists were not responsible for this about-face, neither was the government, although some politicians, such as Health Ministers Bernard Kouchner and Philippe Douste-Blazy played important roles in the change. More important was that new players had arrived on the field in the early 1990s. Led by the compassionate and articulate Anne Coppel, several new organisations including World Doctors (*Médecins du Monde*) began the propogation of harm reduction unifying themselves as, *Limiter la casse* ('limiting damage').[116] Generally, *Médecins du Monde* works in poor, southern countries, but it considered the health situation of French drug users serious enough to begin harm reduction projects in France, such as needle exchange. Progressive general practitioners led by Jean Carpentier and Clarisse Boisseau began prescribing substitution substances to heroin users before this practice was officially sanctioned, actions which meant criticism from their colleagues and temporary loss of medical authority by the French Order of Medicines. Their actions led to a declaration of solidarity by hundreds of general practitioners published in *Libération* and *Le Monde*.[117]

By the mid-1990s, the new players had won the now public debate over harm reduction policy. Stimulated by the findings of the 1995 report of the Henrion Commission, which received a lot of attention in the media who labelled it a *commission des sages*,[118] the government started to substantially increase substitution treatment. The French did this in their own way: instead of opting for the commonly prescribed methadone, they chose another substance as the primary prescribed: buprenorphine (under the brand name Subutex). The French made this U-turn at full speed, making it possible to substantially expand

---

115 See Boekhout van Solinge (1996), *L'héroïne, la cocaïne et le crack en France*, 186-189.
116 See her account of the rise of the French harm reduction movement: Coppel (2002), *Peut-on civiliser les drogues?*
117 See also his book on GPs and heroin users: Carpentier (1994), *La tocixomanie à l'héroïne en médecine générale.*
118 Some of the commission's hearings were broadcasted on French television.

substitution treatment in a short period. From fifty-two people on substitution treatment in 1993, their number was expanded to 90,000 in 2002. As Anne Coppel notes, this makes France the European leader in drug-substitution.[119] These 90,000 prescriptions fit more consistently with the overall rate at which French doctors prescribe drugs.

3.5 State Traditions of Law Enforcement and Central Rule

Although the French drug problem slowly shifted more towards a health approach, the punitive and repressive aspects of French drug policy did not disappear. In the late 1980s the French government opened the way for the sales of syringes in pharmacies as a way to prevent the further spread of infectious diseases, but drug users did not always go there to buy them. While the government decided to increase the number of care and treatment centres and shelters, this did not immediately mean more drug users went there. The reason for user reluctance was that the police patrolled areas surrounding pharmacies and treatment centres. In some cases their patrol extended to the doorsteps of these. Users going to the pharmacy to purchase needles ran the risk of being arrested. Carrying drugs is not the only condition of arrest, a syringe in the pocket can be enough to presume that someone is a drug user.[120] This problem of the incompatibility of care and repression existed until the end of 1995, although harm reduction had already become part of official French policy more than a year before.[121]

During the 1980s and 1990s the Ministry of Justice issued several guidelines to the prosecutors – the last one dating June 1999 – recommending non-penal answers to people arrested for the offence of drug use. Such guidelines included recommendations that drug dependent users undergo care and treatment, alternately giving the occasional or socially well-integrated drug user a mere warning. In practice however, drug users have continued to be arrested and their numbers have been steadily on the increase. Part of the explanation is that in the French judicial model, police and prosecutors have substantial discretionary powers to decide whether to follow a guideline or not. Prosecutors may judge that a guideline is not adapted to the local circumstances, which means in practice he has the power to adapt the guidelines to the local specificity – to the extent that the prosecution practice can be contrary to the guideline. Moreover, because the court district division is outdated, some tribunals are found in small

119 Coppel (2002), *Peut-on civiliser les drogues?*, 181.
120 So declared magistrate and later advisor to the Minister of Justice, Jean-Paul Jean for the Henrion commission.
121 See Boekhout van Solinge (1996), *L'héroïne, la cocaïne et le crack en France,* 228-229. Even at Olievenstein's famous Marmottan centre, the author witnessed the presence of police near the entrance of the consultation hour for drug users by the end of 1995.

towns and villages, where the use of drugs is rare, and severely condemned. Prosecution for carrying small amounts of cannabis in these tribunals is considered a serious offence and the prosecutor may ignore the national guidelines in favour of local opinion and punitively apply the law.[122] This explains why prosecution practice can differ substantially between tribunals – despite the centralist tradition in France. For example, the prosecutor of Nice decided to not prosecute the use of cannabis at all, while his colleague from Versailles does prosecute small quantities, as he states not having received any particular instructions for doing otherwise.[123] In any case, there is no uniformity of policy which makes it possible for someone carrying two hundred grams of cannabis may be taken into custody, whilst others with six kilos of heroin or nine kilos of cocaine are not.[124]

In general terms it can be said that the 1970 drug legislation is being strictly enforced. Paradoxically, since the official drug policy became health oriented in 1994, the number of drug arrests has only been on the rise. Whereas in 1985 the total number of arrests was nearly 30,000 (of which 21,000 for drug use), in 1995 this had more than doubled to almost 70,000 (52,000 of which was for use). In the last years of the 1990s, the number of drug arrests rose to over 90,000 a year, and in 2000 it broke through the 100,000 barrier (of which 83,000 was for use). What is striking about these statistics is that the number of heroin arrests went down substantially after 1995 when harm reduction was introduced. By contrast, the number of arrests for cannabis has been rising rapidly. The French Drug Observatory (OFDT) report speaks of an "explosion" of cannabis arrests. The OFDT notes that from 1990 to 2000 the number of cannabis arrests nearly quadrupled. Whereas in 1990, one in two drug arrests concerned cannabis, ten years on this holds for nine out of ten cases.[125] Since cannabis arrests now represent the bulk of all drug arrests, it can be said that policing drugs in practice essentially means policing cannabis. This led French sociologist Michel Kokoreff to say that the police are essentially a cannabis police.[126]

122 For a thorough description of the judicial guidelines and the application of the law in practice, see respectively chapter three and four of Boekhout van Solinge (1995), 'Le cannabis en France'.
123 *Libération* interview with prosecutors Eric de Montgolfier in Nice and Yves Colleu in Versailles. See *Libération* (2001), 'Un peu de cannabis, et la justice divague. Les risques pour les usagers diffèrent selon les tribunaux, en attendant un vrai débat'.
124 As Minister of Justice Marylise Lebranchu remarked in an interview with *Libération* of 8/9 December 2001, referring to two cases of traffickers not taken into custody: in Versailles a Congolian heroin trafficker (because of having minors) and in Bobigny two Israeli young women with nine kilos of cocaine. See *Libération* (2001), 'Un peu de cannabis, et la justice divague. Les risques pour les usagers diffèrent selon les tribunaux, en attendant un vrai débat'.
125 ODFT (2003), *Drogues et dependences. Indicateurs et tendances 2002*, 50.
126 Interview with sociologist Michel Kokoreff of Lille I University in *Libération*, 8/9 December 2001 by Santucci (2001), 'L'analyse d'un sociologue sur les interpellations: Réprimer l'usage, une stratégie'.

This tendency of increasing cannabis arrests is in contrast to the general European trend. In many EU countries, the more pragmatic and softer attitude towards heroin users – resulting from the introduction of harm reduction policies – was followed in the second half of the 1990s by a tendency towards cannabis decriminalisation.[127] In France the trend is the opposite: the decrease in heroin arrests seems to have given police and gendarmerie the opportunity to spend more time pursuing cannabis users. The fact that law enforcement agencies are able to pursue policies that neglect or entirely negate the spirit of the guidelines given by the Ministry of Justice, demonstrate enough autonomy and power to do so. The explanations for the rise in cannabis arrests may be that they are generally easy to make, or that drug arrests are a means of social control. In any case, I.D. checks and drug controls are important tools for police enforcement of law and order. In order to understand the law enforcement practice more fully, it is essential to look at a more fundamental point, France's tradition of stringent law enforcement.

Generally speaking, France has a large police force. Its police force is larger than countries such as the United States, or in Europe, the United Kingdom.[128] The French police system is of a dual nature. The older of the two, the *Gendarmerie Nationale*, is under the ministry of Defence, while the *Police Nationale* is under the Ministry of Interior.[129] The gendarmerie is the most visible and ubiquitous of the two as it polices some 90% of the French territory, and many foreigners have the misconception that they are the only French police.[130] As a general rule, the gendarmerie polices communities with less than 10,000 inhabitants, while the police operate in urban areas with more than 10,000 inhabitants. This means approximately that both police half of the population.

The strong law enforcement tradition can be traced back to Napoleon, who introduced the penal code and created a police force responsible for maintaining order and preventing offences. During the Napoleonic period, the *police générale* was made into an effectively operating organisation, suppressing any opposition or publicly expressing dissatisfaction, giving the French police a bad

---

127 As observed by the European Drug Observatory EMCDDA since the late 1990s. See EMCDDA (1998), *Annual report*, 77-78, and see EMCDDA (1999), *Extended annual report*, 19.

128 Kurian (1989), *World Encyclopedia of Police forces and Police Systems*, 127, writes France has a population/police officer quote of 630, while according to another source, France has 403 policemen per 100,000 (with the EU average being 375). See Ministerie van Justitie (2000), *Juridische infrastructuur in international perspectief*, quoted in Lissenberg (2001), *Tegen de regels IV*, 75. The two sources are not compatible as they lead to a totally different number of police officers, but they agree on France having a relatively large French police force. It should be noted though that the UK and US have more private security, which lead them to have more 'security personnel' than France.

129 The gendarmerie are the premier regiment of the French Army. They work in units of between five and fifty-five which are normally stationed in barracks in the main town of the canton. They are heavily equipped with tanks and armoured vehicles. See Kurian (1989), *World Encyclopedia of Police forces and Police Systems*, 129.

130 Kurian (1989), *World Encyclopedia of Police forces and Police Systems*, 130.

reputation in Europe.[131] Napoleon had an aversion to criminal proceedings because of the attendant publicity, and Fouché, his Minister of Police generally knew how to touch enemies of the state in a sore spot without the verdict of a judge.[132] In 1810 Fouché was dismissed but after 1815, under Louis XVIII, regained his position as Minister of Police.[133] In the further course of the nineteenth century, which witnessed the rule of Napoleon III and during which two revolutions took place (1848 and 1870), the French central state kept its large police apparatus.

In the 1960s, Paris was confronted both with a series of terrorist attacks, which increased its demand for policing for which riot police were deployed. Although the riot police CRS are civil, their modus operandi is military, they are a highly trained professional force who are based in barracks, and are given military titles and military address.[134] Because of their excessive use of force, the riot police carry a bad name and poor reputation. In May 1968, the CRS reacted with gratuitous violence, while earlier in 1961, Paris' police used extreme violence against Algerians who were protesting peacefully. Thousands of protestors were arrested, some were shot dead while many were thrown in the Seine River and drowned. The number of people killed in the police massacre is estimated somewhere between several dozens and more than two hundred.[135]

The French police have a notorious reputation for 'incidents' of power abuse. The French media regularly print stories of police abuse: maltreating, battering and sometimes torturing detainees at police stations, all of which give the French police a bad reputation amongst human rights organisations. These abuses of power are in many cases directed towards people of minority groups, especially those of Arabic origin. In 1997 European Court on Human Rights gave its verdict in the Salmouni case, in which the seventeen judges unanimously convicted France for torture of a forty-nine year old Dutchman of Moroccan origin sentenced to thirteen years for heroin trafficking. It was the first time a Western European had been found at fault for torture.[136] It was particularly painful that this concerned a country which considers itself the cradle of human rights. Police violence and the unnecessary use of firearms have led to a number of deaths. The UN Human Rights Committee adds that

---

131 Boek (1999), 'De politiefunctie', 30.
132 Boek (1995), *Organisatie, functie en bevoegdheden van politie in Nederland*, 46. Boek briefly discusses the French police, both in France and in the Netherlands that was conquered by Napoleon.
133 Kurian (1989), *World Encyclopedia of Police forces and Police Systems*, 127.
134 Kurian (1989), *World Encyclopedia of Police forces and Police Systems*, 129.
135 According to the official version held during thirty years, only three people died on 17 October 1961, but later in the 1990s, in court cases such of war criminal Maurice Papon (found responsible for the deportation of Jews) who then the responsible *prefet de police* of Paris during the massacre, the number was found to be much higher. The exact number still remains unknown though, as not all archives are accessible while some other were destroyed.
136 European Court of Human Rights (1999), *Case of Selmouni v. France,* or see Uildriks (1999), 'Police Torture in France', 411-423.

such a risk is much greater in the case of foreigners and immigrants. The UN also expresses concern over the virtual impunity of such behaviour, as in most cases where a complaint was filed there was little, if any, investigation. Moreover, it found that prosecutors failed or were reluctant to investigate allegations of human rights violations, and if they did, the investigations and prosecutions were unreasonably lengthy. A similar image appears from reports by Amnesty International, and by the European Commission for the Prevention of Torture (CPT), publishing a report on the treatment of suspects in different locations in France. The report states that it has not heard of any allegations of torture or bad treatment by the gendarmerie, but only by the police. Police violence predominantly involves people from (Northern) African countries. It is especially prevalent in the cities, for example Marseille and Montpellier, with Greater Paris having the most notorious reputation. From the various reports it appears that inhuman and degrading treatment is endemic within routine police work, especially when questioning suspects.[137]

French police violence can also be seen in some films, especially those showing life in one of the many lower class suburbs, the *banlieues*, the best known one which is Matthieu Kassovitz's *La Haine* ('Hate').[138] Police violence is also a recurring subject among the many French hip hop songs, or *rappeurs*, many of whom come from the same socially deprived areas which house many immigrants and where violence is the game of the day.[139] Considering the nature and scale of this poverty, ghettoised areas are characterised by an accumulation of social problems – unemployment, lack of future, an underground drug economy, and (police) violence – the French lower class housing situation is the nearest European equivalent of American ghettos.[140] For many years, violence,

137 Uildriks (1999), 'Police Torture in France', 416 and 419. Uildriks mentions that of one judicial medical centre in Paris (*Urgence Médico-Judiciaires*) medical records indicated that eleven percent of all visits concerned with serious injuries were related to allegations of police violence.

138 The film is a good endeavour to show this other side of France, but as Chavannes (2000a) notes in *Frankrijk achter de schermen,* 122-123, it has been criticised by people and film makers from the *banlieues*, for being too superficial and having too many clichés.

139 A clear example is the popular group NTM, which stands for *nique ta mère,* ('fuck your mother'). Their first CD was *1993. J'appui sur la gachette* ('1993. I pull the trigger') with a gun and bullet on the cover. The CD also contains other topical songs that reveal something of life in France's lower class suburbs, such as (translated in English) 'For a new massacre', 'Who pays the damage?' and 'Police'. The latter song ends with the line 'Fuck the police' and it calls for the use of violence against them. This led in November 1996 to the condemnation of two NTM singers for an offence against public authority by the Tribunal of Southern Toulon (which has a mayor of the Front National), where the offensive words were spoken during a concert. NTM was banned for six months for performing on French territory.

140 More than five million people, almost ten percent of the total population live in lower class housing schemes, some of which have developed into no-go areas. Every weekend riots break out in some or several French suburbs, especially in summer, varying from setting fire to cars to attacking and fighting with firemen and police. Every few years the French government announces a new *Marshall plan pour les banlieues,* but considering the scale of the housing schemes and the problems occurring there, and the little money made available, it can be seriously questioned if the real political will exists to really improve the situation.

immigration, and security have been among the main themes in electoral campaigns. One of France's leading sociologists, Michel Wieviorka, has dedicated books to this subject, *La France raciste* and *La violence*. The typical reaction to a threat, such as the 1995 bombings in the Paris metro, is to deploy large number of police and military in all public places. Even though the soldiers cannot use their machine guns in the event of an attack as they are not always loaded, their presence reassures the French public.

The general importance French governments attach to the police is clear.[141] It appears to be substantiated, for example, by the fact that the Minister of Interior usually is held to be of high rank in the government, and is given relatively large say in policy. Additionally, the person assigned as Interior Minister is typically a hard-liner who stands for law and order. This can first be explained by understanding the French political tradition of having a strong state.[142] It serves a strong state to have personnel that ensure its rules are respected and lived by. Secondly and more fundamentally, is the French republican tradition born out of the revolution, which is that of the state as a social institution. In this political tradition, the notions of law and citizenship both occupy important places. The law is the expression of the general interest, which is represented by the state. In the typical French conception of citizenship, citizens have to sacrifice their personal interests for the sake of the common good. Ehrenberg explains that it is a paternalistic concept, part of a more general vision of state-society relationships, in which the law is used to regulate diverse practices, as well as to fix interdicts and norms.[143] Laws thus have the role as beacons of society, giving direction to citizens and it is the civilians' duty to respect the rules that the state has set. Breaking laws, in that sense, is like defying the state. Even if not everyone always respects the law in practice, it is still good to have the laws, as a standard to which reference can be made, or fallen back upon. This explains why French politicians find it so hard to de-penalise cannabis use, or worse, to decriminalise small possession. A phrase that is frequently employed in the political debates when the government is trying to set forth its rationale for not liberalising policy, reminds citizens of the importance of the law ("*rappel à la loi*"). This refers to the norms that have been set – lest the beacons fall out of sight and society loses its direction. It is within this context that Ehrenberg considered the 1970 drug legislation, voted unanimously by Parliament, a republican law.[144]

---

141 In 1933 a Dutch overview on police forces in several countries, the remark is made that the French government is still to a considerable extent interested in the police. See Haarman (1933), *Geschiedenis en inrichting der politie in Nederland. Met eenige aantekeningen omtrent de politie in andere landen*, 164.

142 Jacobinism places the interest of the state on the first place.

143 Ehrenberg (1995), *L'individu incertain*, 102-104. A page further Ehrenberg explains that this state role explains the important administrative infrastructure, namely to form the citizens, the nodal role of the school teacher, and the importance of republican education.

144 Ehrenberg (1995), *L'individu incertain*, 75 and 102-104.

The psychiatrists then came into play to explain why young people were not respecting the law anymore. Their drug use was considered a transgression of the civic norms of the law, which also has as symbolic function, as a *loi du père*, law of the father. Ehrenberg commented that this has led to a confusion of the clinical and the political, with penal law having the same role as the symbolic 'law' of psychoanalysis. Hence, the relationship between the state and citizens is modelled after a father figure and the citizens are placed in a position of children who have to be educated.[145] The fact that young people were using drugs and thus transgressing the norms set by society was interpreted as an indicator that the life of these young people was not sufficiently structured. The remedy was to restructure their lives, for which penal law was employed.

Finally, there is also a political dimension at play that influences the law enforcement tradition with regard to drugs, the role of presidents. In the history of France, the role of its rulers, whether they were kings, emperors or presidents has always been more important than in most other European countries. With the French political tradition of centralised power, rulers had the ability to personally influence the political position and viewpoints of their country. In the history of international drug control, Bruun et al. identify France as a country that emerged as a traditional advocate for a total ban on drugs, which it has consistently argued for in international forums and made a series of proposals in this line.[146] Over the last decades, some French presidents have been particularly active in promoting anti-drug measures in international bodies. Part of the reason why they were able to do so is explained by the political structure which has been in place since the Fifth Republic was founded in 1958. While the new constitution had been drawn in the context of the Algerian crisis and had been drafted especially for De Gaulle, his successors have used these presidential powers as well.

In 1971, President Pompidou launched the Pompidou Group, an expert consultative committee organised by the judicial authorities and met in the framework of the Council of Europe.[147] In 1989, at the Strasbourg European Council, President Mitterrand took the initiative to launch a European Committee to Combat Drugs, Mitterrand had hoped it would carry his name, but

---

145 Ehrenberg (1995), *L'individu incertain*, 102.
146 In *The Gentlemen's Club*, Bruun et al. (1975: 130) describe France as one of the main countries (after the US and the UK) that have actively pursued the cause of international drugs control. And, unlike the UK, which has tended to favour regulation, France emerges as a traditional advocate of a total ban on drugs.
147 It cannot be ruled out that U.S. President Nixon influenced Pompidou in this regard. Bruun et al. (1975: 141) observe that when Nixon placed the drugs issue near the top of the domestic political agenda in the early 1970s, it was soon increasingly being brought into diplomatic relations. "Indicative of the importance attached to the drug issue is the appointment of a Cabinet Committee in International Narcotics Control in 1971 and the inclusion of the item of drug traffic control in negotiations at a high political level, such as those between Nixon and Pompidou". In the same year, Pompidou took the initiative to set up the European Pompidou Group.

eventually it was given the more neutral name of CELAD.[148] His successor Jacques Chirac, having been elected in 1995, immediately demonstrated a fierce aversion to drugs and became a passionate advocate of a harmonised European policy on drugs, based on a ban and strict punitive measures. At the Cannes European Council he placed drugs on the agenda by launching the European Global Plan of Action in the Fight against Drugs (1995-1999). And it was this European summit that inaugurated the periodic progress reports that made drugs a fixed theme at every European Council.[149]

Whereas Pompidou and Mitterrand founded consultative bodies, Chirac seeks more restrictive policies in France, Europe, and the world. Shortly after being elected President in May 1995, he put the drug issue high on the political agenda, both domestically and in Europe. He started attacking the Netherlands for its liberal drug policy which he said was "poisoning" French youth and he demanded the Dutch to be more repressive. Chirac began dogmatically propagating a more repressive policy, which stood in contrast to the pragmatic policy his country had initiated just a few years earlier. The years 1993 and 1994 had represented a turn in French drug policy as it was fully acknowledged that the repressive drug policy had had disastrous results. This happened under the Presidency of Mitterrand with both right and left wing governments. But with Chirac coming to power, less room was left for those voices to be heard, and the emphasis was again placed on repression and fighting the evil of drugs.

The reasons for Chirac's tough stance are both personal and electoral. Drug-related family dramas appear to have created within him an emotional interest as well as having generated very negative ideas about drug use.[150] Additionally, drugs are also a subject he can easily exploit politically. Since the security theme has become so important in French politics, especially for right wing parties, fighting drugs has become a theme through which he can present himself. By beating the security drum, he tries to get more votes from the right side of the political spectrum, especially from the extreme right which historically addresses and exploits the feelings of insecurity in French society. Chirac regularly speaks out against drugs in his speeches, characterising them as evil, and stressing the importance of fighting drug use.

---

148 CELAD is the French acronym ('Comité Européen de Lutte Anti Drogue') for European Committee to Combat Drugs. In October 1989, Mitterrand wrote a letter to the other eleven EU government leaders and to the President of the European Commission, a letter that Georges Estievenart called a milestone in the history of the European fight against drugs, and Mitterrand's initiative recalled the efforts of Georges Pompidou in 1971. See Estievenart (1995), *The European Community and the global drug phenomenon: current situation and outlook*, 60.

149 Boekhout van Solinge (2002), *Drugs and Decision-Making in the European Union*, 23.

150 The exact story of the drug dramas in the Chirac family remains unknown, as French media, unlike for example the British, usually do not write about politician's private life. That a drug drama in the family does not necessarily have to lead to a political tough stance on drugs is shown by the example of President Jorge Sampaio of Portugal, who now supports drug legalisation.

The UNGASS speech quoted in the introduction of this study is only one example of the many dramatic speeches or references to drugs Chirac has made. They are often full of references to crime, disease, and death; drugs are described as a menace and a gangrene that has to be fought on all fronts. The speeches indeed seem influenced by his personal views as they sometimes have the character of war declarations and are in contrast to the more pragmatic stance both left and right wing governments have been taking since the mid-1990s.[151]

However, since De Gaulle's Fifth Republic was created, French Presidents have had substantial powers, which has enabled Chirac to put forward some of his own ideas and exert influence upon national drug policy. The extent to which this is possible is dependent upon the political colour of his government. In the French political system it is possible for the president to hold a different political stripe than the Prime Minister and the rest of the government. The term used for it *cohabitation*.[152] Right wing president Chirac 'cohabited' twice with a left wing government. In such cases, the right wing president and left wing government must manage to find a balance through pragmatism. The President and Prime Minister are then almost automatically in competition over certain issues and the President usually concentrates on defence and foreign affairs, which had been the intention of the Fifth Republic. If however, the right wing president has a right wing government under him, it becomes much easier to govern and the President almost automatically becomes the leader of the government, acquiring more possibilities to have his say on domestic affairs too.

The extent to which Chirac is able to push through his own ideas therefore actually depends to a great extent upon the government under him. Working with a left wing government, he more or less has to back off from the drug dossier, and the policy becomes less restrictive and more oriented toward health and harm reduction. But when he has a right wing government, he is not only able to personally influence policy, but in more general terms, law enforcement and security become more important political themes, which in terms of the drug policy means the emphasis is once again placed on repression.

---

151 See for example his speech presented on 22 May 2003 in Paris at the opening ceremony of the international conference on drug routes.
152 The reasons are that Presidential and Parliamentary elections are not held simultaneously, although every new president has the possibility to call new elections. Another reason is that the French presidents were elected for seven years – under Chirac changed into five – while Parliament is voted for four years. So it can happen that the President and the parliamentary majority (usually forming the government) are of different political parties. And, since the left- right schism is one the fundamental aspects of French politics, cohabitation has meant in practice having a left wing president with a right wing government such as happened to President Mitterrand and Prime Minister Chirac (1986-88), and vice versa, a right wing President and left wing government, which happened to the then President Chirac and Prime Minister Jospin.

For example, when Chirac was elected in 1995 he had a right wing govern-ment which took a tough stance on drugs, and less was heard of France being internationally behind on harm reduction. The emphasis was put on fighting drugs and the root of the problem was sought internationally, particularly in the Netherlands which was too little to fight drugs.[153] The pragmatic progress that had been made on harm reduction was again turned into ideological drug fighting. But when the left won the 1997 parliamentary elections, harm reduc-tion was on the agenda again. Prime Minister Lionel Jospin nominated harm reduction proponent, Bernard Kouchner, as Health Minister. He, in turn, appointed a new head of the inter-ministerial drug co-ordination body MILDT, Nicole Maestracci, the first appointee who was not formerly a politician, but a well-versed professional on the subject.[154]

Under Maestracci several scientific studies were conducted which had a significant effect on French drug policy. The study of Parquet (1997) tried to develop a prevention policy for all psychoactive substances, both legal and illegal.[155] A year later, in 1998, the Roques Report on the danger of both licit and illicit drug use became public.[156] Shortly after, another study was published by economist Pierre Kopp on the social costs of drugs. He found that the social costs of illicit drugs (2 billion euro) were much lower than those of tobacco (13,6 billion euro) and particularly alcohol (17,6 billion euro).[157] A few years earlier, Kopp and Palle found that by far most of the public money spent on drug control went to repression. They calculated the public money spent in 1995 and estimated that some 412 million euro were spent on law enforcement, while some 96 million euro was devoted to care and treatment.[158] These different scientific studies served as a basis for new French drug policy. In January 1999 Maestracci's MILDT presented the plans, which *Le Monde* described in a big front page article as "Drugs: The Report That Changes Everything".[159] Breaking

---

153 This question will be fully discussed in the final chapter.
154 Maestracci had dealt with drugs before as a magistrate working in Bobigny, a suburban city just outside Paris. She was the first head of the inter-ministerial governmental body MILDT (formerly known as DGLDT) responsible for co-ordinating the national drug policy whose nomination was not on political grounds, but on professional ones. Before that, another person occupied the post almost every year. It was usually a political nomination of either a politician needed to be 'placed' somewhere temporarily, or one close to the Prime Minister or President. They had usually no knowledge of the subject matter.
155 Parquet (1997), *Pour une politique de prevention en matière de comportements de consommation de substances psychoactives.*
156 The Roques report first circulated in a report version and was immediately intensely debated before being officially published as a book a year later. See Roques (1999), *La dangerosité des drogues,*
157 Kopp (2001), *Calculating the social cost of illicit drugs,* table 34.
158 The estimate for the drug-related expenditures for the Ministry of Interior and Justice were estimated at respectively 183 million (1.2 billion French Francs) and 229 million euro (1.5 billion French francs). See Kopp & Palle (1999), 'Economistes cherchent politique publique efficace', 258-259, or see Kopp & Fenoglio (2000), *Le coût social des drogues licites (alcool et tabac) et illicites en France.*
159 Folléa (1999), Drogues: le rapport qui change tout', *Le Monde* 8 January 1999.

with the classical approach based on the legal status of products, a new more pragmatic policy would be introduced, taking into account all addictive behaviours, irrespective of the legal status of the product used. One of the recommendations was to redefine the penal policy, for example by avoiding incarceration as a penalty for drug use, and by giving more law enforcement priority to the drug trade. The MILDT report recalled that guidelines from the Ministry of Justice from 1978 and 1984 had recommended not prosecuting drug users. A few months later, in June 1999, Justice Minister Elisabeth Guigou, issued a similar guideline recommending that cannabis users were given a warning because obligatory care and treatment were deemed inappropriate.

In 2002 new presidential elections were held, during which the French electorate had to choose in the second round between Jacques Chirac and Jean-Marie Le Pen of the extreme right *Front National*.[160] Chirac easily won the elections and called for new parliamentary elections that were comfortably won by his rightwing party. During the campaign Chirac focused much on the security theme and with his new government headed by Jean-Pierre Raffarin and hardliner Nicolas Sarkozy on Interior Affairs he put this into practice.[161] Possibly influenced by the New York City zero tolerance policy instigated by the then mayor, and now 11 September icon, Rudolf Guliani, Chirac initiated his *tolérance zero* policy shortly after his re-election, which also had its effect on drug users and small drug traders. In a speech held in May 2003, Chirac made clear that since heroin users were now looked after by the care and treatment sector, more than ever before, it was now a priority to efficiently fight against the consumption of cannabis and ecstasy among the youth. France, believing in the educational virtues of sanctions, would remain firm in not legalising or de-penalising the use of drugs.[162] In the same period a Senate drug report came out under the title *Drugs, the other cancer*, which only served to promulgate their more repressive approach.[163] Sarkozy put forward a phrase that received media attention: "There are no soft or hard drugs; there are only forbidden drugs".

In September 2003 the French government announced a new policy towards cannabis users. At first glance, the document appeared to offer a relaxation of current legislation as it proposed to abolish prison sentences in favour of fines. The new laws were created to make the drug legislation more effective and to see that it be applied more appropriately, based on the premise and practice that the use of drugs no longer justifies a prison sentence. It is possible, however, that the new system will make it easier to punish cannabis users. It remains

160 Chirac and Le Pen were first and second in the first round of the elections.
161 The position of Nicole Maeastracci as head of MILDT was replaced by physician Didier Jayle.
162 A speech of 22 May 2003 in Paris at the opening ceremony of the international conference on drug routes.
163 See the report of the senators Nelly Olin (president) and & Bernard Plasait (rapporteur): Sénat (2003), *Drogue: l'autre cancer*.

unclear whether the law also means that violators will be punished less severely once a system of fines are in place.[164] How the new approach will work out in practice will depend on whether Prime Minister Raffarin opts for the harsh plans supported by his Interior Minister or the more tolerant approach favoured by the Health Ministry.[165] This ambiguity is exemplary for French drug policy, over which politicians still have not clearly decided. It also remains to be seen whether the government wants to be repressive or whether they are willing to move further in a more pragmatic, harm reduction approach.

164 The French legal system has five different types of fines.
165 Gentleman (2003), 'Smoking them out', *Guardian*, 17 September 2003.

Chapter 4

Doing Drugs the Dutch Way

4.1 Introduction

When you hear the word 'Dutch' the first thing to come to mind might be drugs. When visitors arrive in the Netherlands they often include a stay in the capital city, Amsterdam, which may include some kind of an encounter with illicit drugs. Amsterdam has almost three hundred *coffee shops* where ~~many varieties of hashish and~~ marijuana are available for purchase and consumption either within the shop or outside on its terrace. When strolling through Amsterdam's historical tourist areas, coffee shops can be easily be seen and smelled. The use of other drugs such as heroin and crack-cocaine is also quite visible. Users can be seen in the city centres, somewhat concentrated in the main tourist areas, such as Amsterdam's red light district, the country's main prostitution area. A more recent phenomenon, dating from the late 1990s, is the proliferation of *smart shops*, selling different kinds of 'smart drugs': usually legal, often plant-based, psychoactive substances, varying from energy drinks to psychedelic (magic) mushrooms.

The easy association of Dutch tolerance and drug use is typically encountered by younger Dutch nationals when they travel or Dutch students when studying at foreign universities. It is often assumed that being Dutch equals 'doing drugs'. In fact, some non-Dutch people find it unimaginable that someone from this 'coffee shop country' does *not* smoke cannabis. This stereotypic bonding of the image of Amsterdam and drugs extends to the cliché of young backpackers, for example, who travel through Europe determined to make a visit to Amsterdam as part of their tour, in order to experience coffee shop culture, much as others would go to Paris to visit the Louvre, or Rome to visit the Coliseum.

For serious cannabis users, a visit to Amsterdam takes on the character of a pilgrimage. Whereas in their home country they are criminalised, in the Netherlands drug use behaviour can be freely expressed. Some find the climate in their home country so repressive that they decide to move to the Netherlands permanently, where they consider themselves political drug refugees. In the 1980s, when the United States intensified its War on Drugs, some Americans moved to the Netherlands, thereby also bringing with them the latest Californian techniques for growing cannabis indoors, which in turn made the Netherlands the

European incubation ground of indoor cannabis cultivation.[1] The American cannabis magazine *High Times* has relocated its yearly contest 'The Cannabis Cup' to the city of Amsterdam. Every year, for Thanksgiving Day, approximately two thousand Americans cross the Atlantic to attend 'The Cannabis Cup'.

Cannabis users are not the only drug users to find a safe haven in the Netherlands. A 1987 survey revealed that per month, approximately two thousand non-Dutch heroin users could be found in Amsterdam.[2] Most of these were Western European, the largest group being German. In the 1990s, French heroin users found a refuge in Rotterdam. Some stayed permanently, while others were drug tourists coming from France on a regular basis to buy cheaper heroin. The great migration of French and German addicts has ceased to flow but in the summermonths Amsterdam is still a hot destination for international cocaine or heroine users because drugs can be bought and used under relatively comfortable circumstances.[3]

Despite this drug tourism, the majority of tourists do not visit the Netherlands for the specific purpose of using drugs. The majority of tourists visiting Amsterdam are under 35, but only a minority of them actually visit a coffee shop.[4] Some visitors to the Netherlands view it as the modern equivalent of Sodom and Gomorra where the authorities have relinquished any hope of 'law and order' and taken an 'anything goes' attitude towards the presence and open 'availability' of drugs and prostitution.

Drugs are undeniably visible and easily obtainable in The Netherlands. Cannabis and so-called 'smart drugs' can be bought in coffee shops and smart shops, comparatively, amphetamine, cocaine, heroin, and ecstasy can be found with relative ease from either street or house dealers. Generally, drug users do not experience harassment; judicial and law enforcement agents follow a policy of non-interference. In 1976, Dutch drug legislation was altered to create a legal difference between cannabis and other illicit drugs. For the 'soft drug' cannabis, a *de facto* decriminalisation policy developed, which later grew into the coffee shop phenomenon where the adult consumer may purchase cannabis in small quantities. In regard to other 'hard drugs', policy is based on harm reduction.

---

1   Jansen (2002), *The economics of cannabis-cultivation in Europe.*
2   See the survey by Korf (1987), *Heroïnetoerisme II*, 45-56, where he explains that the drug tourists came for different reasons, the main ones being judicial problems at home, while others were the more tolerant climate (towards drugs, as well as alternative lifestyles, squatting included), easier access to methadone, and cheaper heroin.
3   This demand for drugs in turn has also led to situations in which bogus or bad quality drugs are being offered to tourists in some of the Amsterdam tourist areas. Of course, this only fuels the city's drugs image.
4   The Amsterdam Tourist Board reports that although coffee shops are one of the reasons mentioned by foreign tourists to visit the city, it is not a primary consideration. A majority of these are under 35 years old, yet only a quarter of them report visiting a coffee shop (based on 1997 data). The city of Amsterdam aims to attract older tourists, who spend more and give the city a more refined image. See the special of *NRC Handelsblad*: Weeda (1997), 'Een acht bij vertrek'.

The general policy for hard and soft drugs alike is based upon the principle of not criminalising drug users, which translates practically into decriminalising possession of small quantities. The Chief Prosecutors Office has established standards for criminal enforcement which preclude small quantities of drugs destined for personal use – in effect decriminalising small quantities. Per substance the amounts monitored by the Chief Prosecutors Office as decriminalised are: 5 grams of cannabis, 0.5 grams of heroin and cocaine, and for pills such as ecstasy there is a one tablet maximum.[5] As a general rule, Dutch police do not actively pursue drug users; it is only when groups of users are creating a public nuisance that law enforcement becomes involved.

A common misconception is that drug consumption is high in the Netherlands. This perception has more to do with drug *visibility* in the forms of coffee shops, smart shops, presence of heroin and (crack-)cocaine users and dealers. The decriminalisation of small-scale possession removes the necessity of covert behaviour from users.[6] This is clearly evident in Amsterdam's red light district where there is a concentration of problematic drug users. Ironically, while being one of the Netherlands dodgiest areas in terms of prostitution and drugs, the red light district is one of the main tourist destinations.

The ready availability of drugs in the Netherlands has not led to high(er) domestic drug use. A survey of the Dutch population above the age of twelve reveals that only 17% have ever used cannabis, which means that 83% has never used cannabis despite it's being readily available in nearly 900 coffee shops throughout the country.[7] In a European context, Dutch recreational drug use of substances such as cannabis, cocaine, amphetamines and ecstasy can be positioned in the middle range.[8] Where problematic drug use is concerned, the Netherlands has the lowest registered figure of the EU countries, with 2.6 problem users per 1000 inhabitants aged 15-64.[9]

Some place question marks behind Dutch drug use statistics. They suppose drug use must be substantially higher, considering the access to it as a result of the liberal policy. And, since drug use is so visible in the Netherlands, particularly in Amsterdam, the presumption is that drug use must be higher than in

5 Openbaar Ministerie (2000), *Aanwijzing opiumwet* ('Opium Law Guidelines by the Public Prosecutor').
6 However, drug users who have caused some kind of a nuisance can be subjected to a personal interdiction in the Amsterdam's red light district for a period of one to several months.
7 For data on the prevalence of drug in the general Dutch population, see Abraham et al. (2002), *Licit and Illicit Drug Use In the Netherlands, 2001*.
8 See the EMCDDA table 'Last-12-months (LYP) prevalence of drug use in recent nationwide surveys among the general population in some EU countries'. This statistical table of the EMCDDA data library can be downloaded from the EMCDDA web site and gives more precise data than the annual report and allows for some comparisons comparisons (see «annualreport.emcdda.et.aint»).
9 As mentioned in chapter two, the EMCDDA defines 'problem drug use' as "injecting drug use or long-duration/regular use of opiates, cocaine and/or amphetamines". See the annual EMCDDA reports, e.g. EMCCDA (2001), *Annual Report*, 11. The country reporting the highest problem drug use is Luxembourg, with nine problem drug users per 1.000 inhabitants aged 15-64.

other countries. Governmental anti-drug institutions in the United States, where drug use is approximately twice as high as in the Netherlands, take their scepticism a step further by systematically refuting those statistics. They even go as far as to attempt to characterise Dutch drug policy as a 'dismal failure', suggesting that it has led to higher drug use, and subsequently, higher homicide rates than in the United States.[10] From a public health point of view, problematic drug use is considered to be under control. They report few new cases among this steadily ageing population.[11] The levels of recreational drug use also have been studied extensively, especially cannabis use, and the "overall picture indicates that no significant changes in cannabis use have occurred since statutory decriminalisation".[12]

Shortly after modern drug use started to manifest itself in the late 1960s and early 1970s, the Netherlands has pursued a drug policy that is primarily health oriented and, significantly, less based on law enforcement. In practice this has translated into a wide array of harm reduction measures. One argument in favour of coffee shops is that it separates the cannabis market from that of drugs that are considered more dangerous. Consequently, the cannabis consumer is not put into direct contact with these other substances, at least not in coffee shops. If on the other hand the entire drug scene would be completely illegal and underground – as it used to be – this 'gateway' would become more likely.

Of the three government ministries most directly involved in drug policy, Health, Interior and Justice, the first is considered the primary and co-ordinating ministry. In the 1980s, the concept of 'normalisation' was developed by the Dutch Health Ministry. Normalisation means that drug problems should be considered common social issues; not that it should be considered normal to use drugs. Therefore, problematic drug use can be looked at minus stigmatisation or moral judgements just as alcohol is not vilified because of problematic alcohol use. Normalisation is in line with the primary aim of Dutch drug policy being to protect the health of individual users and their environments by reducing the harms associated with drug use. Within that context, experimental drug use,

10 The American Drug Enforcement Administration (DEA) systematically describes the Dutch drug experience as a disaster, by direct or suggestive assertions that decriminalisation led to more drug use and more drug-related problems (see 'Assertion VI: Legalization and Decriminalization of Drugs Have Been a Dismal Failure in Other Nations' on on-line DEA web site: «www.usdoj.gov/dea/demand/drug legal/14dl.htm»). See further the final chapter.
11 For a brief overview of the epidemiology of heroin use in the Netherlands, see Van den Brink et al. (1999), 'Medical Co-Prescription of Heroin to Chronic, Treatment-Resistant Methadone Patients in the Netherlands'.
12 Korf et al. (1999), 'Windmills in Their Minds? Drug Policy and Drug Research in the Netherlands', published in the 1999 special issue of *Journal of Drug Issues* on Dutch drug policy. Interestingly, Dutch drug use trends are comparable to those of Germany. Surveys show the number of Germans who use cannabis virtually parallels the peaks and troughs in Dutch surveys between 1970 and 1990, even though Germany prohibited cannabis throughout the period. See *New Scientist* (1998b), 'Vraag een politieagent . . . Go ahead, ask a cop for dope. The Dutch don't mind'. See also Reuband (1992), *Drogenpolitik und Drogenkonsum*, or chapter four of Korf (1995), *Dutch Treat*.

although discouraged, is not necessarily considered a problem. In the 1990s, the 'healthy school' programme was initiated into secondary schools to make teenagers aware of numerous 'risky behaviours' involved in certain activities that they might encounter. Keeping with the normalisation concept, drugs are not set apart as a separate category, but are discussed along side the categories of alcohol, tobacco, gambling, and sex.

This chapter will discuss Dutch drug policy and the reasons for its historical development. As this chapter will explain, it is neither the extent of drug use, nor drug problems, that explain Dutch drug policy. It is, instead, the product of several historical, political, and social processes.[13] Some of these factors are directly 'drug-related', others are more structural and rooted in Dutch society, its history, and geography.

4.2 Geography, History, and the People

Undoubtedly, geography is one of the Netherlands most distinct features. The Dutch word *Nederland* signifies low country and refers to the fact that the Netherlands is Europe's lowest part, with half of the country, and more than half of the population living below sea level. Several European rivers such as the Rhine and Meuse flow to the Netherlands, which makes it, in fact, a delta. Dutch history is characterised by their struggle against the water. The Dutch have had to protect themselves from water from rivers and inland lakes, particularly the North Sea.

Eventually they were able to turn from passive protection from the water to the pro-active enterprise of land reclamation into arable land, polders.[14] In order to fight the common enemy, the water, people from all classes and belief systems had to work together for the higher good, keeping the land dry. The Dutch consultative society or 'polder model' is the pragmatic, co-operative Dutch attitude that may stem from the constant fight against the water. Where the fight against the water contributed to a certain mentality, the consultative society got a formal moment in 1917, the moment of the so-called pacification of the different 'pillars', the distinct and self-contained population groups that formed Dutch society.[15] Born out of necessity, the different groups found a way for mutual accommodation, which is often taken for tolerance. The consultative tradition is strong: if groups in society have different or conflicting interests, such as the Airport Board and environmental groups or employer organisations

13 Korf et al. (1999), 'Windmills in Their Minds? Drug Policy and Drug Research in the Netherlands', 451.
14 First a canal was dug around the water of marshy area to be reclaimed and dikes built, then windmills pumped the water out of the area into the canal. See Shetter (1997), *The Netherlands in Perspective*, 20.
15 See section 4.4 where this political model will be further explained.

and trade unions, they sit around the table and try to make arrangements together. How the Dutch dealt with their most natural problem, water, is sometimes used as a metaphor for the Dutch drug policy: Rather than having a constant battle with an insurmountable opponent, it is better to live with it, canalise it, and maintain some level of control.

It was in the seventeenth century that the Dutch fully exploited their water-front position. The nearness and inevitability of the water made the Dutch go overseas, resulting in the seventeenth century Dutch republic becoming the first hegemonic state, and its main city Amsterdam the first world city.[16] During this Dutch 'Golden Age' an economic empire was built that was the staple market and financial centre of the world.[17] During the peak, in the mid of the seventeenth century, the Dutch United Provinces were the leading agricultural and industrial producers, and they managed to establish undisputed ascendancy in the world's carrying trade to become the 'packhouse' of the world'.[18] Amsterdam was the most important trading city:

> "It was a European distribution centre, not only for bulk goods like timber, grain, fish, sugar, and tobacco, but also for luxury goods including East Indian spices, Chinese silk and muslin from India. (…) It was a glittering metropolis, bulging from wealth, where the economic strings of the continent were coming together, an emporium stacked full of products from throughout the world, a city that earned a living through trade, the provision of services and the processing of raw materials. It was also a pocket of free-thinking liberalism, where a wide variety of lifestyles and principles were tolerated, without which the city would have been unable to flourish".[19]

Amsterdam was an international city, with traders, writers and artists from different corners of the world. The Dutch Republic was rather modern; no other country in the world was as urbanised – in 1622, 60% were townsfolk[20] – and it had a relatively large number of smaller cities. The country was not centrally organised, but was instead divided into hundreds of relatively autonomous regions.[21] Citizens also had a local form of governance. In Amsterdam for example, citizens could submit a petition to the mayor for things like odour nuisance coming from a shop.[22]

Attracted by the economic prosperity, tolerant reputation, and religious freedom, many foreigners settled. In the sixteenth and seventeenth century Jews came from the Iberian Peninsula, the first wave fleeing the Spanish Inquisition

16 See Taylor (1996), *The Way the Modern World Works: World Hegemony to World Imperialism.*
17 Schama (1987), *The Embarrassment of Riches*, or Wallerstein (1980), *The Modern World-System II.*
18 Wallerstein (1980), *The Modern World-System II*, 42 and 46. For a more general account, see his chapter 2.
19 Van der Horst (1996), *The Low Sky. Understanding the Dutch.*
20 Wallerstein (1980), *The Modern World-System II.*
21 Van der Horst (1996), *The low sky. Understanding the Dutch*, 35.
22 Kloek & Mijnhardt (2001), *1800. Blauwdrukken voor een samenleving.* See also the interview with Mijnhardt in the Utrecht University's *U Blad* of 4 October 2001 in which he comments on the seventeenth century.

of 1492, and were followed, in another wave, after 1580, by wealthy Jewish traders from Portugal, which had come under Spanish rule. Jews and Protestants arrived from Antwerp, while other Protestants, the Huguenots, came from France. Around 1648, there was a growing influx of Askenazi Jews from Central and Eastern Europe. In the Netherlands, Calvinism was the most predominant religion – in particular its 'reformed' branch – but there has always been a large minority of Catholics, forming almost half of the population.[23] The combination of a Calvinist culture and a large Catholic minority, led to some freedom of conscience (religion) in the late sixteenth century. The official churches in the sixteenth century were reformed and identifiable by their towers. Non-reformed were not allowed to have a public service but it was permitted to gather in spaces that were not recognisable as a church.[24] This led to the existence of the so-called clandestine churches, for which a construction regulation and tax rules existed in the form of 'recognition money'.[25]

The relative freedom in the Dutch republic also made it a haven for writers and intellectuals from all over Europe, such as Spinoza and Descartes. The latter wrote about Amsterdam in 1631: "In which other country can one enjoy such a feeling of freedom".[26] Some writers sought political exile in the Dutch Republic, such as John Locke in the 1680s, while others went there to have their books published, such as Voltaire. Many bookshops and publishers were found in the Dutch Republic, of which Elsevier was the most known. "Thanks to the Elsevier presses in the Calvinist Netherlands, Catholic philosophers such as Galileo and Descartes could make major contributions to a new form of public knowledge that reshaped human culture throughout the entire world".[27]

When the Dutch colonised the Indonesian archipelago, they soon discovered the Asian opium trade and its high commercial value and in the late sixteenth century, the Dutch began trading it.[28] In 1602 the world's first multinational the United Dutch East Indian Company (VOC) was founded and granted privileges by the Dutch Republic. In the seventeenth century most opium was traded

---

23 The Dutch culture is so drenched by Calvinism, that it is sometimes, ironically said even the Dutch Catholics are Calvinist.

24 Taken from the web site of one of the seventeenth century clandestine churches Amsterdam: Ons' Lieve Heer op Solder ('Our Lord in the Attic'), now called Museum Amstelkring («www.zeedijk. nl/heeropsolder-eng.html»).

25 Herman Pleij in a television documentary on the pros and cons of the Dutch cannabis system in the programme 'DNW' of VPRO television, 2001. Pleij is professor of historical Dutch literature and author of several books on Dutch history and culture, such as *Het Nederlands onbehagen* ('Dutch Uneasiness') in 1991 and seven years later *Hollands Welbehagen* ('Dutch Well-Being') in which he describes (37-48) the Dutch tradition of tolerance ('gedogen') and the clandestine churches.

26 Written by Descartes in a letter to his friend M. de Balzac in 1631. On the Westermarkt 6 in Amsterdam, where Descartes lived, a fragment of the letter can be read on the front: "Quel autre pays où l'on puisse jouir d'une liberté si entière".

27 Eisenstein (1985), *The Printing Press as an Agent of Change*, quoted in Dommering (2003), 'Grensoverschrijdende censuur: het EHRM en oude en nieuwe media'.

28 See Vanvugt (1985), *Wettig opium*, 36, or Van de Wijngaart (1991), *Competing Perspectives on Drug Use*, 14.

through the VOC.[29] By the end of the eighteenth century, the VOC had been dissolved, the employees had been turned into civil servants and the opium trade took was taken over by a state controlled system.[30] In the Dutch colony of Indonesia the recreational use of opium had a longer history, resulting in huge profits for several centuries. The sale of opium was regulated through a government controlled leasing system which allowed the government the right to sell opium to the highest bidder.[31] At the end of the nineteenth century, when opium revenues were declining, the government decided to implement 'the opium regime', a state monopoly on its sale and distribution.[32] The Dutch experience with opium use and their involvement in its trade has been documented to some extent.[33] Much less known, however, is that in the late nineteenth and early twentieth century, hence before international drug prohibition, the Dutch were growing coca on the Indonesian island of Java, just like the British were doing on Ceylon (Sri Lanka).[34] Production grew such that by 1911 the Netherlands captured a quarter of the world production, destined for the Netherlands Cocaine Factory in Amsterdam.[35]

Just how long cannabis has been used in the Netherlands is a debatable question. Hemp was widely produced and used in the seventeenth century for ropes and sails, but whether recreational cannabis use goes back this far as is sometimes claimed on the basis of Dutch seventeenth century paintings portraying a pipe smoking person, remains to be seen.[36] Simon Schama wrote on this subject:

"The artist who specialised in rustic or lowlife smoking scenes, like Adriaen Brouwer in the 1620s and 1630s, took great care to record the expressions of deep inhalation of drowsy puffing peculiar to the serious pipe smoker. Some of their figures appear so stunned and insensate with smoke that it has been argued speculatively [by Gerard

29 Vanvugt (1985) describes in his study *Wettig Opium,* 36-37, how the Republic's old motto 'Union is strength' was now applied to the to East Asian trade. By organising the different traders and bringing them together under the umbrella of the VOC, forces would be combined.
30 Van de Wijngaart (1991), *Competing Perspectives on Drug Use*, 14-15.
31 De Kort (1994), *A short history of drugs in the Netherlands*, 7.
32 De Kort (1994), *A short history of drugs in the Netherlands*, 7.
33 Van de Wijngaart (1991), *Competing Perspectives on Drug Use*. For a detailed analysis of the Dutch opium trade, see Vanvugt (1985), *Wettig opium*. The *Atlas mondial des drogues* by the OGD (1996) is of general interest for the history of the use of and trade in drugs. That some studies on this subject of opium in the Dutch Indonesia exist, might suggest much is known about it, but the truth is that most is still largely unknown. It would both be of general scientific interest and relevant to today's policy making to have a better understanding of the control and ration systems that long existed. It would also be useful to know more about the extent and the patterns of use during the legal situation, as well as about the medical and social problems associated with opium use. And, since almost no legal system can prevent the existence of an illegal shadow economy, it would be interesting to know more about the size of the black market during the legal opium regimes.
34 OGD (1996), *Atlas mondial des drogues*, 45-48.
35 Gootenburg (2001), *The Rise and Demise of Coca and Cocaine,* 9.
36 The Hemp Museum in Amsterdam suggests that cannabis may have been smoked in those pipes. French magazines and television documentary showed these paintings as a 'proof' that, at the time, cannabis use was already common.

Knuttel (1962), *Adriaen Brouwer: The Master and His Work*] that their tobacco might have been spiked with some sort of opiate or narcotic. The practice of brewers fortifying their products with trance-inducing or hallucinogenic substances like black henbane seed, belladonna or thorn-apples went back to the late Middle Ages and persisted in spite of fierce prohibitions from church and state alike. Tobacco vendors, particularly those catering to a plebeian clientele, merely applied similar formulae to their product though probably with disproportionately narcotic effect. Roessingh, the historian of the Dutch tobacco industry, does not rule the possibility that some of the merchandise might have been 'sauced' with cannabis sativa, familiar to Dutchmen who had travelled in the Levant and Indian Orient."[37]

Considering that goods from all continents arrived in Dutch ports, it seems likely that some of the cannabis sativa from the Levant or India was carried to the Netherlands. It is however, too early to conclude that cannabis smoking was occurring to the extent to which it has been immortalised in seventeenth century paintings. If such were the case, it would be plausible, though, that written documentation would exist, similar to that regarding tobacco and opium smoking.[38]

The possibilities offered by the Netherlands' geographical delta position on the North See, in close proximity to other important European industries and population centres, was further exploited and strengthened in the twentieth century. The rivers connected it to a vast hinterland for trade, facilitated by roads, and later railroads, that stretch as far as Germany's industrial Ruhr area and Italy, Poland, and even Russia. The harbour of Rotterdam has become a main gateway and logistic transport junction for Europe. In tonnage, Rotterdam is the largest harbour in the world with six million containers a year – more than 500 every hour – totalling some 320 million tonnes of shiploads. In other words, every second, twelve tons of shipments arrive in Rotterdam's harbour. Dutch companies are strongly represented in European road transport because of their many waterways, inland shipping has also become a major way or transport, and Schiphol being one of Europe's main airports; being third in freight. In general terms, transport and distribution are core businesses in the Dutch economy, representing 8% of the GNP and 25% of the national income.

Living close to the sea and having exploited the possibilities it offered, the Dutch have for long been exposed to different cultures. In a cultural and political perspective, the Dutch are Atlantic oriented.[39] Owing to the global dominance of American culture, Dutch (mass) culture is heavily American to the extent that the Netherlands is sometimes considered the most Americanised

37 Schama (1987), *An Embarrassment of Riches*, 212-213. And see Roesingh (1976), *Inlandse tabak: expansie en contractie van een handelsgewas in de 17e en 18e eeuw*, 65-88.
38 French writer Pagès (1996), in his ironic *Descartes et le cannabis*, does not rule out the possibility that French philosopher Descartes, who spent 21 years of his life in the Netherlands, had used cannabis.
39 Which is very different from, for example, neighbouring Germany, that is traditionally oriented towards its hinterland, the mainland of Central and Eastern Europe. The Atlantic orientation of the Netherlands is also clear in its foreign policy, where it usually supports the American position.

European country. From a cultural perspective, the Netherlands – including the countryside – is highly urbanised facilitating the exposure and penetration of 'global' and metropolitan lifestyles.[40] This mentality has been influenced by their long historic involvement in international trade. Descartes, during his seventeenth century stay in Amsterdam, theorised rather playfully that there was no one, except him, not involved in trading. Of course, as Weber has described, capitalism – as well as its earlier, seventeenth century form of Dutch mercantilism – goes well together with the protestant religion and its working ethics, in particular with Calvinism.[41] Religion, culture, trade and readily available capital explain the Dutch preoccupation with money and trade. In the Netherlands it is not considered in 'poor taste' to reveal the price of anything, for example, it is a normal practice for television news statements to add the price tags attached to a policy measure or the acquisition of an artwork. Political conflicts in the Dutch coalition governments have more than once been about the budget or the paying off of the national debt. In EU meetings, the Dutch have the reputation of being hard-liners when it comes to budget control.[42] This historically rooted commercial spirit has created a cost-benefit and no-nonsense way of thinking regarding commerce. Overall, these traits have made the Dutch and their country attractive for doing business. In 2000, the Economist Intelligence Unit (EIU) called the Netherlands the best place in the world to conduct business, before the United States and United Kingdom, and it thinks it will remain so for another five years.[43] The Royal Tropical Institute (KIT) in Amsterdam, an international institute with experience in intercultural communication, offers a course to introduce foreigners to the Dutch way of life. In these courses five traits are presented, which would be characteristic of Dutch society: egalitarian, utilitarian, organised, trade oriented, and privacy minded.[44]

Freedom, particularly in respect to individual freedom, has been a long-standing trait of Dutch society. One explanation for this is that the Netherlands have been occupied by the Spanish, French and Germans, which is why, according to Dutch journalist Marc Chavannes, the Dutch are born with a "quasi-sentimental ideal of resistance".[45] The Dutch ardour for freedom can sometimes almost be anarchistic, when Dutch citizens display some kind of resistance against the authorities who, in their eyes, 'mess' too much with their personal affairs. It is, in any case, generally accepted in Dutch society that the

---

40 In the Dutch geography and planning literature, the Dutch countryside is considered to be to a large extent urbanised. This refers not so much to the population density, but more to lifestyles, such as the type of professions, and to which information sources people are oriented, such as media.

41 See the classic by Weber (1958): *The Protestant Ethic and the Spirit of Capitalism* (originally published in 1904).

42 In Brussels, Dutch Finance Minister Zalm acquired the Italian nickname 'il duro'.

43 Economist Intelligence Unit (EIU) in its *Global Outlook* for 2000. See «www.eiu.com».

44 Van der Horst (1996), *Under the low sky. Understanding the Dutch*, 17.

45 See his contribution to the *Public Affairs* Report as a visiting scholar of the Institute of Governmental Studies at University of California, Berkeley: Chavannes (2000), 'Gedogen Allows the Dutch to Manage the Unmanageable'.

government only plays a background role when it comes to religious or moral issues. The Dutch notion of freedom is easily interpreted as tolerance. Since the individual freedom is bounded by where it meets others,[46] many Dutch do not really care about things they are not directly bothered by. "No wonder the facade of tolerance so often conceals a reality of indifference".[47]

One of the areas where the respect of individual freedom becomes most apparent is homosexuality. The subject of homosexuality is not taboo in the Netherlands to the extent that it is not shocking for a homosexual couple to appear on popular quiz shows. Nor is it shocking to see an interview with a homosexual television personality in a popular gossip weekly show, followed by him showing a picture of himself and his male partner in the garden of their house. In the Netherlands known social figures such as television personalities and politicians are openly homosexual. Elsewhere, the taboo of public homo-sexuality could be damaging to one's career, but for the Dutch this has not been negative.[48] Because gays and lesbians are more accepted than elsewhere, they consider the Netherlands the European 'gay country' and the city of Amsterdam as the European gay capital. In 2001, the Dutch parliament opened the possibil-ity of same-sex marriages, which contrary to other countries, hardly caused any controversy.[49]

The Dutch tolerant attitude towards illicit drugs is partially explained by their integral notion of freedom in regard to moral and religious matters. The question whether to consume a substance or not, many Dutch think, is up to the individual, and not up to an authority like the government. And, although the official church was reformed, it allowed other faiths on the condition they were not too overtly displayed. A similar policy is taken towards cannabis: officially forbidden, but the consumption and sales are allowed in coffee shops. However, this cannot be too overtly displayed by means such as advertising. Cannabis' societal integration can be likened to the abundant presence of water being turned into an advantage, by becoming a trading nation. Just as the seventeenth century spice trade covered the four corners of the world, so do today's Dutch cannabis and ecstasy traders. Commerce does not entirely explain Dutch involvement in the drug trade, inevitably pragmatism plays its part as well. Owing to the aforementioned trade and distribution aspects of the Netherlands, it is economically and logistically impossible to stop drugs from entering the

---

46 This concept of freedom is close to that of Mills. See Maris (1999), 'The Disasters of War: American Repression Versus Dutch Tolerance in Drug Policy'.

47 Chavannes (2000), 'Gedogen Allows the Dutch to Manage the Unmanageable'.

48 According to Paul Schnabel in an interview with Weeda (1992), *Vrouwen verlangen mannen*, 175. Schnabel was then professor of Mental Health at Utrecht University and is currently director of the Social and Cultural Planning Bureau (SCP), an interministerial research and advisory body. Schnabel added an anecdote showing to what extent homosexuality is accepted. When the weekly *Vrij Nederland* suggested Dutch singer Gerard Joling was gay, his manager's reaction was: "It is possible, but he himself is not sure, he has not solved it yet".

49 See the highlight 'Same-sex marriages' at Radio Netherlands: Schippers (2001), *Why the Dutch?*

country. Dutch policy makers have taken a 'pragmatic' and more economic attitude: instead of fighting drugs, they opted for regulation, sale and taxation.

These factors do not explain the Dutch drug control system at large. In recent years, Dutch governments have made a number of decisions that have placed this system in a wider perspective of regulating so-called deviant behaviours, such as the same-sex marriages that became legal in 2001. In 2000, the Netherlands became the first country to legalise euthanasia, although under strict conditions.[50] In that same year, prostitution was further liberalised by making it a fully legal profession.[51] If this is added to the fact that in the 1970s the Netherlands became one of the first countries to allow abortions, it becomes understandable that the Dutch have developed a preference to place certain matters in the open where there is the possibility of some control and regulation, rather than forcing the issues underground.[52] For illicit drugs, regulation is only a part of the equation as they remain illegal – with the exception of cannabis. Cannabis is the only illicit substance to be 'semi-legalised', although a majority of the Dutch Parliament and government ministers are, in principle, in favour of the full legalisation of cannabis. That they have not done so, is because of 'the international context'. Other countries are not yet prepared for legalisation of cannabis so Dutch politicians say that it is better to wait, leading to another distinguishing trait of Dutch society – national conceit. Although their Calvinism does not allow them to be openly chauvinistic or proud, the Dutch in fact are proud of the achievement of their small country. The national self-image speaks for itself: "Netherlands, guiding nation".

4.3 Commissions and Professionals

Before the era of modern drug use, the use of illicit substances in the Netherlands itself was rare. In the early twentieth century some opium use was occurring in the Chinese communities, counting some 14,000 around 1914, in the harbour cities of Amsterdam and Rotterdam. The authorities turned a blind eye towards the opium use in these Chinese communities. The few Dutch people who used opiates were primarily physicians, nurses, pharmacists, and artists. Police reports from the 1920s suggested widespread cocaine use by seamen congregating in certain neighbourhoods, to which they were attracted by prostitutes and bars, most of whom obtained these drugs through a physician's

---

50 The Dutch health minister said "the goal of the bill was to bring the practice of euthanasia and physician-assisted suicide out into the open so that it could be more easily regulated and controlled". See Richburg (2000), 'Dutch Vote Clears Way for Legal Euthanasia', *International Herald Tribune*, 29th November 2000.
51 More precisely: prostitution was already legal but in 2000 the ban of brothels was lifted.
52 The Netherlands has the lowest abortion rates of the industrialised world. See Chavannes (2000), 'Gedogen Allows the Dutch to Manage the Unmanageable'.

prescription.[53] In the 1950s, cannabis use was rare, generally occurring among particular groups such as jazz musicians and American soldiers. In 1953, possession of marijuana became prohibited under the Dutch Opium Act, and in 1955, the first arrests were made. Attention was focused primarily on American soldiers based in Germany who would come to the Netherlands on 'pay day'. Dutch people would sell them marijuana, which they had obtained from sailors.[54]

It was during the 1960s that Dutch authorities were confronted with modern drug use. The substances concerned were mostly cannabis (marijuana and hashish), and to a lesser extent amphetamines, and LSD. In the early 1960s the police would hunt intensively for a few grams of cannabis and the penalties were quite severe. Possession of a minimum amount could easily lead to a few months imprisonment. This repressive approach could not prevent a fast increase in the use of cannabis, particularly with the rise in the second half of the 1960s of youth cultures of *provos* and hippies.

These 'provocative' youth movements were very active during the 1960s and received substantial media attention.[55] As Leuw describes it: "The recreational use of illegal substances by sometimes non-conformist, but definitively non-marginal youths gained some prominence, although perhaps more in public awareness than in numbers. The nature of this drug use, a rather inhibited and even somewhat ostentatious smoking of cannabis, implied that value conflicts rather than objective problems were at the core of the initial phenomenon".[56] Particularly in the traditionally liberal city of Amsterdam, the alternative youth culture manifested itself. 'Anti-smoke magician' Robert-Jasper Grootveld, performed ceremonies under the *'t Lievertje* statue, which had been sponsored by a tobacco company. Grootveld performed these 'anti-smoke' ceremonies, which attracted increasing crowds, as a way to protest against the difference in policy towards tobacco and cannabis. As Leuw further describes, the cultural rebels that were the *provos* were highly visible and were generally admired by their otherwise more conformist peers:

> "The movement playfully provoked the Amsterdam city administration and police in various inventive ways. Stretching the borders of social and personal liberty was the movement's explicit aim. Challenging the public order regulations and some penal law prohibitions was its strategy. Weekly 'happenings' downtown delighted the young, partying crowd, while making the authorities quite nervous. Publicly smoking pot was part of the provocation game".[57]

53 De Kort (1994), 'A short history of drugs in the Netherlands', 13.
54 De Kort (1994), 'A short history of drugs in the Netherlands', 13-16.
55 Especially the ('provocative') *provos* in Amsterdam got much attention as they, being republican, announced that they planned to disturb the wedding of Dutch queen Beatrix with German Claus Von Amsberg in 1966, which they did with, for example, smokie bombs. The *provos* had also announced that they would give LSD impregnated sugar cubes to police horses, or to add LSD to the tap water of the city of Amsterdam. Shortly afterwards and before the wedding LSD was added as a prohibited substance in the Dutch Opium Law.
56 Leuw (1995), 'Initial construction and development of the official Dutch drug policy', 23.
57 Leuw (1995), 'Initial construction and development of the official Dutch drug policy', 25.

At the end of the 1960s, the phenomenon of illicit drug use had spread sufficiently to generate widespread confusion, anxiety, and some moral outrage in Dutch society. This centred around "the highly symbolically loaded issue" of cannabis and LSD use by a young avant-garde or different groups, who later were referred to as hippies. The social reactions intensified, Leuw further describes, when it became inescapably clear to parents, educators, and legislators that the hippie lifestyle was appealing to broad segments of the 'normal' young generation, perhaps even to their own children. The phenomenon was met with different reactions. On the one hand, several conservative groups were very much against these new lifestyles. On the other hand, the hippie movement found supporters among liberal new elite groups, such as young university graduates who were taking positions in the rapidly expanding world of (mental) health, welfare and social policy institutions.[58]

From the beginning, the police reaction to provocation and protest (NATO and Vietnam) was in a repressive way and around 1966 the skirmishes became more violent.[59] As Marcel de Kort describes, generally, the reactions of the media on the escalations were critical, not only towards the youth, but also and increasingly towards the repressive and sometimes violent reactions of the police towards their provocative actions. Criticism was expressed in particular to the chief of police and mayor of Amsterdam, who both eventually had to resign.[60] This in turn led to some confusion within the police forces about appropriate reaction, which resulted in an insecure, somewhat passive and reluctant attitude on their side as to how they might enforce the law. This was later described as a kind of accommodation, that is, as essentially, a non-treatment of problems".[61] In short, in a period of a few years it became increasingly clear that repressive (re)actions towards provocative youth were not backed by public opinion.

During law enforcement's moment of insecurity the youth movement took advantage of the situation by pushing the boundaries of acceptability further. In popular clubs such as Fantasio and the Paradiso in Amsterdam, which received subsidies from the municipality, cannabis sales and consumption were openly visible. De Kort describes the criticism in the press of these subsidised youth centres disrespecting the law, but that it was also necessary to acknowledge a social reality. Closing down these premises was not considered a good idea as this could result in trade and use spreading further and becoming even less

---

58 Leuw (1995), 'Initial construction and development of the official Dutch drug policy', 26.
59 A violent incident occurred in June 1966 when construction workers and *provos* demonstrated together and clashed with the police. Two people got injured and one construction worker killed. The next day, the most-read Dutch daily, the *Telegraaf,* suggested the worker had been killed by some of his colleagues, when an angry crowd stormed the newspaper building in Amsterdam.
60 De Kort (1995) describes in detail the situation of the 1960s in chapter six of his Ph.D. study: *Tussen patiënt en delinquent,* 176-183.
61 De Kort, ibidem, quoting Paul ten Have (1975), 'The Counter Culture on the Move. A field Study of Youth Tourists in Amsterdam', 313.

controllable. In 1969, in an attempt to keep dealers away the authorities made a failing attempt to implement a series of rules which resulted in the closure of Fantasio and Paradiso for a number of months. When they reopened, drugs were once again present. At that time, a public prosecutor wrote to the Ministry of Justice that despite the many police checks, they were confronted with a hopeless situation. In practice this amounted to the police intervening occasionally, but generally being hesitant to conduct any real action.

A year later, in 1970, a big pop festival was held in Rotterdam. The police tolerated the use and sale of drugs and restricted its activities to 'collecting facts and events in a discrete manner'. The police later concluded that there was little alcohol use, surprisingly few thefts, no sexual excesses and that the festival goers generally behaved peacefully towards one another. Around 1970, De Kort concluded that large metropolitan areas had adopted a policy of tolerance towards illicit drugs despite its' being unsupported by the national authorities in The Hague.[62] The variety of opinions and the lack of clarity about how to react to the phenomenon of illicit drug use, led to the installations of commissions and study groups around 1970. De Kort finds it striking that none of these studies makes reference to experiences of the past, such as the integrated drug use of the nineteenth century, the opium leasing system, the later opium regime, and the regime from 1920 to 1960 in which drugs were medically prescribed. It seemed these experiences had vanished from the Dutch collective memory and the debates came to centre around the question of that day: cannabis use in the counter culture.[63] To understand the context in which these commissions operated, Leuw writes: it is "of utmost importance that these working groups were established in an era and in a society where drug use had come to the public consciousness against the backdrop of a relatively mild dispute of lifestyles and value systems, and not against a background of criminality, pathology, and deeply rooted social conflict".[64]

In 1967 and 1968 two expert working groups were installed, one private and one state commission. In 1967, the state-sponsored Institute for Mental Health appointed the first commission, chaired by Louk Hulsman, a Professor of Criminal Law and Criminology, who was known for his critical and abolitionist views on criminal law.[65] In 1968, the government installed the second, the Working Group on Narcotic Substances. This commission became functional in 1970, after the number of members was extended and a new chairman was found, following the resignation of the original chairman. The second commis-

---

62 Because of the relative passive and therefore lenient attitude towards the use of especially cannabis, Amsterdam had a magical attraction to young people from elsewhere. In the late 1960s and early 1970s hippies from different countries and continents went there to enjoy freedom and smoke cannabis and Amsterdam became one of the centres of the international counter culture.
63 De Kort (1995), *Tussen patiënt en delinquent*, 184.
64 Leuw (1995), 'Initial construction and development of the official Dutch drug policy', 27.
65 Hulsman became (and still is) internationally known as an abolitionist, a supporter of the abolishment of criminal law.

sion is known as the Baan Commission, after its chairman, Pieter Baan, who was both Chief Inspector of Mental Health and Professor of Psychiatry.

In both the analysis of the drug problem and the recommendations, the two reports largely have the same approach.[66] The Hulsman Report had no officially recognised political status, and was therefore less bound by political or administrative limitations, which rendered it more open and scientific, explaining why in comparison to Baan, it is more theoretical and liberal – and more critical towards the use of criminal law. Since the Hulsman Commission started the job a year earlier, it paved the way for the Baan Commission, which was published in 1972.[67] Add to this that almost half of the Baan Commission (six out of fourteen) had also been sitting on the Hulsman Commission, Hulsman influenced Baan. In fact, the Baan Report largely adopted Hulsman's way of looking at the drug use phenomenon. It is no exaggeration that without the Hulsman Report, the Baan Report would not have been possible. Significantly, Baan wrote the foreword of the Hulsman Report, where he stated that he found it to be a privilege to announce this "important book".

As Leuw puts it, the Hulsman Commission provided an "ideological justification for the much more down-to-earth Baan Commission to break away from the single-minded prohibitionist regime that until that time had seemed to be the most natural Dutch (official) social policy towards illicit drug use.[68] Strictly speaking, Baan had more direct influence. The most striking aspect of the Baan Report, Leuw concludes, was that "its conclusions and recommendations were broadly accepted by the Dutch government as well as parliament, and that its recommendations to the present day have guided the practical implementation and execution of Dutch drug policies".[69]

The Baan Report devoted a lot of attention to cannabis, the use of which it generally described as not being problematic. One of the findings put forward to support this was the quote of a Dutch sociologist who had found that drug-using youths "not only read more about drugs, but also read more about other things than drugs: art, politics, science and philosophy than youths from the two control groups".[70] The report described cannabis as being relatively benign with limited health risks. According to the commission there seemed to be no basis for the idea that cannabis was a gateway drug which led users to other heavier substances. Eventually the Baan Commission made a classification of different drugs on the basis of a 'risk scale' based on medical, pharmacological, socio-

---

66 For a more detailed account and comparison, see: Peter Cohen (1994), *The case of the two Dutch drug policy commissions. An exercise in harm reduction 1968-1976*, and Leuw (1995), 'Initial construction and development of the official Dutch drug policy', 27-33.

67 Both working groups worked for two years on the subject. For the reports, see Van Dijk and Hulsman (Eds.) (1970), *Drugs in Nederland*. The Baan Report was published as Werkgroep Verdovende Middelen (1972), *Achtergronden en risico's van druggebruik*.

68 Leuw (1995), 'Initial construction and development of the official Dutch drug policy', 28.

69 Leuw (1995), 'Initial construction and development of the official Dutch drug policy', 28.

70 Cohen (1994), *The case of the two Dutch drug policy commissions,* 4.

scientific and psychological data. It recommended making a distinction between cannabis and other illicit drugs, as the latter group was considered to pose an unacceptable health risk.

What is striking in both commissions is the presence and influence of sociological views and insights on drug use. Both commissions included several social scientists, and although they did not form the majority, their discipline clearly put a stamp on the commissions' work. The sociological way of looking was very present at the time, both in the law and medical field. Hulsman himself was a lawyer working at the Ministry of Justice when he was asked to become Criminal Law Professor in Rotterdam. He accepted the chair on the condition that it would also include the social science of criminology. The request was granted, which explains why Hulsman became professor in both academic areas It shows that for the lawyer Hulsman, sociological viewpoints and theory were essential elements of his professional outlook. When he was asked to head a commission on the new drug use phenomenon in the late 1960s, the natural thing for him to do was to include sociological thinking. Hulsman also asked the young physician, Peter Geerlings (1939), to join his commission. Geerlings had been working as an assistant psychiatrist at the Jellinek Clinic in Amsterdam. His fieldwork among drug users included professional visits to some of them in their homes, and meetings in the Vondel Park with the hippies from different countries who congregated there at the time. In April 1968, he started a consultation hour for young drug users.[71] Geerlings, who still works at the Jellinek Clinic – now in the position of Medical Director – recalls that around 1970, there was significant influence from the social scientific and sociological theory in the medical and psychiatric field, especially in the then popular anti-psychiatry. The American sociologist, Howard Becker, was known and his book, *Outsiders* (1963), was also read by psychiatrists, who were thus well aware of the mechanisms and effects of stigmatising and labelling deviant behaviour.[72]

Another young member of the Hulsman Commission was the psychologist Herman Cohen (1936) who worked at the Institute of Social Medicine at the University of Amsterdam, where his assignment was the study of deviant drug use. Geerlings and Cohen were the only members of the Hulsman Commission who had had any substantial contact with drug users. Cohen had been conducting empirical research about drug use based upon fieldwork, and had close connections to the drug scene; at a later point in life, he was arrested on cocaine charges. In 1969, Cohen finished a study on drug users, later published as his Ph.D.[73] Cohen was known to have read extensively about drugs and he introduced social scientific literature to the Hulsman Commission. That he was well

---

71   See also the contribution by Geerlings (partly based on a survey among the young drug users of his consultation hour) to the Hulsman Report: Van Dijk and Hulsman (Eds.) (1970), *Drugs in Nederland*, 156-174.
72   Personal Communication Peter Geerlings, 1 April 2004.
73   Cohen (1975), *Drugs, druggebruikers en drug-scene*.

acquainted with the international social scientific literature on drug use, combined with the fact that he was a pioneer in researching the drug scene, allowed him substantial authority. This is a probable explanation for the invitation extended to him to become a member of the Baan Commission as well.

The sociological contribution in both the Baan and Hulsman Reports is that the drug use phenomenon is clearly put in a social and (sub)cultural context. For example, The Baan Report stated that a significant amount of drug use is the short-lived experimentation practised by young persons. The Baan Report further qualifies that there are boundaries and particularities inside youth culture and subculture governing the functions of drug use.[74] In later years, this would scientifically be known as the importance of the 'setting' in understanding patterns of drug use.[75] In both reports, sociological findings such as surveys among drug users were widely quoted. An important finding of these surveys was that youths using drugs did not have objectionable morals. This led the majority of the commissions' members to the conclusion that there was not a problem of social pathology among the drug using population. Although surveys found the drug users to differ from the 'normal' population on a number of issues, this was not interpreted as a consequence of drug use. The idea of drug use being the result of individual or social pathology was therefore abandoned by most members of the commissions.[76] As a result, remedies based on the idea of correcting deviant (pathological) behaviour, such as in France through the use of criminal law, did not gain foothold in the Netherlands.

While the pathological theories lost influence, interactionist theories, such as the labelling theory, that focus on social reactions toward certain behaviours, grew in popularity in the late 1960s and early 1970s. The clearest sign of the sociological influence in the work of both commissions, which was to have the most long-term influence by playing a significant role in shaping Dutch drug policy, was the labelling theory. According to this theory, deviant behaviour does not exist in itself but is defined as such in a particular society at a particular time. It was on the basis of this theory that the reports of both commissions stated that if society stigmatises a (deviant) behaviour like drug use, the risk exists that this behaviour will intensify. This in turn will initiate a spiral, which will make the return of a socially accepted lifestyle more difficult.

It was this interactionist way of conceiving the phenomenon, which led in 1976 to a formal change in Dutch drug policy, a revision of the 1928 Dutch Opium Act. The new drug legislation of 1976 made the legal distinction between illicit drugs posing an unacceptable health risk (List I), and cannabis

74 Cohen (1994), *The case of the two Dutch drug policy commissions.*, 4-5.
75 See the model drug, set, and setting as developed by Norman Zinberg (1984), *Drug, Set, & Setting.*
76 De Kort (1995), *Tussen patiënt en delinquent*, 199. De Kort explains that in the Netherlands, the theory of drug use as a sign of individual pathology was influential before World War II. In the 1950s and 1960s, drugs use was often interpreted as a sign of social pathology. From the late 1960s on, interactionist theories became popular, which also looked at the interaction between 'normal' and deviant behaviour.

products on the one hand (list II), in the law called 'hemp'.[77] From this arose the difference between the so-called hard drugs (amphetamines, heroin, cocaine, LSD, etc.) and soft drugs (i.e. cannabis). The Baan Report did not explicitly recommend what type of different penal regime should be applied for cannabis. This was left for the politicians to decide. Baan only offered three possibilities. The first was to make use, small possession, and small-scale trade a misdemeanour. The second was to not criminalise use and small possession at all, but to continue the criminalisation of the cannabis trade, as either a misdemeanour or an offence. The third was to regulate a legal cannabis supply through a licensing system.[78] Liquor shops were considered as possible outlets. Cafés where cannabis could be used, would not be allowed, according to this third option.

During this early period of the 1970s other governments began creating drug commissions. The United Kingdom set up the Advisory Committee on Drug Dependence, the United States set up its National Commission on Marijuana and Drug Abuse, Canada set up the Commission of Inquiry into the Non-Medical Use of Drugs.[79] These were known respectively as the Wootton Commission (United Kingdom), the LeDain Commission (Canada), and the Shafer Commission (United States). In accordance with the Hulsman and Baan Commissions, all shared the primary focus of cannabis. Similar to the recommendations of Hulsman and Baan these other national commissions recommended the decriminalisation of small quantities of cannabis for private use. Some of the commissions initiated visits and dialogue with their counterparts. Members of the Canadian LeDain Commission came to the Netherlands and the American Shafer Commission visited many countries, including the Netherlands. They met and developed a good working relationship with the Hulsman Commission. The Hulsman Commission member, Geerlings, recalls that members were invited to meet some drug users as well as to visit one of Amsterdam's famous youth centres of the time, *Fantasio*. To their surprise, they encountered quite a few American hippies, with whom an interesting discussion started on the notion of freedom.[80] The Shafer Commission also met Koos Zwart, a key figure in the counter culture, who had made a name for himself through his controversial Saturday morning radio programme, called Stock Market News, which among other topics, gave the latest cannabis market prices.

---

77 The Dutch opium law, of course uses the Dutch word for hemp, which is 'hennep'.
78 De Kort (1995), *Tussen patiënt en delinquent*, 196.
79 In the United Kingdom, Canada, and the United States were published respectively: Advisory Committee on Drug Dependence (1969), *Cannabis*; National Commission on Marihuana and Drug Abuse (1972), *Marihuana: A signal of misunderstanding*; and Canadian Government Commission of Inquiry (1970), *The Non-Medical Use of Drugs*.
80 Dr. Geerlings remembers that when the members of the Shafer Commission met young American hippies in *Fantasio*, they asked them what they were doing in Amsterdam, to which the hippies answered "to be free". The members then replied they were free in the United States, to which the hippies objected, as they stated people were not always allowed to say, write and express what they wished. An interesting discussion followed, in which the hippies quite convincingly made their point of being more free in Amsterdam than in their home country.

In retrospect, it can be said that the Dutch exception lies in the fact that the commissions' recommendations were followed by a formal change in the law.[81] In the year the Shafer Commission published its report (1972), Nixon had been re-elected and he initiated repressive, law enforcement oriented drug policies. Thirty years on, Canada appears to be implementing policy recommendations of the LeDain Commission: Canada is taking steps towards a more liberal cannabis policy as well as towards a heroin prescription programme. That the Netherlands was the only country where the recommendations were translated into real policy, is significant for that period. In the first half of the 1970s, a climate of political and legal culture was in place that allowed for the introduction of these progressive and innovative changes.[82] Sebastian Scheerer adds in his Dutch-German drug policy comparison that in the Netherlands, unlike Germany, there was no conservative opposition party that could oppose and exploit the proposed liberal approach, as the potential candidate, the Catholic KVP, was part of the government coalition. This Dutch government under Social Democratic Prime Minister Den Uijl is considered to be one of the most progressive of the last few decades. It not only included Irene Vorrink as Minister of Health (the mother of Koos Zwart), but also Andries van Agt, a young and progressive law professor of the KVP, who became Minister of Justice.

4.4 Political and Legal Culture

In the 1960s, Dutch society underwent major changes. In many ways, Dutch society opened up. The 'pillarisation' system, a distinctively Dutch form of policy making that had been in place since the beginning of the twentieth century, collapsed and led to increased democratisation with more groups participating in society. Lijphart begins his standard work *The Politics of Accommodation*, which was published in 1968, by stating that the political system of the Netherlands presents a paradox to the social scientist. On the one hand it is one of the most notable examples of a successful democracy, on the other hand it is characterised by an extraordinary degree of social cleavage, with "deep religious and class divisions separating distinct, isolated, and self-contained population groups".[83] The system of pillarisation had been the main characteristic of the twentieth century Dutch political system and to some extent

---

81 De Kort questions though the influence of Baan as having laid the basis for Dutch drug policy. He states that opinions at the different departments had evolved further and even surpassed the rather conservative recommendations of Baan. See De Kort (1995), *Tussen patiënt en delinquent*, 201.

82 In Germany on the other hand, the conservative opposition described drug use around 1970 as a growing danger for which the state of emergency should be declared. See Sebastian Scheerer (1982), *Die Genese der Betäubungsmittelgesetze in der Bundesrepublik Deutschland und in den Niederlanden*.

83 Lijphart (1968), *The Politics of Accommodation*, 1-2.

of Dutch society, as many activities were organised according to these pillars, which are vertical social groups, which can also be designated as 'blocs': i.e. there was a Roman Catholic, an orthodox Calvinist, and a secular bloc.[84] The average citizen was supposed to stay in his pillar. For example, a catholic boy would attend a Catholic school, go to a Catholic football club, listen to the Catholic radio, go to a Catholic grocery shop, and marry a Catholic girl. In a sense, the Netherlands could be called a 'multicultural' society, with separate blocs, whose members were not supposed to mingle with people from other blocs. But at the aggregate, national level, the leading elite of the pillars did meet in order to run the country. That the country functioned as a democratic system, is because these elite made compromises through a process of political accommodation, with pragmatic solutions being forged for all problems.[85] Hence, the pragmatic attitude of the Dutch was also clearly visible in the political culture. Sovereignty in one's domain, the pillar, demanded great tolerance for other ways of thinking.[86]

In the late 1960s, the whole system of pillarisation collapsed over a short period of time. Increased prosperity, de-secularisation, and expansion of the mass media (television) contributed to this process. People no longer felt committed to their ideological pillar, which provided an opportunity for groups outside of the established pillars to play a role in the political and social world. Youth culture was also depillarised, which in this time of social change was not relegated to a marginal social position. As a result, counter cultures with drugs were not marginalised and combated with criminal justice measures.[87] As a consequence of the ambivalent social reactions to the *provos* and other youth movements in the 1960s, law enforcement agencies were reluctant to enforce drug laws. Moral entrepreneurs wishing to stop these developments were not powerful enough to make their voices heard. More influential than the moral entrepreneurs were the voices heard in the media who had criticised the earlier repressive law enforcement efforts.[88]

The 1960s were a decade of transition for the Dutch. The old system of traditional norms and values disintegrated into a new one with more room for alternative moral positions and lifestyles. Hippies and young people from all over the world flocked to Amsterdam during the late 1960s and early 1970s. Thousands of hippies slept in the Vondel Park and on the Dam Square, made possible by several hot summers. Amsterdam's reputation for being a magical

---

84 Some of the blocs could be subdivided, such as the orthodox Calvinist bloc into Reformed (protestant) and fundamentalist Calvinist. As Lijphart (1968: 17-18) explains, the threefold division goes back as far as the birth of Dutch state in the sixteenth century, and can be traced to the three forces of Roman Catholicism, Renaissance, and Reformation.

85 Lijphart (1968), *The Politics of Accommodation,* in particular chapter six ('The Spirit of Accommodation').

86 Van der Horst (2001), *The low Sky,* 53.

87 De Kort (1995), 'A short history of drugs in the Netherlands', 18.

88 De Kort (1995), *Tussen patiënt en delinquent,* 179.

attraction turned it into one of the international counter culture centres. People came from everywhere to experience freedom, but not only in regard to drugs. Sex and abortion tourists came from Southern European countries. On Friday nights gays and lesbians arrived from London in crowded aeroplanes to party in the gay bars.[89] Internationally, the Netherlands was seen as a place to experiment with new lifestyles and new beginnings. The cultural 'revolution' the Netherlands was going through in the 1960s affected a number of issues, ranging from drugs, to women's emancipation, abortion, homosexuality, and student participation in universities.[90] The call for participation was symbolised by the student occupation of the 'Maagdenhuis', the administrative centre of the University of Amsterdam in 1969, a year after the events in Paris. During the Maagdenhuis occupation, the students rebelled against the authoritarian mentality of the universities and demanded increased participation. The demand for increased participation was eventually granted setting in motion a process of democratisation for the entirety of Dutch society. Generally speaking, the 1960s led to significant changes in society. In the Netherlands these changes during the 1960s occurred faster and more radically than in other European countries.[91]

It was against the backdrop of these societal changes that a new Dutch government took office in 1973. The Baan Report had been presented a year earlier and the new centre-left wing government would revise the Opium Act and bring it to Parliament in 1976.[92] Under this new government the winds of change blew in. The liberal idealist Irene Vorrink became responsible for drug and abortion policy at the Health Department where she openly declared support for cannabis legalisation.[93] Her views differed substantially from those of her predecessor, the physician Kruisinga who was very worried about the dangers of cannabis. Under Vorrink's rule the Health Ministry gradually abandoned its conservative position on cannabis. At the Justice Ministry, support for decriminalisation was already dominant, a position that was only reinforced by the ministerial nomination of the Law Professor Andries van Agt. Later however, he would become a Christian Democratic party leader and the Prime Minister of a conservative government. In 2004, when he was retired and looking back on his career, he stated his regret that he had not fully legalised cannabis.

In 1973, the Dutch government – particularly the two ministers most directly involved – supported full cannabis legalisation as the best long-term option.[94] With regard to 'hard' drugs, the government wanted to introduce a policy of decriminalisation. The question of feasibility was raised because legalisation of

89 Leuw (1995), 'Initial construction and development of the official Dutch drug policy', 31.
90 De Kort (1995), *Tussen patiënt en delinquent*, 180.
91 Scheffer (2002), 'Alles van waarde moet zich verweren', *NRC Handelsbad*, 22 September 2002.
92 Leuw (1995), 'Initial construction and development of the official Dutch drug policy', 32.
93 De Kort notes (1995: 225) that at the press conference shortly after her nomination she gave a fully affirmative answer to the question if the supported the legalisation of soft drugs.
94 Personal communication Louk Hulsman, 21 June 2003.

cannabis meant that it had to be removed from the 1961 UN drug convention. At that moment, the Dutch government was faced with criticism from both Germany and Sweden over its liberal approach to drugs. In 1973, the Netherlands was subjected to more international criticism, this time from Arab countries for the (military) support to Israel during the Yom Kippur War, which led to an oil boycott of Israel's main allies, the United States and the Netherlands.[95] The Dutch government had become somewhat isolated, internationally, and as a result, could not permit itself to take up a distinct position in another policy domain. Because of these foreign policy considerations, cannabis legalisation seemed politically unwise and unattainable; therefore compromise was reached by sending a letter to the UN, a letter "nobody talks about, although it clearly was a political statement".[96] In April 1975, the Dutch government sent a letter to the president of the International Narcotics Control Board (INCB), asking for leeway to interpret the 1961 Convention concerning cannabis. The letter made clear that the Dutch government wished to liberalise its cannabis policy and included the remark that "the policy of repression expressed in the provisions of the 1961 Single Convention has failed".[97] A full regulation was not possible, according to the INCB,[98] and the Dutch government followed the middle option of the Baan Commission, that the trade remained criminalised, but not the use and possession of small amounts of cannabis. This was translated into concrete provisions with the 1976 Revised Opium Law: a different penal regime was made for cannabis, and possession of small amounts of cannabis was made a misdemeanour.

Social and political change were not the only factors contributing to the position of the Dutch government The new governmental position can also be explained by another trait of Dutch political culture, which is the strong decentralisation tendency and the tradition of local policy making. Decisions and experiences at the local level, particularly in the main cities, trickle up to the national political level. The background of the political culture lies in the seventeenth century when, as was noted earlier, a majority of the Dutch were already urban dwellers. Ever since the seventeenth century, the Netherlands has been a very urban society, with flourishing cities, with the proportion of its

---

95 In the Dutch collective memory the boycott seems to live on as a boycott of 'Western countries' or 'the West', as this is how it is commonly described. It is rare to hear or read about the Arab oil boycott being directed against two countries in particular, the United States and the Netherlands.

96 Personal communication Louk Hulsman, 21 June 2003. Hulsman adds that, a few years later, American president Carter also wrote a letter to the UN, which however did not substantially the way the UN or United States handled the cannabis issue. It shows that UN drug treaties are apparently not easy to change.

97 Letter signed by Health minister Irene Horrink addressed to Professor Paul Reuter, Chairman of the INCB, dated, 15 April 1975.

98 From internal memos it appeared that the strict interpretation by the INCB of the 1961 provisions led to internal discussions and critical remarks among lawyers at Dutch ministries, who considered that the treaty allowed for some regulated use of cannabis leaves (Dossier BuZa DVE 1945-1984, map 4607).

population of town people always being much higher than in neighbouring countries. As Dutch sociologist De Swaan puts it: "Thus cities and city folk have set the tone throughout the centuries in the Netherlands, burghers were the trendsetters and the arbiters of taste".[99] The lack of central rule allowed urban communities to set their own moral codes. Since the major Dutch cities functioned as ports, "these large harbours came to adopt their own standards of policing and toleration, without much interference from royal courts as existed in the capitals of other countries (London, Munich, Paris, Madrid)".[100] The big harbour city Amsterdam went furthest in tolerating certain behaviours: "drinking and whoring have been a feature of the Amsterdam landscape for at least four centuries".[101]

Returning to the second half of the 1960s, it was in the cities of Amsterdam and Rotterdam where a lenient approach towards cannabis first began, as shown by the examples of the clubs in Amsterdam in 1968, and the Rotterdam pop festival of 1970. In the third biggest Dutch city, the Hague, the prosecutor had developed guidelines for prosecution, where a distinction was made between cannabis and other illicit drugs.[102] In 1969, these guidelines were taken over by other districts, which means that in that year, prosecutors in all districts differentiated cannabis from other drugs.[103] It is an example where the national level is being influenced by experiences at the local level.

Another clear example, later in the 1970s, which clearly shows the importance of the local level for policy making, is the care and treatment of drug addicts. The Netherlands is known as being among the first countries to have methadone programmes and to take other harm reduction measures. In 1968 the first Dutch methadone programmes were set up, but they were for opium users. The early 1970s saw the arrival of heroin, and by the mid 1970s, the methadone programmes were expanded to a larger scale. The reason why these programmes were set up so quickly in the Netherlands lies in the tradition of local policy making. Since the late nineteenth century Dutch cities had locally organised municipal health services ('GG&GD') that played an important role in public hygiene and combating infectious diseases. One task of the GG&GD was to offer health care to those who could not be reached by the normal health care system, such as the poor, homeless people, alcoholics, and prostitutes. The approach has always been more practical, seeking pragmatic solutions to

99 De Swaan (1993), *Accommodating Drinking Habits. The Control of intoxicating substances in the Netherlands*, 3. As De Swaan further explains, large estates were rare in the Netherlands and the landed gentry did not count much in the Republic, feudalism hardly existed in the marshy expanses of the early Netherlands, where cavalry did no dare set foot. As a result of this, there was not much of an aristocratic culture or a courtly civilization.
100 De Swaan (1993), *Accommodating Drinking Habits, 4*.
101 De Swaan (1993), *Accommodating Drinking Habits, 4*.
102 The Public Prosecutor in the Hague used three categories: incidental cannabis uses (1), regular cannabis users (2), and users of other drugs and dealers (3).
103 De Kort (1995), *Tussen patiënt en delinquent*, 214.

problems encountered, for which it had to adapt every time to changing situations.[104] Because a local health care system was already in place, the heroin users could relatively easily be added as a new category of people needing specific care and treatment. In the early 1970s, the municipal health authorities in Amsterdam set up mobile outreach teams that went out looking for drug users in need. By the end of the 1970s, the methadone bus was established, a mobile methadone supply system.[105]

In addition to Dutch political culture, the legal culture in the Netherlands has helped shape Dutch drug policy. For example, in the second half of the 1960s, it was possible for public prosecutors to deal with and make distinctions between various drugs, thereby handling them differently in their practice, on the basis of the expediency principle. The expediency principle allows prosecutors in certain cases to refrain from prosecution of criminal offences if this is in the public interest. If they choose not prosecute, there should be ponderous arguments to do so. For cannabis it was decided to apply the expediency principle systematically, if the quantity involved did not exceed thirty grams, the limit that had been defined between a criminal offence and misdemeanour. The rationale behind it is that public health interests (the protection of the citizens) are considered more important than criminalising citizens for the behaviour of consuming or possessing cannabis.

It is no coincidence that the *de facto* decriminalised quantity of thirty grams is almost equal to one ounce. Ironically, the introduction of the thirty grams rule in the Netherlands was inspired by American experiences.[106] The year 1970 saw passage of the U.S. Comprehensive Drug Abuse and Control Act. This act put marijuana in the same schedule of drugs as heroin and LSD, but it also lowered the maximum penalty for cannabis possession of one ounce or less.[107] It was this legal difference, set at one ounce, that was taken by the Dutch and transformed into a decriminalised quantity.[108]

The legal expediency principle not only opened up the way to decriminalising small-scale possession, but would in a later stage also open the way to

---

104 When hippies from all over started flocking to 'magical centre' Amsterdam, the GG&GD reacted to it and, for example, installed a special consultation for people without medical insurance, informally called the 'hippie surgery'. See Israëls & Mooij (2001), *Aan de Achtergracht*, 170.

105 In the early 1970s there were several initiatives of these mobiles teams, not only the GG&GD, but also the Jellinek clinic and Streetcornerwork. See Portegijs (1986), *Drugs in Mokum*, 93-95.

106 Some sources refer to this quantity as being enough or reasonable for a consumer to use for one month, and to be able to share some with friends. While these practical arguments may have been put forward, the thirty grams idea was originally taken from the United States, as can be read in section 4.5 of the Dutch policy paper, *Continuity and Change* by Ministry of Health et. al (1995). With thanks to dr. Peter Geerlings of the Jellinek Clinic for pointing at the American origin of the thirty grams rule.

107 Harrison et al. (1995), 'Cannabis Use in the United States: Implications for Policy', 183.

108 It can be discussed what decriminalisation exactly means. The strict definition is that an act is decriminalised when it is removed from criminal law. In the Netherlands this is not the case. The Chief Prosecutors Office's guidelines made possession of up to thirty grams of cannabis a misdemeanour.

the coffee shops. The policy makers never really meant to introduce a system of outlets selling cannabis. However, in the early seventies, the expediency principle offered some clubs the possibility of having a 'house dealer'– a person permitted to sell small quantities to consumers on their premises. The house dealer could only carry the 'allowed' decriminalized quantity of thirty grams. In a later stage, this system of house dealers opened the way to a new type of selling outlets, the coffee shops, who also started selling cannabis in small quantities, also making sure their stock did not exceed thirty grams. A customer could, in principle, also buy (and have) thirty grams. It was only after 1995, when a new governmental drug policy paper *Continuity and Change* was presented, that coffee shops got a more formal status and were allowed to have more stock, namely 500 grams, and the thirty grams possibility ceased being the basis of their existence.[109]

The expediency principle itself is not unique to Dutch legal culture, but the form it has taken in the Netherlands, called 'gedogen', to decide to systematically allow something that is formally illegal, and to even develop rules for it, can be said to be part of the Dutch legal culture. The Dutch coffee shop system is the most known example. Illegal cannabis is allowed to be sold, under conditions given in a series of guidelines set by the Chief Prosecutors Office. The rules are no advertising, no nuisance, no minors (under 18), no hard drugs, and a stock not exceeding five hundred grams.[110]

The historical example of clandestine non-reformed churches during the sixteenth century was already mentioned. While not officially allowed, they were tolerated and rules were applicable to them. Since the early seventeenth century a comparable situation exists for the brothels and prostitution. Another clarifying example is how the Amsterdam police dealt with homosexual encounters in practice. Since the 1930s, localities existed where homosexuals could find young men ready to accept their propositions in exchange for money. The police were aware of these officially illegal activities but did not interfere. Later, after World War II, the encounter places acquired some kind of semi-legal status and the owners reached an understanding with the police. As long as nuisance for others was kept down, the police would not intervene. Also, the police commissioner regularly consulted the homosexual community, which by then had just come into the open.[111]

---

109 This also gave the owners a more solid basis for existence. Before 1995 they were officially allowed to have only thirty grams but since almost no coffee shop could normally operate with such a small stock, owners always broke run a risk of drugs being seized by the police, or being closed down. And whereas before coffee shops operated in a legal vacuum, since 1995 a licensing system exists, which makes them at least formal selling points – although still of an illegal substance.
110 The rules are strictly applied. If during a police check a customer is found to carry hard drugs, the coffee shop owner has a problem, as it means the rule of no hard drugs was broken with the risk of the shop being closed. This is why certain coffee shop owners refuse access to clients who might be carrying hard drugs.
111 De Swaan (1993), *Accommodating Drinking Habits,* 4.

Gedogen, the systematic and official allowing of illegal practices has become part of the pragmatic Dutch way of dealing with undesirable behaviours. Instead of keeping them underground, the Dutch seem to prefer to have things take place out in the open. As Blankenburg and Bruisma note in their compendium *Dutch Legal Culture*, while illegal practices occur everywhere, in the Netherlands they are usually overt. At times they are explicitly tolerated by the authorities and are to some degree even treated as official policy. Blankenburg and Bruisma give the example of the practice of euthanasia, before it was legalised, as a good example of this dualistic aspect of Dutch legal culture. "The gap between the explicit prohibitions of the criminal code and the permissive medical practice was bridged by the end of 1993 with a by-law which requires every doctor to fill in a questionnaire for each natural death".[112]

As remarkable as the tolerance and pragmatism in criminal law might seem to the foreign observer, an even more discretionary application of legislation can be found in other fields. "In substantive civil law the court can circumvent a legalistic outcome by means of a general escape clause based on fairness and reasonability. If the ordinary civil procedure appears too long and complicated, one may initiate informal summary proceedings, handled by the court's president".[113] Blankenburg and Bruinsma explain that informality in civil law and tolerance in criminal law are not simply unintended and marginal phenomena, but they are deliberate and systematic. For the explanation they look at the working of the Dutch welfare system state and the making of policies. At every level the civil service implements policy, described in Dutch by the term *beleid*. "At a minimum, *beleid* implies a pragmatic use of the rules, which may result in more or less official recognition of authorities that they will not enforce the rules".[114] Peter van Buren, Administrative Law Professor and judge at the Council of State, adds to this that *gedogen* is "a human and understandable matter. It is a typical administrative tool. In order to reach certain administrative goals, one sometimes has to enforce, but sometimes one should not. It is also the task of the government to make certain that society functions. Many mayors and aldermen will then say this it is more readily possible when the rules are not always strictly applied – making allowance for them to be broken, instead of working strictly according to the book".[115]

Besides legal culture, there is also a legal climate. As the earlier section on the geography and history described, (respect for) individual freedom has been a strong sentiment in the Netherlands. Since its inception in the late nineteenth century, Dutch criminal law has been underwritten by the liberal constitutional

---

112 Blankenburg and Bruisma (1994), *Dutch Legal Culture*, 1.
113 Blankenburg and Bruisma (1994), *Dutch Legal Culture*, 2.
114 Blankenburg and Bruisma (1994), *Dutch Legal Culture*, 2.
115 Peter van Buren in a television documentary on the pros and cons of the Dutch cannabis system in the programme 'DNW' of VPRO television, 2001. Van Buren adds that under certain circumstances, Dutch law gives the possibility to even start a legal procedure against the denial of a *gedoog* permission!

state: the citizen's freedom has priority, and the state refrains from interfering.[116] Libertarian thinking was particularly strong in the 1960s and 1970s; John Stuart Mill's maxim from *On Liberty* – that the state should refrain as much as possible from behaviours that have consequences for the individual alone – was popular and used to be quoted a lot.[117] At the time, the Netherlands had the lowest prison population of (Western) Europe. It had, in fact, only been declining since the 1950s.[118] A critical attitude existed towards the use of criminal law as a way to solve social problems. The nomination of the reputed abolitionist Louk Hulsman, in 1968 to chair a drug advisory commission is therefore indicative of the legal climate.[119] Pieter Baan, who was chairman of the official governmental drug commission installed a year later, was, besides his job as chief inspector for mental health, also Professor of Psychiatry at the Criminological Institute in Utrecht and he had studied law as well.[120] The Criminological Institute – now named The Willem Pompe Institute – not only had an interdisciplinary and humanistic way of looking at criminality, but also had expressed a solidarity with the underdog and the delinquent; this contributed to the moderately lenient penal climate. In Baan's work as a clinical practitioner, the notion that the influence of others as a conditional factor for the origin and consolidation of deviant behaviour was already manifestly present in the 1950s, therefore coming well before the labelling theories of the 1960s.[121] This makes it unsurprising that, around 1970, Baan and his commission used the labelling theory as the scientific basis for suggesting a change from the stigmatisation and criminalisation of cannabis users.

4.5 Drug Trade and Drug Tolerance

In the meantime, the Netherlands has become increasingly caught up in international drug trade. The country appears to be a crossroads for international drugs traffic and is considered as one the centres of the European drug trade. In particular, its capital Amsterdam is a place where people from all over the world meet to conclude drug deals. Indigenous Dutch criminals have got a foothold in international trade of cannabis, and became internationally big cannabis traders

116 Kelk (1994), *De menselijke verantwoordelijkheid in het strafrecht*, 24.
117 Leuw (1995), 'Initial construction and development of the official Dutch drug policy', 29.
118 The imprisonment rate in the Netherlands per 100,000 inhabitants (as imprison rates are usually put) went from 50 in 1950 to 25 in 1975. In the 1980s, the Netherlands still had the lowest imprisonment rate of EU countries. But in the 1990s and the first years of the twenty-first century it has been rising very rapidly and the Netherlands now has the fastest rising prison population in Europe. For a broader analysis (in Dutch) on the question how punitive the Netherlands is, see Moerings (ed.) (1994), *Hoe punitief is Nederland?*
119 For his ideas, see for example Hulsman (1986), *Afscheid van het strafrecht* (originally published in French).
120 Kelk (1994), *De menselijke verantwoordelijkheid in het strafrecht*, 33.
121 Kelk (1994), *De menselijke verantwoordelijkheid in het strafrecht*, 27-33.

by smuggling hashish from Pakistan and Morocco, to both Europe and North America. Additionally, some Dutch ethnic minority groups are over-represented in certain drug trade: Moroccans in hashish, Turks in heroin, while cocaine is being smuggled from the Caribbean, either from the former Dutch colony Suriname or the Dutch Antilles such as Curaçao.[122] In 2002 and 2003 the cocaine smuggling (being swallowed or transported in the luggage) from the Caribbean happened on such a large scale that it necessitated special prisons be set up, for which the Dutch tradition of each detainee having his or her own cell, had to be abandoned. Since the 1990s, the Netherlands is considered to be one of the principal centres in the world for the production of ecstasy and other synthetic drugs. Whether the Netherlands is the world's biggest producer of ecstasy, as the American Drug Enforcement Administration (DEA) easily states, is difficult to determine because of the lack of comparable data and independent scientific research. The Unit Synthetic Drugs of the Dutch police, considers the Netherlands as one of the biggest producers of ecstasy in the world.[123]

The question exists, at this point, whether the importance in the international drug trade of the Netherlands, in general, and Amsterdam, in particular, can be explained by its liberal drugs climate and lenient drug legislation. It is a relationship that is easily alleged and often put forward by critics of the liberal approach. This argument is usually employed when other governments or government officials complain about drugs coming into their country, which have been determined to be of Dutch origin. Some argue it is the result of a generally liberal social climate in the Netherlands, as well as a culture which supports a high degree of personal freedom. But most of all, the argument has been put forward that the lenient drug legislation would appear to make the country an attractive place to be for drug traders. It seems tempting to explain the relatively important role of the Netherlands in the European and international drug trade, but in order for the argument to become a theory, it should be able to withstand scrutiny and investigation. The question therefore is to what extent is it correct that the drug trade can thrive in the Netherlands thanks to the Dutch legal culture or legal climate?

It is indeed a practical aspect of a liberal social climate, and importance attached to personal freedom that people in the Netherlands experience more freedom and are not 'bothered' to the same extent as in many other countries by law enforcement officials, such as for example identity checks and (body) searches. Hence, people involved in illegal activities like the drugs trade might have less chance of being caught. And, in the event of being caught, the relatively lenient drug legislation and the good prison conditions would make

---

122 See Fijnaut et al. (1998), *Organised Crime in the Netherlands*.
123 Although ecstasy seizures and law enforcement activity seems successful against trafficking networks connected to the Netherlands, anything that occurs elsewhere is generally unknown. See Gruppo Abele et al. (2003), *Synthetic Drug Trafficking in Three European Cities: Major Trends and the Involvement of Organised Crime*, 27-28 and 40-60.

punishment relatively bearable. In other words, these different factors combined, could make the Netherlands a safe haven for drug traffickers, and explain why this country plays a relatively important role in the international drug trade.

The argument is built on the assumption that (potential) drug traffickers rationally consider and compare countries in order to decide from which to operate. The reality, however, is that professional drug traffickers do not expect to be caught.[124] As a consequence, very few of them will find it necessary to make such a cross-country risk-of-being-caught analysis. The idea that relatively lenient penalties in one country will attract more crime and more criminals, is based on the (same) supposition that tougher penalties – the death penalty being the most extreme case – lead to less crime. However, it has been proven from criminological research that such laws do not have such a deterrent effect. For most professionals involved in organised crime, national borders do not really matter, as they consider the European Union as just one market. Factors other than the toughness of the legislation are determinant for their actions; more specifically, a very important reason for engaging in drug trafficking is the profit motive. And, if drug legislations were really so powerful and as effective as proponents like to claim, fewer people would take the risk of smuggling drugs into the United States where penalties for drug crimes are severe. Traffickers sought by the American authorities for this reason are not even safe in other countries, as it is likely their extradition is to be asked, or otherwise, they may be kidnapped.[125] The reason why people from many nationalities do smuggle drugs into the United States is because it offers so many possibilities: the American drug market is so enormous that a lot of money can be earned. The same is true for some Asian countries where drug smuggling from a certain quantity automatically leads to the death penalty, but it still does not stop people from doing it.

That the liberal policy facilitated the drug trade, appears true for cannabis. Several reasons can be suggested why the Netherlands – and Dutch criminal organisations – have attained an important international position in the cannabis trade. One reason can be found in the tolerant policy towards cannabis since its retailing has become permitted in the coffee shops since the 1970s. This has led to a situation in which the trade in cannabis was also receiving a lower priority by law enforcement. As a result, during the 1970s and 1980s the police barely exhibited any interest in the import and trade of cannabis.[126] Also, the coffee shop system allowed some drug traffickers to have regular and solid sales, enabling them at the same time to launder some of their drug money. Some drug traders were able to construct coffee shop 'empires' through a lucrative chain of

---

124 This was one the findings from interviews with criminals in the Netherlands and the United Kingdom. These interviews were part of a big report on the extent of organised crime in the Netherlands, as part of a parliamentary inquiry into organised crime in the Netherlands.
125 Such events have happened in several countries, for example, in Jamaica. General Noriega, former President of Panama of one of the most known examples of a smuggler being covertly kidnapped and taken to the United States.
126 Fijnaut et al. (1998), *Organised Crime in the Netherlands*, 60.

coffee shops. A parallel can be drawn with the age-old Dutch tradition and skills of commercial trade all around the world.

Another reason can be found in a certain tradition of smuggling, going back to the butter and cattle smugglers in the South of the Netherlands during the post-war period. This trade was well organised and some smugglers shipped cattle as far the United States. In the 1960s, some of these smugglers shifted to the production and trade in synthetic drugs. This was partly to cater to local markets, but most was destined for export to Scandinavia, and Sweden in particular. In the 1980s and 1990s the Netherlands, especially the South, became an important producer of synthetic drugs for the international market. According to the American drug enforcement officers, the Netherlands is responsible for 80% of world production, which would make it the ecstasy equivalent of what Colombia is for the cocaine trade.[127] That the Netherlands has such an overwhelmingly major international role in the ecstasy production is unlikely, however, and has not been supported by hard data. These statements should therefore merely be interpreted as political declarations, part of the 'usual' negative portrayal, by American drug enforcers, of the Netherlands as a country where both drug use and drug trade have got totally out of hand.[128] Still, it remains true that the Netherlands is a major producer of ecstasy and other synthetic drugs. The tradition of producing and trading illicit synthetic drugs cannot explain everything though. Another part of the explanation lies in the fact that the Netherlands is home to several big chemical industries (DSM, Akzo) which facilitated access to ingredients (precursors) of synthetic drugs and their production.

However, the aforementioned factors could not have facilitated the rise of the illegal drug industry without what should be considered the main factor, the Netherlands' geographical position and its dominant role in transport and distribution. Being Europe's main distribution centre, it makes the country highly suitable for drug trade. The argument can then be made that more than its liberal policy towards drug and small drug trade, it is this geographical condition that drug traders have exploited, giving a comparative advantage to the Netherlands. Damián Zaitch interviewed Colombian cocaine smugglers and asked them why they shipped cocaine transports through the Netherlands. The reasons and advantages given for shipping cocaine to the Netherlands were: the huge volumes transported through both airports and seaports, the infrastructure, its central location in Europe, a good business climate as well as financial and banking being well represented and finally the attractiveness of Amsterdam as in international meeting point.[129]

---

127 As a Dutch police officer involved in fighting ecstasy production once described it.

128 A lot of the production of synthetic drugs in the world remains unknown or is not studied a lot, such as production in Eastern Europe, East Asia, as well as for example South Africa, one of the first countries were ecstasy was produced.

129 Zaitch (2001), *Traquetos*, 82-91.

Considering the importance of the Netherlands for the international drug trade, the fight against this trade has become the number one target of Dutch law enforcement authorities. A large part of their capacity is devoted to fighting drug crime. Law enforcement officers sometimes went too far in fighting drug crime, and struck 'deals' with criminals in order to fight bigger criminals, a situation that got out of hand – with drug shipments being imported under the 'control' of the police – which led to a parliamentary inquiry.[130]

Immigrant ethnic minority groups in the Netherlands have also taken advantage of the trade and distribution possibilities of the country they came to live in. This was facilitated by the fact that the main immigrants groups in the Netherlands come from drug production or drug transit countries.[131] Most Moroccans living in the Netherlands originate from the Rif area, the mountainous area in the North, which also is home to the most significant cannabis (hashish) production area in the world. Another important immigrant group in the Netherlands is Turkish. Since Turkey plays a key role in the European drug trade, Dutch Turks have also become involved in this trade.[132] The logistic advantage of the Netherlands as a distribution centre also plays a role here, of course.

Besides cocaine being smuggled to the Netherlands by ships from South America, it also comes in from the former South American colony, Suriname, as well as from the Dutch Antilles. It has become common to transport cocaine by plane, with the contraband hidden in a suitcase, strapped onto the body, or swallowed. This type of cocaine trade is first explained by the proximity of both Suriname and the Dutch Antilles to the cocaine production countries, and as well as transit zones of South America. These factors combine with local factors, such as the weak state government in Suriname. In the 1990s, the military rulers were directly involved in the cocaine trade. This is not unique to countries in this part of the world, but since the same number of Suriname people live in Suriname as in the Netherlands (an estimated 400,000 in each place), it is clear that there exists an abundant travel, back and forth, of both of people and goods, providing a opportunity for the cocaine trade. Cocaine comes in from the Dutch Antilles as well, a trend that has increased considerably around 2002. Since the Caribbean is a major cocaine trafficking zone and the islands themselves are not adequately equipped for fighting this lucrative trade in the Caribbean Sea, cocaine is smuggled from all of the Caribbean islands. This is especially prevalent from those islands that are characterised by corruption and economic difficulties. The worsening economic tide in the Dutch

130 See Fijnaut et al. (1998), *Organised Crime in the Netherlands*. It should be noted that controlled deliveries are common and accepted in some other countries, notably the United States where they are known as stings. There were some indications and rumours of American Drug Enforcement Administration (DEA) involvement in the cases of the controlled deliveries by Dutch police.
131 See Bovenkerk (1998), 'Organized Crime and Ethnic Minorities. Is There a Link?'.
132 See Bovenkerk & Yeşilgöz (1998), *De maffia van Turkije*.

Caribbean since the late 1990s led not only to an influx to the Netherlands of many middle class people who hoped to find better work opportunities, but also led to a sharp increase in (poor) people smuggling cocaine by plane.

In summary, the reason why the Netherlands plays a relatively important role in the European and international drug trade has not so much to do with its drug laws, but more with the country's strategic location, its well-developed port systems, and its major role in trading and distribution of goods in general, of which the trade oriented Dutch, as well as immigrant groups, often from drug producing or transit countries, managed to take advantage. Combined, these factors make the Netherlands an attractive place for trading drugs, as well as producing them before sending them off to the consumer markets.

The question whether the law enforcement policy for the drug trade has been too 'liberal', is difficult to answer. It may be argued that since Dutch drug policy is primarily health oriented, combined with the liberal penal tradition which means the Netherlands does not have a large police apparatus, the drug trade was not the first priority of law enforcers. It is plausible this was to some extent the case in earlier stages, such as with cannabis during the 1970s and 1980s, and ecstasy production and trade in the (early) 1990s. It is also possible that the authorities underestimated the logistic attractiveness of the Netherlands for these types of trade, as well as the business attitude of some Dutch drug dealers and producers, who were more aware of these possibilities. On the other hand, both among law enforcement officers and judges there is a growing body of opinion that considers that fighting drugs already takes too much of their capacity and time, and they think that they should spend more time going after other criminals.

Since the 1990s, the penal climate has changed and more measures have been taken to curb the international drug trade. Harsher penalties for the production and trafficking of hard drugs were introduced, with an additional focus on synthetic drugs, in particular, ecstasy. A special team, the Synthetic Drugs Unit, was created to co-ordinate the efforts of police, public prosecutors, the Economic Investigation Service (ECD), and tax, customs and also intelligence officials.

In 1995, a new three party coalition government published a drug policy paper entitled *Drugs Policy in the Netherlands: Continuity and Change*.[133] This was generally considered to be a major evaluation and review.[134] A major public debate ensued among politicians, government officials and drug specialists, and drug policy regularly made front-page news. It was thought by many that the government would now go forward with the cannabis policy and put an end to the ambiguous situation surrounding coffee shops – which are allowed to sell to consumers, but where the purchase of stocks remains formally illegal, especially

---

133 Ministry of Health, Welfare and Sports et al. (1995), *Drugs Policy in the Netherlands. Continuity and Change*.
134 See Boekhout van Solinge (1999), 'Dutch Drug Policy in a European Context'.

since two of the three coalition parties had clearly advocated its legalisation in their party platforms. It was therefore thought that this government would take initiatives to further regulate the cannabis market, in particular the unregulated supply side. In addition to these political motives, there was also a practical reason to review the drug policy. Most of its underlying principles dated back to the mid 1970s, and during a twenty year period various elements of the policy had been reviewed, although it had never been evaluated in its entirety. The new government seemed likely to undertake such a task.

Ultimately, the policy paper proposed only minor changes in the existing situation. Some of these measures called for more restrictions on drugs, such as lowering the maximum quantity of cannabis purchase from thirty to five grams, which led many foreign commentators to (rightly) conclude that these were a response to international criticism, particularly from France. The simultaneous relaxation of other restrictions attracted far less attention, as they amounted to a restatement of policies already in place, or even moves toward further liberalisation. Although foreign criticism undeniably played a part in some of the stricter measures taken, the overall drug policy did not change in any fundamental way, neither in principle, nor in practice. The harsh criticism expressed by the French president Chirac – already unpopular because of the nuclear tests he reinitiated – on the 'lax' cannabis policy only seems to have reinforced support, even of some of those who previously did not support Dutch cannabis policy.

What remained was the biggest and most fiercely debated issue of Dutch drug policy, the so-called 'front door-backdoor problem' of the coffee shops, the discrepancy between the sanctioned sales to customers and the illegal way these products are cultivated and traded to the coffee shops. Regulating this supply proved to be too sensitive politically in view of the international political context. A political compromise was found in new guidelines for cannabis growing. The more plants being grown and the more professionally it is done, the higher the penalties would be. In reverse, if the cultivation was unprofessional and the number of plants did not exceed five, the plants would still be seized but criminal sanctions would be absent. By introducing these guidelines, the government hoped that many small-scale growers with no more than five plants were going to supply the coffee shops, to the detriment of the larger illegal suppliers. Since the Netherlands is a country with a strong horticultural tradition and 'grow shops' already existed – shops selling equipment for cannabis cultivation – this new policy could be easily implemented.

In retrospect, it can be said that the government's position has been some-what naïve, as it has underestimated the huge financial gains that can be made by growing cannabis. Frank Bovenkerk described how cannabis cultivation has sometimes been taken over by organised crime groups.[135] Politicians and policy

---

135 See chapter six of Bovenkerk (2001), *Misdaadprofielen.*

makers are well aware of the ambiguous status of cannabis, but have had to proceed by moving between two polar realities. The first pole is that of not wanting to criminalise cannabis users, and the other pole is not being able, as yet, to fully legalise cannabis. At the local level, where authorities are confronted with the practicalities of this 'front door-back door problem', politicians call for local experiments. A group of some sixty mayors of Dutch cities, belonging to all main political parties of the Dutch political spectrum, including some political heavyweights, asked the government for authorisation to start local experiments with coffee shops being supplied by licensed growers. A majority in the Dutch Parliament voted in favour of such an experiment – and most parties are, in principle, pro-legalisation – but the government has refused to execute it because of "the international context".[136]

The coffee shops themselves, have become an international symbol of the country's drug policy. While the value of coffee shops is understood they are considered to be too many in number. If there were less, it was decided, they could be more easily controlled. It was then decided to gradually cut down their number by implementing a stricter application of the rules set out by the College of Prosecutors-General. These rules included provisions that no minors would be allowed to frequent coffee shops, even if accompanied by parents, and that no hard drugs were to be sold on the premises, The rule not allowing hard drugs in coffee shops has been widened from not selling, to also include not being allowed on coffee shop premises. This means that the coffee shop is also responsible for visitors carrying hard drugs. The owner therefore has an interest in keeping people out if he suspects they might be in possession of hard drugs. The owner risks closure if the police raid a shop and find cocaine, ecstasy or other hard drugs in someone's possession during a search. Coffee shops have in fact now been closed on this basis. While in 1997 some 1,200 coffee shops were operating in the Netherlands, by 2004 their number decreased to approximately 800.

Although it was decided at the national political level to decrease the number of coffee shops, it is actually at the level of the municipality where the decision is made as to whether a municipality desires to have a coffee shop or not. This is, of course, in line with the tradition of local policy making. The national association of municipalities VNG assists municipalities with the development of a local drug policy, irrespective of the question whether it wants a coffee shop, or not – the latter being the zero option. Some of the bigger cities, like Amsterdam, with some three hundred coffee shops, and Rotterdam, with several dozen, clearly want to get the number down. Many medium sized municipalities, where the demand is big enough to support a coffee shop, decide to allow one to open, as they prefer the cannabis market to be above ground instead of

---

136 This appeared again in 2003 when a retiring court president made a plea for cannabis legalisation, which led to public and political debates and which showed that most major parties (forming a clear parliamentary majority), except the Christian Democrats, in principle supported legalisation.

underground. Some municipalities have advertised to find operators and candidates who can present themselves, while some others have created a non-commercial foundation in order to monitor the business themselves.

With respect to the use of cannabis, a certain number of informal norms have developed. As in most countries, drug use itself is not against the law. Although no formal rules prohibit cannabis smoking in public places, bars or restaurants, very few people do so. If they do, no sanctions are applied; but the person is likely to be asked to put it out by the personnel of a shop, bar or restaurant, or alternately, to smoke outside. The absence of formal regulations for the use of cannabis has opened the way for these *informal* norms, and their existence is an aspect of Dutch drug policy that seems difficult to grasp for foreigners. For example, some young tourists visiting Amsterdam think cannabis can be smoked 'everywhere', not understanding that, generally, it is something that primarily belongs in the private sphere. It is done at home, or in special places like coffee shops.

The Dutch policy on hard drugs is generally quite different, although some aspects of it are based on the same principles as the cannabis policy. One basic assumption is that users of hard drugs should not be punished for that behaviour alone. Consistent with the normalisation model, the police leave drug users in relative peace unless they cause public nuisance. On the same condition, even street dealing is tolerated to some extent. Just as a quantity of cannabis has been defined as being small possession for personal use, the possession of heroin or cocaine in quantities not exceeding 0.5 grams is defined as a petty offence with a low prosecution priority. Depending on the circumstances, such a small quantity of hard drugs, if found on a person, may actually be returned to them.

Since users of hard drugs are treated with relative lenience, this practically means problematic or marginalised drug users are relatively readily visible as compared to countries with more restrictive policies. Rather than retreating into less visible parts of town, Dutch heroin or crack-cocaine users are often seen in the main shopping and entertainment areas of the cities. One result of the public presence of these drug users who appear to be a public nuisance, is that they give heroin a very negative public image. Hence, for most young people, there is nothing glamorous or attractive about heroin. It is now widely seen as a drug for losers. In this sense, the visibility of drug addicts seems to have become an effective prevention measure. Since problematic drug use is considered more a social and medical issue than a criminal one, interventions with drug users are generally non-punitive, with particular emphasis on care and treatment. Because the extensive care system is diversified and offers many low-threshold pro-grammes without too many conditions to enter, it is estimated that the services reach about 70% of all heroin addicts.[137] Methadone and needle exchange

---

137 Van den Brink et al. (1999), *Medical Co-Prescription of Heroin to Chronic, Treatment-Resistant Methadone Patients in the Netherlands.*

programmes are designed for addicts who are not yet 'ready' to quit the habit. Because of the low-threshold nature of such programs, they are a good way of establishing and maintaining contact with the addict population.

The low-threshold availability of methadone has also served to turn heroin addicts into discriminating consumers. The relative stability of both the heroin user population, and in the demand for the drug has caused heroin prices to drop to as low as thirty euros a gram (of some 30 percent purity). The availability of this cheap heroin has led more addicts to prefer 'chasing the dragon', as smoking heroin is known, rather than injection, as their route of administration. Because smoking heroin carries a far lower risk of contracting infectious disease than does injection, this method of utilisation has been encouraged among drug injectors by street health workers, such as of the organisation Mainline which had a special 'switch' campaign. An advantage of the availability of cheap heroin, in combination with the easy availability of methadone supplements has made it possible for drug users to maintain an addiction while earning a low income or subsisting on welfare without resorting to property crime or prostitution. A clear disadvantage is that the cheap heroin attracts consumers from other countries, especially in the summer, which can lead to noise and nuisance. Heroin has for long been the main drug among the population of problematic users, but since the 1990s crack-cocaine has been on the rise and it has in some drug scenes replaced heroin as the main problem drug.[138]

Since the 1990s the term 'drug nuisance' has in general become one of the new key words in drug policy, especially at the local level. Heroin arrived on the Dutch market in the early 1970s. In 2002, the average age of the heroin user was approaching forty.[139] Since the average age rises by almost one each year, the influx of new young users is very low. From a public health point of view, the heroin epidemic is under control. From a public order point of view, however, the situation is not under control. However cynical it may sound, the emphasis on health and harm reduction aspects of Dutch drug policy has led to low morbidity, which practically means that problem users in the Netherlands do not die in the same numbers as elsewhere. However, the tolerance towards deviant lifestyles has gone down. In order to combat nuisance of problematic and criminal drug users, the possibility of compulsory treatment has been introduced.

Besides these repressive measures, more harm reduction measures have been implemented as well. An experiment has started with the legal prescription of heroin to long-term users who tried to kick the habit several times. After a pilot

---

138 Boekhout van Solinge (2001), *Op de pof.*
139 In 1997, the mean age of heroin users enrolled in a methadone programme in Amsterdam was 39; for Rotterdam (in 1995) this was 34. Since the inflow of younger users has been low, the mean age has been increasing by ten months each year since 1984. See Van den Brink et al. (1999), *Medical Co-Prescription of Heroin to Chronic, Treatment-Resistant Methadone Patients in the Netherlands.*

ɔle, which was conducted in Amsterdam and Rotterdam, the ⸻xpanded to other cities and included 750 people.[140] A measure ⸻d with the hope of combating nuisance, and promoting harm reduction, ⸻s the installation of users rooms, where people with a pass can go in and in relative tranquil circumstances, can use the substances they have brought in. Some cities experiment even further, such as Rotterdam where underground places were allowed to sell crack-cocaine in small quantities to people with a pass.[141] Over the course of years, Rotterdam's Reverend Hans Visser has given shelter to homeless and marginalised drug user and he has selected some dealers to sell heroin and cocaine on the premises, a practice that was restricted, though, by the police.

The examples show that Dutch drug policy remains experimental, and open to new approaches. Although it has become more repressive in some aspects since public nuisance has become a policy issue, the Dutch approach has remained primarily health-oriented. The Dutch public health attitude towards drugs also is clearly represented in the attitude towards the latest Dutch drug phenomenon, the smart shop, selling legal psychoactive substances such as stimulants and psychedelics, including psychedelic mushrooms. After a toxicological study ordered by the Ministry of Health showed they posed no danger to public health, the shops were allowed to continue their existence.[142]

---

140 Van den Brink et al. (1999), *Medical Co-Prescription of Heroin to Chronic, Treatment-Resistant Methadone Patients in the Netherlands.*

141 This public prosecutor limited the project when the media got hold of it and started asking questions.

142 According to a court verdict on psychedelic mushrooms and their status in the Dutch opium act, these mushrooms are only legal if they are in a unprocessed form. Hence, in Dutch legal terms, the drying of these mushrooms is considered as processing, which makes them illegal. Dried magic mushrooms are therefore prohibited; fresh, raw ones are not. Smart shops have used this possibility to sell them. The Dutch Ministry of Public Health stated after a study that these psychedelic mushrooms do not pose a health risk that could justify their prohibition. See Bosch et al. (1997), *Psycho-actieve Paddestoel- & Plantproducten. Toxicologie en klinische effecten.*

Chapter 5

The Restrictive Swedish Model

5.1 Drugs in Sweden

Between 1965 and 1975, Sjöwall and Wahlöö authored ten popular crime novels which were translated into several languages. This couple wrote innovative detective novels which integrated popular fiction into a vehicle for social criticism.[1] Their books also contain strong elements of social realism, by which they founded a Swedish tradition of crime fiction. Not only is the police work described in raw detail, but there is also the depth necessary to explore complex social conditions and the economic mechanisms underlying crime.[2] From their first book, *Roseanna* (1965) and onwards, their detectives offer in-depth descriptions of urban Sweden. Their last book, *The Terrorists* (1975), is a bitter analysis of the welfare state which deifies the criminals as revolutionaries.[3] In their books, the modern phenomenon of urban deviance in Swedish society is fairly represented: alcoholics, moonshiners, prostitutes, drug dealers and hashish smokers.[4] Sjöwall and Wahlöö portray Sweden as a modern society where illicit drugs are becoming part of the urban landscape. However, in their books only marginal place is given to drugs compared to the prevalence of alcohol, alcoholics and street thugs.

This is no surprise, as Sweden is a country where drug use is relatively low compared to other EU countries. Swedish teenage drug use is among the lowest of the EU member states.[5] Statistics show that reported recreational or experimental drug use has gradually decreased from the 1970s to the 1990s, but since then the trend has reversed. During the 1990s, the proportion of fifteen and

---

1   As Per Wahlöö said in an interview, their intention was to "use the crime novel as a scalpel cutting open the belly of the ideological pauperised and morally debatable so-called welfare state of the bourgeois type" (see «www.kirjasto.sci.fi/wahloo.htm»).

2   Michaëlis (2001), 'On the Trail of Scandinavian Crime fiction. Scandinavian Crime Novels: too much Angst and not enough entertainment?', 15.

3   At the end of the series, the central figure police officer Martin Beck is ambivalent about remaining a policeman, fearing he is contributing to the violent nature of Swedish society, rather than preventing it. See: «www.kirjasto.sci.fi/wahloo.htm».

4   In *The Fire Engine That Disappeared* (1969) some sings of hash smoking and drug dealing occurs.

5   Portugal and Sweden report the lowest drug use in the EU among 15-16 year school-going teenagers. See «www.emcdda.org».

sixteen year old school students who used drugs has more than doubled, from three and four percent of girls and boys in 1990, to eight and ten percent in 2000.[6] The yearly survey, held among 18 year old male military conscripts, shows a similar trend. Whereas in 1992 seven percent had used illicit drugs, in 2002 this figure had grown to eighteen percent. Surveys show that the majority of those who have used drugs, have tried cannabis; amphetamine is the second most used substance.[7] Despite the increase in teenage drug use in Sweden, it remains among the lowest in the EU.

With respect to problematic drug use, Sweden finds itself in the middle range of the countries of the EU. In 1998, the number of heavy drug users in Sweden was estimated at 26,000.[8] Earlier surveys from 1979 and 1992 estimated their numbers respectively at 15,000 and 19,000.[9] Hence, the 1977 national objective of a drug-free society did not prevent the number of users from rising. What is notable about the Swedish situation in comparison to most European and Western countries where heroin became the main problem drug, is that in Sweden it was amphetamines. In Sweden, the typical problem drug user is injecting amphetamine and belongs to a deviant criminal subculture. Heroin use remained marginal long after its arrival on the Swedish market in the mid 1970s. However, heroin use has increased in the 1990s, particularly in the suburbs of Sweden's bigger cities,[10] low income urban areas, characterised by high unemployment, that are home to many immigrant families. With amphetamines being the traditional problem drug, and heroin use on the rise, the two substances are now on about the same level.

Many Swedes are worried and puzzled by the rise in drug use. They see drugs as being something 'un-Swedish' and belonging outside of traditional Swedish culture. In this country which more or less invented the concept of the welfare state and its social engineering potential, drugs are considered a problem that should be kept at bay. In 1977, the official goal of Swedish drug policy was defined as achieving a drug-free society. This declaration of intent took place during a decade when Swedish recreational drug use was decreasing. Despite this decline, politicians still aim at getting the number down even

---

6   National Institute of Public Health (2001), *National Report Sweden 2001*, 20. In 2002, the figures were 8% for both sexes.
7   CAN (2001), *Trends in alcohol and other drugs in Sweden. Report 2001*, 44.
8   In the Swedish context, a heavy drug user is defined as intravenous drug user or as someone using cannabis on a nearly daily basis. In practice the large majority of problem drug users are drug injectors; problem cannabis users represent 8% of the sample, as stated in the EMCDDA report.
9   Three figures come from the three surveys, based on the capture-recapture method, that were coordinated by Börje Olsson of Stockholm University. The earlier surveys in 1979 and 1992 first estimated the number of heavy drug users somewhat lower, namely at 12,000 and 17,000. These have however been adjusted in the latest survey. See Olsson et al. (2001), *Det tunga narkotika-missbrukets omfattning i Sverige 1988*, or see National Institute of Public Health (2001), *National Report Sweden 2001*, 17. For a discussion of the earlier estimates, see section 6.2 of Boekhout van Solinge (1997a), *The Swedish Drug Control System*, 139-143.
10 CAN (2001), *Trends in alcohol and other drugs in Sweden. Report 2001*, 46.

further with the hope of reaching the desired status of a drug-free state.[11] That a great majority in the Swedish Parliament voted for the objective of a drug-free society only showed that there existed a broad Swedish consensus on the unacceptability of drugs. Figures that showed a decrease in recreational drug use – mostly in the form of decreased hashish consumption and to a lesser extent decreased amphetamine consumption – were interpreted as a sign that Swedish drug policy was effective.[12]

Swedish drug policy became an international model. Unlike the internationally dominant trend of drug policies that only minimally managed to curtail drug use, or worse, were incapable of curbing it at all, Sweden presented itself as the example of a country that had actually succeeded in reducing the number of drug users. The Swedish experience gave hope to those rejecting liberalisation trends and believing in stricter approaches as a way to control drug problems. Swedish drug policy was presented as successful, a policy that 'worked', based on the positive ideal of a drug-free society containing welfare state elements such as treatment programs. The Swedish model became an appealing alternative both to repression and liberalisation and was soon labelled 'the Swedish model'. Tellingly, in the 1930s, the expression 'Swedish model' had initially been used to describe the labour market, and in a later stage, it grew to define the Swedish welfare state as a whole. Since the 1980s, however, it increasingly came to be used for the restrictive drug policy.

The paradox in Swedish drug policy is that in itself, the Swedish drug problem is relatively small, as compared to other European countries, although public opinion perceives it as an enormous social problem. Drugs are considered a larger problem than issues such as pollution or the economic crisis. Drug (ab)use is perceived as almost as serious as assaults and family violence.[13] The use of drugs is generally considered as being very deviant and problematic because officially every instance of use is automatically considered abuse. Most Swedes support the restrictive approach; a more liberal approach, it is generally thought, would result in more drug problems.

In the late 1960s, Parliament laid down Swedish drug policy, based on three pillars: prevention, control measures, and treatment.[14] Prevention is the overriding principle of the drug policy. Drug prevention and so-called opinion formation form an integral part of school programmes. Some children get their first

---

11   The school survey among grade 9 pupils (aged 15-16) is held since 1971, when drug use was estimated at fifteen percent. At the end of the 1970s it had dropped to a little less than ten percent. It should be noted though that problematic drug use was rising in this decade.

12   This was especially based on the survey among military conscripts. The decrease in drug use among them started around 1980, when the restrictive approach was initiated. Supporters interpreted this is as being the result of the policy. A more accurate analysis would show that the decrease in recreational drug use among 16 year olds started already in the mid 1970s, before the restrictive approach. Moreover, problematic drug use also increased during the 1980s.

13   Hübner (2001), *Narkotika och alcohol i den allmänna opinionen*, 217 and 247-248.

14   Tham (1998), 'Swedish drug policy: A successful model?', 396.

drug education at the age of seven, and by the age of twelve almost every child has been informed about drugs. Parents of all school children receive a copy of the *Hash Book* when their child reaches the age of 14-15. This book advises about the dangers of cannabis. Besides structural drug prevention as part of the school curriculum, the occasional big anti-drug campaigns are launched, with billboards announcing the dangers of drugs. Campaigns promoting awareness on the dangers of drug use are generally presented dramatically.

The second pillar of Swedish drug policy consists of control measures. Since the end of the 1960s, there has been substantial tightening of the control related aspects of drug policy, particularly following the 1977 goal of a drug-free society.[15] Earlier in that decade, the police focused on combating big dealers and drug imports; drug use was not criminalised and cases of small quantities of cannabis and amphetamine were dismissed. This changed around 1980, with the focus of law enforcement shifting from the supply to the demand side. At that point, the emphasis was placed on disturbing the market, in particular targeting drug users, considered to be the motor of the 'drug engine'. The Prosecutor-General restricted the possibilities of dismissing drug cases and in 1988 the use of drugs was criminalised as a fineable offence. The penalty was increased in 1993 to include six months imprisonment. The justification behind the last measure was not the desire to imprison drug users, but to make it legally possible to conduct mandatory drug tests on potential drug users, which is only possible under Swedish law for offences that are punishable with imprisonment. This law permits the search of a person who is not possessing drugs, but who, nonetheless, is suspected of being under the influence. Thus, the person can be taken to a police station and be forced to undergo a urine or blood test in order to verify the suspicion of recent drug use.

The reason for introducing the urine tests is that they enable authorities to find new and previously unknown drug users. However, statistics indicate that most alleged drug users brought in for urine tests are in reality older drug addicts who were previously known to the authorities. The police introduced the Rave Police as an addition to their forces; young undercover officers who go to rave parties, pick up drug use suspects and take them to the police station for a urine test. Later in the 1990s these control activities were extended to bars and clubs as well. Approximately 10,000 urine tests are currently performed on a yearly basis. Of all the young people whose blood or urine was tested, one third tested negative. In 2000, in the National Council of Crime Prevention's policy evaluation criticism of the drug detection tests was expressed as violating the personal integrity of the young people subjected to these. In more general terms, Swedish drug control has been stepped up in the 1990s; the number of drug

15   Tham (2003), 'Drug policy and trends in problematic drug use in Sweden', 5.

officers within the police force has almost doubled (to approximately 900) and a steep rise has been observed in the number of young people being arrested.[16]

Finally, the third pillar of the Swedish drug policy is treatment. Large amounts of money are available for treatment, especially in-patient treatment centres on the countryside. A key expression often used is the 'caring chain', which points to various elements within the treatment system, for example, outreach activities, detoxification, outpatient care, and institutional care. Social workers play a key role in this chain. Swedish authorities, some of which are, in practice, social workers, have the right to intervene deeply into people's private life. For the sake of the greater public's good (to reach a drug-free society), individual freedom may have to be scarified. For example, social workers have the authority to decide on coercive treatment, based on the laws that came into effect in 1982, LVM and LVU. Therapeutic communities, however, have for a long time, been the most dominant form of drug treatment. It had not been uncommon for drug users to spend one or two years in these communities that are usually found in rural areas. In the 1990s, however, changes in financing methods, as well as budget cuts, which mean that the burden of paying for drug treatment would then fall to local authorities, has led to fewer people being sent into treatment. In fact, it means that the caring chain has all but been dismantled now.[17] In 2000, in the context of rising drug use, the decision was made to make more money available for treatment again. The option of compulsory treatment, decided upon by social workers, also exists since 1982. This is a system applied not only to drug users, but alcoholics as well. The program duration is a maximum of six months. Although it is often under discussion, this type of treatment is not frequently applied.

Harm reduction is not an element of the official Swedish drug policy. It is considered as 'giving up' and in contradiction with the goal of a drug-free society. This explains why the methadone and needle exchange programmes that exist in Sweden are not labelled as harm reduction. It is for this same reason that Sweden has used its veto power when references to harm reduction measures in the European Union have arisen. Eventually, however, a compromise was struck agreeing that no overt terms could be employed. The agreement was that a euphemism, however, could be substituted.[18] Methadone programmes do exist however, and have a long history, as the first European methadone programme started in Uppsala in 1966. The methadone programmes have relatively strict criteria for participation and all exist on an experimental basis, allowing a maxi-

16 Tham (2003), 'Drug policy and trends in problematic drug use in Sweden', 7-14.
17 Another reason for cutting down on in-patient treatment is that it started when Sweden was afraid of a HIV-epidemic and wanted to get potential spreaders off the streets. Without an epidemic, an important reason for in-patient treatment disappeared.
18 This explains why EU texts use euphemistic terms such as "measures that may stop the spread of infectious diseases", terms that are acceptable for the Swedes. Although in practice they come down to harm reduction, the sensitive words are not employed.

mum of 800 participants.[19] However, since the legal prescription experience of 1965-67 when opiates and, in particular, amphetamines were made available by prescription to a group of drug addicts, there is a strong reluctance to introduce any more legal prescription programmes. Sweden is also reluctant about initiating needle exchange programmes. In the late 1980s, the National Board of Health and Welfare proposed the introduction of needle exchange programmes in light of the HIV epidemic, a position that was adopted by the government. However, this resulted in fierce protests in the form of popular mass movements, as well as protest from professional associations. The proposal was then squashed by Parliament in 1989. The argument had successfully been put forward that a higher availability of needles would not stop the spread of HIV, but on the contrary would increase intravenous drug use.[20] This explains why the two needle exchange programmes that exist in the southern cities Lund and Malmö remain, officially, as scientific projects operating on an experimental basis.

This chapter attempts to explore the origin and development of Sweden's restrictive approach towards illicit drugs. Looking for explanations, it would appear obvious to look first at Swedish alcohol policy. Sweden has a strong temperance tradition and has historically maintained a strict alcohol policy, which makes a restrictive drug policy a logical option. But in order to understand Swedish drug policy, it is also important to look at the Swedish drug experience – or more precisely: the construction of the Swedish drug experience. The Swedish drug epidemic began officially with the 1965-67 drug prescription experiment. Prior to the 1965-67 drug prescription experiment Sweden had several decades experience with legal amphetamines. But in search of the real underpinnings of Swedish drug policy, and the goal of a drug-free society, it is important to take a more fundamental look at certain aspects of Swedish society. This includes the role of popular mass movements, and the strong tradition of a social democratic welfare state.

5.2 Geography, History, and the People

Sweden is one of Europe's largest countries, covering 450,000 km2. Its Nordic location, at a latitude comparable to Alaska and Greenland, means that great contrast exist between the seasons, with long light summer days and short dark winter days. Relative to the country's size, the number of inhabitants is small. At approximately nine million citizens, Sweden has one of the lowest population densities in the EU. A third of the population lives in the country's three

---

19 For example, users must go through a detoxification period of a few days, so that they are drug-free when entering. If drugs have been used, which is regularly checked through urine tests, they are expelled for two years. Section 6.3 of the next chapter discusses the other participation criteria more in detail.

20 Gould (1994), 'Pollution rituals in Sweden: the pursuit of a drug-free society', 86.

urban areas: Greater Stockholm (1.7 million), Gothenburg (800,000) and Malmö (500,000).The urban population is relatively small for a modern industrial country, thus a significant part of the population still live in the countryside or in smaller towns. Many city dwellers cherish their roots in the countryside, which they often visit, and which probably explains the general respect Swedes show for their landscape and natural environment.

The Swedes' Viking past is probably considered, internationally, to be the best known part of their history, although this period was relatively short, lasting from the ninth to the twelfth century. The stereotypical Viking is a tall, blond, physically powerful figure possessed with a raging fury that he unleashes upon other countries.[21] In reality however, not all Vikings manifested this kind of rage. In particular, it has been attributed to a special group of Viking warriors known as the 'berserkers'.[22] Their 'berserker rage' is sometimes associated with the intake of hallucinogenic mushrooms such as the Amanita Muscaria, while others attribute it to the consumption of massive quantities of alcohol.[23] Manoeuvring their ships over seas and rivers, the Vikings both raided and conducted trade through out Europe, including Britain, Ireland, and the west coast of continental Europe (with French Normandy bearing their name to this day.) They ventured as far south as the Mediterranean, Middle East, and eventually set foot in North America.[24] While the Vikings from regions identified today as Norway and Denmark ventured west and south-west, those from Sweden usually set forth in easterly and south-easterly directions. These Swedish Vikings travelled down the Russian rivers to reach the Black and Caspian Sea. In Constantinople, they were to provide bodyguards for the emperors of Byzantium for more than a century.[25] They even made it to Baghdad, exerting an influence so great that 90% of all the Arabic coins from Baghdad and surroundings found in Europe, were actually found in Southern Sweden.[26]

---

21 See «www.luth.se/luth/present/sweden/history/viking_level.html», a Luleå University website on Swedish and Viking history.

22 The berserker did not fight in armour but in bearskin ('ber sark' in the Nordic languages) which gave them their name. The berserker is also closely associated with the god Odin, also known as Wodan, meaning fury.

23 Fabing states that the discordant behaviour of wild rage or 'going beserk', "may not have been a psychologically determined habit pattern, but may rather have been due to the eating of toxic mushrooms. This idea, fantastic though it may appear at first glance, has won general acceptance among Scandinavian scholars according to Larsen (who was then provost at University of Illinois in Urbana and whose personal communication served as a source.) See Fabing (1956), 'On Going Berserk: A Neurochemical Inquiry'.

24 On the East coast of North America, such as Canada's Newfoundland, archaeological evidence of Nordic visits has been found, some four centuries before Southern Europeans would 'discover' the continent.

25 Comparable to the Swiss Papal guards in the Vatican. See Coles (1949), *The Lovely Land. An interpretation of the Realm and People of Sweden*, 95.

26 It is on the island of Gotland in the Baltic Sea where the Arabic coins were found. It is also worth mentioning that more ancient English coins found in Sweden than there are in England. Source: Luleå University website on Swedish and Viking history.

The political history of Sweden over the last centuries was characterised by feudalism and a working class struggling against poverty. In the early nineteenth century the feudal and hierarchical past ended but by the mid-nineteenth century, Sweden was one of the poorest countries in Europe. A very large part of the population (70%) worked in agriculture, many of them under very difficult circumstances.[27] In the second half of the nineteenth century the Swedish economy underwent many profound changes towards industrialisation but this did not mean that the standard of living went up. In fact, the consequences of the agricultural and industrial revolutions were so severe that, around 1900, Sweden still was a country with widespread poverty. "Poverty was becoming rampant in underdeveloped Sweden which could not provide jobs for its burgeoning population".[28] Poverty led to a mass exodus of Swedes hoping to find a better future abroad. The destination in many cases, was North America, and in particular the United States. The first exodus started between 1853 and 1873 when some 100,000 Swedes, representing more than three percent of the population, made the passage. A few years later, after 1879, emigration once more escalated. Between 1851 and 1930 some 1.5 million persons emigrated from Sweden, which was roughly a third of the total population, which totalled 3.5 million in 1850 and 6 million in the 1930s.

This mass migration drew attention to the need for improving social conditions. In order to halt migration, massive efforts were undertaken to increase economic prosperity and improve social conditions in the country. Offering (social) security became what the new Sweden wished to offer its people. The plan succeeded, which makes twentieth century Swedish history remarkable. Sweden experienced a steady development from an agricultural, poor society into one of Europe's most industrialised and wealthiest countries. As Hans-Ingvar Johnsson put it, "it was a dramatic change".[29] From this moment forward, Sweden could offer *trygghet*, a Swedish word, Wijkström notes, more evocative and warm than its translation 'security'.[30]

The Social Democratic Party, founded in 1889, played a central role in this development. The party came to power in 1932. Working in close collaboration with the trade unions, it laid the foundation for the Swedish welfare state, a combination of economic growth and advanced industrial capitalism directed towards export – based on a Keynesian economic policy – and the distribution of the welfare among the people – by conducting a social welfare policy. Since its inception the party had close ties with the trade unions and throughout the development of the Swedish model the latter played their part. Through the organised efforts of the unions, in close interaction with the employers and the social democrats, labour disputes were kept to a minimum and employment was

---

27 Johnsson (1995), *Spotlight on Sweden*, 125.
28 Johnsson (1995), *Spotlight on Sweden*, 21.
29 Johnsson (1995), *Spotlight on Sweden*, 125.
30 Wijkström (1996), *Movements, Members and Volunteers in Sweden*, 4.

offered to most of the work-force, in some periods leading to a full employment situation.[31] Except for a three-month interregnum in 1936, the social democratic party stayed in government until 1976. By that time, the Social Democrats had been governing for 44 years, a period not matched by any other social democratic party. The Social Democrats were in power again from 1982 to 1991 and since the 1994 elections they are governing again. This makes Sweden probably the democratic country with the longest history of social democratic rule.

From the moment the Social Democratic Party came into office, they started developing a programme for the social welfare state, or as it was called, the people's homeland: *folkhemmet*. The society, with an important role to the state, would protect all individuals. No one would have to suffer any longer from distress or poverty, and in the case that someone 'fell out', for one reason or the other, society's safety net would come to the rescue. Because of the exceptionally long period the Social Democratic Party was in power, a strong social democratic tradition has arisen, with some of the traditional social democratic ideas having become generalised and shared by other political parties as well. In the decades following World War II, the welfare model matured, eventually leading to, as Tilton put it, "the Swedish welfare state's distinctive character – provision of largely universal services of high quality affording *trygghet*".[32] It is indeed the *trygghet* (security) that is the most important virtue of the Swedish welfare state. In the second half of the twentieth century, Sweden became an international prototype of the welfare state and modern society. As Gould notes in his recent book on Swedish social policy, modern Sweden was positivistic, technocratic and rationalistic, believing in the malleability of an ideal social order.[33] Sweden's economic and social success, in the central decades of the last century, encouraged outsiders and Swedes to see it as a model for the rest of the world:

> "The commitment to a modern, ordered, rational society became a source of national pride and identity. Sweden was in the forefront of technological and scientific developments, and its art and urban planning were influenced by functionalistic ideals. Its labour movement was disciplined and based on values of sobriety and solidarity. All of this gave rise to an understandable sense of national superiority. Swedish welfare was regarded as a model to follow for others. Their leadership role was not only attributed to Sweden by its outside admirers; it was proclaimed by Swedes proud of what their country had achieved."[34]

---

31 This is why it is sometimes said the trade unions changed the face of Sweden. The Social Democrats are still heavily dependent upon their support, such as the blue-collar trade union federation LO that represents over two million workers or 90% of the blue-collar work-force and a part of the white-collar trade union federation TCO that represents 75% of the white-collar labour. See Tilton (1991), *The Political Theory of Swedish Social Democracy*, 2-3.
32 Wijkström (1996), *Movements, Members and Volunteers in Sweden*, 4.
33 Gould (2001a), *Developments in Swedish Social Policy. Resisting Dionysus*, 16.
34 Gould (2001a), *Developments in Swedish Social Policy*, 26 (see also page 15).

The Swedish welfare state sought to create an ideal social order, improve society, and to elevate its people. The other side of the coin however is that in order to reach an ideal state, its personnel (a term borrowed from Max Weber), usually social workers, have the right to intervene deeply into people's private lives. Whereas the solidaristic tradition of the social democrats had affected most aspects of social policy, social services continued to display characteristics of paternalism, charity, the work ethic, individualism, repression, and Puritanism.[35] Hence, in order to create the ideal people's homeland without too many social problems, it would be, within the Swedish context, possible to take far-reaching measures.

The most drastic example probably was the compulsory sterilisation of thousands, 90% of them women, "to prevent the birth of individuals who, most likely, must become a burden to themselves and others".[36] These measures were taken in the context of a degeneration danger, which became one of the most potent images of social threat in Scandinavia.[37] "Most things were considered hereditary: crime, a propensity to commit rape, mental handicap, but even the inability to be thrifty, masturbation and vagabondism".[38] In total, some 60,000 people were sterilised between 1935 and 1976, when the eugenic project was stopped. Gould notes that many chroniclers of the welfare state have concealed the details and their recent revelation in the late 1990s has encouraged the government to set up a commission of inquiry and propose compensation.[39]

Another example of far-reaching measures is the Contagious Disease Act of 1989. This measure had been enacted to prevent the further spread of infectious diseases. So it was that once an administrative court had considered a person capable of putting others at risk, for example by having unprotected sex or by sharing needles with people carrying an infectious disease such as HIV, they could be forced to enter preventive detention in a hospital ward.[40] This measure has given Sweden a bad name in the international gay community, although it is mostly used for drug users and the mentally ill.

Another example of state intervention introduced in the 1990s is a strict new prostitution policy that aims to rid the country of both prostitution and the exploitation of women. These measures provide for the prohibition of sex for hire. Consistent with the desire to support women's right and to prevent their exploitation, instead of prohibiting the phenomenon itself, only those purchas-

35 Holgersson (1994), 'Building a people's home for settled conscientious Swedes', *Scandinavian Journal of Social Welfare* Vol. 3 3: 113-120, quoted in Gould (2001a), *Developments in Swedish Social Policy*, 19-20.
36 Smith and Zaremba, 'Outcasts from Nordic super-race', *The Observer* 24 August 1997, quoted in Gould (2001a), *Developments in Swedish Social Policy*, 24.
37 It should be noted, though, these types of eugenics projects were not unique to Sweden.
38 Zaremba, 'Delusions of racial purity', *Guardian*, 3 September 1997, quoted by Gould (2001a), *Developments in Swedish Social Policy*, 24.
39 Gould (2001a), *Developments in Swedish Social Policy*, 24.
40 Email Communication of the Swedish Office of the Ombudsman against Discrimination on grounds of Sexual orientation, December 2003.

ing a prostitute's services were criminalised. The measures became a mainstream political issue and were ratified in the Swedish *Riksdag* by a two to one margin.[41]

In order to understand the Swedish approach to dealing with illicit drug use, and deviance is general, it is useful to consider the Swedish culture and mentality. To begin this exploration, it would seem logical to start with an observation of several natural elements that define the country, namely, latitude, and climate and low population density. All are conditions that have either shaped, or to some extent, at least influenced its development. A history of long, cold, dark winters in isolation contributed to the somewhat closed personalities of the Swedes today. In his comprehensive book *Swedish Mentality,* Åke Daun describes Swedes as being rather solitary people. The national stereotype is "a peaceful person who dislikes unruliness and disorder and who prefers calm, and who may be described as clean, quiet, industrious, and modern."[42]

The Swedes can be said to be a combination of modern and traditional. These paradoxical elements manifest themselves in various ways. On the one hand, for example, the Swedes easily embrace new technologies, as is shown by the early and widespread use of mobile phones and the Internet. Another sign of modernity within Sweden is the gender equality. According to the UN, it is the most gender equal country in the world.[43] On the other hand, Swedes are very much attached to their traditions and in some ways reject too much modernity. Many people who live in the city like to spend their weekends and holidays traditionally in a cottage in the country or in nature, where they exchange their modern households accessorised with electronic equipment for a simple cottage minus modern amenities such as electricity and running water. It should also be said that this pattern has become less prevalent among the younger generation.

The strong social democratic tradition has left its mark upon Swedish society. Social democracy in Sweden has connotations of pride and solidarity. Liberalism on the other hand, has a negative connotation. Criminologist Henrik Tham explains that the tradition of liberalism lacks strength in Sweden because in the rest of Europe liberalism as a political philosophy flourished in cities during the nineteenth century when Sweden was still a predominately rural society.[44] On the other hand, social democracy did flourish, and Swedish people are indeed proud of what it has achieved. Older people, particularly those who have experienced the gradual changes, are proud of the Swedish accomplishments and the virtues of the welfare state. Through this system, a long-standing history of poverty was replaced by a new system that brought well-being, welfare and security. This comfort and security led society to feel a great deal of

---

41 Gould (2001a), *Developments in Swedish Social Policy*, 123. See also Gould (2001b), 'The Criminalisation of buying sex: the politics of prostitution in Sweden'.
42 Daun (1996), *Swedish Mentality*, 2 and 22.
43 Gould (2001a), *Developments in Swedish Social Policy*, 110.
44 Tham (1995b), 'From Treatment to Just Deserts in a Changing Welfare State'.

confidence in the Swedish state in accordance with what was perceived as the state's successful social engineering. The Swedish attitude towards the state and 'system' can generally be described as positive, and rarely suspicious or distrustful.[45] This explains why the aforementioned and far-reaching measures for creating the perfect people's 'homeland' did not meet much resistance. Naturally, this extensive Swedish welfare system is, an expensive one, but because Sweden combined economic growth with a progressive tax system, it was affordable. However, in the early 1990s the favourable economic picture of the twentieth century ended and Sweden was faced with the deepest economic crisis since the 1930s.[46] Some elements of the welfare state were no longer affordable, leading to the demise of the security offered by the welfare state. It was in 1995 during this period of economic downturn that Sweden joined the European Union.

The Swedish population is relatively homogeneous. Nearly 90% of the population of Sweden is Lutheran. Although only 10% regularly attend, many of the church traditions are still discernible in society. For example, most children are baptised, and most undergo their confirmation at the age of fifteen. Weddings and funerals generally take place in the church.[47] Also from an ethnic-sociological perspective, Sweden can be labelled as a homogenous society, although more than one million of the population (13%) is defined as immigrant. Within this context, it should be noted most immigrants in Sweden originate from other Nordic countries, Finns in particular, making Swedish multiculturalism appear less colourful than multiculturalism in other European countries. This near-sighted diversity is partially explainable by Sweden's imperial past which did not extend beyond Northern Europe which meant that large groups of non-Nordic immigrants did not arrive until the 1980s.[48] However, this drastically changed in the 1990s. Political refugees began emigrating from the former Yugoslavia, the Middle East (Iranians, Iraqis, and Kurds) and East Africa (Eritreans, Ethiopians and Somalis). The large numbers of these recent arrivals has changed the total composition of the immigrant population considerably.

---

45 Tops (2001), *A society with or without drugs?*, 76.
46 To give some figures: GDP declined by 7.5 %, the national debt as a percentage of GDP climbed from 45% to 80%, and unemployment rose from 1% to almost 9%. For an average European country this may not be very high, but between 1970 and 1990 Swedish unemployment had always been very low, between 1.2% and 3.5%, and had never exceeded 4%. The situation turned out to be chronic; during the rest of the 1990s unemployment stayed around 8-9%, including government-financed or subsidised training programmes, the unemployment rate was 12%-13%. See Lachman et al. (1995), *Challenges to the Swedish Welfare State*, 1 and 134.
47 In the late 1980s two-third of the marriages took place in church.
48 Since the 1960s immigrants started to include groups from further afield, like the Mediterranean (Yugoslavia, Greece, Turkey), and political refugees from the Middle East (Lebanon, Syria) and Latin America (especially Chili), but these numbers were relatively small. In the late 1980s and early 1990s Sweden no longer received immigrant workers; the only immigrants arriving since the late 1980s are family members of earlier immigrants, as well as political refugees.

In addition to its relatively homogeneous population, social values in Sweden are also oriented towards conformity. For example, in the capital city of Stockholm which is home to more than one million inhabitants, there are few signs of a counterculture, eccentrics, or alternative clothing. Many Swedes consider their own views as normal, while eccentricity is not regarded positively. As Daun puts it: "Swedish culture stresses sameness and conformity and plays down differences in encounters with others. (...) Swedes tend to stress similarities and disregard dissimilarities". Deviance from group norms and common group patterns is regarded as a potential threat to the individual.[49] The Swedish emphasis on similarities rather than differences, and the desire not to deviate, which in practice results in conformist behaviour, also helps bring understanding to the general attitude towards deviance. Of course, this is also, or perhaps even more true for drug use, given the explicit official goal of establishing a drug-free society. Swedish drug users are considered outcasts. Traditionally, the common problematic drug user is injecting amphetamine and has ties to the criminal subculture. The extent of their deviance is often symbolised by leather jackets and tattoos as well as in their lifestyle and behaviour. In the Swedish view, the typical problematic drug user might be profiled as someone who participates in nocturnal activities that combine well with their amphetamine use, such as driving around in stolen cars or drinking beer.

In discussing Swedish people and their attitudes towards behaviour they consider non-normative, it is relevant to stress Sweden's geography. International cultural developments are generally strongly related to metropolitan cultures and lifestyles. It is in the 'liberal' cities where new, different and non-conformist behaviour is more accepted than in rural areas. A partial explanation for the Swedish reluctance towards the relatively 'new' and unknown phenomenon of illegal drug use might be found in Sweden remaining a predominantly rural country that has been historically lacking a strong urban tradition with its concomitant liberalism. Swedish life still seems to go at a slightly slower pace than in much of urbanised Europe.

The Swedish emphasis on 'sameness' and the tendency to conform to group norms out of 'solidarity', means that an emphasis upon individualism is not strongly rooted. As Daun writes, the individual is considered weak, except when representing an organisation. Formal groups and organisations, on the other hand, are considered strong and influential.[50] This explains the important role of *folkrörelse,* or popular mass movements, in Sweden. Since their beginnings in the nineteenth century, popular mass movements have played a vital role in Swedish society as means for bringing about change. Traditionally, strong

49 Daun (1996), *Swedish Mentality*, 2-22, and 103-109.
50 Daun (1996), *Swedish Mentality*, 106.

popular mass movements are the Labour Movement,[51] the Free Church Movement, and the Temperance Movement. The Free Church Movement consisted of the formation of new Protestant churches alongside the traditional and established Lutheran state church. The popular movements at the time were progressive and reformist, and occasionally revolutionary. "In an historical sense, the traditional Swedish and Scandinavian popular mass movements were also part of an anti-authoritarian – although comparatively peaceful – struggle against oppressive state and capitalist structures during the formative years."[52]

An official definition of the term *folkrörelsen* does not exist, but it is commonly and widely used in Sweden, without a need to specify its exact meaning. The first attempts to interpret it were made in the 1940s by Thörnberg, who defined the movements as "organised efforts in relation to certain values".[53] An important aspect of these movements is that they are based upon a general conviction that something has to change, sometimes with a touch of rebelliousness, and the belief that it is possible to satisfy these desires.[54] Wijkström adds that the term *folkrörelsen* has a strong positive connotation, implying goodwill, a positive link to the general public, and it could be viewed as a term of honour with an almost ceremonial significance: "The word appears still today to have a tremendously positive ring. There is a smell of participation, active and engaged people, protest and democracy – people on the move towards a goal."[55] The way popular movements function and the importance they have in Swedish society, probably explains the notion of the 'collective' that is so strongly present in Sweden. Popular mass movements are so deeply rooted in Swedish society that the Swedish non-profit sector of today cannot be understood without paying attention to the role of earlier popular mass movements. It is occasionally said that the role played by *folkrörelsen* and their members is of fundamental importance to democracy and welfare in Swedish society and public debate.[56] However, time and change also come to *folkrörelsen* as well, and it can be seen

51 Closely linked to the labour movement were the study circles, the first of which was found in 1860. Socialistic and revolutionary, study circles emerged out of the nineteenth century poor working class. People's education ('folkbildning') was seen as a means to change society. Since the 1930s the socialistic aspect is not very evident, but many study groups are still connected to political parties and the notion still exists it is important to have knowledge and to get organised in order to get something done in society. Obviously, the influence of the organised efforts of the trade unions throughout the economic success period has also played its part in this respect.
52 Wijkström (1996), *Movements, Members and Volunteers in Sweden*, 4.
53 Quoted in Wijkström (1996), *Movements, Members and Volunteers in Sweden*, 3.
54 To be called a Popular Movement, an organisation must be nationally established, having several regional or local branches, which allows them to receive state subsidy. Some of the popular mass movements are politically active and they sometimes have formal links to a political party.
55 Peter Antman quoted in Wijkström (1996), *Movements, Members and Volunteers in Sweden*, 3.
56 In an international perspective, a large proportion of Swedes belong to associations (which includes sport clubs, study circles and popular mass movements). Swedish associations have approximately 32 million members which means that on the average every Swede is a member of almost four associations. Less than one out of ten Swedes are not a member of any association. See Wijkström (1996), *Movements, Members and Volunteers in Sweden*, 8.

that the traditional popular mass movements are losing membership and therefore no longer have the same influence they once had. The Temperance Movement for example, could still claim a membership of more than ten percent of the adult population in the 1950s,[57] but in the following decades they lost membership and consequently have been less able to exert the same kind of influence they once had. On the other hand, because they have had a significant presence for a long period of time, "many of the earlier popular mass movements have become highly integrated with established society and are now part and parcel of that".[58]

Following in the footsteps of the traditional popular mass movements, new popular movements have arisen that are active in new areas, such as the environment, human rights, and illicit drugs. Not only have these new social movements become more influential than the traditional ones, the system seems to have developed to an extent that it is acceptable to speak of a 'social movement industry'. In the words of Wijkström, "the Swedish popular mass movements of today (...) seem to be large *systems* of organisations. Most of the popular mass movements found nowadays are actually a giant complex of organisations (...)".Another concept used is that of the Social Movement Industry, that "comprises all social movements pursuing similar goals".[59] As will be described later in this chapter, it seems that this situation is applicable to the anti-drug popular mass movements. Whereas the popular mass movements against alcohol held long standing influence in Sweden, in the twentieth century they have gradually lost authority with the general public. This has led to a severe decline in the Swedish Temperance Movements that now appear to be slowly dying out; their membership is mainly composed of elderly people and is quickly on the decrease. On the other hand, the twentieth century, more precisely the late 1960s, witnessed the rise of a new category of popular movements, active in the field of illicit drugs, which had a tremendous impact on Swedish drug policy.

5.3 A Restrictive Alcohol Policy

To understand why Sweden has a restrictive drug policy, it is useful to look at the policy aimed toward the most familiar and commonly used drug in Sweden, alcohol. The Swedes have a complicated relationship with the substance. Many Swedes think that they cannot really control it, which explains why the alcohol policy has long been restrictive. Against this background, it is understandable that society would be inclined to opt for a restrictive drug policy. As this section will show, this is indeed the case; an understanding of the policy applied toward

---

57 Gould (2001a), *Developments in Swedish Social Policy*, 156.
58 Wijkström (1996), *Movements, Members and Volunteers in Sweden*, 6.
59 Wijkström (1996), *Movements, Members and Volunteers in Sweden*, 7.

the use and regulation of alcohol sales and use, is essential for interpreting Swedish drug policy. This discussion will begin by taking a closer look at alcohol use in Sweden.

Sweden is said to belong to the 'vodka belt', the zone stretching from Europe to America including countries like Canada, Russia, Poland, and the Scandinavian countries. The most common intoxicant traditionally used in this zone was alcohol, particularly strong or hard liquors. An important reason for the traditional use of stronger liquors is that wine could not be produced due to the climate so beverages like beer and ale could not be stored and were difficult to distribute.[60] Being part of the vodka belt, the Swedes therefore have a tradition of drinking vodka (*snaps*).

It is internationally assumed that Swedes drink a lot. However, compared to many other (European) countries, the total consumption of pure alcohol per capita is not very high; alcohol consumption in countries with a beer or wine tradition is generally higher.[61] However, an important feature of Swedish alcohol consumption that explains the misconception Swedes drink a lot is their consumption *pattern*. As can be read in official publications, the Swedes have a "culturally-established drinking pattern" in which alcohol is widely used "as a means of intoxication rather than a table drink".[62] More precisely, the dominant consumption pattern is a typical Nordic intoxication oriented drinking pattern, which is also found in Sweden's neighbouring countries. When it comes to drinking, the aim is to get drunk. As a matter of fact, the expression 'drinking' in Sweden already expresses that a state of drunkenness will probably be reached. The reason given is that Swedes are not able to use alcohol in a controlled or moderate way, an argument also often put forward by Swedes themselves.

The explanations for the Swedish alcohol consumption pattern vary from naturalistic, to climatological, to social-psychological. For example, it is sometimes said that the intoxication oriented consumption pattern is inherited from the fierce and wild Viking spirit, a theory that could be described as naturalistic. Another explanation puts the emphasis on climatological factors (the cold and dark climate), in other words tedious natural conditions that, in the spirit of Montesquieu, would have led to the Swedish melancholic psyche and, consequently, has generated a desire for intoxication.[63] Another, third possible reason

60 Lenke (1991), *The Significance of Distilled Beverages. Reflections on the Formation of Drinking Cultures and Anti-Drug Movements*, 5.
61 National Institute of Public Health (1995b), *Swedish Alcohol Policy. Background and present situation*, 37.
62 Ministry of Health and Social Affairs (1993), *The Swedish Alcohol Policy. Caring About People's Health*, 4.
63 See the section 'The Influence of Climate on Mood' in Daun (1996), *Swedish Mentality*, 163-165. A clear example of the fact that the climate affects the psyche is that when the dark Swedish winter do not have much snow, more Swedes go into light therapy. When there is snow, it reflects the little sunlight and gives the impression of more light.

for the drinking pattern is related to the traditional work mentality of the Swedes, in which the (social) drink functions as a reward for the work that has been done. Traditionally, Swedes working in the woods were away from home for a long period of time. Coming home, a glass would be raised for the end of the working period, and the start of leisure time.

Supportive for the latter explanation is that the use of alcohol today is still strongly related to leisure time. The clear distinction between the working week and the weekend is symbolised by the fact that Swedes tend to buy their alcohol on Friday afternoon, after work and just before the weekend. Since many people do this, it means of course they have to queue.[64] As a rule, the alcohol bought on Friday afternoon is the amount required for the weekend. For most Swedes, drinking is limited to the weekends. They drink and get drunk on Friday and Saturday night,[65] but are sober on Sunday again since it is followed by Monday. As a result, few Swedes have alcohol in their homes on weekdays. Again, this may lead to the easy conclusion that Swedes are not able to control their alcohol use, but this argument is hardly convincing in view of the cultural fact that they are generally capable of controlling themselves. It is just here where a deeper explanation can be found for the traditional intoxication oriented drinking pattern. The behaviour of the – normally – emotionally disciplined Swedes can change dramatically when alcohol comes into the picture. What people are usually not 'allowed' to do, suddenly becomes possible or can be overcome. As Daun put it:

> "One of the social and psychological functions of drinking in Swedish culture is to lessen the individual's fear of making a fool of him- or herself - for example the anxiety people feel about saying the wrong thing. Instead, under the influence, it is permitted to be 'too' aggressive, 'too' sentimental, 'too' loud or gay. The individual then never – or seldom – is accountable for breaking the norms. (...) What matters to the drinker is less the psychological effects of alcohol than the 'cultural ticket' to a freer and more irresponsible pattern of social interaction."[66]

It is common for the individual to blame abnormal or deviant behaviour on alcohol. Under the influence of alcohol, the individual is no longer responsible for their own behaviour-the alcohol takes over eliminating inhibitions and the ability to behave in a socially acceptable manner. The functionality of this pattern of alcohol use becomes clear by looking at the social rules and obliga-tions of Swedish and Nordic culture. The (internalised) social norms intended to establish how people are to behave, are oriented toward controlling emotions. Foreigners frequently report that they find the Swedes to be 'cold'; Swedes also see themselves as 'stiff'.[67] One interpretation of why The Swedish drinking

---

64 Until recently it was not possible to buy alcohol during the weekends.
65 Another 'typical' moment for drinking is when Swedes (and other Nordic people) leave the country (hence when they get 'out' of their normal working week).
66 Daun (1996), *Swedish Mentality*, 51.
67 Daun (1996), *Swedish Mentality*, 112. Daun's chapter 'Feelings' is very interesting in this respect.

pattern focuses on intoxication could be that it is an appropriate and functional balancing point for the general shyness and inhibitions that characterise the collective timbre of Swedish emotional life. Drunkenness can be said to enable people to let go, to let their hair down, thereby 'stepping out' of the social control system. In their 1969 study, *Drunken Comportment,* a study of the different forms of alcohol intoxication assumes in different cultures, Craig MacAndrew and Robert Edgerton identified this function of drunkenness as 'time out' behaviour.[68] This hypothesis is supported by the observation that Swedes do not always appear to be as physically intoxicated as their exaggerated or dramatised drunken behaviour might indicate.[69] In this respect it is relevant to note that public drunkenness and its corresponding behaviour, are more socially accepted in Sweden than in other Western, and certainly, Southern Europe societies, where alcohol use has different patterns and functions.

Although the ingrained drinking habits of the Swedes are historically and culturally rooted, they are changing. Drinking patterns in Sweden (and other Nordic countries) are becoming more like those in the rest of Europe, especially among younger people. In the 1990s 'European drinking' became the new expression to describe the new pattern of alcohol consumption. This term means drinking one or two glasses after work, without necessarily getting drunk. So, it appears that the traditional intoxication-oriented pattern is becoming modified. It would be too simple, however, to conclude that the new drinking pattern means that self-regulation is developing. In fact, there already was a form of self-regulation, namely limiting drinking to the weekends. The significant change is that alcohol consumption patterns are diversifying. Drinking no longer equals 'getting drunk'; it now also means drinking moderately.

A possible explanation for this diversification could be that alcohol has become more accessible since the 1990s. EU membership and domestic pressure – polls indicated most Swedes were tired of some aspects of the restrictive alcohol policy – led to a gradual liberalisation of the strict alcohol policy.[70] Before there was an external alcohol control policy in place, users did not internalise attitudes that would lead to moderate alcohol consumption. But a lessening of official restrictions, in a broader sense, has ushered in the recognition of a need for change within the individual. In the last decade, these changes in public policy have included the relaxation of rules for obtaining an

68   With thanks to Ted Goldberg of the Institute of Social Work of Stockholm University for signalling the work by MacAndrew & Edgerton (1969), *Drunken Comportment.* In this, in the alcohol field, landmark study it is shown that alcohol intoxication takes different forms in different cultures.

69   See Boekhout van Solinge (1997a), *The Swedish Drug Control System,* a book with more field observations than in this chapter. Robin Room, commenting on drinking as 'time out' behaviour and drunkenness as an explanation of bad behaviour, reminded that the idea of a licence for 'time out' is supported by social psychological experiments among American college students that showed it was the belief they were getting alcohol rather than whether there was actually alcohol in the drink that changed their behaviour. See Room (1993), 'Alcohol and Crime: What Kind of Links, and Can We Break Them?', 2.

70   Gould (2001a), *Developments in Swedish Social Policy,* 159.

alcohol license, a decline in alcohol prices, as well as a substantial increase in the number of bars. Until recently, cafes were obliged to serve food in order to receive an alcohol license. Additionally, restaurants operated with the restriction that 70% of their turnover had to be food-related. Today there are many places such as bars and restaurants that serve alcohol, on the condition that they serve some kind of food. International cultural influences also play their part – which is true for both alcohol and drugs. With alcohol becoming more readily available, people find other use patterns and attribute other function to it. For example, a bar culture is developing which gives alcohol use a different function than solely 'getting pissed'.

When it comes to the Swedish alcohol policy, its main aim is to reduce total consumption. The underlying idea is that this reduces both the social and medical damage that results from alcohol use. Two main strategies used for limiting alcohol consumption are restricting the availability of alcohol through a state monopoly on alcohol, and by manipulating the price mechanism.[71] But before looking more closely into the alcohol policy, some background factors will first be discussed. This includes the temperance movement, Swedish alcohol policy during the twentieth century, and the total consumption model that furnishes the scientific basis of the actual alcohol policy.

It was noted previously that Sweden belongs to the so-called vodka belt, that is, the zone of countries with a tradition of stronger liquor drinking. In the nineteenth century the temperance movement would get a foothold in Swedish society and be of great influence on the creation of alcohol policy. In the alcohol literature, Sweden is considered one of the nine temperance cultures: the English speaking cultures of the United States, Canada, the United Kingdom, Australia, New Zealand; and the Nordic societies of Finland, Norway, and Iceland are the others. It is interesting to note that historically, a considerable portion of the alcohol consumed by people in all these countries was in the form of distilled liquor: vodka, gin, rum, or whisky. Another characteristic of these cultures is that they are predominantly Protestant. But again, what they do not share is heavy drinking. Temperance cultures are not characterised by heavy drinking, because in temperance cultures people consume significantly less (pure) alcohol per capita than people in non-temperance societies.[72]

The rise of the Temperance Movement has to be understood by the high alcohol consumption that occurred at the time these groups emerged. In 1820, alcohol consumption, was about five times higher than it is today, with liquors with strong Vodka-like qualities among the most commonly consumed. People were allowed to distil their own spirits, (*brännvin*), until 1860, when Parliament withdrew this right under pressure from the Temperance Movement.[73] Abundant

---

71 See Ministry of Health and Social Affairs (1993), *The Swedish Alcohol Policy*, 1.
72 Levine (1992), 'Temperance cultures: concerns about alcohol problems in Nordic and English-speaking cultures', 20.
73 Johnsson (1995), *Spotlight on Sweden*, 60.

alcohol use also occurred during the period of industrialisation. "The social dislocation caused by the industrial revolution led many to solve their social misery by resorting to alcohol".[74] The main aim of the temperance movement was to achieve absolute abstinence from alcohol and a complete ban of the substance. The temperance movement had grown particularly strong by the end of the nineteenth century. This movement was one of the main social movements of the time, and had strong links with the labour movement. Temperance Movements emphasised the damaging properties of alcohol. For example, it was argued that alcohol destroyed a drinker's self-control and self-discipline, and that it would weaken the parts of the brain where higher and moral decisions were made. "Temperance supporters in the nineteenth century also maintained that alcohol was an inherently addicting drug (the way people often think of heroin today), and that it eventually enslaved people."[75]

Despite its influence and strong popular roots, the temperance movement never managed to achieve total prohibition in Sweden. Eventually the outcome was a restrictive system consigned to a state monopoly that controlled alcohol sales. In 1917, the 'Bratt System' was introduced, based on the propositions of Dr. Ivan Bratt. This system consisted of a government monopoly on the sale of alcohol, and a ration book entitling people to buy up to a certain quota of alcohol. The control system led to an increase in alcohol prices, especially of the strong liquors. Rules were strict. The minimum age to get a ration book was 25 and before it was issued an examination was carried out to establish whether the applicant was abusing alcohol and whether his financial position was satisfactory. The authorities could reduce the ration or withdraw the ration book if a person was not purchasing in conformity with the rules. The husband as head of family generally was the holder of the ration book, entitling him to buy up to four litres of spirits a month. Married women had no ration books, whilst single women received a smaller ration. Furthermore, the supply of alcohol was restricted in restaurants, in particular for women and young people.[76] This also explains why Sweden has never developed a working class restaurant culture.

In 1922 a referendum was held on the question of whether Sweden should have a total ban on the sale and consumption of alcohol, in other words, an alcohol-free society. A very small majority of 51% voted against. The ration system introduced some years earlier, had actually led to a drop in the support for total prohibition. As an advocate of total abstinence, the temperance movement had from its inception been against this ration system. It was in this period, the 1920s and early 1930s, that society's control was the strongest, with home inspections, anonymous information-gathering, and databanks. The ration system was subjected to growing criticism, especially after the Second World War. For example, it was argued that the ration system created an artificial

74   Gould (2001a), *Developments in Swedish Social Policy*, 156.
75   Johnsson (1995), *Spotlight on Sweden*, 26.
76   Nillson (1995), 'The Current Alcohol Situation in Sweden', 311.

demand for spirits.[77] Following this argument, it was thought alcohol consumption would decline if the ration system were abolished.

Eventually, in 1955, the alcohol ration system was abolished. The initial years following saw a steep increase in consumption, but increased taxation in 1956 and 1958 brought consumption down to its former level. Alcohol consumption rose during the 1960s and 1970s until reaching a peak of 7.7 litres per capita in 1976.[78] Following this peak consumption, there was a gradual decrease in registered alcohol consumption which stabilised in the late 1980s and 1990s to reach six litres per capita of the population. The consumption rate of six litres per capita was maintained for more than 15 years.[79] In recent years, possibly due to EU membership, alcohol use is rising again. It should be noted though that these figures refer only to registered alcohol sales. Unregistered alcohol consumption is assumed to add about 25-30% to the registered alcohol sales, which makes the total per capita (pure) alcohol consumption almost 10 litres in 2002.[80]

Despite the abolition of the ration book, several elements of the restrictive alcohol policy were enforced until recently. As previously said, the primary mechanisms limiting alcohol consumption are availability and price. The state-owned alcohol retailing outlets the *systembolaget*, are central in the implementation of alcohol policy. This changed when Sweden was compelled to liberalise its state monopoly in accordance with EU membership. *Systembolaget* are now also open on Saturdays, although they maintain early closing hours. The sale of alcohol in *systembolagets* is restricted to people who are twenty or older, whilst eighteen is the legal minimum age for purchasing alcohol in a bar. Alcohol restrictions force teenagers to procure alcohol illegally. In Sweden, these clandestine purchases mirror how illicit drugs would be bought in other countries. The staple of these back room purchases has created a systemically embedded paradox: because black market alcohol is usually stronger (sometimes containing 40-50% alcohol) than what is available through legitimate channels, in practice, some teenagers are confronted with the reality of drinking strong liquors instead of weaker alcoholic drinks like beer and wine.[81]

Price control is another essential mechanism of Swedish alcohol policy. The stronger the spirit the higher the tax. The goal of high taxation is multifaceted in that it controls alcohol consumption and raises revenues while encouraging the consumption of lighter alcoholic drinks. In addition to the instruments of availability and price policy, there is a ban on advertising alcoholic products, and the government encourages and supports the distribution of information

77 Ministry of Health and Social Affairs (1993), *The Swedish Alcohol Policy*, 6.
78 Nillson (1995), 'The Current Alcohol Situation in Sweden', 312.
79 For the trend in the total registered alcohol consumption see the graph in: National Institute of Public Health (1995b), *Swedish Alcohol Policy*, 14.
80 The unregistered alcohol consumption is mainly comprised of imports procured on off-shore boats or in other countries.
81 Personal communication Eckart Kühlhorn, sociology professor at Stockholm University, October 1996.

about the health risks associated with alcohol use. In large part, these alcohol prevention measures became the responsibility of non-governmental organisations such as youth groups, sport clubs, scouting, education organisations, unions and church organisations.[82]

The scientific basis of Swedish alcohol policy is found in a 1975 WHO report: *Alcohol Control Policies in a Public Health Perspective.*[83] The theoretical model of this WHO publication, the total consumption model, was used for the Swedish alcohol policy implemented in 1977 following the recommendations of the *Alcohol Policy Commission.* The total consumption model suggests a correlation between the total alcohol consumption and the total damage caused by it, such as liver cirrhosis, pancreatitis, certain types of cancer, as well as alcoholism, itself.[84] Furthermore, the model alleges that the more individuals are drinking, the more people will change from moderate drinking to heavier forms of drinking, including alcoholism. Conversely, the less people drink, the less the alcohol damage will be. Since it is assumed that alcohol consumption is influenced by its availability, the implication is that the policy should focus on limiting availability.

The sum total damage caused by alcohol is, of course, difficult to measure and varies according to drinking patterns. Statistics show clearly that medical injuries like liver cirrhosis are common in wine cultures. On the other hand, it is also true that in countries where intoxication-oriented drinking patterns are dominant, consumers may drink on fewer occasions, but since they often get drunk, the medical damage may be low but the social costs may be high. In Sweden, a clear correlation has been observed between violence and drinking. Alcohol is involved in 70% to 80% of all violent crimes. It can be argued that the Swedish alcohol model focuses more on the medical costs, and less on the difficult to quantify social costs.

In 1993 a research team studied the possible effects of a reduction of alcohol prices in Sweden.[85] If the prices were to be adjusted to the Danish level (meaning a price reduction of 50% for beer, 25% for wine, and 15% for spirits), it was estimated that this would bring about a growth of pure alcohol consumption of 1.5 litre per capita per annum. This rise in alcohol consumption would then lead, conjecturally, to a 13% increase in fatal accidents, a 14% increase in suicides, a 18% increase in murders. Furthermore, alcohol-related deaths would rise with 1,000 per year and the number of alcohol-related assaults by 5,000.[86] Although the price reduction was implemented, the studies merely served to

82 National Institute of Public Health (1995b), *Swedish Alcohol Policy. Background and Present Situation*, 19.
83 Bruun et al. (1975b), *Alcohol Control Policies in a Public Health Perspective.*
84 National Institute of Public Health (1995b), *Swedish Alcohol Policy,* 8. For a more recent publication on the total consumption model, see: Edwards et al. (1994), *Alcohol and the Public Good.*
85 Holder et al. (1993), *Assessment of consequences resulting from the elimination of the Swedish alcohol retailing monopoly (Systembolaget).*
86 National Institute of Public Health (1995b), *Swedish Alcohol Policy,* 41.

confirm the perceived need for a continuation of the strict alcohol policy. Further, these type of studies are revelatory of the Swedish approach to alcohol and drugs as both are viewed as leading towards undesirable effects on society. By extension, it is thought that society can control these undesirable effects by a strict policy.

Since the nineteenth century, notwithstanding some modifications, a constant in Swedish alcohol policy has been characterised by implementation of restrictions, with the emphasis placed on external control rather than on individual self-control. A shift is currently taking place from the external control model to an internal control model. This is partly due to an apparently natural development in which Swedes have moved from intoxication-oriented drinking patterns to more moderate 'European drinking'. With alcohol more widely available at a lower price, the alcohol policy has also become more 'European'. The EU and its regulations make it increasingly difficult for member states to have monopolies, like the Swedish state monopoly on the sales of stronger alcohol beverages. During negotiations for EU membership, Sweden was forced to relinquish its monopoly on the wholesaling, distilling, importing, and exporting of alcohol. The *systembolaget* monopoly for restaurant sales also came to an end retaining only the retailing monopoly. These political developments imply the inevitability that Sweden will gradually move toward the aforementioned alcohol policy with less emphasis on external control, and greater emphasis on internal self-control. In this way, Swedish alcohol policy is becoming more liberal, while maintaining some of the traditionally restrictive elements. It is Sweden's long history with restrictive alcohol policy that makes a restrictive drug policy a logical option. However, understanding alcohol policy is insufficient for understanding drug policy; the advent of rising drug problems also played a part.

5.4 The Swedish Drug Problem

Like most Western countries, Sweden was faced with an increase in drug use during the 1960s. Sweden, unlike other European countries such as France and the Netherlands did not have a colonial past in Asia thereby lacking experience with non-medical drug use. Prior to the 1960s, substances like cannabis and opiates were used primarily for medical purposes. Cannabis preparations were used as tranquillising agents in medications until the 1950s, and opiates were being prescribed for pain relief. The extent of the non-medical use of cannabis and opiates was very limited. The number of people using opiates for non-medical purposes was estimated at about two hundred, and cannabis was rarely smoked by Swedes, but when it was, it was associated, in particular, with jazz

musicians and other entertainers.[87] Generally speaking, until 1965, drug use was
very limited and not particularly regarded as a serious social problem, which
explains why no specific research was undertaken on the subject.[88] By 1965,
however, there were clear signs that drug use was on the rise. Consistent with
the historical Swedish approach, the government took the lead in investigating
this issue. The Committee for Treatment of Drug Abuse was thereby set up,
publishing four reports between 1967-69. These reports included survey data on
the extent of drug use. Young Swedes were found to be using amphetamines,
cannabis, LSD and opiates. Cannabis, in the form of hashish, was the drug most
widely used. The second most widely used drugs were central nervous system
stimulants (CNS), primarily amphetamines. In the 1969 report it was found that
the estimated number of 'heavy drug abusers', mostly amphetamine injectors,
had risen from 6,000 in 1967 to 10,000 in 1969.[89]

One explanation for why amphetamine has become the main problem drug
in Sweden is that Sweden has a history of central nervous system stimulants
(CNS) use, which can be said to have conditioned people to more readily, and
less sceptically, accept them. Introduced in the late 1930s, amphetamines could
be legally bought over-the-counter in pharmacies. At that time, the media
launched amphetamines as slimming pills and stimulants. Newspapers, magazines and radio broadcasts recommended the 'pep pills' for all kinds of people,
from students to tired housewives: "Two pills are better than a month's vaca-
tion".[90] The majority of the consumers were normal people who occasionally
used central nervous system stimulants in a functional way, to lose weight or as
a stimulant drug for students during exams. In the 1940s, the total number of
users was estimated at 200,000, which was 3% of the population.[91]

Amphetamine use began to be considered a problem in the 1950s and 1960s
when a small group of around two hundred users were found to be taking higher
doses, in excessive quantities of up to one hundred tablets a day on a more or
less continuous basis. These people were showing somatic and psychic symptoms.[92] Prescription regulations were introduced to limit excessive amphetamine
consumption. The middle and upper classes were put off from the use of these

87 CAN & National Institute of Public Health (1993), *Trends in Alcohol and Drug Use in Sweden*, 44-55.
88 CAN & National Institute of Public Health (1993), *Trends in Alcohol and Drug Use in Sweden*, 44-55.
89 The Committee on the Treatment of Drug Abuse (Narkomanvårds-kommittén) was installed in
    1965 after signs that drug use was increasing. It published four reports in the period 1967-69. Two
    first reports were published in 1967, the first on the treatment issue, the second on repressive
    measures. The second report served as a basis for the Narcotic Drugs Act that came into power in
    1968. The Committee estimated the number of individuals to be either injecting drugs, or otherwise
    taking drugs on a regular (daily) basis in the Stockholm area at 3,000 and for the country as a
    whole at 6,000. A majority of these 'heavy drug abusers' injected amphetamines or other central
    stimulants. In the two reports published in 1969 the number of heavy drug abusers was estimated at
    10,000. See Tops (2001), *A society with or without drugs?*
90 Goldberg (1968a), 'Drug abuse in Sweden', 3.
91 See for example the table in Boekhout van Solinge (1997a), *The Swedish Drug Control System*, 39.
92 Olsson (1995), 'Utilisation et abus de narcotiques et de drogues illégales en Suède', 172.

central nervous system stimulants by the control measures while the excessive users and the criminal subculture remained outside of the controls. Users outside of the control measures consumed substances by other means in much higher quantities – intravenously. As a result, the more typical and conservative forms of amphetamine use became increasingly rare, while intravenous amphetamine use became a characteristic part of the criminal subculture. Hence, the moderate users disappeared, whereas the users that remained were the deviant, excessive users.

Olsson has pointed out that in the period from the end of World War II until 1965 the partition of different types of amphetamine use underwent important changes. Initial consumption was characterised by widespread (occasional and regular) use, but by a very limited number of problem users. In later periods, after the initiation of more control measures, the number of occasional and regular users decreased, while the number of excessive users grew.[93] The development of the consumption of central nervous system stimulants from the late 1930s to the mid-1960s could be described as the transformation of a socially accepted medicine used by many different kinds of people, into an illicit drug basically consumed in a deviant environment.[94] People involved in a criminal subculture and also known to be using amphetamines, further rein-forced the growing sense that this deviant behaviour, injecting drugs, posed a serious problem and threat to the establishment. Moreover, this drug use became quite visible since this group of users were socially deviant. The Swedish experience with amphetamines can thus be summarised as a process in which the drug users became increasingly deviant and marginal, whereby the deviance of the subculture was seen as a consequence of amphetamine use or closely associated with it, without realising that the existence of the deviant subculture actually preceded the introduction of amphetamine use.

In 1965, an 'experiment' began in which illicit drugs were legally pre-scribed.[95] During a two-year period, beginning in April 1965 and concluding in May 1967, drugs were prescribed to drug addicts in Stockholm. There is some misunderstanding regarding the purpose of the prescription project, which is often presented as a valid scientific experiment. However, it was never intended to be a scientific experiment, nor did it ever become one. It was merely the liberal prescription practices of several physicians, one of whom was Sven-Erik Åhström. These doctors' prescription practices were initially supported by a client organisation for drug users (RFHL). The fact that it was possible to start the liberal prescription practices must be seen and understood within the context of the relatively liberal 1960s when there was, in the words of Bejerot, a more

---

93 Olsson (1994), *Narkotikaproblemets bakgrund.*
94 Olsson (1995), 'Utilisation et abus de narcotiques et de drogues illégales en Suède', 172.
95 The prescription practice has become relevant again in view of the introduction in some countries of legal heroin prescription programmes.

permissive attitude towards non-medical use of drugs.[96] It was only later that the prescription practices received official support from the Health Inspector. Because of the non-scientific status of the project, there was never a control group, which makes it impossible to make a scientific evaluation or to draw more than very limited conclusions.[97]

The prescription practices began in April of 1965 with ten drug addicts to whom narcotic drugs were prescribed. By the end of 1965 this number had grown to 60. In 1966 and 1967, approximately 100 patients were participating in the project. Most of the participants belonged to a criminal subculture. During the two-year period, a total of 120 patients had participated in the liberal prescription practices for at least three months. The substances that were prescribed included methadone, morphine and primarily amphetamines, administered orally as well as intravenously. In the beginning about ten physicians were involved, but by the end of 1965 only one physician remained, police doctor Sven-Erik Åhström who had initiated the project. For most of the time that the experiment lasted, he was the only person writing out prescriptions. Dr. Åhström was known for being outspoken with liberal ideas about drug addiction and treatment. He was of the opinion that the patients themselves were responsible for the dosages they were taking, he delegated part of his work and responsibilities to a few patients who were permitted to prescribe and distribute as well, and he allowed patients to take drugs home for several days and, if this quantity ran out earlier than expected, they could come back and ask for more.

Because of its liberal prescription practices, the experiment became more and more controversial. Halfway through the experiment, all physicians except Åhström had abandoned the prescription practices, and it also lost the support of the client organisation for drug users (RFHL). The police regularly found people with legally prescribed drugs that were not participating in the project, which meant that a lot of the prescribed substances were being distributed to people outside of the project. Other criticisms concerned the high mortality rate amongst the participants and that the crime figures did not decrease, as had been expected. When in April 1967 a 17-year old girl not taking part in the prescription project, died from an overdose of amphetamine and morphine that had been administered by one of the patients, the experiment finally came to an end. During the two-year period a total of four million dosages of amphetamine (15 kilos) and 600,000 dosages of opiates (3.3 kilos) had been prescribed to 120 patients.[98]

---

96 Bejerot (1975), *Drug Abuse and Drug Policy. An epidemiological and methodological study of drug abuse of intravenous type in the Stockholm police arrest population 1965-1970 in relation to changes in drug policy*, 21.
97 Lenke & Olsson (1996b), *Legal Drugs,* 3.
98 Lenke & Olsson (1996b), *Legal Drugs*, 4. Bejerot stated that these quantities were prescribed to an average of 83 patients, see Bejerot (1975), *Drug Abuse and Drug Policy*, 23.

Lenke and Olsson describe how, in the period 1965-69 three different strategies were being debated to tackle the increase in drug use: the legalisation strategy, the treatment and reform strategy, and the control and sanction strategy.[99] Legalisation was the least influential of the three strategies, although this policy option did receive a lot of attention in the media and was advocated by some influential individuals.[100] The proponents had some impact in the sense that their ideas contributed to the 1965-67 prescription experiment, but when this ended, the legalisation option faded away. The treatment and reform strategy, based on the social symptom theory that drug addiction was a consequence of worsening social conditions, had many advocates, especially since it was inspired by criticism of the capitalist society. This strategy had some influence, but eventually it was, as Lenke and Olsson put it, more successful in the debate than in practice.[101] The scheme that had most influence was the control and sanction strategy, which according to Lenke and Olsson, was revitalised in the late 1960s, when the foundation was laid for the (restrictive) drug policy. The control and sanction process began with the 1968 Drug Act, which in itself was not so severe, but was reinforced gradually, in 1969 and 1972.

The Swedish prescription practices of 1965–67 heavily influenced the construction of the Swedish drug problem. The prescription practices are often referred to as a failed experiment with drastic consequences. Although there was no scientific basis to the prescription practices, the conclusion drawn was that legalising the prescription of narcotic drugs would lead to a rise in new users and addicts, and more drug problems. This project is often blamed for the ensuing drug epidemic which followed. Swedish drug policy pamphlets base their arguments against a liberal drug policy on the devastating results of this 'experiment' as being their attempt at a liberal drug policy. In the ongoing international discussion on decriminalisation and legalisation, this experience is sometimes referred to as one of the very rare studied and documented examples, indicating where legal prescription or more liberal tendencies of drug policy can lead. In reality, there was never the question of a legal prescription policy experiment. The prescription project was merely the unmonitored act of one physician, which became uncontrollable. The persistence of the misunderstanding and confusion surrounding the experiment is primarily attributable to the influence of Nils Bejerot, one of the founders of the restrictive Swedish drug policy. In his various writings and speeches Bejerot tried to find proof for his theory of the epidemic character of drug use and he believed that the 1965-67 prescription experiment had been the root of Sweden's drug epidemic.

Nils Bejerot was a police doctor working in Stockholm who conducted a study into the relationship between drug use and drug policy in Stockholm

---

99 Lindgren quoted by Lenke & Olsson (1995), *Constructing a Drug-Free Society*, 3.
100 Lenke & Olsson (1995), *Constructing a Drug-Free Society*, 3.
101 Lenke & Olsson (1995), *Constructing a Drug-Free Society*, 4.

during the period of 1965-1970. Working as a psychiatric consultant to the Stockholm police force since 1958, he became supervisory medical officer at the detention centre in Stockholm. Bejerot decided to start a study into the occurrence of injection marks on the arms of arrested people, assuming that this group was well suited to be studied: the identity of the arrested people could be determined with accuracy and intravenous use could be simply and objectively observed. The method which followed was simple: trained nurses would inspect the arm veins of every person arrested for crime and taken to the police premises in Stockholm.[102]

One of the goals of Bejerot's investigation was to "organise a study of a possible connection between drug policy in general and the spread of intravenous abuse in the arrest population which we knew from experience was highly infected".[103] The prescription project was of special interest because it enabled a comparison of a permissive drug policy, in effect during the period of 1965-67, with a more restrictive drug policy, in effect during the period prior to 1965 and after 1967. Bejerot considered this highly relevant to his argument that drug use had an epidemic and contagious character. "Once a group of abusers has formed and a drug culture has arisen in society, the availability of the drugs is the most important factor in the spread of this form of abuse. (...) According to this theory, society must follow a restrictive drug policy for both preventive and therapeutic reasons".[104]

Throughout his dissertation and other publications, Bejerot explains his concept of drug use and addiction.[105] He makes distinctions between several types of addictions, of which the *epidemic addictions* take the most prominent place and are most relevant in regards to illicit drugs. His definition of epidemic addictions is as follows: "Mainly among young, psychologically and socially unstable persons who, usually after direct personal initiation from another abuser, begin to use socially non-accepted, intoxicating drugs to gain euphoria".[106] The point of departure for this definition is the scientific meaning of epidemics, which basically means that a disease has an unusually high incidence defined in time, place and persons and compared with previous experience. Bejerot however, goes further in his concept of epidemic addictions since this definition does not mention contagion, an aspect Bejerot considers of eminent importance when it comes to illicit drug taking. In Bejerot's view, drug abuse epidemics have a high psycho-social contagiousness whereby "the availability of the drug is the most important factor in the spread of this form of abuse, once a group of drug abusers has been formed and a drug subculture has

102 Bejerot (1975), *Drug Abuse and Drug Policy*.
103 Bejerot (1975), *Drug Abuse and Drug Policy*, 22.
104 Bejerot (1975), *Drug Abuse and Drug Policy*, 214.
105 Bejerot (1975), *Drug Abuse and Drug Policy* or see Bejerot (1988), *The Swedish Addiction Epidemic in Global Perspective*.
106 Bejerot (1975), *Drug Abuse and Drug Policy*, 24.

arisen in society".[107] This means that one drug user can contaminate another with similar psychological and social characteristics. This explains the expression Bejerot uses for the spread of drug use, 'psycho-social contagion'.[108] Contagion (C) can be considered as a function of susceptibility of the individual (S) and exposure (E), which can be put in the formula: C= S x E.

According to Bejerot, the drug epidemic spreads quickly, with the potential of becoming exponential over longer periods of time. Bejerot stated that "in most countries" it has been possible to observe such an exponential growth.[109] He supports his thesis by pointing to statistics in Sweden, indicating that between 1946 and 1965, intravenous amphetamine use doubled every thirteen years, and that in England, between 1959 and 1968, the number of heroin users doubled every sixteenth months. One of the problems Bejerot sees in drug epidemics is that they do not respect international borders. He referred to the Swedish epidemic of intravenous amphetamine use that spread quickly and extensively. After developing in the 1940s in the centre of Stockholm, it spread rapidly to the rest of Sweden (Gothenburg in 1956), and to other countries, such as Finland (1965), Denmark (1966), Norway (1967) and Germany (1972).

Bejerot's dissertation data on 1965-70 suggest that changes between 'permissiveness' and 'restrictiveness' in Swedish drug policy is reflected in the rates of intravenous drug use.[110] In other words, he found data supporting his hypothesis that the 'permissiveness' had led to an increase of intravenous drug use resembling an epidemic-like spread effect. Bejerot found a remarkable expansion of intravenous drug use among people who were arrested during the liberal or permissive period. In 1965, 20% of arrested people were intravenous drug users, this figure rose to 25% in 1966 and 33% in 1967. The increase was particularly high among the youngest and oldest detainees. When after 1967 a (gradual) shift occurred towards a more restrictive policy, Bejerot observed a decreasing percentage of intravenous users among the arrested people. Hence, Bejerot saw his hypothesis confirmed.

Bejerot's assumptions and conclusions have been thoroughly analysed and criticised, particularly by criminologists. The first criticism is that his injection mark figures are based on police statistics, which he used as an indicator for the incidence of drug use. As is often the case with police figures, their limitation is that it is unknown whether they reflect actual behavioural trends (in drug use), or whether they reflect police activity (for example, arresting more people with injection marks). A second criticism is that even if a rise in the number of arrested people with needle marks is observed, this cannot immediately lead to the conclusion that this is related to drug policy. Lenke and Olsson commented

107 Bejerot (1975), *Drug Abuse and Drug Policy*, 25. On the other hand, Bejerot considers the availability of little importance if an epidemic has not arisen.
108 The term is somewhat close to peer pressure.
109 Bejerot (1988), *The Swedish Addiction Epidemic in Global Perspective*.
110 See Bejerot (1975), *Drug Abuse and Drug Policy*, 218-224.

on the increase in detainees with injection marks in 1965, by stating that this figure was already increasing prior to 1965. They argue it is more plausible to see the increase in the context of a larger and longer-lasting development – the growing drug use of the 1960s. This hypothesis is endorsed by the fact that in the period 1965-67 (intravenous) drug use was not only rising in Stockholm and Sweden, but in many other European cities as well. The third and probably most fundamental criticism to Bejerot's arguments concerns its statistical significance. The Norwegian researcher Ole-Jorgen Skog, who made a thorough analysis of Bejerot's findings, also including later data (1970-77), found that there was no evidence for the hypothesis that the change from a liberal to a restrictive policy in 1967 had any reducing effects.[111]

Apart from these more fundamental arguments, there are some other points of criticism concerning the effects of the experiment on health and criminality. With regard to health it is sometimes said that the legal prescription experiment resulted in a high death rate of eleven deceased people in the follow-up study in December 1969. However, Lenke and Olsson, after a closer look into the original data, concluded the number of deceased was only four; seven of the eleven people died after the project had terminated.[112] Confusion also exists on the effect on criminality. One of the aims of the project was to decrease criminality, supposing that the drug users would no longer have to commit crimes to finance their habit. Apart from the fact that the desired effect of crime reduction is probably too ambitious considering most participants belonged to a criminal subculture, such an analysis also neglects other facts. Lenke and Olsson recall that the 1969 report of the Committee on the Treatment of Drug Abuse stated that many of the patients involved in the project had spent at least part of the year *prior* to the project in prison, and were therefore physically incapable of committing crimes.[113] Considering the fact that amphetamine use at the time developed primarily within a criminal subculture, and that criminal behaviour is an integral part of the life style, it may come as no surprise that a rise in criminal acts was observed when some of the patients left prison and entered the project.

Although Bejerot's thesis that the prescription experiment had a fatal, triggering effect on the further spread of drug use is not valid in scientific terms, the idea is still politically widely accepted in Sweden. Criminologists Lenke and Olsson point to the fact that the police, already unhappy about the legal experiment, seized upon the conclusions offered by police doctor Bejerot in order to ask for a stricter approach. When a national police board was created in 1965, the police gained a stronger lobby and became an important factor in influenc-

111 Skog (1993), 'Narkotikamissbrukets utvikling i Sverige 1979 -1992'. By applying the Box-Jenkins time series analysis (a common technique to measure correlation over time), it is found that the correlation is not statistically significant. See also Lenke & Olsson (1996b), *Legal Drugs*, 5.
112 Lenke & Olsson (1996b), *Legal Drugs*, 5.
113 Lenke & Olsson (1996b), *Legal Drugs*, 6.

ing Swedish drug policy.[114] Bejerot's conclusions were "given massive support and promotion by a police organisation that probably has no equivalent in Western society when it comes to the degree of centralisation and political influence in society".[115] Until now, Bejerot's analysis of the 1965-67 experiment is widely accepted by government officials and can be found in government documents.[116] His political influence is remarkable, considering that internationally and in Sweden, members of the scientific community rarely share his ideas and conclusions.

In more general terms, Bejerot's ideas have been very influential in the Swedish drug policy debate. Since his appearance on the scene in the 1960s, he has argued for a more restrictive drug policy by writing many articles and giving interviews to newspapers (particularly tabloids). Initially his opinions were easily dismissed and lacked influence because of his fanaticism and impression of being an angry old man – for which he was disliked by many.[117] Over the course of time, Bejerot's influence grew to the extent that he became a national celebrity. When it was assumed his house had been burnt down by some angry drug users, most newspapers turned the event into front page news. Hence, his role in the drug policy debate gradually shifted from an extremist in a marginal position to the founding father of the restrictive Swedish drug policy.

In Bejerot's view, drug use has a contagious character. Considering the earlier mentioned formula of C=SxE, Bejerot suggested that in order to limit contagion (C), individual susceptibility (S) is difficult to influence through policy making. Contrary to this, restrictive drug policy could limit exposure (E) to illicit drugs, meaning that the prevalence, and more specifically the incidence of drug use (new users) should be kept down. With regard to street level law enforcement, Bejerot argued that drug users should be targeted, since they are the irreplaceable elements of the 'drug chain'. Drug dealers can and will be replaced by other dealers in the event of arrest; the drug user on the other hand is not replaceable, but can be considered as the motor of the system. To break the chain it is therefore important to target the drug users: "We have to accept the painful fact that we cannot win decisive advances unless drug abuse, the abuser and personal possession are placed in the centre of our strategy."[118] An additional reason to focus on the user, is that by association, they are encouraging the spread of drug use to others. As an intervention measure for Swedish drugs users, Bejerot suggested manual labour as a punishment for drug offences. First time offenders were met with one month of forest clearing, second time offenders would be punished with two months forest clearing duty, and so forth.

---

114 Lenke & Olsson (1996b), *Legal Drugs*, 4.
115 Lenke & Olsson (1996a), 'Sweden: Zero Tolerance Wins the Argument?', 111.
116 See for example the chapter 'Is Swedish Drug Policy Successful?' in: National Institute of Public Health (1995a), *Drug Policy. The Swedish Experience*, 31.
117 Personal communication Ola Sigvardsson of the newspaper Dagens Nyheter (Stockholm, October 1996), and Per Johansson of RNS (Stockholm, October 1996).
118 Bejerot (1988), *The Swedish Addiction Epidemic in Global Perspective*, 8.

Furthermore, Bejerot believed governments are not able to tackle the problem without popular support, which can be achieved through "broad political agreement and massive information which leads to something like a popular uprising against drug epidemics".[119] One of the ways he would try to realise this was by founding in 1969 the popular mass movement for a drug-free society RNS.

5.5 The Symbolic Importance of the Drug Threat

It was mentioned earlier that popular mass movements play an important role in Swedish society. The Swedish drug policy cannot be understood without taking into account the role played by some of these popular movements. In the 1960s the main popular movement working in the field of drug policy was the Swedish Association for Assistance to Drug Users (RFHL). The RFHL was founded during the same year as Dr. Åhström's prescription project – which it supported initially. In the Swedish context, RFHL views are generally quite progressive, as the organisation supports needle exchange programmes and opposes compulsory treatment and the criminalisation of drug use. During the 1970s and especially the 1980s however a shift took place. RFHL lost a lot of its influence and power in favour of three other popular movements that developed as the most influential popular movements in this field and were to leave their stamp on Swedish drug policy: the Association for a Drug-Free Society (RNS), Parents Against Drugs (FMN), and Hassela Solidarity.[120] All three strive for a drug-free society and correspondingly strict drug policy. They can be regarded as the driving force behind Sweden's drug policies as they managed to get their principles of a drug-free society adopted by the Swedish authorities.

The *Association for a Drug-Free Society* (RNS) is the most militant popular movement in the field of drugs. The RNS is a popular movement with a somewhat revolutionary and combative character which was once described by its founder (Bejerot) as a guerrilla movement which explains why RNS does not accept any government funding, although it is entitled to do so. RNS is dependent upon member contributions by its 10,000 members, a number that which increased during the 1990s door-to-door membership campaign. The membership increase can be explained by the rise in drug use during the 1990s, which was presented as a threat. During discussions for joining the EU, RNS presented Europe as a source of potential danger to their country because it is where both drugs and the drug legalisation lobby originate. In RNS magazine *Narkotikafrågan* references are often made to the decadent hippie culture of which drugs could be a part. In an extreme comparison, RNS also accused rock groups of

---

119 Bejerot (1988), *The Swedish Addiction Epidemic in Global Perspective*, 10.
120 In the 1980s RFHL became involved in therapeutic communities and partly became a treatment institution.

advocating drug use, which would typify a permissiveness reminiscent of to the cabaret shows in the liberal Weimar Republic.[121] This way, RNS points to the danger of liberalism, by drawing a comparison between the deterioration of Sweden and the liberal Weimar Republic. RNS' members are active in capacities such as writing newspaper articles, organising petitions, demonstrating all of which result in their being a powerful lobby locally and nationally.

Parent's Against Drugs (*FMN*) was founded in 1968 and is primarily composed of the mothers of problematic drug users (addicts). FMN is a national organisation with some forty local branches and a few thousand members. Its main activities are supporting parents of drug addicts, setting up self-help groups, and organising training courses. FMN also has two therapeutic communities and many smaller family care centres. Although FMN is merely working on a local level, it is an important pressure group on the national level, trying to get its views through to politicians and being influential upon public opinion. FMN has the same objectives as RNS, a restrictive drug policy, but FMN is less militant and also shares some of its ideas with RFHL, like the client's perspective.

Hassela Solidarity is a popular movement that was founded in 1969 by the teacher and military veteran, K.A. Westerberg. In 1969, an educational community was founded in the village of Hassela, 350 kilometres north of Stockholm. Hassela now has expanded to several communities in Sweden, with a program dedicated to re-educating problem teenagers. Hassela considers that taking drugs is "like doing the wrong things in life", and Hassela is there to "teach how to live an ordinary life".[122] Most students in the communities were sent there through LVU, the compulsory treatment programme for young people. The communities' strict rules have led to considerable criticism. In addition to offering re-education, Hassela offers satellite prevention programmes in some schools throughout Sweden. Still more important is its active role in the drug policy field, where it continually argues the need for a restrictive drug policy. Hassela's power and influence derives, in part, from the ideological background it shares with the Social Democratic Party. Since its founding, Hassela has had a working class and social democratic background and it presents drug use as an attack on the traditional working class values of order, discipline, solidarity, and decent behaviour. It has such a strong lobby that it often deals directly with the politicians who are usually social democratic, rather than with lower-ranking civil servants. They leverage their appeal by using leftist, social democratic rhetoric. Thus, Hassela claims that "intoxicated, ignorant and disorganised people are easy to manipulate and oppress and quite often they do not take any part in the creation of a future society".[123]

---

121 See: Tham (1995a), 'Drug Control as a National Project: The Case of Sweden', 117.
122 Interview Mia Sundelin, Hassela Solidaritet, (Stockholm, December 1996).
123 Peterson (1993), brochure *Hassela Solidarity Sweden*, 4 and 9.

Popular mass movements like RNS, FMN, and Hassela continually work to rally support for their ideas because of the necessity of being influential upon the general public which is made quite possible through good mass media contacts. By using traditional Social Democratic rhetoric, they were able to play on people's feelings. Their message not only appeals to the social democrats, but even more so to the conservative parties. They also influenced the Bourgeois Government (1991-1994), when Liberal Party chairman Bengt Westerberg was Minister of Social Affairs.[124] In the 1990s, the popular mass movements capitalised on the declining *trygghet* (security) which Swedes faced because of the economic crisis. It was presented as if the Swedish haven was under threat from the outside, in particular by (continental) Europe, the alleged source of illicit drugs. EU membership therefore triggered a re-activation of these popular movements explaining why they continue their struggle, not only in Sweden, but now also in Europe. This prompted the creation of its *European Cities Against Drugs* (ECAD), which was founded in Stockholm, which remains its base of operations.[125]

A recurrent question that arises when discussing Sweden's restrictive drug policy is why an atmosphere of moral panic exists around drugs. This question becomes even more intriguing when considering the aforementioned fact that illicit drug use in Sweden is among the lowest in the EU.[126] Yet, opinion polls show that people continue to consider drugs as one of the major threats to society.[127] How is it possible that drugs provoke such extremely strong reactions, to a degree that parliament and state commit themselves to the goal of a drug-free society? Criminology Professor Henrik Tham of Stockholm University states that these strong reactions need to be seen "in light of the notion of drugs as a contagion that can afflict anyone at any time and that is sweeping through younger and younger age groups in society".[128] The risks related to cannabis are perceived as especially dangerous, besides being considered a gateway to heroin and other hard drug use, which, in turn, can lead to extensive criminality, marginalisation, and death.[129] Drug use, as a problem, falls into a different category from all other social problems; it can be said that drugs are seen as *the* threat, and the main enemy of the Swedish people.

---

124 See Westerberg (1994), Reply to Arthur Gould: "Pollution rituals in Sweden: the pursuit of a drug-free society'.

125 European Cities Against Drugs (ECAD) was founded as a reaction to the 1989 Frankfurt Resolution of a number of European cities pronouncing themselves in favour of cannabis decriminalisation and harm reduction. ECAD is based on the Stockholm Declaration, which means the signatory cities adhere to a restrictive drug policy, and oppose to discussions on cannabis decriminalisation or heroin prescription.

126 Supporters of the restrictive approach would argue this is because of the restrictive policy.

127 See Hübner (2001), *Narkotika och alcohol i den allmänna opinionen*. Hübner's opinion poll shows that drugs are generally perceived as a serious social problem, bigger than 'pollution' or the 'economic crisis'. Drug (ab)use is perceived as almost as serious as assaults and family violence.

128 Tham (1995a), 'Drug Control as a National Project: The Case of Sweden', 114.

129 Tham (1995a), 'Drug Control as a National Project: The Case of Sweden', 114.

It is difficult to accurately pinpoint the root cause of the Swedish moral panic over drugs. Several factors can be presented that might have played an important role in the formation of Swedish opinions. As early as the 1960s and continuing through the 1970s, a well-known Swedish documentary maker, Stefan Jarl, made three documentaries. His first film, *Mods,* about people living 'outside society', lent a somewhat romantic image of drug users. At the time of this first film, Jarl did not yet know which direction his subsequent films would take. A few years later, in his second film, the same drug users reappeared, but in worsened conditions. Some of the subjects of the first film reportedly had died as a result of drug abuse. The third film, *The Social Inheritance*, focused upon the next generation – children of the drug users from the first films – some of whom were themselves also using alcohol and drugs. Jarl's documentaries have had a big impact in Sweden and may have contributed to the very negative opinions about drugs.[130]

The media have also played their part in contributing to building up a pubic perception of drugs as frightening and menacing. Bergmark and Oscarsson have analysed the descriptions of drug and drug users in fifteen different daily newspapers in the period 1981-1983. Their research indicates that newspaper articles that address the drug issue, tend to stress the psychological and physical consequences of drug use: "There is a strong emphasis on the changing of the individual drug users, both mentally and physically".[131] They conclude that the contents of images predominantly featured in the press can be summarised fairly briefly and succinctly:

> "The abuse of drugs leads to extensive alterations of the abuser's body and mind in an obviously negative way; psychosis, distorted reality conception, anxiety, apathy, brain damage, impaired immune defence, genetic lesions, and so forth, are all possible consequences of drug abuse. The governing image of the abuser in the press seems to be a person more or less 'out of his mind' and at the same time a 'physical wreck'."[132]

In a more recent article on criminal policy, Henrik Tham makes a similar point. Tham states that it is "clear the media has been very active in the definition of drugs as a major social problem". He points out that, together, four daily newspapers have published more than 12,000 articles on drugs in the period 1981-1991.[133] Not only have the media played an important role in highlighting the public concern about the drug problem. The government has also played its part as well. It was around 1980, when Gertrud Sigurdsen was Minister for Health and Social Affairs, that a new way of looking at drugs took shape. A new theoretical model or even paradigm arose. However, it is difficult to say whether Sigurdsen introduced new material, or whether she adopted a trend that

---

130 Personal communication Ola Sigvardsson of the newspaper *Dagens Nyheter* (Stockholm, October 1996).
131 Bergmark & Oscarsson (1988), *Drug Abuse and Treatment*, 61.
132 Bergmark & Oscarsson (1988), *Drug Abuse and Treatment*, 63.
133 Tham (1995b), 'From Treatment to Just Deserts in a Changing Welfare State', 106.

had already been put in motion by Nils Bejerot. Sigurdsen emphasised the dangers of drugs and their properties by invoking, for example, catch phrases such as it 'could happen to any family'. In essence, this was a break with the traditional social welfare theory, the so-called symptom theoretical perspective, that had previously emphasised the socio-economic conditions of the people (like poor housing conditions) as explanatory factors for social problems, like alcohol and drug abuse. As a matter of fact, Sigurdsen even drew criticism from the working class temperance association, *Verdandi*, for adopting this new approach. Under Minister Sigurdsen, the role of the client organisation RFHL diminished in the 1980s. Sigurdsen's views about alcohol and drug policies created a situation where she was increasingly at odds with some members of the government commission, who themselves were responsible for keeping an eye on the operation of the new compulsory treatment Act (LVM) passed in 1982. This led, in 1986, to the replacement of the commission's liberal chairman by a senior member of the Parents Against Drugs (FMN).[134]

As outlined in the beginning of this chapter, advocating drug prevention and shaping public opinion are primary elements of Swedish drug policy, and are aimed toward furthering the goal of full realisation of a drug-free society. The government is not the only body involved in spreading drug prevention information; social movements such as Hassela, FMN, and RNS, as well as the police and social workers are also active in this regard. In an attempt to achieve these goals, the government occasionally organises big public anti-drug campaigns using billboards. More important, however, are drug prevention programmes in schools. Some school children are exposed to their first drug prevention by the age of seven, and by the age of twelve, most have already taken part in a programme. Between the ages of 12 and 13, the Alcohol, Narcotics, and Tobacco (ANT) courses begin. From that point on, these courses are a recurring element of the school curriculum, with one day every year devoted to them. The next school year, parents of children between 14 and 15 are all sent the *Hash Book*, which attempts to provide an overview of cannabis' dangers. The focus of prevention is placed on cannabis since this is usually the first illicit drug people encounter. The primary aim of the course is not to inform the school children in a differentiated and rational way about the effects of these substances, but to teach them about the dangers. Since this is often done in a dramatised manner, it serves to set the character of drug scare messages, that is, frightening children away from drug experimentation. However, these messages about the dangers attributed to illicit drugs, and cannabis, in particular, can be said to be predicated upon a weak or controversial scientific basis. For example, mention is made of both short-term and long-term dangers of cannabis use. Thus, hashish psychosis and an increased suicide risk are presented as short-

---

134 Gould (1989), 'Cleaning the People's Home: recent developments in Sweden's addiction policy', 735.

term risks, while leukaemia and degenerative second and third generation effects are presented as long-term risks.[135] The impact of these different drug prevention programmes should not be underestimated. When the drugs topic is discussed with Swedes, they usually come up with what they have been taught, repeating the messages about the hashish psychosis, higher suicide risk, and second and third generation effects. In this respect, the information campaigns seem to have had the desired effect.

This raises the question why the drug-scare campaigns seem to work in Sweden, at least until the 1990s if drug use figures are taken as an indication. The question that arises next is how it can be that Swedes tend to believe the cannabis scare messages? Authorities of others countries – France, for instance, but especially the United States – have used similar drug scare techniques, but they do not succeed in promoting cannabis abstinence. Part of the explanation can be that drug scare messages only work when drug use rates are low, such as in Sweden, with relatively few people who have personal drug use experience. However, if more people have used a drug such as cannabis – which in France and the United States is about half of the older teenagers – then governmental information has to 'compete' with the personal experiences of users and those who know users. Since scare messages tend to point at the negative effects, and since most people experience cannabis use as positive, the more drug use increases, the less likely it will be that drug scare messages are taken seriously.

Another reason why Swedes tend to believe in the authorities' anti-drug messages might be found in the state-citizen relationship of the social demo-cratic welfare state, in which, to put it bluntly, the government is considered to know what is good for the citizens, who in return accept it with disciplined behaviour. Arthur Gould, the British social policy expert who specialised in Sweden, notes that the development of the restrictive line against alcohol – and in recent decades drugs, is an important feature of Swedish social policy and holds great cultural significance. "The restrictive line represents an authoritarian and disciplined aspect of Swedish society, which most accounts of the welfare state neglect to mention or make light of".[136] To this should be added that most Swedes seem to have a generally positive attitude towards state and government, unlike some other countries where citizens have developed varying degrees of reluctance or suspicion about their governments. The positive Swedish attitude is based upon the twentieth century experience of the Swedish welfare state, as previously cited, in which it can be seen that Sweden was transformed from a poor into a rich country. As a result, many people have experienced the virtues of

---

135 Cannabis use is also said to pose a higher suicide risk. As an official publication puts it: "People who have used cannabis on its own, without simultaneous consumption of other substances, have frequently died in connection with impulsive and unforeseen acts of violence. The predominant form of death is suicide". See Rajs (1994), *Narcotic-Related Deaths in Stockholm 1986-1993*, 1. These findings were used in a prevention video issued by the National Institute of Public Health, in which a person suddenly falls from a balcony after smoking a joint at a party.
136 Gould (2001a), *Developments in Swedish Social Policy*, 156.

the social democratic welfare state, which put an end to inequality and poverty, and replace these with guaranteed security. This has created a foundation of trust, and a willingness to believe in what is set forth from 'above' by the state.

Yet the prevalence of illicit drug use has been rising since the 1990s, suggesting that, at least part, younger Swedes no longer accept uncritically the government's drug scare messages. Young Swedes travel more, regularly tune into international media such as TV (MTV), and use the Internet freely. This has led to increasing exposure to other behaviours and other information about drugs beyond what the government issues. Obviously this has had an influence upon them. The new phenomenon of European drinking already shows the effect of international influences, and there is no reason to believe that this should not be true for drugs as well, especially since drug use is significantly higher in most western countries than it is in Sweden. It is indeed the "international cultural context," of "intense international promotion of illicit drug use (…) accompanied by music and fashion" that worries Swedish politicians, as the speech at UNGASS clearly shows (see chapter one).

At a deeper level, it is the strong tradition of the Swedish welfare state that may partly explain the strong negative reactions to drugs. As described earlier, Sweden was for most part of the twentieth century a relatively homogeneous, non-urban society on the outskirts of Europe where the people were familiar with most social problems. In principle, both alcohol and drugs are seen as threats to public health which, if neglected, endanger the stability of society itself,[137] but through a restrictive approach the alcohol problem is considered to be under control. For the drug problem the situation is different. Illicit drugs were something unknown and strange, which makes it more easily understandable that they triggered strong reactions and fear.

In the welfare state tradition, a firm belief exists in the social engineering capacities of society. It was thought to be possible to eliminate the drug problem, for example, by offering care and treatment to the drug users and through setting up restrictions. However, Swedish drug users exist, and it has proved very difficult, if not impossible, to eliminate drug use from Swedish society. In a manner of speaking, drugs were seen as an irritating, atavistic nuisance, that is, a phenomenon which fell outside of the control of the idealistic social democratic welfare state, and over which the state had insufficient influence and control. Jan Myrdal, one of Sweden's leading intellectuals, wrote in the 1970s that drug addicts were disruptive to the general morality and that criminality and drug use prolong the oppression of the working class. They must first lift themselves out of their 'lumpenproletariat' before they can be seen as comrades.[138] Thus, the persistent problem of drug use not only showed the

---

137 Gould (2001a), *Developments in Swedish Social Policy*, 156.
138 Tham (1995a), 'Drug Control as a National Project: The Case of Sweden', 117.

limitations of the social engineering approach of the welfare state, it also enabled drugs to be singled out as a threat.

Den gode fiende (The Ideal Enemy) is regarded as one the best books about the background of drug policies in Nordic Europe.[139] In their books, the authors, Nils Christie, a Criminology Professor at Oslo University, and the late Kettil Bruun, a Finnish professor specialising in alcohol research at Stockholm University, describe how drugs and drug addicts, from 1985, came to be seen as the society's ideal enemy. They characterise Scandinavian drug policy as a war fought with an escalating intensity, and identify Sweden as one of the hawks in this war.[140] Christie and Bruun state that this war against drugs is merely a symbolic war, fought against the easy target of drugs, using the drug issue as a scapegoat for society's ills and drawing attention away from other social problems in society that are more difficult to solve. The strong reactions that followed the book publication, Bergmark and Oscarsson write, indeed suggested that for some people a war was being waged.[141]

The characterisation of an issue as a problem is highly subjective. Christie and Bruun argue that the drug issue is an ideal target to be defined as a major social problem or enemy. Their explanation is that this war takes on a highly political tone. It is easier to declare a war on drugs, than on unemployment, or alcohol use, they argue, because of one significant factor: the lack of power of the 'enemy'. Christie and Bruun consider the ideal enemy to have the following traits: nobody defends it; the struggle against it gains a lot of kudos; the costs connected with the battle become a burden mainly for non-privileged groups; and the lifestyle of the majority is not disturbed. Finally, the ideal enemy is of the kind that it can explain other problems in society, such as problems among youth groups, poverty, criminality, and homelessness. Drugs tend to be an answer that leaves the powerful elite and the great majority of people alone, distracting attention away from other, urgent social problems. In short, drug users are an ideal 'enemy' or scapegoat to blame social problems on and to draw attention to.

Using the same theoretical concept, Swedish Criminology Professor, Henrik Tham, conducted an extensive analysis of the Swedish restrictive drug control model and its functionality. Additionally, he analysed the drug debate in the media, political platforms, and parliament during the 1980s and early 1990s. Tham comes to the conclusion that the struggle against drugs is so strong and widespread because it serves "the function of strengthening a threatened national identity in a situation where the traditional 'Swedish model' has come under increasingly hard attack from both inside and outside the country".[142]

---

139 The original Norwegian publication was translated into German: Christie & Bruun (1991), *Der nützliche Feind*.
140 Bergmark & Oscarsson (1988), *Drug Abuse and Treatment*, 168.
141 Bergmark & Oscarsson (1988), *Drug Abuse and Treatment*, 168.
142 Tham (1995a), 'From Treatment to Just Deserts in a Changing Welfare State', 113.

Gould offers a detailed description of the many changes that occurred in Sweden during the 1980s and 1990s. In particular, he notes the chaotic and competitive atmosphere of the free market that was threatening the Swedish economy. National sovereignty was being eroded and national boundaries weakened, and Sweden had become multi-cultural with ethnic minorities arriving from different continents. In this perspective, "the outside world could only appear threatening to those living in a pristine laboratory. It seemed dirty, chaotic and diseased. Order was threatened by disease".[143]

Tham's thesis that the fierce Swedish struggle against drugs acts as a reinforcer of the national identity, is supported by the fact that drugs are so often presented as a threat to Swedish society. "The idea that the entire society is facing a threat has come to mean that it is the Swedish society itself that is at risk. Swedishness is expressed in the indignation that drugs are spreading to what is typically Swedish – our small towns and rural areas." In this perspective, the struggle against drugs gains another dimension, surrounded by a large degree of moral panic. For example, the chairperson of the Christian Democratic Party, Alf Svensson, stated that the Swedish national radio and television should transmit regular prime-time broadcasts with information about drugs. Swedish television granted the police and customs time slots to announce a telephone number where people can give anonymous tips about drug crimes. Tham ends his analysis by concluding: "Drugs (...) have come to represent something more than themselves. Drugs have been perceived as an attack on cherished Swedish values. In a period of national uncertainty, the struggle against drugs has been broadened into a more general national project for the defence of 'Sweden'."[144] In what has become a national struggle, dissident opinions are not welcome. Drugs remain such a highly politicised subject that no major political party dares to speak in other than dramatic terms about drugs. The dissident voices are mostly academic; drug policy experts who are mainly social scientists, who have been critical of the drug 'problem' as well as the strict drug policy.[145] Because of this relativism they have become politically marginalised.

The drug threat is often portrayed as something coming from outside Sweden. A recurring theme in Tham's media analysis is that drugs come from abroad and are alien to Sweden, whereby "the enemy image and the struggle's popular support have taken on a clear national(istic) complexion: drugs represent an attack on the Kingdom of Sweden – both culturally and territorially".[146] Newspapers, in particular the tabloids, tend to emphasise the foreign origin of

143 Gould (2001a), *Developments in Swedish Social Policy*, 196.
144 See Tham (1995a), 'From Treatment to Just Deserts in a Changing Welfare State', 118-122.
145 See Gould (1994), 'Pollution rituals in Sweden: the pursuit of a drug-free society', Goldberg (1997), 'The Swedish Narcotics Control Model - A Critical Assessment', or Boekhout van Solinge (1997a), *The Swedish Drug Control System*, 172-178.
146 Tham (1995a), 'From Treatment to Just Deserts in a Changing Welfare State', 120.

both drugs and drug dealers. This 'relationship' between drugs and foreigners has even led the newspapers to abandon their tradition of not publishing names and photographs of suspects. Tham mentions that the tabloid *Expressen* carried a month-long special about drugs, including articles on a man of Greek origin who was said to be organising consignments of drugs whilst in one of Sweden's prisons. Other articles featured stories about a shipment of heroin from Turkey, the leaders of an international crime syndicate, the role of the Iranian security police in the trade, the 'deadly harvests' in Thailand, and Chinese triads. One member of Parliament, who later became Minister of Defence, claimed on television that Sweden should be protected from drugs and terrorist immigrants.[147]

Not only are drugs themselves alleged to be coming from abroad, but the liberal ideas and approaches to the drug problem are also considered exogenous. The 'European debates' about decriminalisation, legalisation, and harm reduction are seen as threats to the restrictive Swedish drug policy. Therefore, the membership of the European Union could, in the long run, means that Sweden has to adapt its drug policy to the rest of Europe. EU membership however was a very delicate matter and the political decision to join the EU had been preceded by a referendum and a long fierce debate. Ironically, several of the hot issues in this debate had to do with drugs, both licit and illicit: alcohol, *snus*, and drugs. The alcohol debate centred on the state monopolies on alcohol and the membership implication that more alcohol was to be legally imported from other member states. *Snus* is a smokeless tobacco, somewhat similar to chewing tobacco that is used quite widely in Sweden.[148] Since the EU at first did not allow *snus*, membership would imply that *snus* would be declared illegal. This prospect led to a lot of protests, such as people having stickers on the car bumpers saying 'EU? not without my snus'. Eventually Sweden was allowed to keep *snus*. Drugs were another hot topic in the debates about the EU. It was thought that EU membership meant that more drugs would come into the country, resulting in more drug use and drug addicts. Indeed, the increase in drug use in the 1990s is sometimes attributed to the EU membership. Some people go further and attribute many changes in Swedish society since the 1990s to EU membership, not only the increase in drug use, but also the economic crisis, the rise in unemployment, and the decline of the welfare state. Drugs are seen as an invader stirring up disorder and excess, in what was the calm and clean people's home.[149]

The rise in drug use over the last decade is irrevocable. It implies that cracks have appeared in the Swedish model that had long based its success on the decreasing number of (recreational) drug users. The rise of both experimental and teenage use created such concern among the authorities that in 1998, at the

---

147 Tham (1995a), 'From Treatment to Just Deserts in a Changing Welfare State', 119-120.
148 Snus is taken orally, placed on the gum under the top lip.
149 See Gould (2001a), *Developments in Swedish Social Policy*, 196.

same time as UNGASS was being convened, a governmental drug commission was installed that published its report in 2000. The commission's report showed the degree to which Swedish academic drug policy experts – who are mostly social scientists and criminologists, in particular – were politically marginalised, as the report stated that criminological and other social scientific data were not taken into consideration.[150] It so appears that these specialists are (systematically) excluded from official reports. The governmental commission reached the conclusion that Sweden had arrived at a crossroads: the choice was either a significant augmentation of devoted resources, or the acceptance of drug abuse.[151] The commission clearly choose the first option. It was concluded that two of the three pillars of Swedish drug policy (prevention and control) had received sufficient financing, whereas the third pillar, (the treatment sector), had undergone budget cuts, implying, politically, that more should be invested in treatment.

Still, however determined politicians seem to stick to the goal of a drug-free society, some of the most recent measures indicate that some politicians are taking a more pragmatic stance as well. The nomination of Björn Fries as the new drug National Drug Policy Coordinator is significant, as he is not one of the traditional drug fighters but has shown an inclination toward a pragmatic and research-oriented policy. The government's decision in 2004 to make the needle exchanges programmes Malmö and Lund permanent (after having operated on an experimental basis since the early 1980s) indicate a start of a change of course in Swedish drug policy. Fries also called for provisions permitting needle exchange in the rest of the country. Meanwhile, the National Board of Health and Welfare passed rules that allow for more substitution treatment with methadone and buprenorphine.[152] Politicians are becoming less dogmatic about measures that are not totally in line with the drug-free society. A new development in the media is that popular mass movements have become less influential over the last few years, whereas scientists get more room to voice their concern and criticism. It shows the academic specialists are no longer as marginalised as in 2000, when the government did not even want to look at their data.[153] The media also report differently – both more compassionately and critically – about the Swedish drug situation as well as the policy, especially since the number of lethal overdoses has risen considerably over the

---

150 Another sign of the marginal position of critics of Swedish drug policy is that the press almost devoted no attention to the publications of a number of them, edited by Tham (2003), *Researches on Swedish Drug Policy*, which was published during the mid-term review of UNGASS in April 2003.
151 National Institute of Public Health (2001), *National Report Sweden 2001*, 11.
152 Goldberg (2004), 'The evolution of Swedish Drug Policy', 572 (written just before the decision to implement the two measures).
153 Indicative of this change, some of the academic drug experts who were first marginalised have since been granted research funding from the National Drug Policy Coordinator Björn Fries.

last years, from 99 in 1995 to over 400 in 2002 and 2003.[154] Considering these hard data, it becomes more difficult for policy makers to present the Swedish approach as a humane care and treatment oriented policy that is part of the wider social policy as is the Swedish tradition.

For the coming years, Swedish drug policy is likely to remain based upon the restrictive concept. In view of the high-rising number of drug deaths, however, the question is whether the modern Swedish welfare state can maintain a strict drug policy in its current form with its detrimental effects. It should be questioned if sticking to the goal of a drug-free society is really feasible and workable in the long term. The Swedish statistics – of both rising drug use and overdoses – may force the authorities to give some of their principle firmness and mould it into a new form that is more compatible with Sweden's drug use situation. It might be found necessary to adjust the policy to changing conditions, as well as some of the theoretical assumptions on which the policy is based, which date from the 1970s. In order to respond to these rising drug problems, mainly young immigrant heroin use in lower-income suburbs, Sweden can fall back on older theoretical concepts of the social welfare state, such as the symptom theoretical perspective. This theory, which used to be popular in the Swedish welfare state, emphasises poor, or worsening social conditions as explanatory factors for alcohol and drug problems. This is a very different perspective than the current Swedish drug policy paradigm, which is based on the theories of Nils Bejerot, according to which drug use spreads like an epidemic.[155] Bejerot's model puts much emphasis on the substances themselves and does not look at the wider socio-economic context. Considering the recent rise in problematic drug use, that model appears to have become obsolete and unpractical.

---

154 As was brought by the Swedish TV1 News of 11 February 2004.
155 See Tops (2001), *A society with or without drugs?*, 149-150.

Chapter 6

The Study of Drug Control Systems

6.1 Three Countries, Three Approaches

The three previous chapters dealt with defining and giving clarity to the question of how France, the Netherlands and Sweden have each developed their individual drug control systems. These three countries share common characteristics regarding the issue of illicit drugs. Each of these countries has signed the three UN drug conventions: the 1961 Convention on Narcotic Drugs, the 1971 Convention Against Psychotropic Substances and the 1988 Convention Against Illicit Traffic in Narcotic Drugs and Psychotropic Substances. Each of these countries' leeway in the area of illicit drugs is further restricted by their European Union memberships. While none were immune to the confrontational character of the modern drug use phenomenon as it emerged in the 1960s each has since developed individual responses towards the phenomenon of modern drug use. This final chapter will summarise the three approaches by discussing them through various themes and angles, and by providing some comparisons and concluding remarks. This chapter will also provide further analysis of drug policies and discuss the concept of drug control systems.

Through comparison and analysis the approaches of France, the Netherlands and Sweden possess considerable differences although each nation's approach to illicit drugs developed in the 1960s during the initial phase of modern drug use. Why is it that the social responses per country were entirely different form the start? Section 6.2 will clarify these differences on the basis of popular perception and will also evaluate the particularities of the role of scientific knowledge in relationship to these social factors. Significantly, the scientific theory that is used to interpret the drug use phenomenon, has varied from country to country. This shows that scientific knowledge in regards to drug use and drug policy is a floating factual reality, bound by scientific disciplines or currents as the exist within national borders – thus demonstrating the relativity and limitations of scientific knowledge and how it is used.

How drug control works in practice in each of the three countries, and what happens when the user meets the controller, will be the subject of section 6.3. Three types of drugs use will be discussed for this purpose: first cannabis, the most popular of illicit substances; second, the more problematic usage of amphetamines, crack-cocaine, and heroin; and third, the use of ecstasy and other designer drugs in the rave culture.

Differing views, ideologies, and practices can and have led to friction or policy collisions between countries. As countries are finding themselves further obliged to reach consensus as EU member states, policy disagreements are bound to arise from their differing views, ideologies and practices. Frequently, the Netherlands has been at the centre of this type of row because of differences in approach. Therefore, Section 6.4 will describe drug policy conflicts, and attempt to evaluate these conflicts as either practical or ideological in nature.

Section 6.5, the last in this chapter, will endeavour to develop a 'schema' for drug control systems. Is it possible to draw from the three country chapters the components necessary to create a national drug control system? The final question of this study is: are drugs an actual sacramental presence or a panacea for other social ailments? Before delving further into this analysis of drug control systems, the three approaches will be summarised briefly.

Despite the prohibitionist, law enforcement based approach that France has upheld since the 1970 drug law, a more pragmatic harm reductive and health oriented policy has begun to preside in the mid-1990s. This shift towards a harm reduction approach was observed in nearly all EU countries from 1985 onwards, but France was one of the last European countries to officially embrace it because Frances specialists (mainly psychiatrists) considered such approaches to be insufficient and unnecessary. This view was changed by the large number of AIDS cases related to drug use which led to an 'about face' in the mid-1990s. The shift to harm reduction was initially unsuccessful owing to the police force continuing its repressive approach. Gradually however, harm reduction measures were introduced – mainly through large scale substitution treatment programmes (methadone and buprenorphine). Following the medicalisation of the heroin problem, drug law enforcement shifted their attention towards 'chasing' cannabis smokers – despite Ministry of Justice guidelines that recommended the issuance of caution. Law enforcement's resistance towards implementing the Ministry of Justice' guidelines only serves to illustrate the point that the older, more repressive tactics still continue.

In the 1960s when the Netherlands was confronted with modern illicit drug use, its initial response was to apply a repressive approach. However, this tactic was short lived because the counter culture won public favour altering the prevailing views within the political culture and social climate. Shortly thereafter, a more pragmatic, non-penal approach was instituted – a policy that was actually more in line with the attitude toward substance (opium) use in earlier decades of the twentieth century. In 1976, drug legislation was changed to establish a distinction between cannabis and other drugs with the assistance of two advisory commissions that were proven to be highly influential in shaping this policy. Based on the sociological labelling theory that was popular at the time, it was recommended that drug users not be stigmatised or criminalised.

This meant that a policy of *de facto* decriminalisation was instituted for cannabis. For the other substances, a harm reduction approach was developed. In the 1990s, some repressive elements were added to Dutch drug policy, including compulsory treatment, which suggests a setback to the non-punitive, health-oriented approach. Still, despite increasingly repressive measures, the Dutch approach continues to be largely based on harm reduction and non-punitive means. This extends to other more recent measures that include increased regulation of cannabis retail, medical cannabis, and heroin prescription programmes.

From the late 1960s, Sweden has taken a restrictive approach in drug policy. During the 1960s there still existed some leeway for exploring alternate views and measures, such as the prescription experience of 1965-67 and including the inception of the first European methadone programme in 1966. The officially unsanctioned prescription drug 'experiment' from 1965-1967 is considered to have been the onset of the Swedish drug epidemic. In 1977, the end goal of drug policy was explicitly defined as a drug-free society. In the 1980s and 1990s drug policy gradually became more restrictive, based on the philosophy that it should be hard to be a drug user, owing to the perception that users were held accountable for the further diffusion of drug use within Swedish society. In 1982 compulsory treatment was introduced, and in 1988, the use of drugs was criminalised by becoming a fineable offence, in 1993, the penalty became six months imprisonment. Along with this penalty, nearly 10,000 people (yearly) have been forced to comply with the far-reaching measure of compulsory urine and blood tests. Local harm reduction efforts remain controversial and limited as they carry the implication that drug use is accepted, contrary to the objective of a drug-free society. Harm reduction measures will expand in 2005.

6.2 Diverging Perceptions and Constructions

From the beginning of the modern drug phenomenon, France, the Netherlands and Sweden have each developed individual and culturally viable solutions in their drug policy. In the 1960s as drug use began to rise among younger segments of the population the modern drug use phenomenon began bringing with it new drug legislation that was shaped by the types of substances used and by the 'types' of drug users.

In all three countries the most widely used drug during the 1960s was cannabis. In Sweden (intravenous) amphetamine was perceived as the most serious drug problem, drawing the most attention. As Tops notes, the user profiles were unclear but experience thus far had shown that it was largely a "collective phenomenon of loosely organised sub-groups (...) whereby rituals surrounding the use and the sense of coherence seemed to exert a strong suggestive effect on the members".[1] Their asocial, deviant status, combined with their intravenous drug use, did not facilitate their social acceptance. The Dutch and French drug using youth had a different social position then their Swedish counterparts. They were deviant in the sense that their use was part of a subculture that opposed the dominant values in society. Generally however, these users were not in a socially marginal position; on the contrary, many had a middle-class background, were well educated, and went for example to university.

Although there were certain similarities between Dutch and French drug users, the societal perceptions and reaction towards them were not the same primarily because of the very different political contexts in which drug use were placed. Drug use in both France and the Netherlands was generally seen in the context of the counter culture, but the French viewed drugs as the symbol of a threat to law and order and the Dutch considered it troublesome but they had a certain degree of public sympathy for it. The French government's reaction was ferocious as if the very republic itself was at stake while the Dutch government's reaction began with violent skirmishes that were modified greatly after public outrage over hurting the youth. Dutch policy makers did not consider these youth as outsiders or deviants, but merely as representatives of a younger generation and this was reflected in their policy making. Dutch policy makers were influenced by the sociological labelling theory that was fashionable around 1970, according to which it was felt that stigmatisation and criminalisation would only serve to exacerbate the situation. This perception, combined with the circumstances and players immediately involved, had a major influence on the non-penal Dutch approach towards drugs.

The relevance of the sociological labelling theory in creating the Dutch drug approach points to the general significance of scientists and scholars in defining the drug question. French parliamentarians consulted with psychiatrist such as Claude Olievenstein whose theories and intellectual stardom monopolised drug care and treatment. This explicitly Lacanian approach was easily integrated into French drug policy making because of the importance it attached to laws that would sufficiently structure those who transgressed social and legal norms. Employing a term devised by Foucault, it could be said that these specialists had 'definition power' and contributed to how the question of illicit drug use was perceived and consequently dealt with. Moreover, because of the view that drug problems were an expression of deeper individual suffering, the specialists ignored the practical problems of many drug users (i.e. infections) by declining harm reduction measures that could alleviate those problems. In short, focusing upon a diagnosis of individual pathology, they ignored the larger social and public health context of the French drug problem until the mid-1990s.

In the Netherlands, views based upon fieldwork studies became influential on Dutch policy formation. Here, Herman Cohen's up-to-date data on the

---

1   Tops (2001), *A society with or without drugs?*, 82.

demographics of drug users dispelled the French and Swedish perceptions of deviance being the core issue by finding that not only were users not victimised by objectionable morality but that they were generally quite normal. Although Cohen was influential as his place on the Hulsman and Baan Commissions suggest, he was not deified as Olievenstein and Bejerot. The presidents of the two Dutch drug advisory commissions, Hulsman and Baan, played an important role in placing the drug use phenomenon within a social context. For example, the Baan Report stated that most drug use consists of short-term experimentation by young persons. Further, it stated that the special characteristics of youth culture and subculture are important determinants of the functions drug use has.[2] Hulsman pointed at greater social consequences of criminalising drug users with the long term consequence that it would become increasingly difficult for the user to return to a socially accepted life style.

The Swedish perception of the modern drug use phenomenon in the 1960s differed from that of the French and Dutch. According to reports by the Swedish Commission on the Treatment of Drug Abuse, intravenous drug use was rapidly increasing. These statistical findings were later explained in the thesis of police doctor Nils Bejerot in his 1965-1967 study of injection marks on the arms of detainees in the Stockholm detention centre. This study led him to establish a relationship between the amount of injection marks he tallied and the orientation – permissive versus strict – of drug policy which supported his hypothesis that the permissiveness of the 1965-1967 prescription drug 'experiment' had led to the epidemic spread of intravenous drug use.[3] In this early period of the mid-1960s, when the Commission had been newly installed, Bejerot's influence was not yet pervasive, but once he began more active involvement in drug policy formation, urging a restrictive approach, his influence grew gradually. In the 1970s and 1980s, his theories found increasing acceptance, and eventually came to serve as the theoretical basis for establishing the increasingly restrictive Swedish drug policy. Until now, his conclusions regarding the 1965-1967 prescription drug 'experiment' had found official acceptance. Further, certain policy implications that he advocated, such as putting the emphasis upon heavy law enforcement to crack down on drug users, became official policy in the 1980s.

A comparison of these three drug policies shows the disparities amongst them. It appears that initial perception of modern drug use, in the very early stages of its emergence, were decisive in the construction of the varying drug problem perspectives in the three countries. Each has its own approach which is in contrast to the rest thereby making it difficult to agree upon a communal approach. None have reached a consensus on the exact nature of the drug use itself, nor on whether and when drug use is really a problem, and if so, what kind of problem.

2   Cohen (1994), *The case of the two Dutch drug policy commissions*, 4-5.
3   Bejerot (1975), *Drug Abuse and Drug Policy*, 218-224.

The French developed a law enforcement approach emphasising the need for the French constitutional state to set clear moral standards about what a citizen is allowed and what not. The French model could be described as a 'call-for-order' drug control system. The Dutch developed a non-penal and health-oriented approach, giving room for the drug use phenomenon by practically arranging it into their society, mainly at the local level. The Dutch model could be described as an 'accommodating' drug control system. The Swedes decided to keep their welfare state 'clean' from drugs and developed a comprehensive care and control response aimed at 'containing' the undesired modern drug use phenomenon. Their model could therefore be described as a 'containment' drug control system.

6.3 Different Policies and Practices

The previous section reviews the histories of France, the Netherlands and Sweden on their interpretations of the drug phenomenon and their policies to handle it. The directions taken in drug policy formation in each of the three countries, differ considerably. Each country has taken its own distinct direction in drug policy formation. This section will look at drug control in the three different countries in practical terms, the law enforcement and (health) care system and the implications for both the drug users and the 'controllers' directly involved.

Cannabis
In France, despite the repressive nature of French drug policy a cannabis culture exists that is comparable to the 'wine cult' of the older generation. Cannabis culture can be said to be quietly making its way into French society in an analogous manner. Cannabis can be easily purchased in apartments, parks and on the street. The media regularly report about cannabis – with celebrities speaking out and openly declaring that they have also used it. Debates on the de-penalisation of cannabis use have been going on for years: should the traditional law enforcement approach be followed, or a more liberal attitude be adopted? Proponents say the 1970 drug law is out-dated and too severe, especially since it penalises the consumption of drugs. Politicians are reluctant to liberalise the drug laws and sometimes put forward the 'transgression' theory, which suggests that drug use is an expression of the desire to transgress norms; break rules. If cannabis use were to be de-penalised, they argue further, young people will then seek transgression in other, more dangerous drugs. Besides that, they add, it is good for a country and state to set a norm (drug prohibition), otherwise other illegal acts could just as well be de-penalised. French cannabis users are arrested in large numbers. The number of arrests has been steadily increasing since the 1970 drug law took effect. For many years the bulk (some two thirds) of the arrests were cannabis users. Historically, heroin users ranked second in the number of arrests. Since the mid-1990s (when the heroin problem

was 'medicalised') drug enforcement has increased its focus on cannabis users. Despite guidelines issued by the Ministry of Justice, recommending less emphasis on arresting cannabis users, these now represent approximately 90% of all drug arrests, amounting to more than 100,000 a year. A police arrest does not necessarily lead to the prosecution of the user, but it does entail a trip to the police station. If lucky enough to be picked up by an officer who adheres to the Justice Ministry guidelines, the cannabis user's name only ends up in a written register (*main courante*) of the police station in question. This means that no official report is filed. Being less lucky, a report is made, and users might have to spend the night in a jail cell and could be detained until the next morning, sometimes forcing them to be late for school or work.

In the Netherlands, with the *de facto* decriminalisation of possession and purchase of cannabis in coffee shops, cannabis users have nothing to fear from the police. A 'cannabis culture' exists here but is different than the French one. Since cannabis in the Netherlands attracts many foreign customers, and is a profitable sector, it has a more commercial feel. Cannabis use has been normalised to the extent that it has become a non-issue from a moral point of view. The prevailing attitude among many Dutch is one of indifference, as it is considered to be part of people's private life. Dutch authorities see cannabis use and experimenting as being inevitable. It is considered a fact of today's life that youngsters will eventually encounter alcohol, tobacco, gambling, and drugs, and that some will experiment. All of these just-mentioned potentially risky behaviours are therefore put together in Dutch prevention policies. Supplying sound information on the enjoyment and advantages of drug use, as well as on the risks and disadvantages, is part of the policy program. Cannabis itself is regarded as having a relatively low health risk, and its consumption and possession are not considered worth criminalisation, which is considered more damaging. Retail sales are therefore allowed to adults (eighteen and older). The *de facto* decriminalisation in itself is no longer debated, and it is generally thought not to have led to a significantly higher cannabis use as compared to neighbouring countries. It is further argued that the cannabis sales from coffee shops have led to a separation of the markets of cannabis and hard drugs, resulting in a relatively low number of drug addicts. In recent years, treatment demands for cannabis use increased, which suggest that its use is not as harmless and innocent as thought. The main subject of discussion is the 'half baked' and contradictory character of the coffee shop system which allows cannabis sales in the front door while it must be purchased illegally by coffee shops at the back door.

In Sweden, attitudes towards cannabis are strict. The substance is not only regarded as dangerous in itself, but its use is also considered as the start of a drug career involving other drugs like amphetamines and heroin (the stepping stone or gateway hypothesis). As a result, it is thought that the best way to limit the use of amphetamines and heroin, is by limiting the number of people experimenting with cannabis. One strategy is the on-going use of big drug prevention campaigns, in which the emphasis lies upon the dangers of cannabis use. It is a widely shared idea among officials that the dangers of cannabis are underestimated in many other countries. The dangers usually referred to are cannabis psychosis, loss of fertility, genetic modifications, flashbacks (the cannabis 'high' can come back at an unexpected moment), and a higher suicide risk. Psychosis is often presented as the major risk of cannabis use, while the correlation between violent deaths and cannabis use comes second. These possible dangers of cannabis use are one reason for most Swedes not to try cannabis. Another reason is that using cannabis is so socially deviant, that most people will not even consider it. Another way to prevent cannabis experimentation is by limiting cannabis supplies. To this end, the police try to follow the market movements, such as by cracking down on sales in the streets and in parks (where it could still be bought in the 1970s). Law enforcement has increasingly put the focus on drug users and the police may insist upon a urine or blood test to verify if someone has used cannabis. Using drugs will not lead to a jail term (although it is formally penalised with six months imprisonment). Someone found using or carrying cannabis will have a criminal record though and will have to discuss the cannabis problem with their parents or a professional social worker. There also might be social repercussions, since cannabis use is almost automatically considered problematic. Attitudes and behaviours are slowly changing – especially among young Swedes who have become increasingly internationally oriented. This may also explain the rise in cannabis use since the 1990s, although Swedish cannabis use remains among the lowest in the EU.

Amphetamine, Crack-Cocaine, Heroin
The primary problem drug in France is heroin, but the use of crack-cocaine has increased since the 1990s, especially in the bigger cities. French heroin use partly results from the 'epidemic' of the 1960s and 1970s, but it also includes younger users of the 1980s and 1990s. It seems that the latter category correlates with difficult socio-economic circumstances, particularly in some of the lower class suburbs. French drug law is primarily repressive in character although it also offers the alternative of treatment (*injonction thérapeutique*). However, availability of treatment options for long remained limited, which meant that the treatment option existed more in theory than in practice.[4] Moreover, the French care and treatment model ignored the urgency of introducing more pragmatic measures. The worsening health situation amongst French (intravenous) heroin

---

4   Since many opiates are sold as over-the-counter drugs in French pharmacies, Néocodion, a
     coughing tablet, gained top popularity among heroin users as a substitution opiate. Approximately
     ten million boxes of Néocodion were sold annually, mostly to heroin users. Ingestion of several
     boxes of tablets, at the cost of a few euros each, was known to take away the craving for heroin, but
     also led to other health problems, such as constipation. See Boekhout van Solinge (1996),
     L'héroïne, la cocaïne et le crack en France, 251 (and see footnote 248).

users forced the introduction of harm reduction measures in the mid-1990s – a high morbidity rate with approximately one-third of them HIV infected and a high mortality rate of hundreds of heroin overdoses annually. Needle exchange, 'steri-kits', and substitution programmes became available, but were not always easily accessible because law enforcement agents could be waiting outside pharmacies or near care and treatment centres. After harm reduction entered official policy, substitution treatment was widely extended in a short period of time. Methadone treatment became available, but only specialists (psychiatrists) could prescribe it. Potential participants in these programs had to be enrolled in a specialised care and treatment centre. Another substitution substance, buprenomorphine (usually known under its brand name Subutex) could be prescribed much more easily, by General Practitioners. So many French heroin users are currently under substitution treatment that France is now the European leader in substitution treatment. This 'medicalisation' of the heroin problem significantly increased the health conditions of many French heroin users; resulting in a significant reduction in the number of new HIV infections and overdoses.[5]

In the Netherlands, heroin has been the most widely used substance among problem drug users since the 1970s. Some users have been known to combine it with cocaine. Few of them inject, and most use the 'smoking' technique of 'chasing the dragon', which lowers the risk of infection and overdose. Since the 1990s, crack-cocaine use has been on the rise and has in some places replaced heroin as the primary problem drug. Problem drug users are a steadily ageing population now approaching the average of forty years. They are quite visible in the streets, in particular in the bigger cities. An important reason for this visibility is that the authorities generally adopted a non-punitive approach in which the emphasis is on care rather than on law enforcement. Although the possession and sale of these substances remain illegal, small quantities destined for personal use, have been *de facto* decriminalised.[6] The public health emphasis of Dutch drug policy means that different treatment possibilities are available. Generally it is easy for heroin users to get methadone; this way methadone treatment is used as a tool to establish contact with heroine users. For those who are 'ready' to quit, other treatment programmes are available. As a scientific project, a medical heroin prescription programme has started for users with a long drug use career and several failed attempts to kick the habit. It involves approximately 700 participants and has been positively evaluated by the responsible medical doctors, but at the national political level, there is reluctance to extend it. A consequence of the non-punitive health approach has been

---

5   For the quantitative effects of French harm reduction on the HIV infections and overdoses, see ODFT (2003), *Drogues et dependences*, 48-49.
6   The defined quantities for heroin, cocaine, and amphetamines are half a gram, the amount a user is supposed to consume on an average daily basis. Guidelines for law enforcement are found in the Dutch Opium Act.

that relatively few users die from drug use, and many of the 'old' and marginalised addicts are still 'around', sometimes creating a public nuisance. As public
tolerance for this kind of behaviour seems to have declined, Dutch drug policy
has become more repressive, particularly since the second half of the 1990s.
Moving from being a predominantly public health based policy, public order
became another policy focus, with 'nuisance' as the new policy key word. It has
resulted in more police presence in order to intervene in the cause of public
nuisance caused by drug addicts and in the introduction of compulsory treatment
for drug users committing many petty crimes. Local politicians are pushing for
an extension of the heroin prescription programmes, which they see as a way to
reduce crime and public nuisance.

In Sweden, the typical and traditional problem drug user is an amphetamine
injector who is part of a criminal subculture. Heroin use has long been marginal
but it increased during the 1990s, especially in socially deprived suburban areas
around the bigger cities. In the 1980s the focus of law enforcement shifted from
the dealer to the user, with the aim of disrupting the market. Although the
principal aim of Swedish drug policy is not to punish drug users but to offer
them help and treatment, in practice the policy has taken an increasingly
repressive form, as the recent measure of the urine tests shows, which is mostly
applied to the 'old' and known addicts.[7] In the 1990s, the number of officers
assigned to drug related matters almost doubled to 900.[8] The police however are
not the only 'controllers' whom drug users may encounter; social workers play
an important role as well; they can, for example, decide about (compulsory)
treatment. In the 1980s, sufficient financial means were made available so that
a drug user could easily be placed in a therapeutic community. The economic
crisis of the 1990s dictated that less money be allocated for treatment, resulting
in a shift toward short-term programmes. In 2000, it was once again decided to
devote more money to treatment. Harm reduction is not part of official strategy,
but some limited programmes do exist that fit under that heading, such as
methadone and needle exchange programmes. Participation criteria for methadone are strict, the aim is abstinence and users are quickly excluded when it is
found out (through urine checks) that they have used drugs.[9] Since no substantial harm reduction measures are taken and the general idea of policy is that
using drugs in Sweden should be difficult, the increased heroin use of the 1990s
has led to a substantial rise in overdoses. In 2003 they were more than four
hundred overdoses, which meant that the figures have quadrupled in nine years.
The irony of the restricted methadone prescription in Sweden, and the subse-

---

7   Although the aim of the urine tests was to find new users who were previously unknown.
8   Tham (2003), 'Drug policy and trends in problematic drug use in Sweden', 7 and 10.
9   If traces of heroin are found the patient is expelled and excluded from the programme for two
    years. Use of other illicit drugs is not permitted and alcohol only moderately. Before entering the
    programme patients must first go through a detoxification period of a few days, to make sure they
    are drug-free.

quent high mortality rate, is that it was Swedish research a decade earlier that demonstrated how methadone treatment could substantially reduce mortality.[10] This research was used in other countries as their justification for creating or extending methadone programmes. In 2004, it was decided to significantly extend substitution treatment programmes. The needle exchange programmes in the south that so far only operated on an experimental basis were made permanent. Other needle exchange programmes will also be made available, which allow drugs to be used under safer circumstances. Substitution treatment through methadone and buprenorphine will also be extended and be made more accessible. The new measures take effect in 2005.

Ecstasy and Other Designer Drugs in the Rave Culture

In France, the rave culture attracts many enthusiastic acolytes, but the attitudes of those outside of the cultural phenomenon are far more ambiguous. France is one of the main countries at the centre of the rave culture. The French even have their own name for rave music: *techno*. Some French techno DJs have acquired international fame. Several techno festivals are held every year, such as in the ten-day *Rendez-vous electronique* and the *Techno Parade* in Paris that attracts some 200,000 people. Some television advertisements now have techno music, which indicates that it has become an accepted cultural phenomenon. Former Minister of Culture Jack Lang, while still in office, defended techno music and rave culture by stating that drugs and techno are not the same. He also argued for pill testing at parties. Despite the formal support of this well-known politician, governmental reactions to this young cultural *techno* phenomenon remain generally repressive. The French techno movement therefore remains an underground phenomenon. Since France has a lot of countryside, many parties – called 'free parties' – are organised in rural areas or deserted industrial areas. It is common in summer, and especially in the south, to have illegal 'free parties', which are a bigger phenomenon than techno parties in clubs.[11] Police and gendarmerie in the countryside take a repressive attitude towards these illegal parties which are sometimes combined with intimidation techniques (dogs and riot police) and they may conduct body searches for drugs.[12] Repression of the raves sometimes leads to clashes between ravers and Police. In 2001, an anti-rave amendment to a public safety law tried to allow the seizure of sound equipment from raves and giving the organisers fines for their failure to pre-register their events with the local authorities, was followed by protests of ravers in several French cities. In Toulouse it led to serious clashes with the police, who used tear gas on the rioters. Yet also at authorised parties, police sometimes arrive looking for users and dealers. Another sign of how authorities are trying

---

10 Grönbladh et al. (1990), 'Mortality in heroin addiction: impact of methadone treatment'.
11 The book by Colombié et al. (2000), *Drogue & Techno* focuses on the drug trade in the rave culture but it also gives a good description of the French techno movement itself.
12 Colombié et al. (2000), *Drogue & Techno*, 181-183.

to clamp down on the phenomenon is the trial of former *Techno* + President for disseminating pro-drug information on the Internet, which was intended as harm reduction material.[13] Still, at the local level some harm reduction takes place at 'free parties', such as 'Mission Rave', a drug-testing and information service organised in 1998 by *Médecins du Monde*, which operates with public funding but which nonetheless drew criticism from the Interior Ministry.

In the Netherlands rave culture is also big but in contrast to France's underground movement, the scene is more mainstream and commercialised, resulting in large, highly organised and regulated parties. Although in the first stages of raves, in the late 1980s, there were illegal parties, Dutch authorities quickly took a pragmatic and public health attitude towards the rave phenomenon. They considered the use of illicit drugs at these parties inevitable, and it was decided that it is preferable to have it occur in the open rather than forcing it underground where there is less control and more risk. A harm reduction approach was set up with regards to the rave culture. The Ministry of Health issued a memorandum for local authorities recommending the best way to deal with rave parties.[14] The recommendations were aimed at limiting health damage to ravers. In furtherance of this goal, potential users were offered information about the risks involved, but more importantly, an effort was made to modify the circumstances under which drugs like ecstasy were being used, aimed at limiting fatal accidents. The policy recommendations included an obligation on the part of the party organisers to make free water available, to create a quieter and cooler 'chill out' space and to have first aid workers on the site.[15] For some time, pill testing was also part of this package, but this measure became controversial under recent conservative governments.[16] Monitoring the rave phenomenon has also been part of the Dutch public health approach. Surveys were held at both small and large rave parties in order to monitor drug use and accidents, as well as the circumstances under which they occurred.[17] The police are not always present at parties, but if they are, they go after dealers, not users. Party organisers usually work together with local governments, who define the exact rules and the quantities of drugs that are allowed for personal

---

13 See the introduction of chapter three on the *Techno* + trial.

14 Ministry of Health, Welfare and Sports (1995), *Stadhuis en house ('Townhall and Rave')*.

15 For example, it is known that ecstasy use increases body temperature. When combined with long hours of dancing, an increase in (fatal) accidents can occur, particularly when there is inadequate availability of water or ventilation.

16 Part of the monitoring was measuring the differences in the level of drug use at parties with and without pill testing, in order to determine if pill testing led to increased drug use (which apparently it did not, as most people decide beforehand if they want to use or not). Pill testing became controversial because ecstasy is now considered to be more harmful (on long term) than some years ago. Also, pill testing has become an ethical issue for the Christian Democrats, who consider it stimulates drug use and gives out the wrong message. Although it is no longer possible at parties, it is still possible to have pills tested at drug information centres.

17 Van de Wijngaart et al. (1998), *Ecstasy and the Dutch Rave Scene*.

use.[18] This is enforced by private security guards hired by the organisers and it is therefore normal to be searched for drugs at the entrance. In case party organisers or club owners systematically allow more drugs, their premises run the risk of being raided by the police, which can lead to (temporary) closure.[19]

In Sweden the rave culture is less popular than in France and the Netherlands. Swedish authorities demonstrate far more reluctance and difficulty in relating to this phenomenon, as the Swedish UNGASS speech made clear. That the authorities seem to have a strong resistance to rave culture can be gauged by their creation of special rave police squads: the Rave Commissions. This police team mainly consists of young undercover officers, including women, who either look for drug users or for behaviour that might be drug related. When they find someone whom they suspect is under the influence, they have the authority to take the person to the police station for a mandatory drug test. In the mid-1990s, the police started targeting rave parties in Gothenburg. Although dealers were the prime target of the Gothenburg police, Ravers were taken to the police station as well for urine or blood tests. By 1996, not long after the inception of this policy, five hundred people had been arrested. From September to November of that year, approximately seventy-five party visitors were drug-tested by the Gothenberg police, most of whom tested positive.[20] In that same year, 1996, the police anti-rave actions were extended to the whole of Sweden. In the winter of 1996, police operations at Docklands, a club in Stockholm, received wide media attention after ninety policemen raided a rave at Docklands where one thousand people were present. When the police arrived, everyone was forced to leave immediately. Hundreds of people were forced outside into the cold night dressed in T-shirts, without being allowed to get their coats.[21] Eventually seventy-two people were arrested and forty-eight 'drug samples' were found at the raid, later named 'razzia' by some newspapers. A week later, the police raided Docklands again and of the three hundred visitors present that night, two were arrested. In the following months Docklands became a popular topic in the Swedish media. At the end of the 1990s, the Rave Commissions were renamed Night Club Commissions, extending their drug control activities to night clubs, bars, concerts, or anywhere else where young people might come into contact with illicit drugs. One favoured strategy in order to identify those who appear under the influence of drugs, is to shine a flashlight into a suspect's eyes to see if their pupils are dilated.[22] The police's clamp-down on suspected

18 Generally speaking cannabis is permitted and for synthetic drugs like ecstasy one or two pills are allowed. Some municipalities, however, do not allow any drugs at all, or only allow cannabis.
19 If the police have indications that many drugs are used at certain parties, they observe the situation for some time with undercover officers and if proof is found that organisers do not make enough efforts to halt drugs coming in and being sold, the police organise a nocturnal raid.
20 The most commonly detected drugs found in the urine were amphetamine and hashish; ecstasy and LSD were also found. See Boekhout van Solinge (1997a), *The Swedish Drug Control System*, 117.
21 Olsson (1996), *Drug Trends in Sweden - Spring 1996.*
22 Goldberg (2004), 'The Evolution of Swedish Drug Policy', 560-561.

users at has inevitably led to extended caution by (potential) drug users; they stop their use or no longer use in public. Although the raids have received criticism, particularly because many young people are now being stigmatised by criminal records, the fact that they continue indicates the degree of official resistance to rave culture.

6.4 Colliding Principles and Practices

As earlier explored upon, the policy differences between France, the Netherlands and Sweden are so profound, both in their principles and practices, that it comes as no a surprise that their approaches sometimes collide. This has increasingly been the case since all three are now members of the European Union and therefore required to work together and reach agreements in more and more areas, including the question of illicit drugs. From the perspective of the UN drug conventions, the Netherlands is the exception. However, from the perspective of practical measures taken as part of drug policy, it could also be argued Sweden is the exception. Sweden resists the EU trend towards harm reduction, as this is contrary to the goal of a drug-free society. Sweden wishes to remain firm in its refusal to accept any drug use.

All things considered, the Netherlands remains the most outstanding of the three under study, in the sense that the Dutch do not appear to support the total international ban of drugs through prohibition, and are therefore refusing to fully comply with the current international drug control system. This can be seen through their open and visible system of coffee shops, which Dutch politicians seem unwilling to abandon. This attitude can also be seen in how Dutch politicians and diplomats present their position within the international political arena, such as the speech given by the Dutch foreign minister Hans van Mierlo at UNGASS, as cited in chapter one. Although Van Mierlo used diplomatic terms, his message challenged the general goal and slogan of UNGASS, which was to achieve a drug-free world. International drug prohibition is fundamentally criticised by many specialists – not only at UNGASS – but the Netherlands is one of the very few *countries* that has challenged and criticised it by openly questioning its efficacy and principles at a UN drug summit such as UNGASS. More importantly, it is the only country where this attitude has been translated into the practice of openly selling an internationally prohibited substance in most major cities throughout the country. And, if they could, a majority of Dutch politicians would even go further, by fully legalising cannabis.[23] That they do not put this into practice, is always explained by the

---

23 Several major political parties have declared to be, in principle in favour of cannabis legalisation. What is regarded as the coffee shop's main problem, is the semi-legal status of cannabis which leads to a discrepancy: it is allowed to be sold to customers, but the supply to the coffee shop remains totally illegal. Especially from the local, municipal level, politicians wish to go further, to

'international context', which refers both to international treaties and to diplomatic problems with other countries. Dutch drug policy indeed puts the country and its representatives regularly into diplomatic difficulties: government ministers, diplomats and even the officially politically neutral Queen are sometimes targets of difficult questions such as why the Netherlands has this liberal policy. As the noted Dutch journalist H.J.A. Hofland noted ironically, drug policy is the only area where the Netherlands has its own foreign policy.[24]

In essence, Dutch drug policy presents a challenge to the international drug control system, which has been in place for almost a century. From the perspective of those strongly supporting this system, Dutch drug policy can be considered a threat.[25] The international drug control organs International Narcotics control Board (INCB) and the UN Office on Drugs and Crime (UNODC) are generally negative about Dutch drug policy. Almost every year, the Netherlands is among the countries that are rebuked in the annual report of the INCB for not fully respecting the international drug treaties. The UNODC generally writes in a negative way about the 'Dutch experience'. In the United Nation *World Drug Report 2000*, the UNODC misrepresented EU data on problematic drug use: the Netherlands shifted from being a country with the lowest prevalence, to the category with the highest prevalence of problem drug use. These distortions of data were revealed by Carla Rossi, Italian Mathematician Professor and member of the EMCDDA Management Board. Rossi stated that it "can only have been decided upon to obscure the Dutch data, which are much more positive than all the others, by using a shameful trick".[26] She also found other examples of data being misrepresented or misused in the UN *World Drug Report*, all suggesting

start with an experiment to legally produce and sell cannabis to coffee shops. Such a proposal, supported by many mayors from all major political parties, got a parliamentary majority, but the government refused to execute it for reasons related to the international context In any case, in political terms, there is, in most times, a Parliamentary majority in favour of cannabis legalisation.

24 Hofland (1996), 'Joseph Luns en de coffeeshop'.

25 History has shown that if case interests (in the broad meaning of money, jobs, social prestige or power) are being threatened, the powers whose interests are being challenged, generally react by defending them, and thus oppose situations, or even facts that might threaten them. In more practical terms this means that the powers with interest prefer the status quo, and resist change. Applying this to drugs and the international drug control system, as well as the different interests that have been developed over the last century by having a stake in the current system (such as those actively involved in and dependent on the system), changes and new 'facts' that might place the validity of the system into question automatically encounter opposition.

26 The *World Drug Report 2000* contained a table with the EU countries and their rate of drug addicts. The UNDCP copied the EMCDDA figures, but instead of having fifteen countries listed in the table as the original one, only thirteen were listed, as Belgium, Luxembourg and the Netherlands were put together. No statistical reason exists to reduce a table of fifteen to thirteen countries. More important is that this would be methodologically strange, since it means extremes are put together in one cell: the Netherlands with one of the lowest, and Luxembourg with the highest rate. Even if the three countries were put together, the correct mean should be the weighted mean. Since this was not done, the relative high number of problem users in Luxembourg (three times higher than the Netherlands) changed the ranking of the Netherlands from a country with few to a country with many drug addicts.

that restrictive drug policies 'work' and that liberal approaches have negative effects, which led her to conclude that the report contains "propaganda and misinformation under the guise of scientific data".[27]

Dutch drug policy also leads to problems with and criticism from other countries; first and foremost from the United States, the driving force behind international drug prohibition and the War on Drugs.[28] It therefore comes as no surprise that the most negative epithets about Dutch drug policy have been coined in the United States.[29] It has almost become routine for a senator or drug czar to slander Dutch drug policy and present the 'Dutch experience' as a disaster. One American drug czar made the claim that in Amsterdam's Vondel Park all of the Dutch you were "stoned zombies", whereas another proclaimed "you can't walk down the street in Amsterdam without tripping over junkies".[30] In 1998, American drug czar Barry McCaffrey, a four-star general, just before leaving for a European drug policy 'fact finding tour', stated on CNN that one of the consequence of the liberal drug policy was a Dutch murder rate twice as high as the American. When Dutch officials and journalists confronted him with the accurate figures (which showed the Netherlands murder rate to be four times lower than the American rates) McCaffrey refused to retract his statements. As Reinarman noted, it is said that truth is the first casualty of war, and drug wars are no different in that regard.[31]

In 1988 an influx of over 1,000 wayward German heroin users led to a diplomatic conflict between the Netherlands and Germany over the liberal Dutch policy which led to this influx of Germans to Amsterdam. Few Amsterdammers were pleased by this major influx of German heroin users

---

27 Rossi (2001), *World Drug Report 2000: Contents, Omissions and Distortions*. Rossi found more examples of data being misrepresented; in such a way that the data suggest only restrictive drug policies 'work' and that liberal approaches have negative effects. She concluded: "To bring this brief critical analysis of the World Drug Report 2000 to an end, we can conclude that the volume cannot be considered of any value in terms of information, and even less so in terms of scientific rigour: it is principally a work of propaganda and misinformation under the guise of science; it presents distorted data, covering itself by attributing the data presented to bodies and agencies which enjoy international respect, with the sole imaginable aim of twisting the data in order to support pre-established theses that are not corroborated at all by real epidemiological observations".

28 The irony of it is that while some Europeans consider the Netherlands culturally the most Americanised country in Europe – it certainly is one of the most Atlantically oriented as far as foreign policy is concerned; when it comes to illicit drugs, it is the country that is most removed from the United States.

29 On 22nd February 2001, the American CNN show 'The Spin Room' concerned the question 'Should the government legalise drugs?'. When host Bill Press suggested that it was time for a totally different policy, co-host Tucker Carlson reacted: "You know, it appeals to my libertarian instincts, but people who love socialism go to the Soviet Union and North Korea. See how it actually works. If you love drug legalisation, go to Amsterdam. It's a very depressing place; lots of drooling people. Everyone looks like he's just shot up, which is, in many cases, the truth. It's not pretty in its effect."

30 Reinarman (1998), 'Why Dutch drug policy threatens the U.S.', published in Dutch in *Het Parool*: 'Morele ideologie V.S. haaks op drugsbeleid Nederlands'.

31 Reinarman (1998), 'Morele ideologie V.S. haaks op drugsbeleid Nederland'.

swarming the city who were held responsible for the increase in petty crimes such as car radio theft. Why did German heroin users go to Amsterdam? Was it caused by 'pull' factors such as the climate created by liberal policies that drew them to the Netherlands, or were they pushed out of Germany by the restrictive nature of German drug policy? It became clear that the liberal Dutch policy was not so much the 'cause' of this problem, but that the more repressive climate vis-à-vis drug users in Germany, combined with a few of care and treatment facilities, were more important. In other words, the German 'push factors' were actually more important than the Dutch 'pull factors'. The availability of care and treatment facilities in Amsterdam – especially methadone – was a reason, however, for German users to not go back home.[32] What followed in Germany was the implementation of more care and treatment facilities and reduced emphasis upon law enforcement. Gerrit van Santen, a physician from the Amsterdam Municipal Health Service set up a methadone programme in the late 1980s in Frankfurt. Following the creation of a more health oriented drug policy in Germany, the pattern of German heroin users migrating to the Netherlands faded.

The Dutch-French drug conflict
Before Jacques Chirac became the President of France, it was commonly acknowledged within France and the EU that France was lagging behind in its care and treatment policy for drug users. This had prompted the quick adoption of harm reduction policies just before his election. In 1995 after Chirac came into office, those arguments were no longer supported, and the emphasis shifted to fighting the drug trade, in particular drugs coming from the Netherlands. Chirac's motivation for this change in policy emerged from political circumstances to private considerations such as the dramatic family events which led to the President having a fierce aversion to drugs. The political aspect intensified to the point where the French exaggerated the role of the Netherlands in the drug trade to France.[33] It was an attempt to 'externalise' the root cause of the French drug problem. In 1995, Chirac began to plead for a harmonised European drug policy. Chirac was convinced that his stricter policy was the way to go, and that the liberal, 'lax' policy of the Dutch was an obstacle to the effectiveness and success of his European answer. Therefore, from 1995 onward, he initiated a policy of confronting the Dutch.

The Dutch-French drug conflict dominated all bilateral political relations between 1995 and 1997 making this one of the biggest diplomatic problems for the Dutch in recent history. President Chirac used the considerable powers given to the office of president under the Fifth Republic to compel French government ministers and officials to discuss the drug problem with their Dutch

---

32 See Korf (1987), *Heroïnetoerisme II*.
33 Boekhout van Solinge (1996), *L'héroïne, la cocaïne et le crack en France*, 164-173. See also Boekhout van Solinge (1997b), 'Drugs in France: Prevalence of Use and Drug Seizures'.

counterparts. The French preferred that the Dutch give up their liberal approach that was poisoning French youth by the ready availability of drugs. The Dutch disagreed with this view and considered their policies as being more effective in limiting drug use and drug problems.

One of Chirac's strategies to force the Dutch into giving up their liberal drug policy, was by focusing on the necessity of a harmonised European policy. The harmonisation debate arose during negotiations on the implementation of the Schengen Agreement. Although the EU countries had already decided in principle that complete harmonisation was not essential – provided that measures were taken to reduce imports and exports of drugs – France continued to stress the importance of harmonising drugs legislation, and made no effort to conceal the fact that the liberal policy pursued by the Netherlands was its main target. Within Council working groups in Brussels, Spain, Portugal and Ireland supported the French proposals for harmonisation. Other countries, notably Denmark, the Netherlands, Austria and Sweden, opposed the plan. However, France continued to raise the drug issue whenever possible which gradually created irritation among other member states.[34]

Chirac not only seized virtually every opportunity to attack the Netherlands' policy, but he also tried to gain support for his position from other EU leaders. Chirac's argument was successful with Chancellor Helmut Kohl and Prime Minister John Major. Chirac, together with Kohl, planned a visit to Dutch Prime Minister Wim Kok, in an effort to 'solve' the drug question. It was clear that Chirac had taken the initiative in setting up this meeting, managing somehow to involve his ally Kohl. At the same time that Chirac and Kohl were planning their visit, the health ministers of eight of the fourteen German *Ländern* – the drug policies come under their domain – wrote a letter to their Dutch colleague, Ms Els Borst, expressing their support for Dutch policy and implicitly asking her not to give in to foreign criticism, putting Chancellor Kohl in a difficult position, as he could no longer speak on behalf of the whole of Germany which partially led to the annulment of the joint Kohl and Chirac visit. Beyond the immediate reasons for the cancellation of this meeting, it would have been highly irregular for foreign government leaders to attempt to change Dutch national policy. In the Netherlands, some interpreted this move as an attempt to interfere in the internal affairs of the country, leading to further criticism of this meeting taking place, putting Dutch Prime Minister Wim Kok in the position of not being able to give in to any of the 'foreign demands'. In the end, all three parties concluded that it was best to cancel the meeting.

There were also political-electoral reasons for Chirac to put drugs high on the agenda. As mentioned earlier, 'security' is a popular theme in French politics, especially among populist politicians. The term *discours de securité*

---

34   For the Schengen Agreement and EU drug policymaking, see Boekhout van Solinge (2002), *Drugs and Decision-Making in the European Union*, 36-37.

refers to the bold and uncompromising rhetoric that politicians adopt when speaking about certain problems or threats to society, such as violence, terrorism, or drugs. Part of the reason for this is historical, a tradition of a strong and visible police and army. The chief spokesman is generally the Minister of the Interior, a job that therefore tends to go to a forceful, unyielding individual. By claiming that he will rigorously tackle the problem, and by creating a strong police presence on the street, he set out to reassure the public. The far right parties (representing 20% of electorate) have skilfully used this *discours de securité*, to attract voters away from traditional right-wing parties, which responded in kind. This is part of the explanation for President Chirac's rigid stance on drugs and his unflagging efforts to harmonise European drug policy along French lines. An underlying aspect of the French drug problem is economic, or what the French call *'la fracture sociale'*. The existence of many disadvantaged suburban neighbourhoods creates a hotbed for a variety of social problems. It is in these neighbourhoods that a relatively large proportion of the drug problems takes root: high drug use, related infections such as AIDS, and (drugs) crime. Ethnic minority groups are well represented in these communities where a flourishing underground drug economy exists. Most politicians, however, prefer to speak of drugs as the primary problem, typically refusing to address the underlying social circumstances that lead to these drug problems.

The City of Lille, located in the Department Nord, near the Belgian border, and only 200 kilometres from Rotterdam had seen a rise in relatively young heroin users and small dealers who travelled to Rotterdam for cheap heroin, which they would then resell locally. French customs was confronted with many French citizens returning from the Netherlands with drugs, particularly heroin from Rotterdam. Lille was characterised by high unemployment and rampant heroin use, users and small dealers funding their own habits by petty dealing, and or by making a small business out of it *running* between Rotterdam and Lille. Generally, the smuggled quantities were only several to twenty grams and rarely more than a few dozen grams. In review of overall smuggling patterns, total smuggled quantities in this trafficking scenario were neither significant nor very important. Despite the quantities being smuggled the number of petty smugglers attracted a great deal of attention and stir created by these small-scale dealers and users going to Rotterdam. The extent of the trafficking was such that the word 'Rotter' became a common word heard in Lille's drug scene, which later led French customs and politicians naming it 'ants trafficking' which drove French citizens to be angry at the Dutch for this heroin supply.[35] Dutch-Moroccan drug runners waited for French customers on the highway between Lille and Rotterdam which occasionally led to dangerous and unpleasant nuisance situations on the highway as the drug runners approached many

---

[35] For the situation in Lille, see Boekhout van Solinge (1996), *L'héroïne, la cocaïne et le crack en France*, 241-244.

French car coming into the Netherlands – particularly at night when the passengers were young.[36] From the highway they would pick up clients and direct them to an apartment in Rotterdam to buy drugs.[37] Rotterdam residents were then frustrated by these French drug tourists leaving needles in their streets, being noisy and creating a public nuisance. Some residents blocked French cars, and some of the cars were demolished or rolled over. Some of these users never left Rotterdam and remained as wayward users. Among these were people with serious health problems, such as AIDS. Eventually this led to the establishment, in Rotterdam, of a French care and treatment centre that could help them repatriate.

This Dutch-French drug trade created problems on both sides. The main question was, what brought French heroin users to Rotterdam in the 1990s? The price of heroin in France was several times higher in France than in Rotterdam, which encouraged users and especially dealers to go to Rotterdam. The Netherlands public health approach towards drugs aided in its heroin market remaining stable and the market being saturated with many older heroin users kept it from expanding. Methadone's availability lead to a much more discerning attitude on the part of heroin users,[38] which also kept heroin prices low. The lenient law enforcement approach also helped in keeping prices low.[39] In this stable and non-expanding drug market, the local practice in Rotterdam of tolerating dealers, on the condition that they did not cause a public nuisance, seemed mostly to work without creating serious problems. But, problems were created when a larger influx of buyers suddenly arrived on the market from outside the Netherlands. This influx created business opportunities both in Lille and Rotterdam which was made easier by the reality that many of the French users and dealers were of the same Berber-Moroccan origin as most Dutch-Moroccan drug runners.[40]

The main reason the conflict calmed down was that France softened its criticism after the 1997 elections, when Chirac's bid to increase the majority of his right-wing government by calling an early general election backfired. To the surprise of many, the socialists won the election. As a result, France invoked the *cohabitation* rule.[41] Besides the personal loss of face this meant for Chirac, the

36 It actually happened several times to the author driving into the Netherlands in a French car.
37 See the study by Van der Torre (1996), *Drugstoeristen en kooplieden. Een onderzoek naar Franse drugstoeristen, Marokkaanse drugsrunners en het beheer van dealpanden in Rotterdam.*
38 The great availability of methadone has led to a more critical heroin demand as users will not spend the little money they have on bad heroin in the case of craving, as they can always take refuge in methadone.
39 If there is more risk (of being caught) involved, somewhere along the line this has to be paid for, which leads to higher street prices.
40 In the Netherlands most Moroccans originate from the Rif area in the north. In France, Moroccan immigrants come from the whole of Morocco but many of those in the Lille area come from the Moroccan Rif as well.
41 *Cohabitation* refers to a situation in which the president and prime minister are from opposing parties.

changeover also clipped his wings. He was forced to form a government with his political adversaries, the socialists, with the result that some cabinet ministers were actually in favour of a more liberal drug policy. Thus, with the installation of his new state secretary for health Bernard Kouchner, a firm advocate of drug policy liberalisation and warm supporter of the Dutch approach, Chirac had less political possibilities to quarrel over Dutch drug policy. The 1997 *cohabitation* government is therefore the main reason that the Dutch-French conflict calmed down. France's position clearly changed after the election, and its representatives in Brussels received instructions from Paris to adopt a milder stance, with the effect that the question of harmonising drug policies no longer figured prominently on the EU's agenda. The new policy of the French was to leave the issue of harmonisation alone for the time being and to focus on practical problems that countries had in common, as well as on finding workable solutions. France's increased flexibility, geared towards cooperation rather than confrontation, restored its credibility.

Netherlands versus Sweden: Two Self-Assured Models
While the French diplomatic crisis was putting Dutch drug policy on the agenda, another development began which would change the European drug policy landscape. In January of 1995, Sweden joined the EU becoming the most ardent opponent of liberalisation drug policy. In the EU, the Netherlands and Sweden formed the two poles of the current drug policy spectrum; the Dutch were devoted to a pragmatic and liberal approach towards dealing with the issue of drugs in their society whereas the Swedes were devoted to the principle of creating a drug-free society by enforcing their restrictive drug policy.

Sweden's arrival in the EU changed the landscape in the sense that before 1995 there was a tendency towards a more pragmatic approach towards drug use in all of the member states – especially in major cities where harm reduction had become an accepted practice. And, with the enforcement of the Amsterdam Treaty in 1999, harm reduction was placed on a firmer footing in the EU treaties. Following Sweden's arrival it became increasingly more difficult to come to unanimous decisions regarding harm reduction because Sweden was the only country resisting any open reference to harm reduction. Gradually, however, Sweden became more receptive to accepting harm reduction policy, on the condition that a euphemistic term was used for it.

The Dutch-Swedish differences over drug policy more often manifest themselves at the bureaucratic level of the EU. They no do not have a practical origin, as in the Dutch-French case – although it did during the 1960s and 1970s when some of the amphetamines on the Swedish market were being produced in the Netherlands. Generally speaking however, the Dutch and Swedish policies each operated far from each other, without the differences manifesting themselves practically. The Dutch-Swedish controversy over the drug issue is of an ideological nature. First and foremost, the Swedes have a problem with the message Dutch drug policy sends out by allowing cannabis sales. The Swedish message about how dangerous this substance is, looses part of its strength if the Dutch are allowing it to be sold in shops. Swedish officials often condemn the liberal Dutch approach on moral grounds, saying that liberalising drugs is 'giving up'.

The Dutch and Swedish drug control systems collide on principle and ideological grounds. In the Swedish model, prevalence, and even more so incidence figures, are considered the main indicators for their policy's success. The emphasis is on keeping the incidence of use as low as possible. This explains the problems Swedish policy makers have with the model in the Netherlands, where experimental drug use is not considered to be such a problem. The Dutch for their part focus on limiting the harm associated with drug use. Although the Dutch view includes discouraging teenagers from experimenting with drugs, such experimentation is also seen as an inevitable phenomenon of youth culture. The implication for policy is to steer the inevitable experiments in the right direction by offering information that is credible. This includes not only emphasising the negative effects. Moreover, it is thought that the distinction between soft and hard drugs works as a deterrent in that it can lead to the reduction of the number of future drug addicts. In the eyes of the Swedes however, this must have been the result of a situation that has got out of hand, which resulted in the authorities 'giving up' and taking a 'laissez-faire' attitude. Since it is part of the Swedish drug-free society concept that it should be hard to be a drug user in Sweden, few measures are taken to make life easier for drug users, or to reduce the health consequences of their drug use; the only option is abstinence. The policy to not make it 'easier' for drug users, has resulted in Sweden having the highest per capita number of overdoses in the European Union. For the pragmatic Dutch, this is difficult to understand; in their harm reduction approach one of the primary policy goals is to keep the damage related to drug use as low as possible. For them, the high number of Swedish overdoses is a sign that the restrictive approach does not work and produces greater harm.

Ironically, both Swedish and Dutch policy makers think they are on the right track: the number of drug addicts is thought to be relatively low as a result of the policy that has been conducted. While Sweden considers the restrictive policy to be the basis of its success in limiting drug use, especially cannabis, the Netherlands think their liberal cannabis policy has attributed to a lower number of drug addicts. A more convincing reason for the fact that both countries indeed seem to have a relatively small number of problem users or drug addicts, is that both are rich welfare states, with relatively good social policies, leading to relatively few people living in impoverished conditions and disadvantaged neighbourhoods.

6.5 National Drug Control Systems

Having reached the final section of this study it has become possible to draft a schema from the divergent elements which when pieced together form a national drug control system. This is an attempt to study and dissect the necessary organisms from the body of European national drug control policies for the purpose of understanding why European countries have developed different approaches towards the modern drug use phenomenon.

One of the premises outlined in chapter one of this study is that governmental drug policies are not based upon the degree of problematic drug use. Available EMCDDA statistics indicate that there is no observable correlation between the robustness of a drug policy and the prevalence of drug use across the fifteen EU member states. In other words, drug policy is not a product of drug use; nor is there evidence that drug policy can substantially control the level of drug use – despite politicians' and policy makers' desire to do so. However, drug policy is influential in determining the *conditions* that drugs are used under. Drug policy may effect dominant patterns of drug use that occur under each drug regime, and they certainly influence the social, legal, and health consequences of drug use.

The term 'drug control systems' was used in this study, because the specific way in which societies 'deal' with the question of illicit drug use, is the result of a series of processes; cultural, social, traditions and political factors. Therefore, 'drug control system' is a more appropriate phrase to cover societies' ways of dealing with drugs over the term 'drug policy'. The French, Dutch, and Swedish chapters have shown that societies' reactions to illicit drug use are based on various assumptions about drugs and drug use, and are built on various national traditions. A national drug control system can be regarded as a multifaceted process that has social, political and cultural dimensions. A drug control system refers to the complex whole of assumptions and traditions underlying drug policy, as well as to the practical outcome of what have become general responses to drugs. The values of a drug control system are generally shared by most people involved: politicians and policy makers, law enforcement officers, attorneys and judges, social workers and care and treatment personnel, and to some extent the drug users and drug dealers.

Which of these three drug policies works 'best' is not directly answerable. A country's drug policy does not substantially impact the prevalence of drug use although it does influence the conditions under which drugs are being used. Which type of policy works 'best', is therefore dependent on what a drug control system aims to achieve and how it wishes to control the drug use phenomenon. Different drug control systems produce differing results. The effects of a particular drug control system are dependent upon the powers and traditions that shape it and establish its direction – it depends on what is the aim and function of a drug control system.

The French – 'call-to-order'– drug control system has a powerful law enforcement component, emphasizing the moral standards and norms that have been defined by the constitutional state, outlining allowable boundaries for citizens. Considering the strong law enforcement component this drug control system produces many arrests. The law enforcement apparatus has been set up with the aim of setting standards, enforcing laws, confirming and protecting the states norms. Law enforcement is not willing to easily disburse these powers. France has the highest drug use figures of the three countries under study, despite the strong drug law enforcement. That many young French people use drugs seems mostly related to a general culture of ingestion. It may be hypothesised that the high prevalence of cannabis (hashish) use among French teenagers is first explained by the high rates of tobacco smoking among them. The use of prescription drugs is also high in France. Since the implementation of Frances 1995 drug policy France has formally shifted towards a large scale harm reduction, substitution treatment plan.

The Dutch – accommodation – drug control system has a weak law enforcement, but strong public health component, pragmatically arranging and accommodating modern drug use into society. The Dutch drug control system aims to accommodate modern drug use by offering a certain degree of freedom to people, and making drug use 'open' and visible. The primary concern of the Dutch system is not drug use, it is keeping the drug-related damage low. The strong harm reduction orientation therefore produces relatively low morbidity. Cannabis use is accommodated by allowing and regulating the retail market. Coffee shops have to pay income tax over the profits, and the personnel pay tax like any worker in the Netherlands. Cannabis in itself remains a totally illegal product, and the larger scale cannabis trade is illegal. The Dutch accommodation model's possibilities are used and abused. The Dutch drug tolerance delta obviously attracts consumers, but it also attracts illegal drug traders who follow the money trail. Some traders have grown big and since their trade remains illegal, trade arguments are often settled through informal and illegal means, such as by the use of violence. That drug use is lower than might be expected in view of the freedom to 'do drugs' is possibly explained by the strong beer culture. Amsterdam and Holland are also home of the beers Amstel and Heineken and beer has remained the preferred intoxicant for young Dutch people.

The Swedish – containment – drug control system has a powerful idealistic welfare state tradition and has developed a comprehensive care and control response aimed at physically and socially 'containing' and keeping away the undesired modern drug use phenomenon. Drug control in this system takes the form of a combination of social state intervention through social workers, but increasingly law enforcers. Since the main focus of this drug control system is on banning the phenomenon of drug use, this is where the efforts have been put. This drug control system was able to contain drug use among its homogenous population to some extent until the 1990s, but it required many drastic prevention and control efforts. Most 'normal' or 'straight' people stopped using drugs which partly explains the decrease in recreational use. The increased containment and control measures, however, hardly decreased use among the deviant population, who pay the price for the containment policy: they are criminalised and marginalised and are 'paying' with their health. With the further internationalisation of youth culture, young people are now exposed to other sources of information outside the traditional governmental ones, and they have become more interested in drugs. More drug use may mean increased excessive use – since alcohol use patterns are often excessive, so may the use patterns of illegal drugs.

Now that three drug control systems of France, the Netherlands and Sweden have been described and analysed in detail, this final section of this last chapter further examines the question of whether it is possible to distil from the country descriptions some of the elements that together form a national drug control system. Is it possible to identify the factors that should be looked at in a particular country in order to get an understanding of its drugs policy? Eventually this might serve as a model or blueprint of different components through which other national drug control systems can be better understood as well.

The first component consists of the drug users during the 1960s, without whom there would be no policy. Their social characteristics and their interplay within society made a substantial difference: the 'revolutionary' drug users in France, the 'normal' drug users in the Netherlands and the 'deviant' amphetamine injectors in Sweden. The drug users themselves generally did not have much voice in the debate, except in the Netherlands.

The second component is the role of the professionals, the scientists who interpreted drug use and who drew conclusions that suggested – directly or indirectly – strategies for handling the phenomenon. In France, psychiatrists predicated their understanding of drug use upon a psychoanalytical (Lacanian) theoretical basis. Claude Olievenstein took a central role in formulating the specifics of this perspective. In the Netherlands, sociological thinking held sway, and in particular, the labelling theory was influential in interpreting the drug problem. Professor Hulsman paved the way for decriminalisation through his leadership of the first advisory drug commission. Sociologist Herman Cohen, who had been a member of both the Hulsman and Baan Commission, played an important role in supplying data on drug users. In Sweden it was a police doctor, Nils Bejerot, and his theory of contagious drug use that had a major influence on Swedish drug policy. It is difficult to determine whether the central place of these scientists is a 'coincidence', of being at the right spot at the right time thereby being able to fulfil a demand for knowledge, or whether larger social or political structures allowed them to acquire that influential position.[42]

---

42 This touches an epistemological question: is history explained by and written through 'big' and influential individuals, which is the traditional historiography, or is history better understood through larger social and political structures, which allows certain individuals to acquire influential positions? Influenced by twentieth century French historiography such as the *Annales* School, the latter is the more modern historiography, which also includes describing the history of mentalities.

A third component of the drug control system is geography. According to Montesquieu, latitude and especially climate influence people's morality, liberty, religion and also the political system.[43] While his theories might seem extreme for this discussion, the point remains that latitude and climate have some influence on moods,[44] and may also be influential on mentalities and behaviours. Accordingly, alcohol use represents a striking example that stronger liquor drinking traditions occur more frequently in the higher latitudes – the so-called Vodka Belt. This social pattern of hard liquor consumption also led to abuses and a perception of social ills caused by alcohol consumption, which is why more than half of temperance cultures are in the Vodka Belt.[45] Conversely, the warmer climates of the lower latitudes consume lighter alcoholic drinks, like wine, which were better tolerated by society, leading to broader cultural acceptance in Christian Europe.

Geographical patterns can also be identified with regards to illicit drug use. Culturally dominant and trend-setting western countries in the area of youth culture – music, (M)TV, fashion and trends – such as the United Kingdom and the United States have higher rates of experimental drug use than places that are more peripheral in that sense, such as Greece and Scandinavia. And despite the fact that much of the world is now electrically 'wired', physical distance still plays an important role in the diffusion of cultural phenomena. This makes it understandable why drug use is also high in countries that are close to the 'cultural centres' of youth culture, such as Canada to the United States, and Ireland to the United Kingdom. Sharing the same language of course helps in the cultural transmittance. The level of illicit drug use is also related to the degree of urbanisation. Cities have always been places where different customs and cultures exist and meet, and where more freedom exists to have different lifestyles, also making them centres of innovation.[46] Modern drug use is also more of an urban phenomenon, being more prevalent and accepted among people with urban or metropolitan lifestyles. The correlation between urbanisation and the prevalence of drug use is clear in both the European Union and the

---

43 Baron de Montesquieu, in his famous *Esprits des lois* (1748) translated as *The Spirit of the Laws*, considered climate to be one of the most important natural laws. See MacFarlane (2000), *The Riddle of the Modern World: Of Liberty, Wealth and Equality.*

44 Of the three countries the effect of climate is the clearest in the most Nordic Sweden. The cold and dark winters become much more bearable when there is snow, as it reflects the little light there is. In winters with little snow, more people are depressed and go into light therapy. In the Netherlands the weather is so variable that it is has become a very common subject of social talk. In France, people love going to the warmer, sunny south, *le Midi*, especially in the August holiday month.

45 As a reminder from chapter five: the 'vodka belt' stretches from Europe to America and includes Canada, Russia, Poland, and Iceland, Norway, Sweden and Finland. The background is at least party related to climate: it is too cold to produce wine, and beverages like beer and ale could not be stored and were difficult to distribute. The nine temperance cultures are the United States, Canada, the United Kingdom, Australia, New Zealand, as well ad Finland, Iceland, Norway, and Sweden.

46 As compared to the countryside where tradition is more important.

United States.[47] Even in the small and largely urbanised country of the Nether-lands a remarkable correlation was found between the level of drug use and population density.[48] The urbanisation factor may also explain why in some countries and certainly in their bigger cities drug use has grown and normalised to the extent that a majority of young people have used illegal drugs. These geographical factors could explain why experimental drug use has never been very high in Sweden, and why it is higher in the Netherlands and France – especially in their capitals Amsterdam and Paris.[49]

The fourth component of the drug control systems is formed by what is called state or policy traditions which are certain aspects of policy making that are present or absent in each of the three countries. This could include the role of the Church,[50] but in this study these components refer more specifically to law enforcement, (health) care and welfare systems. In France, the police and the Ministry of Interior are traditionally powerful, a power that derives from France's turbulent history and was predicated upon the need to guarantee law and order. Police and *gendarmerie* form a powerful and almost independent force with its own dynamic, to the extent that despite guidelines recommending the contrary, law enforcement agencies continued arresting cannabis users. In the Netherlands, there is no strong law enforcement tradition. The police have a different role in society; not so much as operatives for the state, but as an extension of the people.[51] The fact that there is no centralised police force – but twenty-five regional forces – may limit its power. Sweden saw the creation of a national police force in 1965, which gave it a stronger political lobby. The national police embraced the conclusions of police doctor Bejerot and actively promoted them.[52] Sweden has a strong social democratic welfare state tradition, combined with influential popular mass movements and a temperance culture. The influence of popular mass movements was evident in the nineteenth century when they managed to push through a restrictive alcohol policy, although they did not fulfil their real aim, an alcohol-free society. In the twentieth century popular mass movements became the driving force behind their restrictive

---

47   See EMCDDA (2002 and 2003), *Annual Report*, and the U.S. national drug use survey: SAMHSA (2003), *Results from National Household Survey on Drug Abuse.*

48   See Abraham et al. (2002), *Licit and Illicit Drug Use in the Netherlands, 2001.*

49   In Amsterdam, (experimental) drug use is twice as high as in the Netherlands as a whole.

50   For example, if Italy and Greece would be subject of this study the Catholic and the Orthodox Church would constitute powerful lobbies in their national drug control systems.

51   This may be a bit of a blunt way of characterising the difference, but it touches the essence of the different roles of police in the two countries.

52   Lenke & Olsson (1996a: 111) note in 'Sweden: Zero Tolerance Wins the Argument?' that after the national police board was created in 1965, Bejerot's conclusions were "given massive support and promotion by a police organisation that probably has no equivalent in Western society when it comes to the degree of centralisation and political influence in society". It is not sure if the latter statement included the French police, but in another paper Lenke & Olsson make the convincing point that the "organisation's central bureaucracy numbers over 1,000 people, which constitutes a substantial force for lobbying due to its strong connections with the media, especially the tabloid press". See Lenke & Olsson (1995: 4), *Constructing a Drug-Free Society.*

approach towards drugs. This time popular mass movement managed to get their viewpoints across completely, as the governments took up their position to strive for a drug-free Sweden. The Netherlands has a strong tradition of local policy making, with local municipalities having significant power. Some policies are mostly decided at the local level. This was the case with the early cannabis policies of the late 1960s, and continues to be so today.[53] Dutch local health services also played an especially important role in the early development of harm reduction policy.

A fifth, related factor for the understanding of national drug control systems is what can be called the state-citizen relationship. This relationship can take many forms within countries, and determines the extent to which citizens have the freedom to adopt new behaviours such as drug use – or whether the state has the authority restricts this form of personal freedom. The question arises of how much freedom and deviance is allowed in a country which can be understood within a relative context. As the country chapters have shown, considerable differences exist on this point. In France, the law has a symbolic importance as an extension of the norms established by the strong central state. To openly disrespect this law, leads to a strong corrective reaction from the part of the state. Part of the Dutch political tradition is the consultative society, in which all parties are heard. This was especially so in the Dutch 1960s, when a process of democratisation and emancipation was given an extra push, furthered by the void that emerged with the collapse of the political pillarisation system. For the drugs field, this meant that Dutch drug users had a voice since the 1960s, as the advisory commissions demonstrated a willingness to listen to them as well. The strongly rooted Dutch notion of individual freedom gave people some liberty to be 'different'. This liberty is however limited and seems to have gone a bit too far, as the concept of nuisance became important since the 1990s. In that sense, the liberty principle of John Stuart Mills seems to apply to the Dutch situation: liberty is limited by other people's liberty.[54] In Sweden, the welfare state tradition means that the state can intervene into people's private lives in the name of the common good, the people. This contrasts with France, where these interventions are made in the name of the state. However, unlike France, which also has a strong state, interventions in Sweden are not only performed by the police but also by social workers. The Swedish social democratic tradition of 'solidarity', combined with a culturally homogenous society, places a great deal of emphasis on 'sameness'. Eccentricity and deviance are not positively regarded and receive quick disapproval, with the risk that what is first a little deviant can quickly spiral into marginalisation and further deviance.

---

53 For example, it is up to the municipality, the town council, whether or not to have a coffee shop, and it is the triangle of mayor, police chief and prosecutor that is an important body where decisions are made for local policing and law and order.

54 Maris (1999), 'The disasters of war: American repression versus Dutch tolerance in drug policy'.

The final and most important component of drug control systems is defined as culture and cultural identity. Each of the country chapters started with a rather extensive section on geography, history and the people, in which a large part was devoted to people and culture. In this study it is argued that countries have fundamental cultural characteristics that have historically evolved. This is maybe truer for those European nations that invested heavily in constructing national identities in their process of nation building during the nineteenth and twentieth century. The national self-image, and the ways people define and actually construct themselves as belonging to a nation is part of this cultural process. The ways people define themselves, influences what they consider to be part of their identities and culture, as well as that which they feel should be excluded. This is relevant to the illicit drugs phenomenon, as this process of self-definition also determines whether drug use can become an accepted part of the cultural realm, and be absorbed into it, or whether it is considered too different and deviant to be allowed. The French view on modern drug use in the late 1960s was that it posed a threat to law and order. As drug use occurred openly in groups, the suggestion on the part of the state was that law and order itself were being challenged. It was interpreted as a sign of revolt, of which French history is full. The pragmatic Dutch, on the other hand, saw drug use as inevitable, and not enough of a problem to justify legal sanctions, and they gradually accommodated the cannabis use and trade. The Swedes saw drug use as threat, too, just like the French, but one that is more cultural in nature, as being un-Swedish.

Now that the issues of culture and cultural self-definition have been touched upon, a more fundamental question can be addressed, namely whether drug control systems are really only about drugs and containing the drug problem. This is what they appear to be about at first sight, but at a deeper, more abstract level, this chapter as well as the previous ones have shown, that public policies are not only, and maybe not truly, about drugs. At the end of this study the idea will be put forward, somewhat speculatively, that national drug control systems, at least partly, serve another function of contributing to the national cultural identity. As such, the public responses towards drugs are not only a function of cultural self-definition; they also contribute to that process. To illustrate the last point, it is best to first discuss it in respect to the most obvious Swedish case, before addressing the more subtle cases of the Netherlands and France.

Chapter five on the Swedish drug control system ended with a deeper explanation for the restrictive approach. While there were no signs that the drug problem was on the increase in the 1970s and 1980s, Swedish drug policy gradually became more restrictive. In order to understand this, it was argued, primarily based on the publications of Scandinavian criminologists such as Henrik Tham, the restrictive policy should be understood within the context of decreased security, whereby the restrictive drugs approach served to reinforce a national identity. Tellingly, the term, 'Swedish model', today refers specifically to Swedish drug policy, and no longer to welfare state or, as in its original meaning, to the labour market model. For the outside world, this worked too, as Sweden came to be known as a country where a restrictive policy bore fruit and decreased the number of drug users. For decades, Sweden had been the example of a successful welfare state that managed to combine economic prosperity, but without overtones of the 'hard' capitalist way, but instead, in a softer, social democratic, welfare state manner. Many Swedes had long considered their country to be (among) the best in the world, but the economic downturn of the 1990s resulted in declining economic and social security, to some extent shattering the perfection held within this view. EU membership in 1995, along with increasing numbers of immigrants, found the Swedes entering a time of increasing uncertainties. The notion of the success of Swedish drug policy had been relentlessly hammered into the heads of most citizens, and since the 1990s has been held up by the Swedes as an international prototype. In the difficult times the Swedes have been facing, this could be seen to offer the ancillary effect of boosting national pride and perhaps offering Swedish citizens something to hold onto in changing and uncertain times.

In the Netherlands, the national drug control system also helped define a national identity. Being one of the original founders of the European Union, the increasing number of member states, gradually decreased Dutch political influence and independence. Also, being a relatively small country with an internationally oriented economy, combined with the disappearance of certain national symbols such as the Dutch currency, and several prestigious companies either going bankrupt or being bought by foreign companies, the Dutch also experienced some alterations in national identity. In the ever important economy, whose prosperity is more dependent on international market fluctuations than on interior markets and national political decisions, a climate encouraging increased internationalisation has emerged, simultaneously bringing with it problems often faced by smaller countries, specifically, an increasing difficulty in determining a home-grown sense of national identity.[55] One of the few remaining areas where the Dutch still exercise some degree of autonomy is in their drug policy. This point was made earlier as a somewhat sarcastic remark, but this time it is used as a serious argument. Coffee shops happen to be one of those very few things that the Dutch have to distinguishes themselves, and confers, especially upon the younger generation, a degree of respect when they visit other countries.[56] Internally, the liberal Dutch approach, exemplified and symbolised by the coffee shop, helps keep up the self-image of a tolerant

---

55 The craze over the Dutch football team, although this is not unique to the Netherlands, shows how 'needy' the Dutch are for national symbols and prestige.

56 This is not only true in progressive, left wing circles, but also in the conservative ones. An anecdote may help to clarify this point. In November 2001 the youth branch JOVD of the (liberal-) conservative VVD party organised a forum on drug policy. When the international secretary of JOVD was asked about his international experiences and reactions towards Dutch drug policy in the political circuits he frequented, he explained that they, being Dutch, were sometimes treated as 'heroes' by representatives of like-minded political parties for the liberal Dutch cannabis policy.

people. Some of this Dutch tolerance is a myth, and much of it is built upon public indifference. Yet, it remains to be related to the Dutch notion of individual freedom: allowing behaviours as long as they do not harm others. As Dutch drug policy came under criticism from the French, Dutch policy makers and bureaucrats defended the Dutch coffee shop system as an achievement that had to be preserved. The French attacks on the Dutch coffee shops only reinforced this internal support for Dutch drug policy.[57] As such, Chirac's constant criticism was counterproductive and eventually gave a boost to the coffee shop as a symbol of Dutch tolerance.

The French drug control system also serves a deeper function. Officially, France embraced a policy of harm reduction, but in practice many of the traditional repressive elements remained in place. For example, although the political decision was to have a less punitive approach towards cannabis, in practice this guideline has not been followed and users continue to be arrested. This reluctance to actually liberalise the cannabis policy in practice, or put differently, the persistence of a repressive response can be explained by the strong law enforcement tradition, which in turn represents a strong state. In the French republican tradition, laws play an important role, and respect for the law is vital. Laws are some kind of extension of the state and are regarded as highly important defenders and safeguards of republican values. They are like the beacons of state and society, giving direction to the citizens. What is allowed and what is not, is imposed upon the citizens from 'above', by the state.[58] In the Republican tradition, if the law is no longer respected, the republic itself is at stake, as it means the points of orientation are lost and society risks going adrift. In the absence of clear laws or rules, there will be chaos and anarchy.[59] Following that logic, defending the drug laws actually becomes defending the Republican state. This explains why, despite the ongoing discussions on liberalisation in the 1970s drug legislation, politicians remain reluctant to do so, as they generally feel bound to defend the republican tradition.

---

57 By 1996 the French had a lower position on a Dutch 'ladder of trust' which shows how much they like other nationalities. The lower French position is most likely explained by the French attacks on Dutch drug policy. See Dekker (1999), *Nationaal favoritisme, germanofobie en Europees burgerschap,* footnote 42.

58 A recent example of this is the governmental decision, announced by president Chirac in December 2003, to ban conspicuous religious signs from schools, such as the Christian cross, the Islamic head scarf and the Jewish skull cap. In the French republican tradition, state and religion are clearly separated. The state is secular – in an address to the nation, president Chirac called secularism one of the great successes of the republic – and as a consequence, so too must be state schools.

59 In the areas of drugs, the law has much symbolic value (see chapter four). As Belgian philosophers Stengers and Ralet (1991: 64-65) explain in their *Drogues. Le défi hollandais,* French drug law is like a symbolic father as it is supposed to structure and give direction to people, especially the young. In that sense, the state takes a parenting role, by putting borders and by structuring the subjective life of 'the child'. The intervention has a structuring effect on young people, especially on those who are weakly structured, according psychiatrists, an argument that is also put forward in the governmental report Trautmann (1990), *Lutte contre la toxicomanie et le trafic des stupéfiant.*

In closing, it has been shown that national drug control systems are far more complex manifestations than they appear to be at first glance. National drug control systems refer to the way countries handle illegal drugs in all their facets. This includes not only their underlying philosophies – the ideological and scientific foundations on which the general approach towards drugs is based – but also the role played by citizens and practitioners who keep the policies alive and play their part in perpetuating the system by executing it, and if necessary, defending or promoting it. National drug control systems are interwoven complexes that evolved in historically and culturally specific ways that are related to the country with great specificity. Of course, the systems are designed primarily about drug problems, but inevitably are implicated within the larger cultural and political contexts of the societies in which they emerge. The phenomenon of modern drug use in the 1960s was the primary reason to establish national responses. But the individual ways these responses further developed and the ways they would operate, demonstrated that they involved a wide range of other factors.

As national drug control systems evolved, they gradually became 'systems of thought'.[60] A system of thought includes ideas about the characteristics of substances, what drugs do to people, why people use them, what makes them continue or quit, and how the drugs issue should be handled for those who do not use drugs. The practitioners from the different corners of the drug control systems familiarise themselves with their own particular system of thought. In the next phase they internalise it, start finding it normal, and eventually it becomes their reference. This is possible since every drug control system has its own internal logic, its own form of rationality. This is perfectly possible, as different forms of rationality exist and practices do not exist without a certain form of rationality.[61] This is why a drug control system seems totally rational to most of the people and practitioners executing it or being otherwise involved in a national (or international) drug control system.

Since a drug control system is also a system of thought, it is interesting to look at the discourse, the language that is used by the practitioners of the drug control system. This is why this study started by looking at the three drug discourses of France, the Netherlands, and Sweden which were presented at the UN General Assembly Special Session (UNGASS) in 1998. Taking a phenomenological view of a drug discourse, these discourses are an expression of drug control systems, since they stand for a way of thinking, a system of thought, determining what is being said, which words are allowed to be used, and which are not. Ultimately, a discourse can be considered to be "constituted by the difference between what one could say correctly at one period (under the

---

60 It was Foucault's way of studying the histories of 'ideas' and 'sciences' that brought up the term 'system of thought'. See Foucault (1991), 'Politics and the study of discourse', 58.
61 Foucault (1991), 'Questions of method', 79.

rules of grammar and logic) and what is actually said".[62] This indeed applies to the three drug control systems in this study; each of them has its limits of what can be articulated politically or culturally. In that sense, drug control systems also act as filters, only allowing certain information to pass through. Michel Foucault described these mechanisms and used them as a method for his archaeology: the limits and forms of the 'sayable', conservation and memory; what is allowed to be said, conserved (and what disappears), and remembered (and what has been abandoned or excluded as foreign).[63] Examples of information that are not allowed and 'filtered out', can be found in each of the three drug control systems.

In France, politicians often talk about the drug problem, but in the French drug control system, these problems are never addressed within their proper social economic context which would indicate that drug problems occur more frequently in the lower class suburbs, and that they are attended by a wide array of other serious social problems, including an underground drugs economy that for many offers opportunities and provides an alternative for the normal jobs that are difficult to find. Additionally, part of the French drug control system is that it encourages the dismantling of drug trafficking networks, therefore necessitating that police initiate arrests of drug users for information gathering purposes. Although it is rare that big networks are dismantled through this 'bottom up' strategy, law enforcers continue using this argument to justify their actions. Another French example is that illicit drugs are usually set apart in a distinct category, different and separate from several popular legal drugs. The fact that cigarettes and alcohol are more damaging than illicit drugs was, until recently, very much a taboo subject. A 'heavy weight' scientific commission (Rocques) was necessary to open the debate on legal and illegal drugs, but many French people still find it hard to accept that their cherished wine is now considered a 'drug'. The fact that the debate has broadened and taboos are being broken, indicates that the drug control system is changing and opening up. In France there is now much more (fundamental) debate – which also fits into the wider French intellectual and discussion culture – compared to the Dutch and Swedish drug control systems that are more solid, firm and also inert. In that respect, the limits of what is 'sayable' are therefore more clearly defined in the Netherlands and Sweden.

In the Dutch drug control system, the fact that problems related to cannabis use, such as (young) people developing problematic use patterns, or having psychological or psychiatric problems related to the use of (potent) cannabis, in worst cases schizophrenia, is not particularly open to discussion. There was, in fact, an apparent taboo placed upon discussing them, even though these problems are not intrinsic to cannabis use in the Netherlands. Another example

---

62   Foucault (1991), 'Politics and the study of discourse', 63.
63   See Foucault (1991), 'Politics and the study of discourse', 59-60.

of what is not really 'sayable' in the Dutch drug control system is that the half-way *de facto* legalisation of cannabis has also created problems. Users can no longer be arrested for possessing and buying cannabis, but the owners of coffee shops still have to operate in an illegal market, which has the disadvantages of every illegal economy: not being able to go to the police or take an attorney when someone did not deliver what he promised.[64] That illegal substances have been allowed to be sold for some thirty years now, also has created problems of black money, and has offered opportunities for others with black money, too, as they could open a coffee shop. Hence, the longer this ambiguous policy endures, the more black money and criminals it will attract, a phenomenon that is called the 'Las Vegas Effect'.[65] Dutch politicians too easily regard Dutch drug policy as innovative and successful, without realising its internal contradictions, which also leads to problems. The same argument can be made to the drug trade and central role of the Netherlands in it. Although it is true that its central place in the trade of cannabis and ecstasy and to some extent cocaine, is mainly explained by the geography and economy of the Netherlands, Dutch politicians seem to have underestimated the very attractive role – not only logistically – of the Netherlands for drug dealers and traders. They might also have underestimated the strong Dutch tradition of doing business and trading over the world oceans, for which the liberal attitude towards drugs offered opportunities.[66]

In the Swedish drug control system there are also examples of the 'unsayable'. To begin with, the expression 'drug use' is taboo, as the correct expression is 'drug abuse', just like in the United States and in UN texts. An example of something that is not said, is the prevalence of the use of toxic solvents like paint thinner and glue amongst Swedish youth. Swedish officials like to emphasise the low prevalence of cannabis among their teenagers, but they do not mention that the prevalence of solvents is actually higher.[67] It seems that low illicit drug use goes together with some teenagers taking refuge in substances such as solvents as glue and paint thinner, psychoactive substances that are more associated with street children in cities like Nairobi, Managua and more

---

64 In worst cases this means fire arms are being used in the larger trade, as big dealers run the risk of being ripped and they might feel they have to protect themselves. This has not so much to do with the cannabis trade itself, nor with the Dutch situation, but is a characteristic of an illegal sector.

65 Among other things, the Las Vegas effect refers to the fact that legalised gambling also attracted criminal elements, as the big gambling sector offered opportunities for money laundering.

66 As a top European civil servant involved in many international projects once remarked in an interview (for *Drugs and Decision-Making in the European Union*): every where you find certain people or certain countries that have a certain business mentality, have a nose for that sort of thing, who see and seize opportunities for doing business. He thought this was true for the Dutch in Europe, the Colombians in South America and the Nigerians in West Africa, and he found it no coincidence all three were more involved in the international drug trade.

67 Of Swedish teenagers of 15-16 years olds, eight percent had used solvents and seven percent cannabis. Of the fifteen EU countries, it is only in Sweden and Greece where the prevalence of solvents among teenagers is higher than that of cannabis. See the statistical tables of the EMCDDA at «www.emcdda.org».

recently also Baghdad, rather than with Stockholm.[68] Another example of what is filtered out by the Swedish drug control system is what could be described as called a quite successful Swedish amphetamines control policy. Amphetamines were legally available from the 1930s to the 1960s and generally did not seem to cause much problems or lead to abuse. There was abuse, but this was especially by deviant youth who started injecting the pills in large quantities, a phenomenon which led to stricter control measures. However, the number of these 'severe abusers' were small, in 1959, estimated at 500-1,000, out of a total number over 300,000 consumers.[69] It could be concluded that the number of abusers was relatively small and that most Swedish amphetamine users managed to control their use. A clearer example of data or knowledge not being welcome as part of history are the 1965-67 Swedish prescription practices that got out of hand, entering official history as an 'experiment' that had devastating effects. The most recent example of unwelcome information in the Swedish drug control system is the high number of overdoses.

Finally, a concept of drug control systems as systems of thought, only allowing certain information to go through, explains why these different drug control systems so often lead to confusion of tongues among professionals and politicians. When discussing the drug issue with colleagues from other countries, they are under the impression that they are talking about the same matters, but this study has shown that the language each of the participants of a national drug control system use, actually stands for different systems of thought and different drug control systems through which information is interpreted and filtered. All drug control systems have their internal logic. For politicians, policy makers and professionals, their national drug policy often appears to be the most logical one. They have grown up with 'their' drug control system, have acquainted themselves with it, and it has become part and parcel of their professional outlook. As a result they find it hard to 'step' out of this belief system and to step outside of the 'box'. This explains why it is difficult to understand one another's national drug control system, as each party does not comprehend the unsaid premises and assumptions on which the other system is built.

68 About glue sniffing in Managua, see Van Heijningen & Van der Winden (1999), *Los Huelepegas*. About glue sniffing in Baghdad, see Beaumont (2003) in *The Observer and Guardian Weekly*: 'Drug craze is fuelling murder on streets of Iraqi capital'.
69 For data, see table 3.1 in Boekhout van Solinge (1997) *The Swedish Drug Control System*, 39, taken from Olsson (1994), *Narkotikaproblemets bakgrund*. See also Goldberg (1968a), 'Drug abuse in Sweden', and Goldberg (1968b), 'Drug abuse in Sweden (II) '.

References

Abraham, Manja D., Hendrien L. Kaal, Peter D.A. Cohen (2002), *Licit and Illicit Drug Use in the Netherlands, 2001*, Amsterdam: CEDRO/Mets &Schilt.

Adelaars, Arno (1991), *Ecstasy*, Amsterdam: In de Knipscheer.

AFP – Association France Presse (2002), *La CRIIRAD publie un atlas des retombées de Tchernobyl*, press release of 24 February 2002.

AFP – Association France Presse (2003), *Cannabis, héroine, ecstasy: la hausse de la consommation en chiffres*, press release 4 June 2003.

Aquatias, S., H. Khedim, N. Murard, K. Guenfoud, and G. Fournier (1997), *l'usage dur des drogues douces. Recherche sur la consommation de cannabis dans la banlieue parisienne*, Paris: GRASS-IRESCO.

Bachman, Christian & Anne Coppel (1989), *La drogue dans le monde. Hier et aujourd'hui*, Paris: Albin Michel.

Barker, Chris & Dariusz Galasinski (2001), *Cultural Studies and Discourse Analysis. A Dialogue on Language and Identity*, London: Sage.

BCC News (2003), *French death report points finger*, 8 September 2003 («news.bbc.co.uk»).

Beaumont, Peter (2003), 'Drug craze is fuelling murder on streets of Iraqi capital', *The Observer*, 14 September 2003, also published in *The Guardian Weekly*.

Beck, François, Stéphane Legleye & Patrick Peretti-Watel (2000), *Regards sur la fin de l'adolescence – Consommations de produits psychoactifs dans l'Enquête ESCAPAD 2000*, Paris: Observatoire français des drogues et des toxicomanies (OFDT).

Beck, François, Stéphane Legleye & Patrick Peretti-Watel (2001), *Santé, mode de vie et usage de drogue à 18 ans – ESCAPAD 2001*, Paris: Observatoire français des drogues et des toxicomanies (OFDT).

Becker, Howard S. (1963), *Outsiders. Studies in the Sociology of Deviance*, New York: The Free Press.

Bejerot, Nils (1975), *Drug Abuse and Drug Policy. An epidemiological and methodological study of drug abuse of intravenous type in the Stockholm police arrest population 1965-1970 in relation to changes in drug policy*, Copenhagen: Munksgaard (Acta Psychiatrica Scandinavica, Supplementum 256).

Bejerot, Nils (1988), *The Swedish Addiction Epidemic in Global Perspective*, Speech given in France, the Soviet Union and USA, Stockholm: the Carnegie Institute (10 pages).

Bell, Jonathan (1999), 'SEITA : Consolidated Cigar's French Connection', *Smoke Shop* Vol. 26, Number 2, April 1999, «www.smokeshopmag.com».

Bennett, Chris (2002), 'The Plant of Kindness: Cannabis and Christianity', *High Times*, June 2002.

Bergeron, Henri (1999), *L'État et la toxicomanie. Histoire d'une singularité française*, Paris: Presses Universitaires de France.

Bergmark, Anders & Lars Oscarsson (1988), *Drug Abuse and Treatment. A Study of Social Conditions and Contextual Strategies*, Stockholm Studies in Social Work 4, Stockholm: School of Social Work, Stockholm University.

Bernat de Célis, Jacqueline (1992), *Fallait-il créer un délit d'usage illicite de stupéfiants. Une étude de sociologie legislative*, Paris: Centre de recherches sociologiques sur le droit et les institutions pénales (CESDIP).

Berridge, Virginia & Griffith Edwards (1981), *Opium and the People. Opiate Use in Nineteenth Century England*, London: Allen Lane.

Bewley-Taylor, David R. (1999), *The United States and International Drug Control, 1909-1997*, London & New York: Pinter.

Bewley-Taylor, David (2002), 'Habits of a Hegemon. The United States and the Future of the Global Drug Prohibition Regime', Transnational Institute (2002), *Breaking the Impasse. Polarisation and Paralysis in UN Drug Control*, TNI Briefing Series no. 5, Drugs and Democracy Programme, Amsterdam: Transnational Institute.

Bisiou, Yann (1999), 'Histoire des politiques criminelles. Le cas des régies françaises des stupéfiants', in: Claude Faugeron (ed.) (1999), *Les drogues en France. Politiques, marchés, usages*, 89-98, Geneva: Georg.

Blankenburg, Erhard & Freek Bruisma (1994), *Dutch Legal Culture*, Deventer/Boston: Kluwer Law and Taxation Publishers.

Boek, J.L.M. (1995), *Organisatie, functie en bevoegdheden van politie in Nederland. Juridische beschouwingen over het politiebestel en het politiebedrijf in historisch perspectief*, Politiestudies 17, Arnhem: Gouda Quint & Antwerpen: Kluwer Rechtswetenschappen.

Boek, J.L.M. (1999), 'De politiefunctie', in: C.J.C.F. Fijnaut, E.R. Muller & U. Rosenthal (eds.) (1999), *Politie. Studies over haar werking en organisatie*, Alphen aan den Rijn: Samsom.

Boekhout van Solinge, Tim (1995), *Standpunten drugsproblematiek (standpoints on the drug question)*, Report for the Royal Dutch Medical Society (KNMG).

Boekhout van Solinge, Tim (1995), 'Cannabis in Frankrijk'/'Le cannabis en France', in: Peter Cohen & Arjan Sas (eds.) (1996), *Cannabisbeleid in Duitsland, Frankrijk en de Verenigde Staten* (Cannabis Policy in Germany, France, and the United States), Amsterdam: CEDRO, University of Amsterdam.

Boekhout van Solinge, Tim (1996), *Heroïne, cocaïne en crack in Frankrijk. Handel, gebruik en beleid/ L'héroïne, la cocaïne et le crack en France. Trafic usage et politique*, Amsterdam: CEDRO, University of Amsterdam.

Boekhout van Solinge, Tim (1997a), *The Swedish Drug Control System. An in-depth Review and Analysis*, Amsterdam: Mets.

Boekhout van Solinge, Tim (1997b), 'Drugs in France: Prevalence of Use and Drug Seizures' in: Dirk Korf & Heleen Riper (eds.), *Illicit Drugs in Europe – Proceedings of the Seventh Annual Conference on Drug Use and Drug Policy in Europe*, pp. 68-73, Amsterdam: SISWO & Bonger Institute of Criminology.

Boekhout van Solinge, Tim (1999), 'Dutch Drug Policy in a European Context', *Journal of Drug Issues* 29 3 1999: 511-528.

Boekhout van Solinge, Tim (2001), *Op de pof. Cocaïnegebruik en gezondheid op straat*, Amsterdam: Rozenberg/Stichting Mainline.

Boekhout van Solinge, Tim (2002), *Drugs and Decision-Making in the European Union*, Amsterdam: Mets and Schilt.

Bosch, J.A., E.J.M. Pennings, F.A. de Wolff (1997), *Psycho-actieve Paddestoel- & Plantproducten. Toxicologie en klinische effecten*, Leiden: Laboratory for Toxicology.

Bovenkerk, Frank & Yücel Yeşilgöz (1998), *De maffia van Turkije*, Amsterdam: Meulenhoff/Kritak.

Bovenkerk, Frank (2001), *Misdaadprofielen*, Amsterdam: Meulenhoff.

Brink, Wim van den, Vincent M. Hendriks, Jan M. van Ree (1999), *Medical Co-Prescription of Heroin to Chronic, Treatment-Resistant Methadone Patients in the Netherlands*, *Journal of Drug Issues* 29 3 1999: 587-608.

Bruun, Kettil, Lynn Pan and Ingemar Rexed (1975), *The Gentlemen's Club: International Control of Drugs and Alcohol*. Chicago and London: The University of Chicago Press.

Bruun, K. (1975), *Alcohol Control Policies in a Public Health Perspective*, Helsinki: The Finnish Foundation for Alcohol Studies.

Burroughs, William (1953), *Junky*, New York: Penquin.

CAN – Swedish National Council for Information on Alcohol and Other Drugs (2001), *Trends in alcohol and other drugs in Sweden. Report 2001*, Summary of *Drogutvecklingen i Sverige, Rapport 2001*, Stockholm: CAN Report nr. 63.

Carpentier, Jean (1994), *La toxicomanie à l'héroïne en médicine générale*, Paris: Ellipses.

Chavannes, Marc (2000a), *Frankrijk achter de schermen. De stille revolutie van een trotse natie*, Amsterdam/Rotterdam: Prometheus/NRC Handelsblad.

Chavannes, Marc (2000b), 'Gedogen Allows the Dutch to Manage the Unmanageable', *Public Affairs Report* Vol.41, No. 4, September 2000, Institute of Governmental Studies, University of California, Berkeley.

Christi, N., and K. Bruun (1991), *Der nützliche Feind. Die Drogenpolitik und ihre Nutznieber*, Bielefeld: AJZ.

Clark, Norman H. (1976), *Deliver Us From Evil. An Interpretation of American Prohibition*, New York: W.W. Norton & Cy.

Clinard, Marshall B. & Robert F. Meier (1979), *Sociology of Deviant Behavior*, New York: Holt, Rinehart and Winston.

Cohen, Herman (1975), *Drugs, druggebruikers en drug-scene*, Alphen aan den Rijn: Samsom.

Cohen, P.D.A. (1994), *The case of the two Dutch drug policy commissions. An exercise in harm reduction 1968-1976*, Paper presented at the 5th International Conference on the Reduction of Drug Related Harm, 7-11 March 1994, Addiction Research Foundation: Toronto.

Cohen, Peter (2003), 'The drug prohibition church and the adventure of reformation', *The International Journal of Drug Policy* 14 (2003) 213-215.

Cohen, Peter D.A. & Hendrien L. Kaal (2001), *The irrelevance of drug policy. Patterns and careers of experienced cannabis use in the populations of Amsterdam, San Francisco and Bremen*, Amsterdam: CEDRO, University of Amsterdam.

Coles, S.F.A. (1949), *The Lovely Land. An interpretation of the Realm and People of Sweden*, London: Chapman & Hall.

Colombié, Thierry, Nacer Lalam and Michel Schiray (2000), *Drogue & Techno. Les trafiquants de rave*, Paris: Stock.

Conseil National des Villes (1994), *L'Économie souterraine de la drogue*, Paris: Conseil National des Villes & Maison des Sciences de L'Homme.

Coppel, Anne (2002), *Peut-on civiliser les drogues? De la guerre à la drogue à la reduction des risques*, Paris: La Découverte.

Daun, Åke (1996), *Swedish Mentality*, University Park, Pennsylvania: Pennsylvania University Press.

Dekker, Henk (1999), *Nationaal favoritisme, germanofobie, en Europees burgerschap. Socialisatie van emoties*, inaugural lecture University Utrecht.

Descartes, René (1631), *Letter to M. De Balzac*, 5 May 1631.

Dijk, W.K. van & L.H.C. Hulsman (eds.) (1970), *Drugs in Nederland*, Bussum: Paul Brand/Unieboek.

Dommering, Egbert (2003), 'Grensoverschrijdende censuur: het EHRM en oude en nieuwe media', pp. 177-217, in: Censures/Censuur. *Actes du colloque du 16 mai 2003 – Referaten van het colloquium van 16 mei 2003*, Bruxelles: Larcier.

Doyle, Mark (2003), *New drugs laws 'send wrong signal'*, BBC News, 26 February 2003 («news.bbc.co.uk»).

Duprez, Dominique & Michel Kokoreff (2000), *Les mondes de la drogue*, Paris: Odile Jacob.

Durkheim, Emile (1982), *The Rules of the Sociological Method. And selected texts on sociology and its method*, London: Macmillan (originally published in 1895 as *Les règles de la méthode sociologique*).

Ecoiffier, Mathieu (2002), 'Alain Labrousse, auteur d'un rapport sur la production de chanvre au Maroc: "Tout remettre à plat sur le cannabis"', *Liberation*, 12 March 2002.

Edwards, Griffith (1994), *Alcohol and the Public Good*, Oxford: Oxford University Press & World Health Organization (WHO).

Ehrenberg, Alain (1995), *L'individu incertain*, Paris: Calmann-Lévy.

Ehrenberg, Alain (1996), 'Comment vivre avec les drogues? Questions de recherche et enjeux politique', in: Communications (1996), *Vivre avec les drogues. Régulations, politiques, marchés, usages,* Paris: Seuil.

Eisenstein, Elisabeth L. (1985), *The Printing Press as an Agent of Change,* Cambridge: Cambridge University Press.

European Court of Human Rights (1999), *Case of Selmouni v. France*, Application no. 25803/94, judgment 28 July 1999, Strasbourg: Council of Europe.

European Monitoring Centre For Drugs and Drug Addiction – EMCDDA (1996), *Annual Report on the state of the drugs problem in the European Union*, Lisbon: EMCDDA.

European Monitoring Centre For Drugs and Drug Addiction – EMCDDA (1998), *Annual Report on the state of the drugs problem in the European Union*, Lisbon: EMCDDA.

European Monitoring Centre For Drugs and Drug Addiction – EMCDDA (1999), *Extended annual report on the state of the drugs problem in the European Union*, Lisbon: EMCDDA.

European Monitoring Centre for Drugs and Drug Addiction – EMCCDA (2001), *Annual Report on the state of the drugs problem in the European Union*, Lisbon: EMCDDA.

European Monitoring Centre for Drugs and Drug Addiction – EMCCDA (2002), *Annual Report on the state of the drugs problem in the European Union and Norway*, Lisbon: EMCDDA («annualreport.emcdda.eu.int/»).

European Monitoring Centre for Drugs and Drug Addiction – EMCCDA (2002), *Prosecution of drug users in Europe*, Lisbon: EMCDDA.

European Parliament, Spanish Presidency & European Commission (1996),*Conference on Drugs Policy. Summary of discussions and conclusions*, Brussels: European Commission.

Fabing, Howard D. (1956), 'On Going Berserk: A Neurochemical Inquiry', *The American Journal of Psychiatry* Vol. 113, 409-415.

Fazey, Cindy (2002), *The INCB and the Wizard of Oz. Usurping the Role of the Commission on Narcotics Drugs: The Politicisation and Unauthorised Expansion of the Role of the International Narcotics Control Board (INCB)*, Working Document for the Drug Policy Advisory Forum 'The Senlis Council'.

Fazey, Cindy S.J. (2003), 'The Commission on Narcotics Drugs and the United Nations International Drug Control Programme: politics, policies and prospects for change', *International Journal of Drug Policy* 14 (2003) 155-169.

Fijnaut, Cyrille, Frank Bovenkerk, Gerben Bruinsma & Henk van de Bunt (1998), *Organised Crime in the Netherlands*, The Hague: Kluwer Law International.

Folléa, Laurence (1999), 'Drogues: le rapport qui change tout', *Le Monde* 8 January 1999.

Forbes, Jill, Nick Hewlett & Francois Nectoux (2001), *Contemporary France. Essays and Texts on Politics, Economics, and Society*, Harlow: Pearson Education Limited.

Foucault, Michel (1972), *The Archaeolgy of Knowledge,* London: Tavistock.

Foucault, Michel (1991), 'Politics and the study of discourse', in: Graham Burchell, Colin Gordon and Peter Miller (eds.) (1991), *The Foucault Effect. Studies in Governmentality. With two lectures by and an interview with Michel Foucault*, London: Harvester Wheatsheaf.

Foucault, Michel (1991), 'Questions of method', in: Graham Burchell, Colin Gordon and Peter Miller (eds.) (1991), *The Foucault Effect. Studies in Governmentality. With two lectures by and an interview with Michel Foucault*, London: Harvester Wheatsheaf.

Foucault, Michel (1991), 'Politics and the study of discourse', in: Graham Burchell, Colin Gordon and Peter Miller (eds.) (1991), *The Foucault Effect. Studies in Governmentality. With two lectures by and an interview with Michel Foucault*, London: Harvester Wheatsheaf.

Friman, H. Richard (1996), *NarcoDiplomacy. Exporting the U.S. war on Drugs*, Ithaca/London: Cornell University Press.

Gentleman, Amelia (2003), 'Smoking them out', *Guardian*, 17 September 2003.

Gerritsen, Jan-Willem (1993), *De politieke economie van de roes*, Amsterdam: Amsterdam University Press. Also published in English (2000): *The control of fuddle and flash: a sociological history of the regulation of alcohol and opiates*, Leiden and Boston: Brill.

Goldberg, Leonard (1968a), 'Drug abuse in Sweden', *Bulletin on Narcotics* Vol. XX, No. 1, January - March 1968, 1-31.

Goldberg, Leonard (1968b), 'Drug abuse in Sweden (II)', *Bulletin on Narcotics* Vol. XX, No. 2, April - June 1968, 9-36.

Goldberg, Ted (1997), 'The Swedish Narcotics Control Model - A Critical Assessment', *The International Journal of Drug Policy* Vol. 8, No. 2, 1997.

Goldberg, Ted (2004), 'The evolution of Swedish Drug Policy', *Journal of Drug Issues* Vol. 34 03: 551-576.

Gootenburg, Paul (2001), *The Rise and Demise of Coca and Cocaine: As Licit Global 'Commodity chains', 1860-1950*, (preliminary) paper presented at conference on 'Latin America and Global Trade', Social Science History Institute, Stanford University, 16-17 November 2001 («sshi.stanford.edu/GlobalTrade2001/gootenberg.pdf»).

Gould, Arthur (1989), 'Cleaning the People's Home: recent developments in Sweden's addiction policy', *British Journal of Addiction* (1989) 84: 731-741.

Gould, Arthur (1993), *Capitalist Welfare States. A comparison of Japan, Britain & Sweden*, London/New York: Longman.

Gould, Arthur (1994), 'Pollution rituals in Sweden: the pursuit of a drug-free society' in: *Scandinavian Journal of Social Welfare* (1994) 3: 85-93.

Gould, Arthur (1998), 'Nationalism, immigrants and attitudes towards drugs', *International Journal of Drug Policy* (1998) Vol. 9, nr 2: 133-139.

Gould, Arthur (2001a), *Developments in Swedish Social Policy. Resisting Dionysus*, Hampshire: Palgrave.

Gould, Arthur (2001b), 'The Criminalisation of buying sex: the politics of prostitution in Sweden', *Journal of Social Policy* (2001) 30 3: 437-456.

Gramont, Sanche de (1970), *the French. Portrait of a People*, New York: Bantam.

Green, Jonathon (2002), Cannabis: *The Hip History of Hemp: Cannibis Indica; Cannabis Sativa*, London: Pavilion.

Grinspoon, Lestern and Peter Hedblom (1975), *The Speed Culture: Amphetamine Use and Abuse in America*, Cambridge: Harvard University Press.

Grönbladh, L, L.S. Öhlund & L.M. Gunne (1990), 'Mortality in heroin addiction: impact of methadone treatment', *Acta Psychiat Scand* 1990: 82, 223-227.

Gruppo Abele, in cooperation with TNI-IECAH (2003), *Synthetic Drug Trafficking in Three European Cities: Major Trends and the Involvement of Organised Crime*, Turin: Gruppo Abele.

Haarman, J.W. (1933), *Geschiedenis en inrichting der politie in Nederland. Met eenige aantekeningen omtrent de politie in andere landen*, Alphen aan den Rijn: Samsom.

Heijningen, Hans van & Bob van der Winden (1999), *Los Huelepegas. Vivir en el Callejón de la Muerte*, Managua: Asociación TESIS.

Henrion, R. (1995), *Rapport de la commission de réflexion sur la drogue et la toxicomanie*, Paris: La Documentation française.

Herer, Jack (2000), *The Emperor Wears No Clothes. Cannabis and the Conspiracy Against Marijuana*, Van Nuys: AH HA Publishing.

Herodotus (1992), *The Histories*, London: Penguin (originally written 450 BC).

Hewlett, Nick (2001), 'Politics in France', in: Jill Forbes, Nick Hewlett & Francois Nectoux (2001), *Contemporary France. Essays and Texts on Politics, Economics, and Society*, Harlow: Pearson Education Limited.

Hofland, H.J.A. (1996), 'Joseph Luns en de coffeeshop', *NRC Handelsblad*, 11 December 1996.

Horst, Han van der (1996), *The Low Sky. Understanding the Dutch*, Schiedam: Scriptum/ Nuffic.

Horst, Han van der (2001), *The Low Sky. Understanding the Dutch. The book that makes the Netherlands familiar*, Schiedam: Scriptum/Nuffic.

House of Commons, Home Affairs Committee (2002), *The Government's Drugs Policy: Is it working?*, Third Report of Session 2001-2002, London: The Stationery Office.

Hoyles, André (1971), 'Social Structures', in J.E. Flower (ed.) (1971), *France Today. Introductory Studies*, London: Methuen & Co Ltd.

Hübner, Lena (2001), *Narkotika och alcohol i den allmänna opinionen*, Stockholm: School of Social work, University of Stockholm.

Huisman, W. & C.M. Joubert (1998), 'Gedogen: een typisch Nederlands verschijnsel?', *Regelmaat* 1998:3, 145-152.

Hulsman, Louk (1986), *Afscheid van het strafrecht. Een pleidooi voor zelfregulering, met medewerking van Jacquline Bernat de Célis en Hans Smits*, Houten: Wereldvenster (Dutch translation from French publication of 1982: *Peines Perdues. Le système pénal en question*).

Inciyan, Erich (2001), 'Selon Alain Labrousse, "l'opium n'a pas été le nerf du terrorisme"', *Le Monde*, 20 October 2001.

International Narcotics Control Board – INCB (1997), *Report of the International Control Board for 1996*, Vienna: INCB.

Inzake Opsporing (1996), Appendix VIII, The Hague: Sdu (Report of the parliamentary inquiry into organised crime in the Netherlands).

Israëls, Han & Annet Mooij (2001), *Aan de Achtergracht. Honder jaar GG&GD Amsterdam*, Amsterdam: Bert Bakker.

Jansen, A.C.M. (2002), *The economics of cannabis cultivation in Europe*, Paper presented at the 2nd European Conference on Drug Trafficking and Law Enforcement. Paris, 26-27 September, 2002.

Jelsma, Martin (2003), 'Drugs in the UN system: the unwritten history of 1998 United Nations General Assembly Special Session on drugs', *International Journal of Drug Policy* 14 (2003) 181-195.

Johnsson, Hans-Ingvar (1995), *Spotlight on Sweden*, Värnamo: Fälths Tryckeri.

Johnstone, Barbara (2002), *Discourse Analysis*, Oxford: Blackwell.

Kelk, C. (1994), *De menselijke verantwoordelijkheid in het strafrecht*, Arnhem: Gouda Quint.

Keyser, Jason (2002), 'Israel center of ancient drug trade', *Jerusalem Post*, 12 August 2002.

Kloek, Joost & Wijnand Mijnhardt (2001), *1800. Blauwdrukken voor een samenleving*, Den Haag: Sdu.

Knapp, Andrew & Vincent Wright (2001), *The Government and Politics of France*, London/New York: Routledge.

Kopp, Pierre & Christophe Palle (1999), 'Economistes cherchent politique publique efficace', in: Claude Faugeron (ed.) (1999), *Les drogues en France. Politiques, marches, usages*, 249-267, Geneva: Georg.

Kopp, Pierre & Philippe Fenoglio (2000), *Le coût social des drogues licites (alcool et tabac) et illicities en France*, Paris: ODFT.

Kopp, Pierre (2001), *Calculating the social cost of illicit drugs. Method and tools for estimating the social cost of the use of psychotropic substances*, Strasbourg: Pompidou Group.

Korf, Dirk J. (1986), *Heroïnetoerisme I. Veldonderzoek naar het gebruik van harddrugs onder buitenlanders in Amsterdam*, Amsterdam: Stadsdrukkerij.

Korf, Dirk J. (1987), *Heroïnetoerisme II. Resultaten van een veldonderzoek onder 382 buitenlandse dagelijkse opiaatgebruikers in Amsterdam*, Amsterdam: Instituut voor Sociale Geografie, University of Amsterdam.

Korf, Dirk J. (1995), *Dutch Treat. Formal control and illicit drug use in the Netherlands*, Amsterdam: Thesis.

Korf, Dirk J., Heleen Riper & Bruce Bullington (1999), 'Windmills in Their Minds? Drug Policy and Drug Research in the Netherlands', *Journal of Drug Issues* 29 3 1999: 451-471.

Kort, Marcel de (1995), *Tussen patiënt en delinquent. Geschiedenis van het Nederlands drugsbeleid*, Hilversum: Verloren.

Kurian, George Thomas (1989), *World Encyclopedia of Police forces and Police Systems*, New York & Oxford: Facts on File.

Labrousse, A. & M. Koutouzis (1997), 'Drugs: the risks for the year 2000', in: D. Korf & H. Riper, *Illicit Drugs in Europe. Proceedings of the Seventh Annual Conference on Drug Use and Drug Policy in Europe*, Amsterdam: University of Amsterdam & SISWO.

Labrousse, Alain & Luis Romero (2001), *Sur la situation du cannabis dans le Rif marocain*, juin-août 2001, Paris: Observatoire français des drogues et des toxicomanies (OFDT).

Lachman, Dennis, Adam Benett, John H. Green, Robert Hagemann & Ramana Ramaswamy (1995), *Challenges to the Swedish Welfare State*, Washington DC: International Monetary Fund.

Lakoff, George & Mark Johnson (1980) *Metaphors we live by*, Chicago/London: University Of Chicago Press.

Lemaire, Ton (1995), *Godenspijs of duivelsbrood. Op het spoor van de vliegenzwam*, Baarn: Ambo.

Lemoine, Françoise (2001), 'Un jeune sur deux a déjà fumé du hasch', *Le Figaro*, 5 February 2001.

Lenke, Leif (1991), *The Significance of Distilled Beverages. Reflections on the Formation of Drinking Cultures and Anti-Drug Movements*, paper presented at the meeting of the Kettil Bruun Society for Social and Epidemiological Research on Alcohol, Sigtuna, Sweden, June 1991.

Lenke, Leif & Börje Olsson (1995), *Constructing a Drug-Free Society. Swedish Drug Policy in Perspective*, unpublished draft.

Lenke, Leif & Börje Olsson (1996a), 'Sweden: Zero Tolerance Wins the Argument?', in: Nicholas Dorn, Jørgen Jepsen and Ernesto Savona (eds.) (1996), *European Drug Policies and Enforcement*, Wiltshire: Macmillan.

Lenke, Leif & Börje Olsson (1996b), *Legal Drugs. The Swedish Legalizing Experiment of 1965-1967 in Retrospect*, Paper presented at the Conference on Drug Use and Drug Policy, Amsterdam, September 26-28, 1996.

Leuw, Ed & I. Haen Marshall (eds.) (1994), *Between Prohibition and Legalization. The Dutch Experiment in Drug Policy*, Amsterdam/New York: Kugler.

Levine, Harry G. (1978), *Demon of the Middle Class: Self-control, Liquor, and the Ideology of Temperance in 19th Century America*, Ph.D. thesis, Berkeley: University of California.

Levine, Harry G. (1992), 'Temperance cultures: concern about alcohol problems in Nordic and English-Speaking cultures', 15-36, in: M. Lader, G. Edwards and D.C. Drummond (eds.) (1992), *The Nature of Drug Related Problems*. New York: Oxford University Press.

Levine, Harry G. (1997), *Drug prohibition and demonization in the twentieth century*, Proceedings, International Conference on the Reduction of Drug Related Harm, Paris.

Levine, Harry G (2001), 'The Secret of World-Wide Drug Prohibition. The Varieties and Uses of Drug Prohibition', *The Independent Review. Journal of Political Economy* Vol. 7: 2 (fall 2002).

Levine, Harry G. (2003), 'Global drug prohibition: its uses and crises', commentary in *International Journal of Drug Policy* 14 (2003) 145-153, special issue on UN drug conventions.

Li, Hui-Lin (1975), 'The Origin and Use of Cannabis in Eastern Asia: Their Linguistic-Cultural Implications', 51-75, in: Vera Rubin (ed.) (1975), *Cannabis and Culture*, The Hague and Paris: Mouton.

Libération (2001), 'Un peu de cannabis, et la justice divague. Les risques pour les usagers diffèrent selon les tribunaux, en attendant un vrai débat', *Libération*, 8/9 December 2001.

Lijphart, Arend (1968), *The Politics of Accomodation. Pluralism and Democracy in the Netherlands*, Berkeley & Los Angeles: University of California.

Lissenberg, Elisabeth (2001), *Tegen de regels IV. Een inleiding in de criminologie*, Nijmegen: Ars Aequi Libri.

Lyman, Michael D. & Gary W. Potter (1996), *Drugs in Society. Causes, Concepts, and Control*, Cincinnati: Anderson.

MacAndrew, Craig & Robert B. Edgerton (1969), *Drunken Compartment: a Social Explanation*, Chicago: Aldine.

Macfarlane, Alain (2000), *The Riddle of the Modern World: Of Liberty, Wealth and Equality*, London: Macmillan.

Maris, C.W. (1999), 'The Disasters of War: American Repression Versus Dutch Tolerance in Drug Policy', *Journal of Drug Issues* 29 3 1999: 493-510.

Martineau, Hélène & Émilie Gomart (2000), *Politiques et expérimentations sur les drogues aux Pays-Bas*, Paris: ODFT.

McGlothlin, William H. (1975), 'Sociocultural Factors in Marihuana Use in The United States', 531-547, in: Vera Rubin (ed.) (1975), *Cannabis Cultures*, The Hague and Paris: Mouton.

McKenna, Terrence (1993), *Foods of the Gods: the Search for the Original Tree of Knowledge. A Radical History of Plants, Drugs, and Human Evolution*, New York: Bantam.

Michaëlis, Bo Tao (2001), 'On the Trail of Scandinavian Crime fiction. Scandinavian Crime Novels: too much Angst and not enough entertainment?', *Nordisk Litteratur/Nordic Literature* 2001: 12-17, Copenhagen: Nordbok.

Mignon, Patrick (1993), *Les 'toxicomanies légales' (alcool, tabac, médicaments)*, Paris: La documentation Française.

Ministère de l'Intérieur (1999), *Circulaire du 17 juin 1999. Les réponses judiciaires aux toxicomanies*, Paris: Ministère de l'Intérieur.

Ministry of Health, Welfare and Sports, Ministry of Justice, and Ministry of the Interior (1995a), *Drugs Policy in the Netherlands. Continuity and Change*, The Hague: Ministry of Health, Welfare and Sports.

Ministry of Health, Welfare and Sports (1995b), *Stadhuis en house ('Townhall and Rave'). Handreikingen voor gemeentelijk beleid inzake grootschalige manifestaties en uitgaansdrugs,* The Hague: Ministry of Health, Welfare and Sports.

Ministry of Justice (2002), *European City Conference on Cannabis Policy*, The Hague: Ministry of Justice, International Criminal Law Affairs.

Moerings, M. (ed.) (1994), *Hoe punitief is Nederland?*, Arnhem: Gouda Quint.

Montesquieu, Charles de Secondat (1748), *Esprits des lois*, Paris: Livre de Poche.

Musto, David E. (1997), 'International drug control: historical aspects and future challenges', in: United Nations International Drug Control Programme (1997), *World Drug Report*, Oxford: Oxford University Press, 165-167.

Musto, David (1999), *The American Disease. Origins of Narcotics Control*, New York: Oxford University Press (first published in 1973 by Yale University Press).

Nadelmann, Ethan A. (1990), 'Global prohibition regimes', *International Organization* 44 4, 1990: 479-526.

National Institute of Public Health (1995a), *Drug Policy. The Swedish Experience*, Stockholm.

National Institute of Public Health (1995b), *Swedish Alcohol Policy. Background and Present Situation*, Stockholm.

National Institute of Public Health (2001), *National Report Sweden 2001*, Report of Swedish focal Point to EMCCDA, Stockholm: National Institute of Public Health.

New Scientist (1998a), 'High anxieties. What the WHO doesn't want you to know about cannabis', issue 21st February 1998 ('Marijuana Special Report'). On-line: «www.newscientist.com/hottopics/marijuana/news.jsp».

New Scientist (1998b), 'Vraag een politieagent ... Go ahead, ask a cop for dope. The Dutch don't mind', issue 21st February 1998 ('Marijuana Special Report').

Nillson (1995), 'The Current Alcohol Situation in Sweden', in: Timo Kortteinen (ed.) (1989), *State Monopolies and Alcohol Prevention*, Report and Working Papers of a Collaborative International Study, Report No. 181, Helsinki: Social Research Institute of Alcohol Studies.

NRC Handelsblad, Profile: The Netherlands (2nd July 1998), Appendix in English, Rotterdam: NRC Handelsblad.

Observatoire français des drogues et des toxiomanies – ODFT (2000), 'Drogues et dependences: Indicateurs et tendances', *Tendances* nr. 19, January 2002.

Observatoire français des drogues et des toxiomanies – ODFT (2003), *Drogues et dependences. Indicateurs et tendances 2002*, Paris: OFDT.

Observatoire Géopolitique des Drogues – OGD (1994), *Rapport d'enquête sur les enjeux politiques, économiques et sociaux de la production et du trafic des drogues au Maroc*, Report published on at the request of the European Commission, Paris: OGD.

Olafsdottir, Hildigunnur (1999), 'The Entrance of Beer into a Persistent Spirits Culture', *Contemporary Drug Problems* 26:4 545-576 (Winter 1999).

Olafsdottir, Hildigunnur (1998), 'The Dynamics of Shifts in Alcoholic Beverage Preference: Effects of the Legalization of Beer in Iceland', *Journal of Studies on Alcohol* 59:1, 107-114.

Olsson, Börje (1994), *Narkotikaproblemets bakgrund. Användning av och uppfattningar om narkotika inom svensk medecin 1839-1965 (The Background of the Drug Problem. Use of and conceptions about narcotic drugs in Swedish medicine 1939-1965)*, Stockholm: CAN.

Olsson, Börje (1995), 'Utilisation et abus de narcotiques et de drogues illégales en Suède', in: Bulletin de liaison du CNDT, No.21, *Pays nordiques - Etats de lieux sur les toxicomanies*, Lyon: Pierre Guette.

Olsson, Börje (1996), *Drug Trends in Sweden - Spring 1996*, Report to the Pompidou Group, April 1996, Strasbourg: Pompidou Group.

Olsson, B., C. Adamsson Wahren & S. Byqvist (2001), *Det tunga narkotikamissbrukets omfattning i Sverige 1988*, Stockholm: CAN.

Openbaar Ministerie (2000), *Aanwijzing opiumwet ('Opium Law Guidelines')*, The Hague: Openbaar Ministerie ('Public Prosecutor').

Pagès, Frédéric (1996), *Descartes et le cannabis*, Paris: Editions mille et une nuits.

Parker, Howard, Judith Aldridge & Fiona Measham (1998), *Illegal Leisure. The normalization of adolescent recreational drug use*, London: Routledge.

Parquet, P.J. (1997), *Pour une politique de prevention en matière de comportements de consommation de substances psychoactives*, Vanves: CFES.

Pelletier, Monique (1978), *Problèmes de la drogue*, Paris: La Documentation française.

Peterson, Torgny (1993), Brochure *Hassela Solidarity Sweden*.

Pleij, Herman (1991), *Het Nederlands onbehagen*, Amsterdam: Prometheus.

Pleij, Herman (1998), *Hollands Welbehagen*, Amsterdam: Prometheus.

Police Nationale, Gendarmerie & Direction Générale des Douanes et Droits Indirects (1994), *Argumentaire antidrogue*, Limoges: Service Diffusion Gendarmerie.

Portegijs, Nico (1986), *Drugs in Mokum*, Amsterdam: Mozeshuis.

Rajs, Jovan (1994), *Narcotic-Related Deaths in Stockholm 1986-1993*, Stockholm: Ministry of Health and Social Affairs.

Reinarman, Craig & Harry G. Levine (eds.) (1997), *Crack in America. Demon drugs and social justice*, Berkeley: University of California Press.

Reinarman, Craig (1998), 'Morele ideologie V.S. haaks op drugsbeleid Nederland', *Het Parool*, 30 July 1998, (original English version, 'Why Dutch drug policy threatens the U.S.'.

Reynolds, Simon (1998), *Energy Flash: A Journey through Rave Music and Dance Culture*, London: Pan Macmillan.

Richburg, Keith B., 'Dutch Vote Clears Way for Legal Euthanasia', *International Herald Tribune (Washington Post Service)*, 29th November 2000.

Rocques, Bernard, (1999), *La dangerosité des drogues*, Rapport au secretariat d'État, Paris: Éditions Odile Jacob/La Documentation française.

Roesingh, H. K. (1976), *Inlandse tabak: expansie en contractie van een handelsgewas in de 17e en 18e eeuw*, Wageningen: Ph.D. Wageningen University.

Room, Robin (1993), 'Alcohol and Crime: What Kind of Links, and Can We Break Them?', in: Justin Russell (ed.) (1993), *Alcohol and Crime*, Proceedings of a Mental Health Foundation Conference, London: Mental Health Foundation.

Rossi, Carla (2001), *World Drug Report 2000: Contents, Omissions and Distortions*, on-line: «www.mat.uniroma2.it/~rossi/wdr_2000_english.htm».

Ruck, Carl (2003), 'Was there a whiff of cannabis about Jesus?', *Sunday Times*, 12 January 2003.

Ruyver, Brice De (1996), *Identification of differences in drug penal legislation in the member states of the European Union*, Ghent: University of Ghent.

Ruyver, Brice De, Gert Vermeulen, Tom Vander Beken, Freya vander Laenen & Kim Geenens (2002), *Multidisciplinary Drug Policies and the UN Drug Treaties*, Antwerp: Maklu.

SAMHSA (2003), *Results from National Household Survey on Drug Abuse*, Rockville: SAMHSA.

Santucci, Françoise-Marie (2001), 'L'analyse d'un sociologue sur les interpellations: Réprimer l'usage, une stratégie', *Libération*, 8 /9 December 2001.

Schama, Simon (1987), *The Embarrassment of Riches. An Interpretation of Dutch Culture in the Golden Age*, London: Fontana.

Scheerer, Sebastian (1982), *Die Genese der Betäubungsmittelgesetze in der Bundesrepublik Deutschland und in den Niederlanden*, Göttingen: Otto Schwarz.

Scheffer, Paul (2002), 'Alles van waarde moet zich verweren', *NRC Handelsbad* (Opinie), 22 september 2002.

Schippers, Arjan (2001), *Why the Dutch?* (highlight 'Same-sex marriages' at Radio Netherlands (on-line: «www.rnw.nl/society/html/dutch010815.html»).

Schiray, Michel (1992), *Penser la drogue, penser les drogues II. Les marchés interdits de la drogue,* Paris: Descartes.

Schultes, Richard Evans & Albert Hofmann (1979), *Plants of the Gods: Origins of Hallucinogenic Use*, New York: McGraw-Hill.

Sénat (2003), *Drogue: l'autre cancer. Rapport de la commission d'enquête sur la politique nationale de lutte contre les drogues illicites, créée en vertu d'une résolution adoptée par le sénat le 12 décembre 2002*, rapport d'information 321 - tome II (2002-2003) - commission d'enquête 2003, Paris: Sénat.

Setbon, M. & J. De Calan (2000), *L'Injonction thérapeutique. Évaluation du dispositif légal de prise en charge des usagers de drogues interpellés*, Paris: OFDT, collection Études, nr. 21.

Shetter, William Z. (1997), *The Netherlands in Perspective. The Dutch way of Organizing a Society and its Setting,* Utrecht: Nederlands Centrum Buitenlanders.

Shulgin, Alexander & Ann (1991), *PiHKAL (Phenethylamines I Have Known And Loved): A Chemical Love Story*, Berkeley: Transform Press.

Siegel, Ronald K. & Murray E. Jarvick (1975), 'Drug-Induced Hallucinations in Animals and Man', in: R.K. Siegel & L.J. West (eds.) (1975), *Hallucinations. Behavior, Experience, and Theory,* New York: John Wiles & Sons.

Siegel, Ronald K. (1989), *Intoxication. Life in the Pursuit of Artificial Paradise*, New York: E.P. Dutton.

Skog, O-J (1993), 'Narkotikamissbrukets utvikling i Sverige 1979 -1992', in: O. Olsson et al. (1993), *Det tunga narkotikamissbrukets omfattning i Sverige 1992*, Stockholm: CAN.

Smillie, Shaun (2001), 'Did Shakespeare Puff on "Noted Weed"?', *National Geographic News*, 1st March 2001.

Smith, William (1997), 'Introduction. France in the Making', in: Sheila Perry (ed.) (1997), *Aspects of Contemporary France*, London/New York: Routledge.

Smith, Huston (2000), *Cleansing the Doors of Perception. The Religious Significance of Entheogenic Plants and Chemicals*, New York: Jeremy P. Tarcher/Putnam.

Stefanis, C., C. Ballas, and D. Madianou, 'Sociocultural and Epidemiological Aspects of Hashish Use in Greece', 304-326, in: Vera Rubin (ed.) (1975), *Cannabis Culture*, The Hague and Paris: Mouton.

Stengers, Isabelle & Olivier Ralet (1991), *Drogues, le défi hollandais*, Paris: Delagrange, collection 'Les empécheurs de penser en rond'.

Stoddard, Ed (2001), *Pipes Show Cocaine [and other psychoactive substances] Smoked in Shakespeare's England*, Johannesburg: Reuters press release (1st March 2001).

Swaan, Abram de (1993), *Accomodating Drinking Habits. The Control of intoxicating substances in the Netherlands*, Speech held for the 34th Assembly of the 'Union Européene des Alcools', Amsterdam, 21 September 1993.

Taylor, Arnold H. (1969), *American diplomacy and the narcotics traffic, 1900-1939. A study in international humanitarian reform*, Durham: Duke University Press.

Taylor, Peter (1996), *The Way the Modern World Works: World Hegemony to World Imperialism*, Chichester: John Wiley.

Thackeray, J.F., N.J. van der Merwe & T.A. van der Merwe (2001), 'Chemical analysis of residues from seventeenth-century clay pipes from Stratford-upon-Avon and environs', *South African Journal of Science* Vol. 97 No. 1/2 January/February 2001, 19-21.

Tham, Henrik (1995a), 'Drug Control as a National Project: The Case of Sweden', in: *The Journal of Drug Issues*, 25 (1), 113-128, 1995.

Tham, Henrik (1995b), 'From Treatment to Just Deserts in a Changing Welfare State', in: A. Snare (ed.) (1995), *Beware of Punishment*, Scandinavian Studies in Criminology Vol. 14, 89-122, Oslo: Pax Forlag.

Tham, Henrik (1998), 'Swedish drug policy: A successful model?', *European Journal on Criminal Policy and Research*, Vol. 6, no. 3, 1998: 395-414.

Tham, Henrik (2003), 'Drug policy and trends in problematic drug use in Sweden', in: Henrik Tham (ed.) (2003), *Researches on Swedish Drug Policy*, 7-14, Stockholm: Department of Criminology, Stockholm University.

Thompson, Tanya (2001), 'One in 50 a heroin addict', *Scotsman*, 15 November 2001.

Tilton, Tim (1991), *The Political Theory of Swedish Social Democracy. Through the Welfare State to Socialism*, New York: Oxford University Press.

Titscher, Stefan, Michael Meyer, Ruth Wodak & Eva Vetter (2000), *Methods of Text and Discourse Analysis*, London: Sage.

Tocqueville, Alexis de (1981), *De la démocratie en Amérique I*, Paris: Flammarion.

Tops, Dolf (2001), *A society with or without drugs? Continuity and change in drug policies in Sweden and the Netherlands*, Lund: Lund University, Lund Disserations in Social Work.

Torre, E. J. van der (1996), *Drugstoeristen en kooplieden. Een onderzoek naar Franse drugstoeristen, Marokkaanse drugsrunners en het beheer van dealpanden in Rotterdam*, Dordrecht: Kluwer.

Trautmann, Catherine (1990), *Lutte contre la toxicomanie et le trafic de stupéfiants*, Paris: La Documentation française.

Uildriks, Niels (1999), 'Police Torture in France', *Netherlands Quarterly of Human Rights*, Vol. 17: 4, 411-423.

United Nations International Drug Control Programme (1997), *World Drug Report*, Oxford: Oxford University Press.

United Nations General Assembly (1998), *20th Special Session Official Records*, New York: United Nations.

United Nations Office for Drugs Control and Crime Prevention – UN/ODCCP (1999), *European-United Nations partnerships against perils*, Vienna: UN/ODCCP.

United Nations Office for Drug Control and Crime Prevention (2000), *World Drug Report 2000*, Oxford: Oxford University Press.

Vanvugt, Ewald (1985), *Wettig opium. 350 jaar Nederlandse opiumhandel in de Indische archipel*, Haarlem: In de Knipscheer.

Wallerstein, Immanuel (1980), *The Modern World-System II. Mercantilism and the Consolidation of the European World-Economy*, 1600-1750, New York: Academic Press.

Wasson, R.G., S. Kramkrisch, J. Ott & C.A.P. Ruck (1978), *Persephone's Quest: Entheogens and the Origins of Religion*, New Haven/London: Yale University Press.

Weber, Max (1958) *The Protestant Ethic and the Spirit of Capitalism*, New York: Scribner's Press (originally published in 1904).

Weber, Eugen (1979), *Peasants into Frenchmen. The modernization of rural France*, London: Chatto & Windus.

Weeda, Iteke (1992), *Vrouwen verlangen mannen*, Schoten: Anthos.

Weeda, Frederiek (1997), 'Een acht bij vertrek', *NRC Handelsblad*, supplement on tourism and the image of the Netherlands, 9 January 1997.

Weil, Andrew (1986), *The Natural Mind. An Investigation of Drugs and the Higher Consciousness*, Boston: Houghton Mifflin (revised edition of the 1972 publication).

Weil, Andrew & Winifred Rosen (1993), *From Chocolate to Morphine. Everything you need to know about mind-altering drugs*, New York: Houghton Mifflin (revised and updated edition of 1983 publication *Understanding Mind-Active Drugs*).

Werkgroep Verdovende Middelen (1972), *Achtergronden en risico's van druggebruik*, The Hague: Staatsuitgeverij.

Wesseling. H.L. (1987), *Vele ideeën over Frankrijk. Opstellen over geschiedenis & cultuur*, Amsterdam: Bert Bakker.

Westerberg, B. (1994), 'Reply to Arthur Gould: "Pollution rituals in Sweden: the pursuit of a drug-free society"', *Scandinavian Journal of Social Welfare* (1994), 3, pp. 94-96.

Wieviorka, Michel (1992), *La France raciste*, Paris: Seuil.

Wijkström, Filip (1996), *Movements, Members and Volunteers in Sweden*, Paper presented at the Third Research Conference on the Nordic Nonprofit Sector, Oslo 22-23 1996.

Wijngaart, Govert Frank van de (1991), *Competing Perspectives on Drug Use [the Dutch Experience]*, Amsterdam/Lisse: Swets & Zeitlinger.

Wijngaart, G. van de, R. Braam, D. de Bruin, M. Fris, N. Maalsté & H. Verbraeck (1998), *Ecstasy and the Dutch Rave Scene. A socio-epidemiological study of the nature and extent of, and the risks involved in using ecstasy and other party drugs at dance events*, Utrecht: Addiction Research Institute (IVO).

Williams, Raymond (1983), *Keywords*, London: Fontana.

WISE (1991), Worldwide Contamination. Environmental monitoring since Chernobyl, WISE News Communique, Vol. 349/350, 5 April 1991, on-line: «www.antenna.nl/wise/349-50/enviro.html».

World Health Organisation – WHO (1997), *Smoking, drinking and drug taking in the European Region*, Copenhagen: WHO.

Zaitch, Damian (2001), *Traquetos. Colombians involved in the cocaine business in the Netherlands*, published in 2002 under the title *Trafficking Cocaine: Columbian drug entrepreneurs in the Netherlands,* published by Kluwer Academic Publishers in Dordrecht.

Zinberg, Norman (1984), *Drug, Set, & Setting. The Basis for Controlled Intoxicant Use*, New Haven: Yale University Press.

Index

Abortion 116, 126
Abstinence 62, 71, 84
Accommodating drug control system
    192, 210
Accommodation 109, 118
Acquis (of EU) 19, 54, 55
Addiction 2, 4, 10, 86, 88, 170, 194-197,
    298
Africa(n) 11, 36, 38, 52
African slave trade 34
Afro-Americans 28
Agt, Andries van 124, 126
Åhström, Sven-Erik 167-168, 174
AIDS 23, 60, 84, 88, 90, 91, 188, 205
Alcohol 6, 9, 11, 12, 16, 17, 26, 67, 69,
    108, 109
Alcohol damage 164
Alcohol use in Sweden 163-164
Alcohol-free society 162
Alcohol policy 148, 161-164
Alcohol prohibition 11, 13, 28, 35-36,
Algeria(n) 98
Amanita Muscaria 149
America 9, 10, 60, 73
American Temperance Society 34, 35
Amnesty International 96
Amphetamines 9, 15, 49, 56, 57, 59, 60,
    117, 144, 145, 165-168, 194-196
Amsterdam 105, 110, 125-126, 133, 202,
    207, 213,221
Animal drug use 6, 7
Anslinger, Harry 41, 50
ANT courses 178
Anti-alcohol movements 35-39
Anti-depressants 78
Anti-drug abuse act (US) 22
Antilles, Dutch 136
Anti-opium movements 36-38, 41, 42
Anxiolytics 78
Annan, Kofi 1, 17, 19, 53

Anti-psychiatry 85
Apes and drugs 6
Aramaic 7
Arlacchi, Pino 50, 52
Artaud, Antonin
Asia 38, 165
Assemblée nationale 82
Atlantic 113
Australia(n) 23, 43, 51, 52, 60
Austria 33

Baan, Pieter 120, 132
Baan Commission 120-123, 127, 191,
    211
Babylon 10
Bad (LSD) trip 57
Baghdad 149, 221
Balanced approach 4
Balzac, Honoré de 66
Bandol drama 82
Barbiturates 15, 49
Baudelaire, Charles 66
Bayer 13
Becker, Howard 57, 121
Beer 9, 158, 164, 210
Bejerot, Nils 169, 17-174, 178, 191, 211,
    213
Bergeron, Henri 82, 85, 86
Bernat de Célis, Jacqueline 82
Belgium 59, 63
Bergmark, Anders and Lars Oscarsson
    177, 181
Berseker 149
Bewley-Taylor, David 21, 22, 44
Bhang 11
Birds and drugs 6
Bisiou, Yann 21
Black drop 12
Black market alcohol 163
Blankenberg, Erhard 131

Blood test   146, 189
Board of Health and Welfare   148
Bohemian underground   57
Boisseau, Clarisse   91
Bonaparte   73
Bordeaux wine   12
Borst, Els   204
Boulin, R.   85
Bovenkerk, Frank   138
Brazil   34
Bratt System   162
Brent, Bishop Charles   39, 42
British, *see* United Kingdom
Brouwer, Adriaen   112
Bruinsma, Freek   131
Bruun, Kettil   14, 16, 45, 49, 98, 181
Brussels Conference (1889-90)   34
Buprenorphine   91, 188, 196, 197
Buren, Peter van   131
Burroughs, William   58

California   28, 40
Call-to-order drug control system   192,
   210
Calvinism   111, 114, 116
Canada   23, 52, 124, 158, 211
Cannabis   3, 6, 7, 9, 11, 12, 26, 56, 82,
   102, 107, 113, 115, 117, 120, 165,
   192-194
Cannabis cultivation   106
Cannabis culture   79, 105-106, 193
Cannabis Cup   106
Cannabis legalisation, *see* Legalisation
Cannabis prohibition   47, 48, 50
Cannabis trade   132-133, 138
Cannabis vapour bath   8
Cannes European Council   99
Carpentier, Jean   91
Caribbean   4, 44, 133, 136
Catholic (Church)   10, 12, 40, 91, 111
CELAD   99
Central Nervous System Stimulants
   see Amphetamines
Central rule   72, 75, 87, 92
Champagne   78
Chavannes, Marc   114
Chasing the dragon   59, 195
Chen-Nong   7
Chernobyl   89
Chicago   62
China/Chinese   7, 9, 14, 28, 36, 41, 45,
   110, 116, 183

Chinatown   40, 41
Chinese opium question   45
Chirac, Jacques   1, 2, 3, 4, 99-101, 138,
   203, 206, 216
Christie, Nils   181
Cigarettes   10, 11, 58
CIRC   66
Citizenship   97
Civil Liberties   83
Clandestine churches   111, 130
Classification of drugs   69, 120
Clinton, Bill   1, 18
Club des Hachichins   66
Coca   9, 12, 38, 48
Coca-Cola   12, 40
Cocaine   3, 9, 12, 13, 28, 116, 136, 139,
   142
'Cocaine crazed negroes'   40
Cocainism   13
Code Napoleon   73
Code of Hammurabi   10
Coffee   7, 10, 58
Coffee shops   23, 105, 106, 107, 108,
   115, 130, 134, 137-139, 193, 216
Cohabitation   100, 206, 207
Cohen, Herman   121, 190
Colonial powers   11
Columbia(ns)   43, 135
Compulsory treatment   141, 147, 196
Consultative society   109
Contagion/contagiousness   170-171, 173,
   176
Contagious Disease Act   152
Containment drug control system   192,
   210
Content analysis   3
Continuity and Change   130, 137
Control and sanction strategy   169
Conventions *see* Drug conventions
Convention against Psychotropic
   Substances (1971)   15, 48
Convention against Illicit Traffic (1988)
   15, 49
Coppel, Anne   90, 91, 92
Corruption   4
Costa, Mario   50, 52
Council of Crime Prevention   146
Council of Europe   98
Counter culture   17, 56, 58, 188
CND   48, 49, 51, 53, 55
Crack-cocaine   23, 59, 105, 140, 141,
   194-195

Crack in America 22, 39
Cradle of Human Rights 76
Crime 4, 5, 119, 143,196, 205
Criminalisation 25, 190
Criminalised prohibition 25
Criminologists 86, 132, 171, 172
Crop Eradication 4
Crozier, Michel 80
CRS (riot police) 95
Crusade 2
Cuba 41
Cuellar, Perez de 18
Culture 28, 209, 215-221
Cultural exception 77
Cultural values 5
Curaçao 133
Curtet, Francis 86, 88

Daun, Åke 153, 155
DEA 44, 133
Debray, Régis 80
Death Penalty 10
Declaration of Paris (1856) 33
Declaration of the Rights of Man 73, 76
Decriminalisation 22, 26, 62, 94, 106,
    108, 126, 129-130, 189, 192
Definition power 30, 190
Delacroix, Eugène 66
Delinquency 4
Demand reduction 4, 146
Depenalisation 68, 97
Depressants 48
Descartes 111
Detoxification 84
Detroit 62
Diderot 66
Discourse analysis 3-6, 29
Dissident voices 182
Docklands 199
Dogs and drugs 6
Doors of Perception, The 66
Douste-Blazy, Philippe 91
Dreyfus affair 76
Drinking and driving 69
Dutch (drug policy), *see* Netherlands
Drug arrests in France 68, 93-94, 192
Drug chain 173
Drug control systems 29, 187, 188, 192,
    208, 209-221
Drug Conventions 14, 15, 19, 45-49, 51,
    54, 126-127, 187
Drug culture 67

Drug-free world 1,2, 5, 19
Drug-free society 2, 5, 144, 145, 147,
    184, 185, 189, 208
Drug policy discourses 29
Drug prohibition 15-28, 43, 48
Drug reform 53
Drug scares 39-41
Drug tourism 106
Drug trade/trafficking 4, 15, 132-134,
    137, 205, 219
Drug use tolerance 26
Drunken Comportment 160
Dumas, Alexander 66
Durkheim, Emile 14
Dutch East Indies 45
Dutch-French drug conflict 203-206
Dutch-Swedish controversy 207-208

Eastern Europe 58
East Indian Company, *see* VOC
ECAD 176
Ecstasy 60, 62-63, 102, 135, 139,
    197-200
Egypt 8, 9, 10
Ehrenberg, Alain 84, 97, 98,
Elephants and alcohol 6
Elsevier 111 6
EMCDDA 24, 27, 59, 61, 201,209
Emigration from Sweden 150
Enlightenment 34, 37, 73
Entheogens 8
Epidemiology of drug use 61
Ephedrine 9
Epidemic addictions 170
Ethiopia 7
European Court on Human Rights 95
European drinking 160, 165
European drug control 53-55, 99
Europe 1, 12, 20, 23, 34, 60
European Union 8, 19-20, 24-27, 30,
    53-55, 59, 114, 134, 200, 207
Euthanasia 116, 130
Exodus 7
Expediency principle 129
Experiment, *see* Prescription 'experiment'
Experimental (drug use), *see* Recreational
Extradition 15, 49

Fantasio 118, 123
Fazey, Cindy 52
Federal Bureau of Narcotics 41
Fifth Republic 74, 98, 100, 203

Finland/Finnish 11, 35
FMN 147, 175, 178
Folkhemmet 151
Folkrörelsen, *see* Popular mass
   movements
Foucault, Michel 29, 190, 219
Fouché 95
France/French 2, 3, 25-27, 29-30, 33, 63,
   65-103, 188, 190-195, 197-198
French drug policy *see* France
Free Church Movement 156
French Connection 65
Freud, Sigmund 13, 86
Fries, Björn 184
Front National 102
Fruits (fermenting) 6, 9
Function(s) of drinking 159

Galileo 111
Gambling 40, 108
Gastronomy 77
Gateway drug 108, 120, 192
Gaulle, Charles de 74, 75, 76, 100
Gautier,Théophile 66
Gay, *see* Homosexuality
Geerlings, Peter 121, 123
Gendarmerie 94
Gender equality 153
Geneva Opium Convention 47
Gentlemen's Club, The 14, 16, 43, 50
Geography 31, 71, 109, 155, 212
Gerritsen 9
German(y) 46, 59, 63, 202
GG&GD 128
Ghettos 96
Ghodse, Hamid 52
Giscard d'Estaing, Valéry 86
Glue 220
Global Drug Prohibition 14-20, 22-24, 30,
   33, 36-38
Goa 62
Goats and drugs 6
Gothenburg 149, 199
Gould, Arthur 151, 179, 182
Government monopolies 21
Gramont, Sache de 65, 72
Greece/Greek 8, 9, 212
Grootveld, Robert-Jasper 117
Grow shops 138
Guideline (Judicial) 70, 92-93, 107, 128,
   138,139, 188, 213
Guigou, Elisabeth 102

Guliani, Rudolf 102

Habits 2, 13
Haemophilia affair 89
Hague Opium Convention(s) 15-16, 39,
   45-47
Hallucinogens 9, 15, 49, 113
Hallucinogenic mushrooms 6, 142
Hammond, William 13
Harmonisation of drug policies 19, 20, 55
Harm reduction 3, 4, 24, 60, 62, 64, 70,
   71, 86, 88, 91, 106, 108, 128, 141,
   142, 147, 188, 194-196, 207
Harm reduction movement 60
'Hash Book' 146
Hashish 61, 65, 67, 117, 136
Hassela Solidarity 174, 175, 178
Health risks 16, 122-123
Healthy school programme 109
Hebrew 7
Hegemon(ic) 16, 38, 110
Hemp 112, 123
Henrion Commission/Report 82, 90, 01
Henrion, Roger 70
Herodotus 8,
Heroin 2, 3, 7, 12, 13, 21, 26, 57, 59,
   105, 140, 142, 194-197
Heroin prescription 88, 141, 195, 196
Heroin prices 141
Hip hop 96
Hippie(s) 56, 117, 125
Hippocrates 8
History 31, 109
HIV 27, 60, 89, 152, 195
Hofland, H.J.A. 201
Homer 8
Homocide 108
Homosexuality 115, 126, 130, 152
Hoyles, André 81
Huguenots 111
Hugo, Victor 66
Hulsman Commission 120-122, 190
Hulsman, Louk 119, 121, 132, 211
Human Rights violations 96
Huxley, Aldous 66
Hypnotics 78
Hypodermic injection 12

Ibiza 62
Iceland 11, 35
Ideal Enemy, The 181
Ideal social order 151

Iliad 8
Immigration 39, 69, 95-96, 133, 154
INCB 48, 49-53, 127, 200
India 10, 11, 21, 110, 113
Indivudual freedom 114, 131, 133, 214
Indochina, French 21
Indonesia(n) 21, 111
Industrial Revolution 162
Injection mark study 170, 191
Injonction thérapeutique 83, 194
Inquisition 110
International Drug control 14-20
Internationalism 33
Intoxication 6, 10, 35, 58, 65, 158, 159, 165, 170
Intravenous drug use 59, 60
Ireland/Irish 28, 34, 204, 212
Islam(ic) 11, 12, 35, 36
Israel 7, 127
Italy/Italians 28, 40, 46, 50, 59
Ivory Coast 52

Jacobinism 75
Jarl, Stefan 177
Java 112
Jellinek Clinic 121
Jesus Christ 8
Jew(ish) 110, 111
Johnsson, Hans-Ingvar 150
Joint actions (of EU) 19, 54, 55
Jospin, Lionel 101

Kaneh bosm (cannabis) 7
Kassovitz, Matthieu 96
Khatami, President 12
King Juan Carlos 12
Kohl, Helmut 204
Kok, Wim 204
Kokoreff, Michel 93
Kopp, Pierre 101
Kort, Marcel de 118, 119
Kouchner, Bernard 91, 101, 207
Kruisinga 126

Labelling theory 122, 188, 190
Labour Movement 156
Lacan 87, 190, 221
Lang, Jack 197
Las Vegas Effect 220
Latin America(n) 38, 44
Laudanum 12
Language (and linguistics) 3-6

League of Nations 34, 36, 47
Ledain Commission 123
Legal culture 130, 131, 133
Legalisation 62, 116, 126, 169, 220
Lenke, Leif and Börje Olsson 169, 171
Leuw, Ed. 117, 119
Levant 113
Levine, Harry 16, 22, 23, 24, 39
Liberalism 153
Libération 91
Lille 205
Limiter la casse 91
Linguistics, *see* Language
Lijphart, Arend 124
Locke, John 111
Loi d'exception 68, 82
London 62
Louis XIV 72
Louis XVIII 95
LSD 49, 56, 57, 63, 82, 118, 166
Lumpenproletariat 180
Lund 184
Lutheran 154
Luxembourg 59
LVM 147, 178
LVU 147, 175

Maastricht Treaty 54
MacAndrew, Craig and Robert Edgerton 160
Maestracci, Nicole 101
Mafia 4
Major, John 204
Malmö 149, 184
Mandatory drug test *see* Urine test
Mandatory sentences 22
Marijuana 28, 57, 61
Marketing (of drugs) 5, 180
Marmottan 85
Matthei, Jan-François 90
May 1968 75, 79-82, 84, 85
Mazarin 72
McCaffrey, Barry 202
MDMA, *see* Ecstasy
Médecins du Monde 91, 198
Media 15
Medical drug use 12,13
Mercantilism 114
Mesopotamia 8
Methadone 4, 60, 86, 91, 128, 140, 147, 188, 195-197, 203
Methadone bus 129

Metaphors 5
Mexico/Mexican 18, 28, 79
Mierlo, Hans van 2, 200
MILDT 101, 102,
Mill, John-Stuart 132, 214
Mind-altering substances 6, 9, 56
Misdemeanour 129
Mitterrand, François 98
Modern drug use 17, 26, 108, 187, 209,
    215
Monde, Le 88, 91, 101
Money laundering 15, 54
Mongooses and drugs 6
Monopoly 10, 13, 21, 45, 87, 112, 162
Montesquieu 73, 158
Moral entrepreneurs 37, 39, 125
Moral panic 39
Morbidity 27
Moreau, Jacques-Joseph 65
Morocco 21, 133
Morphine 9, 12, 13
Morphinism 13
Moses 7
Multicultural 125, 154
Mushrooms, *see* Hallucinogenic
    mushrooms
Muslim 10, 36, 38, 91
Musto, David 12, 40, 41, 42
Myrdal, Jan 180
Myristic acid 9

Nadelmann, Ethan 33, 37, 42
Nanterre, University of 80
Napoleon 65, 94-95
Napoleon III 95
National identity 215-217
National Police 172, 213
NATO 118
Needle exchange (programmes) 4, 60, 88,
    140, 147
Nerval, Gérard de 66
Netherlands, the 2, 4, 5, 22, 23, 25-27,
    29-30, 34, 52, 59, 63, 105- 142, 188-
    191, 193, 195, 198-199
New Scientist, The 44
New Testament 8
New York Times 53
Night Club Commission 199
Nixon, President 124
No-go areas 69
Normalisation 108, 140
Norms 17, 33, 37, 38, 97, 140, 159, 214

Northern (consuming) countries 3
Nuisance 130, 141, 142, 196, 205
Nutmeg 9

Oceania 21
OECD 77
OFDT 93
OGD 66
Old Testament 7,
Olievenstein, Claude 83, 84-86, 190, 211
Open letter to Kofi Annan 19
Opiates 2,13, 165, 168
Opinion polls 176
Opium (poppy) 8, 12, 13, 15, 113
Opium Act, Dutch 117, 122
Opium monopoly 21, 112
Opium addiction 10
Opium prohibition 36, 39, 41, 48
Opium regime 112, 119
Opium smoking 40, 116
Opium trade 36, 41, 111-112
Opium wars (1840-42) 36
Organised Crime 4
Ottoman High Porte 33
Overdoses 27, 184, 196, 208

Pain killers 9
Paint thinner 220
Pakistan 133
Paradiso 118
Paradis artificiels, Les 66
Paribas 21
Paris 67, 213
Paris Peace Conference (1815) 34
Parquet, P.J. 101
Pathology 122
Pen, Jean-Marie Le 102
Pep pills 166
Permissiveness 171
Peyote 9, 66
Pharmacists 13
Pharmaceutical lobby 16, 50
Pharmaceuticals 69, 78
Philippines 39, 41
Pillar(isation) 109, 124-125, 214
Pill testing 63
Physicians 12, 13
Pillars (of EU) 54
Piracy 33, 34, 37, 38
Plants of the Gods 6, 7
Poland/Poles 28, 40, 158
Polder model 109

Police 94, 95, 196, 213
Police violence 96, 118
Popular mass movements 155-157, 213, 214
Portugal 59, 204
Pragmatic approaches 61, 63-64,116
Precursors 54, 135
Prosecution 93
Prescription 'experiment' (1965-67) 148, 167-170, 189, 191, 221
Prevalence of drug use 27, 56-61, 107, 143-144, 209
Prevention (drug), 4, 70, 109, 145, 178
Privateering 33, 34
Problem drug use 57-60, 194-197
Professionals 211
Prohibition 10, 11, 36, 39, 40, 120
Prostitution 34, 40, 128, 152-153
Protest generation 17
Provos 117, 125
Prussia 33
Psychoactive plants/substances 6, 12, 48-49
Psychoanalysis 86, 98, 211
Psychosis 57, 194
Public health 5
Puerto Rico 41
Punitive prohibition 22-24, 28

Raffarin Government 90, 103
Rapid Risk Assessment 55
Ration book 162-163
Rave culture 62, 197-200
Rave Commissions/Police 146, 199
Recreational drug use 13, 56, 60-63, 107, 117, 144, 192-194, 197-200, 208
Red light district 105, 106
Reefer madness 41
Regulatory prohibition 22-23
Regulatory systems, 21-24, 116, 140
Republican (tradition) 97-98, 217
Reinarman, Craig 22, 24, 39, 202
Restrictiveness 171
Revolution, French 73
RFHL 167, 168, 174, 178
Richelieu 66
Riksdag 153
RNS 174, 178
Roessingh 113
Roman 8, 9
Roosevelt, Theodore 42
Roques Commission/Report 69, 101, 219

Rossi, Carla 201
Rotterdam 113, 119, 205-206
Rousseau, Jean-Jacques 73
Royal Tropical Institute 114
Russia 58, 158

Salmouni case 95
Same-sex marriages 115, 116
Santen, Gerrit van 203
Sardinia 33
Sarkozy, Nicolas 102
Sartre, Jean-Paul 76
Scandinavia(n) 34, 59, 135, 152, 158, 212
Scapegoat (drugs as a) 39, 181-182
Scare techniques 179
Schama, Simon 112
Scheerer, Sebastian 124
Schengen 19
Schwartzenberg 88
Scientific knowledge 187, 189-191
SCOPE 18
Scotland 58
Scythians 8
Sedatives 78
Security Discourse 5, 204-205
Self-image (national) 215-217
Senate, French 83, 102
Senegal 52
Setting 122
Sex(uality) 77, 109
Shafer Commission 123, 124
Shakespeare, William 9
Shanghai Opium Commission 14, 37, 39, 42, 45, 46
Shulgin, Alexander and Ann 63
Siam, Kingdom of 21
Sigurdson, Gertrud 177, 178
Single Convention (1961) 15, 48, 53, 127
Sjöwall and Wahlöö 143
Skog, Ole-Jorgen 172
Slave trade, slavery 33, 34, 37, 38
Smart drugs 105, 106
Smart shops 105, 106
Smith, Huston 8
Smith, Sir Clementi 45
Smoking Opium Exclusion Act 42
Smuggling 205, *or see* Drug trade
Snaps *see* Spirits
Snus 183
Social Democratic (Party) 150, 152, 153-154, 175, 176

Sociological views on drugs 121-122
Solidarity 155
Solvents 220
Sorbonne 80
South America 9, 136
South Korea 79
Southern (producing) countries 8, 18, 55
Spain 34, 62, 204
Spinoza 111
Spirits 158, 161, 162, 164
Spiritual catalysts (drugs as) 8
Sri Lanka 112
State monopolies 10
Sterilisation 152
Stigmatisation 108, 122, 132, 190
Stimulants 48
Stockholm 149, 155, 167, 199
Strasbourg European Council 98
Struggle against water 109
Subcultures 60, 167, 172, 190
Substitution treatment, *see* Methadone
Sumerian 8
Supply reduction 4, 146
Suriname 136
Svensson, Alf 182
Swaan, Abram de 128
Sweden/Swedish 2, 5, 24-27, 29-30, 36,
   59, 144-185, 189-191, 193, 196, 199-
   200, 204
Swedish alcohol policy 148, 157-165
Swedish drug policy, *see* Sweden
Swedish model 145, 215
Swedish welfare state 150, 179, 180
Switzerland 52
Symptom theoretical perspective 185
Synthetic drugs 62, 135
Synthetic Drugs Unit 137
Systembolaget 163, 165
System of thought 218

Tabloids 173, 182
Taylor, Arnold H. 42
Techno 62, 197-198
Temperance cultures 161
Temperance Movement 34-36, 38, 156,
   157, 161
Thailand 21, 183
Tham, Henrik 176, 177, 181, 182
Therapeutic communities 86
Thörnberg 156
Tobacco 10, 11, 17, 67, 108, 110, 113
Tocqueville, Alexis 28

Tolerance 105, 115, 128, 141, 217
Tops, Dolf 189
Torture 95
Toxicity 58
Trace, Mike 27, 53
Trainspotting 58
Tranquillisers 15, 49
Transgression 98, 192
Trade and distribution 113, 136
Treaties, *see* Drug Conventions
Treaty on European Union 53
Treatment (drug) 4
Treatment and reform strategy 169
Trygghet 150, 151, 176
Tunisia 21
Turkey/Turks 133, 136, 183

Uijl, den 124
United Kingdom 21, 33, 36, 38, 45, 46,
   52, 59, 62, 94
United Nations (UN) 1, 2, 4, 14, 25, 34,
   45, 48, 127, 153
United Provinces, Dutch 110
United States 1, 12, 16, 18, 21, 22, 34,
   35, 37, 30-44, 55, 94, 134, 212
UNDCP 18, 19, 50, 49-53, 201
UNGASS 1, 3, 18, 25, 44, 53, 55, 100,
   180, 184, 200, 218
UNODC 49-53, 55, 201
Uppsala 147
Urine tests 146, 189

Varieties of drug prohibition 22, 30
Verdandi 178
Versailles Peace Conference 46-47
Vienna 53
Vienna, Congress of 34
Vietnam 56, 79, 118
Viking 149, 158
Violence 96
Visser, Hans 142
Vodka belt 158, 212
VNG 139
VOC 111
Voltaire 66, 76, 111
Vorrink, Irene 124, 126

Wallström, Margot, 2
War on Drugs 18, 43, 83, 105, 202
WASP 28
Weber, Max 152

Weil, Andrew (and Winifred Rosen) 10,
     57
Weimar Republic   175
Wesseling, H.L.   80
Westerberg, Bengt   176
Westerberg, K.A.   175
White slave trade   33, 34, 35
WHO   44, 48, 49, 164
WHO Cocaine Project   44
Wieviorka, Michel   97
Wijkström, Filip   156, 157
Willem Pompe Institute   132
Williams, Raymond   29
Wilson, Woodrow   47
Wine   9, 26, 36, 63, 67, 77, 158, 164
Wine culture   65, 77-78
Wine production   78

Withdrawal symptoms   58
Wootton Commission   123
World Drug Report (UN)   51, 201
World Drug Summit, *see* UNGASS
World War I   46, 56
World War II   10, 15, 47, 74, 79, 90
Wright, Hamilton   42

Yom Kippur War   127
Youth culture   17, 56-57, 60-63, 117,
     125, 191, 208, 212

Zaitch, Damián   135
Zedillo, President   18
Zero tolerance   102
Zola, Emile   76
Zwart, Koos   123, 124

POMPE REEKS

1. *Facetten van economisch strafrecht*, prof. jhr. mr. M. Wladimiroff (red.), 1990
2. *Buiten de muren*, dr. mr. M. Moerings en mr. G. ter Haar (red.), 1990
3. *De sociale constructie van fraude*, dr. C.H. Brants en dr. K.L.K. Brants, 1991
4. *Om de persoon van de dader*, dr. J.A. Janse de Jonge, 1991
5. *Ziek of schuldig?*, drs. F. Koenraadt (red.), 1991
6. *In de bisnis*, Sari van der Poel, 1991
7. *Strafrechtelijke handhaving van gemeenschapsrecht*, mr. R.M.A. Guldenmund, 1992
8. *Homoseksualiteit en recht*, dr. mr. M. Moerings en mr. A. Mattijssen (red.), 1992
9. *Met schuld beladen*, dr. J.A. Janse de Jonge en prof. mr. C. Kelk (red.), 1992
10. *Binnen de steen van dit bestaan*, J.A. Janse de Jonge, M. Moerings en A. van Vliet (red.), 1993
11. *Strafrecht en milieu*, dr. Th.J.B. Buiting, 1993
12. *Latijnsamerikaanse drugkoeriersters in detentie: ezels of zondebokken?*, Janine Jansen, 1994
13. *De overdracht van de tenuitvoerlegging van strafvonnissen*, D.J.M.W. Paridaens, 1994
14. *Hoe punitief is Nederland?*, dr. mr. M. Moerings (eindred.), 1994
15. *Buitenlandse getuigen in strafzaken*, André Klip, 1994
16. *De menselijke verantwoordelijkheid in het strafrecht*, prof. mr. C. Kelk, 1994
17. *De naam van het feit*, C.M. Pelser, 1995
18. *Allah, Satan en het recht*, Yücel Yeşilgöz, 1995
19. *Een schijn van kans*, M. Gras, F. Bovenkerk, K. Gorter, P. Kruiswijk en D. Ramsoedt, 1996
20. *Er is meer*, C.H. Brants, C. Kelk en M. Moerings (red.), 1996
21. *Ouderdoding als ultiem delict*, F. Koenraadt, 1996
22. *Bedreigde getuigen in het strafproces*, Annemarieke Beijer, 1997
23. *Politie en criminaliteit van Marokkaanse jongens*, Rosan Coppes, Flora de Groot en Alex Sheerazi, 1997
24. *Locus delicti en rechtsmacht*, H.D. Wolswijk, 1998
25. *Voorwaarden voor strafbaarstelling van vrouwenhandel*, Roelof Haveman, 1998
26. *Met recht behoorlijk ingesloten*, Anje Brouwer, 1998
27. *Over levende gedachten*, C.H. Brants, 1999
28. *Morele kwesties in het strafrecht*, M. Moerings, C.M. Pelser en C.H. Brants (red.), 1999
29. *Eerlijke berechting en bijzonder straf(proces)recht*, P.J. Baauw, 1999
30. *Decentraal bestuur vervolgbaar?*, J.A.E. van der Jagt, 2000
31. *Recht voor commuun gestraften*, Miranda Boone, 2000
32. *Misdaadvermogen en internationaal strafrecht*, Roan Lamp, 2000
33. *Nederlands detentierecht*, prof. mr. C. Kelk, 2000
34. *De Wet Terwee*, Renée Kool en Martin Moerings, 2001
35. *De Penitentiaire Beginselenwet in werking*, M. Boone en G. de Jonge (red.), 2001

36. *Opsporing van oorlogsmisdrijven*, A. Beijer, A.H. Klip, M.A. Oomen en A.M.J. van der Spek, 2002
37. *Recht op schrift*, dr. Renée Kool, prof. dr. Martin Moerings en Willem Zandbergen, 2002
38. *Herstelrecht in jeugdstrafzaken*, Ytje Minke Hokwerda, 2004
39. *Voor wat hoort wat: plea bargaining in het strafrecht*, Chrisje Brants en Bart Stapert, 2004
40. *Het psychisch onvermogen terecht te staan*, Peter Bal en Frans Koenraadt, 2004
41. *Discretie in het strafrecht*, M. Boone, R.S.B. Kool, C.M. Pelser en T. Boekhout van Solinge (red.), 2004
42. *Dealing with Drugs in Europe*, Tim Boekhout van Solinge, 2004